P9-AFA-965

The Business of Slavery
and the Rise of American Capitalism,
1815–1860

The Business of

Slavery and the

Rise of American

Capitalism,

1815–1860

Calvin Schermerhorn

Yale
UNIVERSITY
PRESS
New Haven & London

Published with assistance from the foundation established in memory of Amasa Stone Mather of the Class of 1907, Yale College.

Yale University Press books may be purchased in quantity for educational, business, or promotional use. For information, please e-mail sales.press@yale.edu (U.S. office) or sales@yaleup.co.uk (U.K. office).

Set in Electra type by IDS Infotech, Ltd.
Printed in the United States of America.

ISBN 978-0-300-19200-1
Catalogue records for this book are available from the Library of Congress and the British Library.

This paper meets the requirements of ANSI/NISO Z39.48–1992 (Permanence of Paper).

10 9 8 7 6 5 4 3 2

for Margaret

CONTENTS

Acknowledgments

This book started with the idea that some of the most destructive aspects of American history were bound up with some of its most creative. That exploration of the tragic in history has taken several years. Some chapters began serendipitously with a single piece of evidence, such as a curious slave ship manifest of a passage originating in New Jersey. Others began as parts of conference papers, such as the one Seth Rockman invited me to give at "Slavery's Capitalism: A New History of Economic Development," cohosted by Brown and Harvard universities in 2011. That conference marked a turning point in my thinking about historical capitalism, and I owe a correspondingly great debt to Seth and his co-organizer, Sven Beckert, along with Ronald Bailey, Edward E. Baptist, Ian Beamish, Daina Ramey Berry, Kathryn Boodry, James T. Campbell, Eric Kimball, Bonnie Martin, Scott Reynolds Nelson, Daniel Rood, Caitlin C. Rosenthal, Joshua D. Rothman, Amy Dru Stanley, Lorena S. Walsh, Shane White, and Craig Wilder, among many others. I am also grateful for Dylan C. Penningroth's and Shirley E. Thompson's helpful suggestions on this work at the Chicago meeting of the American Historical Association in 2012. In 2012–13 I was fortunate to be part of a slavery seminar cohosted by the School for Advanced Research in Santa Fe and Southern Methodist University. I thank Eric Bowne, Catherine Cameron, Paul T. Conrad, Edward Countryman, Melissa Farley, Mark Goldberg, Andrew R. Graybill, Enrique Lamadrid, Sherry L. Smith, Andrew J. Torget, and Nat Zappia for their suggestions in shaping parts of this project, and especially its organizers, James F. Brooks, Bonnie Martin, and Ruth Ann Elmore.

I owe extraordinary debts to friends and colleagues who read chapters and offered suggestions for improvement. They include Edward L. Ayers, Donald Critchlow, who also came up with the book's title, Scott Nelson,

Katherine M. B. Osburn, Anthony F. Parent Jr., Seth Rockman, and Josh Rothman. All were generous with their time and intellectual investments. For Yale University Press, Robert Gudmestad and three anonymous reviewers digested a great deal more material than appears here, offering excellent recommendations that trimmed chapters and sharpened analyses. I am grateful for their expert guidance and for the thoughtful editorial work of Erica Hanson, Christopher Rogers, Jeff Schier, and Christina Tucker at Yale. Ann Twombly's judicious editing improved the text considerably. Sonia Tycko's early interest and suggestions were also quite helpful. Many others answered questions or took the time to meet and talk about this book, including Erik Alexander, Ed Baptist, Andrew Barnes, Christa Dierksheide, Graham Dozier, Stephen L. Esquith, Susan Gray, Monica Green, Christopher F. Jones, Gregg D. Kimball, Ted Maris-Wolf, Scott P. Marler, Jaime Martinez, Caleb McDaniel, Maurie D. McInnis, Fraser D. Neiman, Scott Nesbit, Catherine O'Donnell, Josh Rothman, Ben Schiller, Andrew Torget, Emily Tenhundfeld, Philip VanderMeer, Henry Wiencek, Gaye Wilson, and Andrew W. Witmer. I am especially indebted to Joseph C. Miller for our many conversations and frequent correspondence. I wish to acquit all quickly of any complicity for errors and mistakes here.

At the University of Richmond's Digital Scholarship Lab, Nathaniel Ayers, Justin Madron, Robert K. Nelson, Stefan St. John, and especially Scott Nesbit adroitly undertook the project of creating a digital map of the United States domestic slave trade, devoting quite a bit of time, resources, and resourcefulness to it. A simple credit cannot capture the work they put into it or the wellspring of innovation that is the DSL. At Arizona State University, Coreen Harris, Kristin Rondeau-Guardiola, and Scott West devoted time to this project as diligent student research assistants. The staff at the National Archives and Records Administration in Philadelphia and Fort Worth helped considerably, and thanks in particular to Juliet Seer Pazera at the New Orleans Notarial Archives Research Center. Mrs. Mary M. White of New Orleans uncovered some surprising and helpful sources. I also appreciate the efforts of Frank Arre of the Naval History and Heritage Command, Mark Brown at Belmont Mansion, Tennessee, Matt Farah of the Wilson Research Center in New Orleans, and Laura Clark Brown and Matthew Turi of the Wilson Library at the University of North Carolina, Chapel Hill.

Special thanks to Bonnie Martin, Susan Eva O'Donovan, and Gautham Rao, who graciously shared the fruits of their archival excavations and contributed their wisdom on various subjects. Their generosity is a model of what is best in scholarship.

Material support for this project came from several important sources, beginning with Arizona State University. I thank Rachel Fuchs and Matthew J. Garcia for relief from teaching during a critical phase of this project. I am grateful for a Joel M. Williamson Visiting Scholar fellowship at the University of North Carolina, Chapel Hill's Southern Historical Collection, a John Hope Franklin fellowship at Duke University, and a residential fellowship at the Virginia Foundation for the Humanities.

The VFH is an outstanding institution and was a wonderful place at which to finish this project. It brings together scholars and writers from a variety of backgrounds who interact in a vibrant and collegial, not to mention beautiful, setting in Charlottesville. I owe a special debt to VFH Senior Fellow Emeritus William W. Freehling for his guidance and friendship, along with the enthusiastic support of VFH President Rob Vaughn and Ann Spencer. I am grateful to Sarah McConnell and the producers of With Good Reason Radio for their interest in this project. A fond thanks to my fellow fellows Don Debats, Faulkner Fox, Jerry Handler, Tom Jackson, Jennifer Mendez, Debra Nystrom, Osayimwense Osa, Hermine Pinson, John Ragosta, and Earl Swift. Besides those of historians, the perspectives of poets, authors, anthropologists, sociologists, and scholars of literature considerably enriched this book.

Greatest thanks go to my family, especially my wife, Margaret, and daughters, Marion and Eva. They supported this project immensely and in ways too numerous to list. Margaret encouraged fellowship opportunities even thousands of miles away, and all tolerated my absences at archives and conferences, my disappearances on weekends to write, and my nattering about some long-dead subjects who seemed utterly reprehensible and others whose sufferings found no earthly redemption. Margaret shared the frustrations and disappointments of missed deadlines and devices that gave up the ghost, taking my files to their cyber graves. She also shared my enthusiasm for the project and the small victories of writing breakthroughs, moments when ideas snapped into focus, and discoveries of exquisite archival tidbits. Margaret's loving sacrifices include working less at a noble medical profession so that I could work more in a vocation whose outputs enjoy less demand. No book can appropriately repay such support, good faith, and sacrifice. Nevertheless, I dedicate this book to her.

THE BUSINESS OF SLAVERY
AND THE RISE OF AMERICAN CAPITALISM,
1815–1860

INTRODUCTION

The business of slavery in the early United States was a symphony of creativity and violence. This book details the interstate United States slave trade at the level of the firm. Slave traders investigated here were business insiders rather than social outcasts and were some of the early U.S. republic's most ingenious merchants. Some of slavery's financiers and shippers fit exquisitely the term "Masters of the Universe" in their time and place.[1] Through their strategies the slavery business quickened the march of American development, and through their stories I argue that ventures that financed, traded, and transported enslaved people chart the progress of nineteenth-century American capitalism more strikingly than any other enterprise. This book delves into individual entrepreneurship, which textured the slavery business and influenced the trajectory of American capitalism. But the business of slavery was never merely business, and the creative destruction that built a commercial republic and helped usher into being a continental empire was one that racked the bodies, splintered the families, and tried the souls of African-descended Americans. Their stories feature here too.

Capitalism has many varieties, but like religious orthodoxy it is ferociously contested among adherents of particular traditions. For this book's purposes it was a highly structured system of trade characterized by debt obligations that bound borrowers' ambitions, expectations, and imaginations to future repayment. Debt instruments represented those obligations, which were durable, mobile, and ultimately transferable, the basis of paper money. Capitalism was built on the trust in promises debtors made to creditors and the expansive resources that those relationships yielded in the service of generating returns on investments. American capitalist development was a promethean process that defies progressive stages unfolding in history. Emphasis on credit and investment, paper money and promises, distinguishes capitalism from a mere market system. Markets have been around for millennia and feature significant complexity. Markets for slaves and land were artifacts of classical antiquity. Second-century Roman Italy underwent what amounts to a market revolution, and later eras experienced persistent inflation. Capitalistic modes of exchange are recognizable in fifteenth-century Mediterranean contexts, but the process has deeper global roots and distinctive if intertwined African, Asian, and European histories. Capitalism and slavery were mutually constituted in the Americas, although not every capitalist was an enslaver and not every slave-holder was a capitalist.[2]

North American capitalism developed in the context of an Atlantic system of exchange most recognizable perhaps in the transatlantic slave trade and the systems of indebtedness responsible for its contours. In its classic eighteenth-century configuration, chains of debt moved around the Atlantic basin in coun-termotion to the trajectories of captives, goods, and commodities. Credit's elasticity was the key to returns from American ventures. Investors financed enter-prises that generated commodities, extracted metals and minerals, and produced goods, which moved from port to port. The Atlantic system grew to rely on bound laborers, most of whom were African-descended captives and their enslaved descendants. Enslavers who marched assemblages of captives from points of capture to the African coast for sale to European strangers tended to treat captives as investments, or at least as debt payments. So did those who bought, shipped, and sold the survivors to Americans. Shipmasters, merchants, investors, bankers, planters, and owners of collateral industries such as distilling, provisioning, and shipbuilding also participated in supply or credit chains linked to slaving. State authorities sought to control and tax much of that activity, consolidating power and expanding empires with the proceeds. At the end of the chain, captives who survived that "way of death" toiled in fields, households, or mines. That process reached its bloody apex toward the end of the eighteenth century.[3]

The British colonies that won independence and became the U.S. federal republic were its byproducts, as were other British and European colonies in the Americas. Nineteenth-century North American legatees of that process tended to be involved in slaving in similar ways, including the brutal business of chaining people together and forcing them across a land- or seascape to sites of sale and toil. Slaving developed in the context of a federal system that gave the U.S. slave market its particular configuration, ostensibly contained within a political nation and its imperial territory.[4]

As slave-reliant commercial agriculture grew in the southern reaches of the U.S. republic, river valleys such as the Mississippi became a distinctive landscape of proslavery expansionists jealous of their political rights and fiercely protective of their economic prerogatives over African-descended bondspersons. That process has been abundantly and fruitfully researched. But investigations of slave trading in the American South usually focus on the commoditization of human beings and a business that begins with the purchase of a bondsperson and ends with her sale. Economic histories of nineteenth-century U.S. slavery have focused extensively on southern plantations and questions of productivity. Complementing that focus, most studies of the North American cotton complex have followed the supply chain from sites of production to the markets in which cotton was sold and the political contexts in which that process developed. Cotton exports and the industries connected to them constituted the greatest financial and geopolitical interest in the early republic. Financial historians of the early republic have examined banking institutions, money markets, networks of debt, and the cultures of confidence that supported them. Far from arcane and quaint systems that circulated dry paper among commercial actors, finance was capitalism's locomotion.[5]

This book draws elements from that scholarship and reassembles chains of goods and credit linked to enslaved people. It investigates decisions at the firm level that responded to the demands of competitive pressures and the drive to gain access to a broader share of the biggest and fastest-growing markets for bondspersons, adding the dimension of geoeconomic development to the study of slavery's capitalism. Exploring commerce in people as business looks beyond debates over whether slavery was part of the march of modernity and shifts focus from sites of commodity production such as plantations. Businesses involved in slavery evolved into organizations of remarkable scale and sophistication. Hands that drew bills of exchange, graded and traded commodities, or trimmed the sails of merchant vessels were as important to the process of slaving as hands that picked cotton or those that grabbed hold of whips, grasped the throats, or groped the loins of African-descended captives.

What follows is a chained history focusing on networks of people, information, conveyances, and other resources and technologies that moved slave-based products from suppliers to buyers and users. The forty-five years following the War of 1812 saw revolutions in transportation and finance that brought market actors closer together even as the distances captives traveled increased. This book examines progressions from sail to steam, rough trails to iron rails, and the financial wizardry that permitted enslavers to leverage their bondspersons on financial markets. The slave market was embedded in social practices of commerce and not limited to enslavers or Southerners themselves. Like those in the eighteenth century, some of the more successful participants in the nineteenth-century slaving business carried it on with strokes of quill pens rather than instruments of personal violence. Four of the seven chapters begin in New York. Following chains of supply and credit leads quickly to shipping lines and financial channels that venture far out of the American South. Often enslavers relied utterly on technology, transportation, and credit available thousands of miles from sites of slave auctions and cries of captives moved about like cattle. Such an approach avoids the muck of contemporary proslavery or abolitionist rhetoric and the consequent mire of debates that take as premises a cavernous divide between a Free North and Slave South, or the United States as an isolated or exceptional place, presuppositions that seep into histories looking backward from Confederate surrender and U.S. Emancipation in 1865.

Yet federal contexts and national borders mattered. Slavers knew that better than anyone. Perhaps the defining characteristic of federal sovereignty in the early republic was authority to control trade at the border. As part of a constitutional compromise over slavery initially prohibiting a federal ban on imports of foreign bondspersons, architects of the federal republic gave the national government power to regulate the importations of enslaved people to the United States. To do so they envisioned a national economy that contained the slave market and, once imagined in law, tasked customs officials and courts with policing it. Beginning in 1808, enslaved people were the main category of property not permitted to be exchanged across national borders, even if those borders were suspended once a ship sailed from the coast or a coffle marched through an Indian nation. Federal restrictions conferred a legal monopoly on sales of slaves who resided in the republic to slaveholders within it. Upper South slaveholders benefited from selling bondspersons to their lower South countrymen. The enormous transfer of borrowed wealth cemented interests in slavery's perpetuation among distinctive regions located in the American South and gave many others outside it reasons to take part in the forced migration of over 1 million African-descended Americans over seven decades.

That was neither the culmination nor the corruption of a founding vision, since the nineteenth-century political economy of slavery radically exceeded eighteenth-century imaginings. But it was no coincidence either that federal support for transportation, liberalization of trade, and land and monetary policies tended to open opportunities for enslavers. The end of the War of 1812 catalyzed the process since legal foreign trade resumed after eight years of embargoes and war. After 1815 the United States committed itself to advancing commercial agriculture that relied on bound labor. The United States practically emptied its treasury fighting and extirpating Native Americans to broaden slaveholding agricultural interests. It provoked war with Mexico and risked war with Britain to extend those interests. Proslavery was the default setting in the federal policy-making machinery.[6] This book draws connections between those big processes and the individual businessmen and enslaved people involved in them.

Each of the following seven chapters narrates a tragedy born of ambition through a discrete set of subjects whose participation in the slavery business illuminates the process of capitalist development and the promise of American modernity. The underbelly of that process is also on display in the shadows of coffle chains and captives' anguished passages. That narrative strategy seeks to personalize seemingly impersonal forces and put a face on the history of slavery's commercial development. It gets at the historical complexity, incremental changes, and unintended consequences of historical subjects' strategies. Firms had human faces and particular histories. They reflected social customs and constructions, including those of race, class, and gender. But they also reveal the ephemeral limitations and deep contingencies in which change occurred.

A narrative approach that follows discrete sets of individuals across the economic and geographic landscape also helps demystify abstractions such as capitalism, expansion, and the market. Using such abstractions as the subjects of historical action defies logic and taxes style. Underlying this strategy is a theory of history in which events continually confounded subjects' expectations and changed their plans and strategies. Historical progression has a seeming inevitability, but the subjects investigated here explored opportunities as they arose, trimming their sails to catch the prevailing breezes.

Few developments detailed here were inevitable consequences of an economic or political system or the results of abstract forces acting in history. Historical actors produced changes incrementally, often unintentionally, and usually with a limited comprehension of the results or alternatives. Market actors had imperfect knowledge of the commercial landscape, for instance, and captives who seemed to cooperate faced a series of choiceless choices. That orientation helps put in perspective the tragedy of the history told here: exceedingly creative people developed strategies that visited untold violence on others in the pursuit of returns. Enslavers were every bit as morally culpable for their actions as abolitionists have charged them with being. Their actions belie the ancient aphorism that money has no smell. The slavery business thrived on intergenerational theft, displacement, humiliation, and misery. But what follows seeks to understand the process that slavers helped create in incremental and often unintentional ways.[7]

Each chapter focuses on a small number of subjects connected to one another, and each examines a challenge of capitalist development. One of the obstacles to the growth and development of an interstate market was that the value of things was locally contextualized and the terrain bristled with obstructions. Chapter 1 follows the long, bitter trail of captives driven by Francis E. Rives and his partners from eastern Virginia to the lower South in 1818 and the economic geography of a slave market serving a booming cotton country. Rives and his partners faced the problem of how to transport assemblages or coffles of captives many hundreds of miles along poor roads, over wide rivers, and through Indian nations. Like captives, bank money and other financial paper typically did not travel well, and Rives's strategy had to account for what amounted to a tax on distance at the point of sale. He and his partners were small traders whose firm serves as a baseline for the business. Poorly capitalized and technologically limited slave traders like Rives continued to drive caravans of captives across the southern United States even into the Civil War, finding niches neglected by more well-organized enslavers.

Success in the slavery business required innovation, and slave traders served financial and not merely agricultural strategies. Chapter 2 traces the rise of an intensely entrepreneurial young businessman, Austin Woolfolk, and his Baltimore-based slaving firm. Woolfolk built a reputation into a brand. Through relentless newspaper advertising he conjured an ongoing slave market before it existed. His firm brokered interstate sales by offering banknotes or liquid assets to debt-burdened Chesapeake slaveholders and sold those captives to countrymen in the lower South who were taking on a mountain of debt in order to expand commodity production. As his firm became a perpetual clearing house for bondspersons, Woolfolk solved problems of supply by cooperating with purchasing agents in places such as Easton on Maryland's Eastern Shore and a sales facility in New Orleans managed by an uncle. To solve problems of transport, his firm bought excess space from merchant shippers, giving Baltimore's maritime community a financial stake in the interstate slave trade. Woolfolk's enterprise accelerated a demographic catastrophe among African-descended families in the Chesapeake, but even those north of the Mason-Dixon Line were affected by the development of the lower South cotton kingdom.

Chapter 3 follows John Craig Marsh's reinvention from failed New York City dry goods merchant to successful Louisiana sugar planter. Changes in Anglo-American trade after 1815 sped that transformation, as did federal tariff protections for domestic sugar. But Marsh and a partner lowered startup costs by smuggling New Jersey bondspeople to the canebrakes of the lower Mississippi Valley, supplementing their labor force with African-descended New York contract workers whose circumstances amounted to indentured servitude. They entered a place in which official toleration of slave smuggling was a tool to rule a state whose inhabitants were notoriously hard to govern. Marsh's eager pursuit and others like it illuminate tensions between a federal legal framework that ostensibly regulated slaving and the political economies of slavery that existed within the federal republic in the late 1810s.

As North American commercial agriculture expanded in the 1820s and 1830s, British and other foreign capital flooded into American financial institutions and, through them, into the hands of enslavers. Chapter 4 explores the banking schemes of Hugues Lavergne, Edmond Jean Forstall, and their colleagues as they gave slaveholders a means to draw equity from the bodies of enslaved people, which they bundled and sold abroad. Slaveholders used that leverage to expand sugar and cotton production while slavery's bankers sold the resulting securities to investors in New York, Britain, and Europe. Louisiana's sugar economy thrived on that foreign investment in property banks' mortgaged-backed securities, many eventually sold to investors who had little idea they were investing in slavery. The money supply expanded, and equity in lands and slaves bought more lands and slaves, improving technology such as sugar refining in the process. Demand for bondspersons increased correspondingly.

As finance and trade grew in sophistication, so did interstate slaving firms. Chapter 5 charts the rise and decline of the most successful U.S. slave-trading firm of the 1830s, Franklin and Armfield. Isaac Franklin, John Armfield, and their partners, including the Richmond trader Rice C. Ballard, built an expansive domestic interlocking partnership that was vertically organized and fiercely competitive. Captives circulated through the company's arteries and capital flowed through its veins at a relentless velocity. Franklin was the apotheosis of slavery's capitalist and solved the problem of interstate remittances by burrowing into the New Orleans banking community and using cotton bills of exchange. In the 1830s Franklin and Armfield's Chesapeake agencies eclipsed Austin Woolfolk's firm while building a dedicated slaving fleet and running the company like a railroad. The firm's fortunes rose during the flush times of the early to mid–1830s, when the Andrew Jackson administration liberalized foreign trade, boosted state banking while killing the Second Bank of the United States, and accelerated the extirpation of the Indians' lands, all of which helped propel enslavers' fortunes.

Following the financial crisis of the late 1830s and ensuing hard times, capitalist social relations became more mechanical. Chapter 6 details the slave trade's 1840s landscape through the ordeals of Solomon Northup. Enslavers' great economizer was violence, which Northup experienced when he was kidnapped and processed through a fragmented market, packed aboard steam-boats, rail cars, and a merchant sailing vessel, and taken from jail to jail in a nightmare odyssey. Orchestrating that loosely organized supply chain and distribution channel was Theophilus Freeman, a conspicuous architect of the new market. The violence he and his allies inflicted on the bodies and families of African-descended Americans mirrored the ecological transformation of the river valleys of the southeastern interior. Northup toiled for a dozen years far up the Red River in a strikingly dynamic zone of cotton and sugar production before a near-miraculous rescue.

South and west of the Red River, Texas slave country beckoned a New York City shipping merchant who built a line linking New Orleans to ports on the Texas coast. Chapter 7 traces Charles Morgan's steamship business as in many ways the culmination of slavery's capitalism. Morgan's commanding advantages on the Gulf Coast resulted in part from federal mail and army contracts, and he was one of the largest shippers of enslaved people in the country in the 1850s. Revenues from transporting bondspersons from New Orleans to Texas, along with passengers, goods, and bags of mail, permitted him to build a company that was able to project private power in foreign affairs. Following the discovery of gold in California, Morgan got into the cutthroat business of linking San Francisco and New York by steam, and partly as a consequence he supported filibustering in Nicaragua. Transportation efficiencies provided by companies like his helped revolutionize a slave market that behaved like a stock exchange, and in the 1850s slave prices became unmoored from commodities prices.

To enliven these narratives and sharpen the points they convey, this book draws on scholarship in geography, sociology, and business studies as well as history and literature. Those tools contextualize capitalist development and place an accent on investment and financial strategies wherein enslaved people served as assets managed as part of an enterprise. Investigating slaving firms and enter-prises involved in slavery permits analyses of strategy and subjects' quests for competitive advantages, which are microeconomic analogues of macroeco-nomic comparative advantages. Early nineteenth-century firms operated in a world without electronic communications and the staggering degree of special-ization that characterizes twenty-first-century enterprises. Some of the main challenges firms faced were the distribution of resources over geographic space and managing the webs of finance that spanned the Atlantic Ocean. Capitalism moved at the speed of sail or steam, where possible, and the agricultural year behaved like the crown wheel in a clock, setting the overall commercial pace.

The system evolved to require extraordinary social trust, a hallmark of capitalist markets. Organizationally, most firms' management cadre was coextensive with partners' adult male family ties and did business in a face-to-face environment. And yet the sociality of market actors and firms' strategies for developing competitive advantages were remarkably similar to those of human organizations today. Success hinged on firms' strategic use of resources, especially human capabilities and knowledge, all in the service of a brutal business that the most successful firms made rote and banal, ignoring or externalizing the human sufferings that they caused.[8]

Slaving or enslaving was the process of generating bondspersons. Despite laws that conferred slave status to babies born of enslaved mothers, slaves were made, not born. As so many ex-slave autobiographers have eloquently argued, *slave* was a legal designation rather than an existential one. Therefore, I use the term *captive* to designate those people who were subject to sale and enforced relocation. *Bondspersons, bondspeople,* and *enslaved people* are all used interchangeably. Each chapter contains narratives of individuals subjected to the slavery business. Slavers commoditized their bodies but did not colonize their consciousness. Typically, the enslaved did not behave slavishly, which was one reason enslavers spent so much time, money, and energy on security.[9]

SOUL DRIVERS, MARKET MAKERS

African-descended Virginians tied together and marching reluctantly through the Virginia countryside in the early months of 1818 embodied a central if tragic act in the human drama of U.S. commercial development. At least twenty-seven souls in a coffle driven by horsemen traveled southwest from Petersburg, a port town of seven thousand residents, to Raleigh, North Carolina, where they would turn right and head west. Their passage was part of a process of modern development, the antecedents of which had uprooted over 20 million Africans, 12 million of whom were embarked on Atlantic passages, the survivors landing in the Americas. Descendants of those forced migrants were embarking on another passage, this one south by southwest to the newest, most robust frontier of global staple crop production. That was the lower South. For the captives, it was an abrupt departure from the lands in which their ancestors' bones were buried and the worlds in which they dwelt with their concerns.

The slaves' burdens were heavy and their road was long. On rutted paths leading from Petersburg, girls and women, boys and men were among a caravan of people, wagons, and horses. Some were already sick. Others were disoriented as they walked to Mississippi for resale. In migrating droves or coffles, men were bound by the hands, often with iron shackles that etched bloody rings on the wrists. Dick and other adults were tied to one another with a heavy rope or chain, women as well as men. Tom and Aggy, husband and wife, accompanied each other. Both were from Prince George County, Virginia, like the men who now owned them. Children and anyone unable to make the twenty-mile daily march were hauled in horse carts. Little China rode in one, perhaps with Lucy, who was too old or perhaps too ill to march many days under her own power. Little China's memories of Virginia would fade in a sea of cotton. Most of the coffle members' lives would end there. John Curtis and Jane plodded along as well but would be sold before the others reached Mississippi.

Each coffle contained a diverse assemblage of human beings whose chronicles of sorrow resounded down the generations. In those days and nights on the road, immediate distresses presented themselves in the forms of chills from fevers, lack of proper clothing, damp or wet ground on which they occasionally rested, thirst and gnawing hunger, and the sharp sticks or stones that too often jutted up from the dirt road through a worn-out boot sole or a calloused bare foot. Yet in the recesses of their consciousness, they were also taking along their ideas of family, their worldviews, their repertoires of literature and ideas, their theologies, and their hopes, each one fatigued and refigured by the North American geography through which they walked. The faces of those bound together on foot registered the heartbreak of separations from loved ones and the anguish of a forced march. It was a thousand miles to Natchez, Mississippi. Inclement weather and stingy provisions complemented the dread of not knowing where or into whose hands one might fall. Armed strangers on horses led and followed the procession, their shadows outlining the fears and anxieties of the travelers. Yet a central component of a new market was taking shape in the troubled space between the captives' miseries and their owners' aspirations.[1]

The men driving the coffle viewed the procession in terms that contrasted starkly with those of the forced migrants. Francis Everod Rives led his enslaved countrymen out from Petersburg in the early months of 1818. The twenty-six-year-old Prince George County resident was a member of a wealthy Virginia family and had served in the state militia during the War of 1812, stationed at Norfolk. In 1818 he partnered with his fellow Prince George County residents Peyton Mason Sr. and Peyton Mason Jr. The trio invested in bondspersons in their corner of an expanding and expansive republic and expected great returns from moving them to sites of sale. They called their enterprise Peyton Mason and Company.

Their wealth had been built over the generations in plantation agriculture, which conferred on their generation perhaps more social status than economic stability. Prince George County was situated on the south bank of the James River east of Petersburg, a port that had served the colonial tobacco trade. That tobacco culture gave way to grain during the American Revolution, but the African-descended families in slavery had flourished. In the colonial and early national period, the value of slaves was influenced by the prices of the commodities they produced. But in the young federal republic that market was changing. In the Chesapeake, grain cultivation required fewer workers than tobacco.

Slaveholding agriculturalists found themselves in possession of a surplus of bondspeople at just the moment their countrymen were demanding slaves on a distant cotton frontier. Rives's enterprise shows little sophistication and no elaborate theory of the firm, but the business of slavery was one of the most knowledge-intensive in the Americas.

The development of American capitalism hinged on an economy of knowledge. Success as an interstate slave trader meant leveraging knowledge of local and distant markets and mastering the complexities of negotiating prices of human beings with other human beings. Slave traders' abilities to accumulate, manage, and deploy intangible assets were at least as important as the flesh-and-blood commodities they drove to market, the men they hired for security, the wooden vehicles that took them there, the steel weapons with which they guarded the captives, and the financial paper that changed hands in the transactions. Successful slavers were nimble in response to changing conditions of markets, technology, and routes of travel, from which they sought to gain competitive advantages.[2]

Peyton Mason and Company was a self-financed venture and one that took advantage of a slave market that faced the North American interior rather than the seaboard and Atlantic markets. Rives and his partners pooled capital and knowledge from eastern Virginia, but they needed to sell one coffle before investing in more slaves. They lacked a corporate organization and the ability to grow beyond the means of the trio of principals. To trim costs, Rives demanded that bondspeople walk rather than board ships. Unlike corn, hemp, or tobacco crops, slave traders' movable property traveled well and, in crude terms, largely hauled itself. That lengthened travel time but limited reliance on third parties such as jailors, shippers, and merchants acting as consignees in distant ports. Rives and the Masons acted as their own accountants, researchers, purchasers, transportation and sales agents, and, most important, bankers. Their business model was brutally straightforward.[3]

Isolating bondspeople and moving them from one regional slave market to another was profitable. Enslaved people sold for much higher prices in the lower South—at that moment about twice as much in Natchez, Mississippi, as in Petersburg, Virginia. Yet the seduction of easy profits obscured a business awash in perils. Runaways, money, and the environment formed a constellation of hazards, and what seemed like a good transaction today might prove to be harmful tomorrow. But as his horse gently trotted the west-leading roads, Rives could figure that at about twenty miles per day his enslaved property increased in value approximately 1.5 percent daily as the distance closed to where the Natchez Trace met the Mississippi River. That was if his perishable human goods made it to market.[4]

Rives's success depended on his ability to compel people to march away from their homelands. Some refused to comply. Before leaving Virginia, Dick escaped and was recaptured. He was later sold out of a jail in Southampton County, a cold consolation for someone seeking to avoid the overland passage to the West. Others faltered. John Curtis was sold along the way too, but his new owner would return him for the defect of "being diseased." Rives and his partners sold a woman and her child in Williamsborough, North Carolina, as they traveled south through Raleigh. Perhaps, like Curtis, she was in no condition to move farther or else caught the eye of a local buyer.[5]

Overland travel was plodding and circuitous. A land rich in resources also had abundant obstacles for anyone seeking to pass through the Appalachian Mountains. Roads were often overgrown with vegetation, and wagons had to pass ways blocked by fallen trees, washed out by winter freshets, or cracked from hard frosts that thrust stones to the surface. Roadside camping was standard. The flood of migrants also on their way west tended to bivouac, throwing up makeshift tents if possible. A country inn or tavern—scarce and correspondingly expensive in the Appalachians—might yield a hot meal for the horsemen at the head of the coffle. More frequently, locals earned money by renting shelter and selling chickens, eggs, vegetables, and other provisions for the road-weary stream of humanity passing through. Captives consumed rudimentary fare, insipid and lacking in nutrition. It would not do, slave traders reasoned, for bondspersons to consume any potential profits in the form of nourishing meat or bread when cheaper substitutes were available. They slept under the clouds and stars.

There were few national highways in the South, and those were often indistinguishable from a well-beaten path out of a port town. The national road leading west from Hagerstown, Maryland, was little more than a gravel-filled ditch. The routes Rives's caravan traveled were intermittently crammed with farmers, preachers, visitors, and letter carriers, some on horseback, some in carriages, and many others on foot. Herds of sheep, swine, or cattle ambled by them. One sojourner traveling with his family and slaves from Norfolk, Virginia, to Alabama in 1818 recorded "bad Roads" leading out from Prince Edward County. "Cart turned over," he recorded, but "no damage of consequence" other than a broken axel and being "low spirited" in consequence of his mother-in-law's suffering an illness.[6]

Some locals recoiled at the traffic. Congressman John Randolph of Roanoke, an early opponent of the interstate slave trade, complained of slave traders' coffles on the road passing through Salem, Virginia. In 1818 he wrote to a fellow congressman that the road through his district "is thronged with droves of these

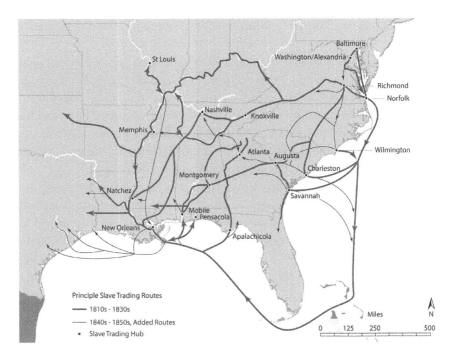

Map of the domestic slave trade, 1810s–1850s (Courtesy of the Digital Scholarship Lab, University of Richmond)

wretches & the human carcase-butchers, who drive them on the hoof to market." The scene brought to mind the British abolitionist Thomas Clarkson's 1786 essay on the transatlantic slave trade. "One might almost fancy oneself on the road to Cal[a]bar," Randolph quipped, comparing southern Virginia to the notorious West African slaving port in the Bight of Biafra.[7]

Federal internal improvements sped the interstate slave trade. They helped reorient it too. In the 1810s federal and state sponsorship of post roads and turnpikes made overland travel less time-consuming, tedious, and expensive than it had been before. It could not have seemed that way from the rude paths Rives and his coffle traveled. Roads leading out of Petersburg, and indeed most American roads, were often nothing more than packed dirt trails, muddy in summer, icy in winter, and ill-marked. Since 1792, citizens had petitioned Congress to establish post routes, and Congress acted to authorize the Postmaster General to establish post roads. Such dirt paths connected otherwise isolated villages, and private companies constructed wooden plank roads and turnpikes. Travelers allergic to tolls often beat paths around toll stations called shun-pikes. In the 1810s southern roads built under the direction of the Post Office and War Department connected riverine ports to entrepôts and cities. Between 1816 and 1820 miles of federal post roads increased nationwide by nearly half, from 48,976 miles serving 4,260 post offices to 72,492 miles serving 4,500 post offices. The benefits were tremendous: "There is scarcely a town, however retired," crowed Baltimore's *Niles' Weekly Register* in 1818, "whose inhabitants cannot converse with the inhabitants of the most remote and distant places of the union, with the same facility as with those of an adjoining town, through the medium of the post-office."[8]

After reaching Fayetteville, North Carolina, Rives's group wound their way westward, crossing in and out of South Carolina as they followed stagecoach routes. Along those roads, they followed many free migrants pursuing opportunities in the newly acquired territories in the West. It was not easy going for any traveler. In late winter and early spring, members of the coffle were subject to icy temperatures at night, and the winter of 1818 would be remembered as cold. The coffle passed through Warm Springs, North Carolina, where the French Broad River cuts through the Appalachians in Tennessee.

As members of the coffle continued to fall ill, Rives and his partners cut their losses by selling them. Jane was one. Her buyer would return her in the fall, claiming that she was "subject to fits," seizures or epilepsy. Her symptoms were probably caused by cysticercosis transmitted by means of pork tapeworms. Meat animals like hogs and cattle, "capital on the hoof," driven along arteries of trade, were vectors of disease. The pork tapeworm was spread to humans in undercooked infected pork and among people in a fecal to oral route. Sanitation was poor along the roads and paths the coffle traveled. All classes of migrant relieved their bodies along the roadside, and not a few streams from which water was drawn were infected. Pork tapeworm symptoms would not show for months as the tapeworm larvae grew to adulthood in the small intestine. Rives and his partners refunded Jane's purchase price when they drove a second coffle along a similar route. Her recovery was unlikely.[9]

The Tennessee border presented no obstacle to Rives's enterprise. It was no crime to carry enslaved human beings into Tennessee, and it would be several more years before the Tennessee legislature contemplated hauling up legal restrictions to the interstate slave trade, however ill-enforced they would be. In the overland slave trade, white skin was the only passport Rives and his partners needed, but in actual appearance the faces of Euroamerican travelers tended to be sunburned to a patina nearly indistinguishable from those of nonwhites.[10] As they traveled deeper into the southern interior, roads linking post offices grew sparse.

Military road projects complemented post roads but tended to cut through Indian lands. At the beginning of the 1810s, the United States built a road for wheeled vehicles along a horse path through the Creek nation. That route served an artery of trade connecting coastal Georgia to the Old Southwest, a highway for slave traders. Some Creek or Muskogee citizens welcomed the road, which helped take their slave-grown commodities to market. Some of their Cherokee neighbors had already built plantations staffed with African-descended bondspersons, and many Native American slaveholders were linked to Anglo-Americans by ties of kinship and trade. But, on the whole, roads that united Euroamericans divided Native Americans, and the federal road through Georgia exacerbated tensions among Creeks, who contended that federal roads were avenues of tyranny and pernicious violations of sovereignty.[11] It was one of several.

Jackson's Military Road was designed as a major artery of trade. It linked Columbia, Tennessee, on the Duck River to Madisonville, Louisiana, on the north shore of Lake Pontchartrain. From its southern terminus New Orleans was accessible by boat. Rives's coffle marched part of the route, which was coextensive with the Natchez Trace between Columbia and Tupelo, Mississippi. The procession of enslaved Virginians would pass army wagons and the occasional engineering group building bridges and widening the path. Congress appropriated the money to build the popular military road, which in the words of War Secretary John C. Calhoun—who still supported federal internal improvements—would "bind this Republic together."[12] In 1819 Calhoun explained that road and canal projects, "highly useful for military operations," were "equally required for the industry or political prosperity of the community."[13] All understood that commercial uses were at least as important as security ones. An army officer working on the road through Alabama in 1819 wrote home to Virginia: "I can with a few hundred dollars capital speculate to a great advantage by going on some fifty or a hundred miles in advance and entering some of the land that this road will pass through." He predicted that "in less than twelve months it will be one of the greatest thoroughfares in the United States." Technology would upend such optimism. Steamboats and river or port improvements would prove more beneficial to farmers and planters seeking to take crops to market, but migrants and slave traders were avid users of such projects.[14]

By scattering some Americans, Rives and his partners were bringing others closer together. Virginia slaveholders and Mississippi cotton planters had increasingly strong complementary interests, and in handing money to Virginia sellers and bondspeople to Mississippi buyers, Peyton Mason and Company was strengthening interregional ties. That was a variation on an old theme.

A British minister in Suriname wrote in the seventeenth century that African-descended slaves were "the strength and sinews of this western world." In the 150 years since that observation, bound labor in British North America had been transformed from scatterings of indentured English workers hoeing tobacco to hundreds of thousands of African-descended bondspersons cultivating cotton in long furrows. They were the strength and sinews of a robust capitalist system. The seemingly abstract market of which Rives's coffle was a small element was populated by people who formed discrete connections to one another. On the long journey from Virginia to the cotton frontier, market connections reinforced and often preceded national ones. That was the essence of democratization in the trans-Appalachian West.[15]

The coffle traveled through a maze of local producers, forging political and economic ties. As Rives directed his caravan of captives downriver from the western slopes of the Appalachian foothills and over the Cumberland Plateau, they ran across locals who took to the market on boats and pathways through the woods, selling their commodities and buying goods. Waterfront villages gathered local produce for transport to bulking centers in towns along the rivers, where they were often sold (or resold) and from which they were distributed. Goods entering a transregional stream of commerce were transported from larger towns down rivers to entrepôts serving overland distribution systems or else ports of international trade. The enslaved would be temporarily relieved of sore feet if transferred to keelboats or flatboats, the latter often nothing more than log rafts fastened together with nails and navigated precariously along the rivers. Thick woodlands flanked much of the route, but in breaks towns with wharves and makeshift warehouses and country stores appeared, the signposts no more than the smoke from village kitchen fires. Men onshore could be seen building broadhorns or flatboats. Most of the population settled within a day's walk of a river, so even the backcountry had access to the emerging markets that riverine routes served.

Goods held value relative to where they were in the market's geographic space. Small producers knew in concrete terms what economic geographers of a later age would theorize as contextualized value. Distances from market centers constituted impediments to trade. That amounted to a tax on distance. Some barriers were political. Before the Louisiana Purchase secured New Orleans for the United States, producers in the Mississippi Valley were at the mercy of whoever controlled that bottleneck to trade. The 1808 Abolition Act, 1809 Embargo Act, and subsequent restrictions on international trade also restricted possibilities for trade even as they promoted economic nationalism. Most barriers on the route Rives took were geographic. Commercial produce of the southern interior river valleys flowed downriver on keelboats or flatboats before steam travel revolutionized the riverine network, cutting the cost and time necessary, along with the prices of those goods. The proceeds of sales and consumer goods traveled the arduous routes back upriver, which before steamboats meant dangerous countercurrent slogs. On keelboats or bateaux men shouldered long poles or harnessed themselves with ropes, swam to shore, and pulled boats along crude towpaths, or grabbed branches and hauled the boat along or bushwhacked their way upriver.[16]

For hundreds of miles, Rives's caravan surveyed great expanses of hardwood forests and occasional farms, the smooth contours of the Blue Ridge Mountains rising in the west and then falling in hindsight as it crossed the Cumberland Plateau. The rocky highlands that appeared at the end of the plateau may have conjured the biblical Mount Ararat or Carmel. The French Broad River flows in the direction of Knoxville and the confluence of the Holston River as it winds its way south to the Tennessee River. The puffing of steam engines powering shallow-draft boats would arrest the attention of future travelers. The first steamboat on the Cumberland River, the *General Jackson*, would arrive the following year; the first steamer on the Tennessee River would not be seen for three more years. It is unclear whether the coffle traveled a river route or kept to overland roads, but they probably walked the Natchez Trace from Middle Tennessee to the Mississippi River.[17] With every mile of river and each labored footstep, the captives were incrementally moving the geographic center of U.S. slavery to the west and south, away from Petersburg, which had been its center at the turn of the nineteenth century.

The nation's fortunes had recently seen a stunning reversal from the economic hard times preceding the War of 1812. It had been just four years since the British burned the national capital of Washington, D.C. In 1814 the Royal Navy blockaded the Chesapeake Bay, encouraging thousands of enslaved Marylanders and Virginians to fly to freedom. In 1818 the U.S. trade with Britain was more robust than at any time in the republic's history, but the growth of the cotton complex corresponded to aggressive expansion into the southern interior. In the 1810s the United States was growing largely as the result of conquest of Indian nations within its territorial empire, which was a tragically ironic outcome of a war begun over trading policies with Britain and France.

The region just to the south of the route Rives and his coffle traveled was the real prize the United States won in the War of 1812. That was an intensification of a process already under way. As president, Thomas Jefferson had contemplated Indian removal, and almost since its founding the U.S. republic had aggressively acquired Chickasaw, Cherokee, and Choctaw lands. Jefferson's administration encouraged debt at Indian trading factories to expedite the process of land transfer to Euroamericans. Succeeding administrations pressured Indians to leave their lands. A significant outcome of the War of 1812 was the forced cession of over forty-three thousand square miles of Muskogee-Creek land to the United States in 1814, which contained most of present-day Alabama. The Treaty of Ghent, ending the war with Britain, ordered the restoration of Indian lands, but Andrew Jackson argued against the provision and Congress ignored it. That land cession was a turning point in American dealings with the southeastern Indians, who had resisted Euroamericans' incursions since colonial times, allied with colonial powers, and sought relationships with Euroamericans on their own terms.[18]

Unbroken sovereignty was an imperial fiction. American conquest of the southeastern interior was far from complete, and the overland interstate slave trade was in that respect not strictly a domestic one. In the 1810s an uncompromised U.S. empire west of the Appalachians was a feat of imagination that existed on American maps and in the political discourse of empire. The vast territory through which the coffle passed included several Indian nations such as the Catawbas, Cherokees, Yuchis, Chickasaws, and Shawnees, each under pressure from Euroamerican migrants, traders, and armies. The Natchez Trace had long been a highway for traders with captives. Indians themselves had been involved in the captive trade since well before Europeans settled the Eastern Seaboard.[19]

Following the War of 1812, the federal government accelerated the process of converting to private ownership lands expropriated from Indians and encouraging the development of import and export markets, along with the inevitable concentrations of wealth (and debt) in the hands of citizen landowners. That system relied on enslaved laborers to produce the staples and Euroamerican residents to consume the goods purchased with the proceeds. The growth of the slave market and the cotton interests it served nourished a political interest that supported slavery's expansion across the Mississippi River. That in turn was a catalyst for the political clashes over slavery that flared first in 1819, when Missouri sought entry into the federal union.[20]

Contrary to myth, much of it homespun, southern planters tended to be more internationally oriented in their economic outlook than their northeastern countrymen. Between 1815 and 1845 the main divisions that emerged between the northeastern and southwestern sections of the republic were what one historian terms "protective nationalism" in the northeast and free trade in the southeast. Protective nationalists viewed a national bank, tariffs, and other protective measures as prophylaxes against the dangers of war with Great Britain or another major European power. They were geopolitical realists who sought to use national authority to foster independence and secure the republic from foreign threats. Free traders voiced more optimism. As a group, cotton planters and their allies held that the market would diffuse the prospect of war with Europe's two largest cotton customers, Britain and France. They voted for capitalism over caution.[21]

Northern manufacturers and other special interests that received support through tariff policies in the twenty-five years beginning in 1816 attracted a near-unanimous opposition from southern agricultural interests invested in slave labor and in the thrall of foreign markets. Sugar producers, who had received increased tariff protections after the War of 1812, constituted a significant exception. But that did not automatically align them with northeastern manufacturers. National debates about the tariff and other protectionist policies turned on whether they would harm free labor in the North, promote slavery in the South, damage farming interests in the West, and thereby cause economic warfare among sections of the United States. But even free traders were deeply embedded in the American political system.

In the forms of security, roads, and "external improvements" such as building of lighthouses and dredging of ports, the U.S. government gave more to landowners and slaveholders in the trans-Appalachian West than it asked of them in taxes and the weight of tariffs. Besides the human and environmental costs, the expense of wars against Indians to conquer strategic regions of the lower South for Euroamerican planters was borne largely by revenues generated by tariffs. Instead of acknowledging their indebtedness to the federal system, southern politicians in the mold of Andrew Jackson argued that their northeastern countrymen ought not to receive direct protections that they lacked, even if the revenues paid for the destruction of their rivals and competitors among Native Americans and the navigation improvements in harbors and along rivers that sped their commodities to market. The relative lack of developed infrastructure did not follow an anti-improvement ethos. To the contrary, southerners living along river corridors welcomed federal navigation improvement projects. The South had an abundance of inland waterways that served as highways of commercial activity and an Atlantic or cosmopolitan orientation to that trade.[22]

Footsore and forlorn, Rives's coffle arrived in Natchez, a bustling hub of commerce on the east bank of the Mississippi River. The entry of a score of enslaved Virginians was a near-everyday occurrence between October and June in the town of 2,200. In the town itself, census takers counted three in ten residents as slaves in 1820. Free males outnumbered free females three to two, yet enslaved females were more numerous by a fifth than enslaved males. While coffles marched in from the eastern part of town, a flotilla of flatboats, keelboats, and steamboats disembarked enslaved people from the Mississippi River. An English visitor, Henry Bradshaw Fearon, arrived at Natchez in 1818 and recalled "observing a great many coloured people, particularly females," exiting flatboats on the Mississippi River. Seeing so many women of color disembark, Fearon "concluded that they were emigrants, who proceeded thus far on their route towards a settlement." He registered shock at the discovery that "fourteen of the flats were freighted with human beings for sale." Slave traders prepared forced migrants for sale before disembarking them. "They were dressed up to the best advantage," or costumed for market, "on the same principle that jockeys do horses upon sale," Fearon contended. As slaves traveled through Natchez, they passed the products of slave labor. "The streets are literally crammed with cotton bales for the Liverpool market."[23]

The town thrived on commerce in cotton, slaves, and just about everything else that could be steamed upriver from New Orleans or floated down it. Named after the Indians who had once lived there, Natchez was situated on a "beautiful commanding bluff rising from one to two hundred feet above the Mississippi river," reported a guidebook. Shouts and calls along the riverbank added to the clatter of horse-drawn carts and coaches along the roads. Elevation protected residents of the upper town from "the noisome exhalations of the adjacent low grounds" thought to cause the malaria and cholera outbreaks that made summers deadly, especially for the newly arrived. Capital of the new state of Mississippi, Natchez was home to its legislature and federal district and state supreme courts. Until 1826 mail from Washington, D.C., to New Orleans went by way of Natchez, along the same routes slave traders routinely traveled. Besides four churches, one each Roman Catholic, Baptist, Methodist, and Presbyterian, one bank and twenty-five dry goods stores were open by the early 1820s. Natchez supported a score of other businesses, from bricklayers, carpenters, millers, and distillers to physicians, goldsmiths, lawyers, and hatters.[24]

Town residents walking the streets could not actually see the river from the bluff, but the sounds, sights, and smells of business were everywhere. Natchez had a steam aqueduct to bring water to the city and two steam-powered sawmills to provide building materials. Members of Rives's coffle could practically hear the city being built. As they trudged through the city's dirt streets, they would also have noticed filth in its roads and alleys, stagnant and standing water, reflections of generally poor sanitation, especially in the lower parts of town. Pavers were at work surfacing roads and, by the 1820s, would build sidewalks as well.[25]

Rives's captives marched into a city that had a coarse, masculine, and unruly veneer, which partially concealed Natchez's role as a shopping center. In the "numerous stores," Fearon reported, "three fourths of the stock of every one consist[s] of British goods," and he was impressed by Natchez's "comparative prosperity exceeding any town which I have ever seen." Tastes for English and European goods were present among all sections of society. Even "the Negro barbers [did] not omit" mention of George Packwood's English razor strops, which they deemed best in the sharpening of razors. Americans consumed such items gluttonously, which by 1818 gave the United States a trade deficit with Britain.[26]

British capitalism thrived on American slavery, and the sad procession of bondspeople was a small link in a global supply chain. Nearly all the captives who were marched to Mississippi would touch the sharp boll of a cotton plant, if they had not already. Demand for cotton in English industrial cities traveled down that chain, tugging at individual members whom enslavers like Rives uprooted from families. The bales of cotton lint that lined Natchez's streets were representative samples of the lower South's primary export commodity. Cotton indirectly paid for the cornucopia of consumer goods so conspicuously on display and the African-descended Americans exiting boats on the Mississippi. Riverfront and backcountry plantations were among the "ghostly acres" that Britain annexed via its trading relationships with the Americas and South Asia, which proved decisive in its competition with other world empires, notably China.[27]

It was more apparent to business insiders than to itinerant slave traders that Natchez was part of England's macroeconomic hinterland. British manufacturers bought cotton from the British merchants that extended credit down the supply chain to planters. Enslavers in the lower South were increasingly reliant on foreign capital to finance the expanding U.S. cotton economy. Consequently, some of the money that reached New York or Baltimore in the form of bills of exchange from London or Liverpool financiers became dollars invested in cotton production in Mississippi or Alabama, a portion of which ended up in the pockets of Rives, the Masons, and their colleagues, and farther down the commercial chain, in the bank accounts of Tidewater Virginia slaveholders like the ones who sold slaves to Peyton Mason and Company in early 1818.[28]

The slave market seemed to sprawl all over town. Starting in the first decade of the nineteenth century, city authorities collected twenty-five cents a head on slaves brought into Natchez, which was a tax on one of the most lucrative commercial activities. Slave sales tended, however, to converge on Natchez-under-the-Hill, a neighborhood fronting the river, which had long been known for gambling, violence, and prostitution.[29] By the 1830s city authorities had expelled slave traders, and the bulk of slave sales took place at Forks of the Road, off the Natchez Trace a mile east of town, which had been a commercial outpost since the 1790s. Isaac Franklin of Tennessee and his partner John Armfield of North Carolina bought the land in 1823 and turned it into the center of the regional slave trade.[30]

When Peyton Mason and Company arrived to sell slaves, they found a thriving market and many willing buyers. But they had to be cautious. Back in Prince George County, Virginia, they were gentlemen of property and standing, but in Natchez they were at best wealthy strangers hawking valuable mobile property. The sole rights they had were those that they could defend, and frontier Mississippi was not known for its residents' dedication to law and order. Estwick Evans, a New Hampshire native, visited Natchez in 1818. He commented, "There is no branch of trade, in this part of the country, more brisk and profitable than that of buying and selling negroes." Plantation owners, aspirants, factors, and other commercial men were all in the market. Slaves, Evans reported, "are a subject of continual speculation, and are daily brought, together with other live stock, from Kentucky and other places." Before 1833 slavers sold their human chattels in town or even off the boats, which saved confinement costs and exposed them to less risk of disease. "So many bullocks, so many swine, and so many human beings in our market!" cried the New Englander.[31]

Traders advertised human beings along with other salable goods, and the market attracted buyers and sellers from near and far. Samuel W. Butler let his customers know he expected from Kentucky 200 barrels of whiskey, 15,000 yards of linen, 10,000 pounds of "good Bacon," and 15 "Likely Negroes," which he offered "at a reduced price for Cash."[32] Like most merchants of his place and time, Butler was not a specialist. Dealers in cotton and other staples, as well as pliers of the Mississippi River trade, diversified so they would be protected if any one part of their business failed. The man who embodied so much of that frontier capitalism was little different. In 1810 Andrew Jackson, in a partnership with two colleagues, sold tobacco and cotton at a store in central Tennessee. The partners invested some of the proceeds in twenty-six slaves the following year, intending to sell the bondspeople in Natchez. The deal went bad, and Jackson assumed responsibility for settling most of the debt, which he had to do by selling the slaves after bringing them back to Tennessee. The episode gave rise to charges that Jackson was a slave trader, but more vexing was his tarnished name and consequent inability to get credit.[33]

Like most businessmen, Jackson understood honor in terms of its being good for his debts. At its core, honor was part of the cadence of capitalism's forward march. Money was a touchy and emotional subject. The honor of one's signature on a bond or bill of exchange had greater bearing on the concept than the performance of mastery and other displays of masculinity. One corollary was that honorable men deserved credit, and much agitation and violence sprang from differences in perception of creditworthiness between would-be borrowers and lenders.

In that sense, being an itinerant slave trader had pronounced disadvantages. Rives was a business outsider with limited means to extend customers credit or borrow the wherewithal to expand the firm. If his customers failed to pay or make good on a bill or bond, the traders could ill afford to sustain the losses. Rives's firm counted hundreds of dollars in legal fees among its expenses for suing buyers over debts. Debt-burdened planters were accustomed to renewing debts rather than paying them, and itinerant slave traders quickly earned contempt.[34]

In the early republic, capitalists marched under a red flag. Soon after arriving at Natchez, Rives and his partners consigned their bondspeople to a respected merchant, Henry Turner, who auctioned most of the coffle members. Turner was the wizard who conjured the magic of returns. He was a general agent operating with his brother Edward out of a prominent brick building between First and Second streets. Red flags appeared outside such establishments with as much regularity as sale signs appear in shop windows today. Turner was a shrewd choice. He bought and sold a variety of goods, including slaves, and was well connected. In 1825 his daughter Eliza married John A. Quitman, a Natchez lawyer and later U.S. representative, governor, and major general. For Rives and his partners Turner sold seventeen young men and women for "an average of $900," throwing in "Lucy an old woman" free of charge. Lucy had ridden over a thousand miles to a market in which her aged limbs were not calculated to make much cotton, serve many plates of food, or scrub many floors. Those Henry Turner did not cry off at auction, Peyton Mason and Company "sold for cash."[35]

Those highly complex acts of sale taxed the knowledge of buyers and sellers. Buyers inspected the enslaved people on sale with as much care as sellers inspected the paper used to pay. Theirs was an age in which no one took money for granted, and assessing the value of the monetary instruments was nearly as important as price. Gold and silver coins were the most desirable monetary items and the last with which anyone would part. Enslaved people too seemed to represent solid value. But judging the value of enslaved people was a matter of experience that put the prestige and often the finances of the buyer on the line. Oiled skin and the threat or use of violence could conceal sickness or a bondsperson's determination to defy mastery. Likewise, a seller hazarded a small fortune when accepting paper. There were enough phony bills in circulation that a vendor had to know that the note was printed back East and signed by a bank official rather than manufactured in a counterfeiter's shop in Kentucky or Missouri and passed down the rivers. Like the bondspersons traded for them, financial instruments had contextualized value.[36]

Rives and his partners realized large profits, at least on paper. The firm doubled their money on Tom and Aggy, selling the couple for $1,200. Most of the other coffle members also sold for nearly twice what Rives and his partners had paid for them. The firm accepted an assortment of paper, including banknotes, promissory notes, and bills of exchange. Their financial ledger registered a profit of $9,060, each of the principals earning $3,020, enough to buy a modest plantation.[37] Negotiating the price of a slave or other item was one step in a commercial transaction, and price varied depending on the medium of payment. Unlike greenbacks of a later age, the money that circulated in the early republic was a hodgepodge of state and national banknotes, checks, firms', merchants', or individuals' promissory notes, drafts, bills, and securities such as deeds or mortgages. Every merchant or storekeeper who touched a market segment beyond her or his neighborhood was an exchange broker of some kind. The same businessman might get away with limited literacy, but numeracy was essential. Despite hard-money backers' claims that paper money was little more than legalized counterfeiting, exchanges of financial paper functioned with a mystifying combination of sophistication and ease.[38]

Despite Natchez's reputation for violence and iniquity, confidence and trust were its commercial cornerstones. Well-regarded market actors could create a piece of locally circulating money by scrawling on a piece of paper a promise to pay the bearer back a sum with interest. The endorsement of a banker or factor could broaden the network in which that financial instrument circulated. A key component of the capitalists' knowledge economy was discerning whose honor was puffery and who was actually good for his debts. In that sense financiers were "confidence brokers" who mediated commercial exchanges and promoted social trust. Merchants and bankers with a sound interregional or international reputation could draw bills of exchange that circulated among port cities as if silver or gold. During the War of 1812 the U.S. government printed treasury notes that circulated as money, but that was an emergency measure. Specie or hard money was scarce and nearly always worth a premium over paper. In 1818, for instance, the U.S. Mint coined less than a quarter million dollars face value in gold coins and just over a million dollars face value in silver coins, mostly half dollars destined to sit in bank vaults. Mexican-milled dollars, or eight reales (or pesos—pieces of eight), were far more common and were legal tender in the United States until 1857.[39] But few merchants could or would use specie.

Paper money was essential, but like economic thought in the early republic, monetary theory was up for grabs. The idea of an organic or natural economic system that existed independently of human choices was in its infancy, along with the idea of business cycles. Instead, issues of money and finance were understood in moralistic terms. Prevailing wisdom of the time was that bills that paid for actual transactions, such as shipments of cotton, were the sole basis of a sound financial system. Economic panics were thought to be the result of overbanking or an unwarranted oversupply of credit and overtrading or trading bills in excess of the real value they supposedly represented. Part of that real-bills doctrine held that sound banking inhered in a responsibly strict relationship between reserves or the liquid assets it owned and the loans it made. Human psychology intervened. In buoyant financial times, like those in the spring of 1818, individual bankers and firms optimistically extended credit or incurred debt beyond the limits of their abilities to repay quickly. Nearly every commercial quarter was awash in paper that did not represent actual assets or obligations.[40]

Banking in the United States was still in an experimental phase. By the time Rives arrived in Natchez, the state banks that opened after 1815 were busy monetizing the country. The number of such banks had exploded since the end of the War of 1812. They were known as caterpillar banks, consuming everything in their paths. State banks supplied banknotes that lowered transaction costs among those who used them as exchange media. They also extended credit to merchants, some of whom behaved like retail bankers when acting as factors to planters. Natchez contained the main branch of the Bank of Mississippi, the sole state-chartered bank. By the time Rives and his coffle entered Natchez, the Second Bank of the United States had been in operation for only a year. It would grow to serve some functions of a central bank through its power to buy and sell foreign bills of exchange and to decide which banknotes were acceptable at the U.S. Land Office. But a Second Bank branch would not open in Natchez until 1830. The sole Natchez newspaper, reflecting the local network of merchants and bankers responsible for allocating credit and mediating financial transactions, printed blank checks, bills of lading, and deeds.[41]

Notes from banks with solid reputations could travel hundreds of miles and be accepted at close to par or face value, whereas notes from local institutions decreased in value the farther they traveled. Virginia state banks opted for strong banknotes rather than liberal loans, a policy that benefited Rives and his partners. Notes from eastern branches of the Second Bank of the United States came close to a national circulating medium, whereas banknotes from unchartered banks and those with reputations for profligacy were traded at deep discounts. Since states had various criteria for chartering banks, banknotes issued by state-chartered institutions in states with weak regulations were almost automatically suspect. Kentucky incorporated forty banks in 1817, for instance, without requiring that they hold actual specie to back prodigious banknote issuances. In a free market such issues would sink to the bottom of the market, but political intrigues kept many leaky financial vessels afloat. Discounts on banknotes and various media of exchange illustrate market difficulties Rives's firm worked to mitigate, and not merely in terms of what to use as money.

Peyton Mason and Company settled on an expedient if inefficient way to take proceeds back to Virginia. The firm avoided banknotes from states like Kentucky, along with local issues or "river money," and collected an assemblage of checks, over $900 in Virginia banknotes, and nearly $8,000 in North Carolina banknotes. Only $60 was in gold. The banknotes had been taken across country by merchants or migrating planters and would complete a circuit in the hands of slave traders. At discounts then available, $900 in Virginia notes from state-chartered banks was worth $890 reckoned in specie or notes from the Bank of the United States. That was as good as any cashier's check or bill of exchange payable in the East. The $8,000 in North Carolina notes the partners received was equivalent to between $7,800 and $7,680 in coin, according to a Philadelphia commercial newspaper. If any of the notes were from unchartered Virginia banks, they traded at 7 or 8 percent below par that spring.[42] Rives and his partners probably scoured the town for Virginia and North Carolina notes to avoid the punishing discounts local notes would impose.

Financial institutions and especially western banks had many reasons to like slave traders. If Peyton Mason and Company accepted Louisiana or Mississippi state banknotes in the lower South, the banks there were happy to see the notes leave the state. The farther a banknote traveled from its issuer, the less likely it was the bank would have to redeem it for gold or silver. North Carolina bankers would just as soon see their notes disappear on the frontier, never to return, but their books still had to account for the notes they placed in circulation. Because of monetary decentralization in the early republic, one's pocketbook often contained a financial travelogue. A Baltimore newspaper advertisement for a lost wallet in 1818 listed the contents as including a $100 note and two $20 notes issued by the Bank of the United States, a $1 dollar note issued by the Bank of Dayton, Ohio, a $100 note (besides smaller denominations) issued by the Bank of Nashville, a $100 note issued by the Bank of Knoxville, over $150 face value "in several notes from 2 to 20 dollars on the bank of N Carolina," $18 "or about, in small notes on the banks of Richmond and Virginia," $50 "in several notes on the Valley Bank of Winchester," Virginia, and $10 notes issued by the Bank of Virginia.[43] That assortment charted the owner's trek across Ohio, Tennessee, North Carolina, and Virginia. Peyton Mason and Company profited from the booming economy underpinned by cheap credit and inflationary policies.

As the enslaved forced migrants were taken to sites of toil, revenues from their purchases began the trek east. After selling members of their coffle, the Masons departed for Virginia. Rives tarried in the Natchez area and reported "having purchased & sold some Negroes after [he] arrivd. in the west, the profits of which defrayed the expenses." Those amounted to a net $14.24. Rives had entered the market at an auspicious time. Back in Virginia, Peyton Mason and Company's money did not sit idle. Using capital deposited in the Farmers' Bank of Virginia after returning from Natchez, the firm bought more enslaved people in the spring and summer of 1818. Rives led a coffle of eighteen to Alabama that fall, returning with a motley assortment of financial instruments, including a collection of promissory notes, banknotes, a gold watch, and two shares of "Marathon" stock—municipal bonds issued by an Alabama boomtown that went bust following the panic that reached American shores the following January.[44]

Henry Watson had an insider's view of the slave trade. Considerations of economic geography, discount rates, and confidence were to him variations on a theme of violence. The humanness of captives like Watson reveals the ugly realities of the market fictions that slave traders conjured and the flimsy banknotes that lubricated the slave trade. Watson was sold in Natchez for $500 within a year or two of Peyton Mason and Company's coffle arriving. He joined the flood of forced migrants who shouldered the burdens of agricultural production on the frontier. Born in slavery outside Fredericksburg, Virginia, in 1813, Watson opened his eyes on a world of tumults. When he was small, his mother disappeared from the manor house on the plantation on which they both lived. The explanation Watson received was that "a slave-dealer drove to the door in a buggy, and my mother was sent for to come into the house; when, getting inside, she was knocked down, tied, and thrown into the buggy, and carried away." In an instant she vanished, never to return. Watson himself was soon sold to a minister—the first of five times he was sold—and spirited off to Richmond, where he was resold at public auction.[45]

If families were not disarticulated before, they were within the confines of the city slave market. Children like Watson, just discovering the contours of life in slavery, witnessed it often in the form of lost parents and disappeared relatives. That was a key part of the process that enabled the business Rives and his partners undertook. More broadly, the abilities of African Americans held in bondage to form families and produce children also held in slavery were necessary to the expansion of North American slavery and the slave market that delivered them to areas where their productive and reproductive labors were in demand. Reproduction was the essence of U.S. slavery's domestication and the consequent move away from the ways of death that characterized slaving elsewhere in the Americas.[46]

Not all experienced the slave market in the same way, and community was correspondingly difficult to maintain or create. "Some were in tears," Watson remembered of the Richmond slave market, although "others were apparently cheerful." The enslaved had no unified understanding of their ordeals. Viewing the condition of his fellow bondspeople "brought to my mind my mother," he recalled, "and caused me to shed many tears; but they fell unheeded." Watson could imagine his mother sold in a similar setting, which intensified the shattering feelings of her loss. He was on his own. "The auctioneer was busy examining the slaves before the sale commenced." After the adults were sold, the children were auctioned. Watson was sold "to a man whose name was Denton, a slave trader, then purchasing slaves for the Southern market." Interstate slave traders like Rives visited local markets to assemble coffles to take south.[47]

Watson's passage out of his native Virginia was indirect. It commenced in a private jail, where, "on entering I found a great many slaves there, waiting to be sent off as soon as their numbers increased." Sixteen-foot walls enclosed a central yard "of but one room, in which all sexes and ages are huddled together in a mass." Watson was in jail for two days before Denton had a full complement of slaves. "Horses and wagons were in readiness to carry our provisions and tents, so that we might camp out at night," he recalled. The drove marched along the roads into Tennessee, "where we stopped several days for the purpose of arranging our clothes." It was harvest time, and as the coffle marched into cotton country, the traders hired out the men as pickers. Meanwhile, "we lost four of our number, who died from exposure on the road." Three weeks later the march southward resumed, "and in about four weeks [it] arrived in Natchez, Miss." Another slave jail awaited "the flock," which was how Denton "would sometimes term us," Watson testified. In Natchez the group was advertised on "a sign-board in front of the house, which informed traders that he had on hand, blacksmiths, carpenters, field-hands; also several sickly ones, whom he would sell very cheap." Those who were half-dead would still fetch a price. "In a short time purchasers became plenty, and our number diminished."[48]

Denton expected his human goods to play the parts he crafted for them in the slave market's commercial theater. Those who refused to get into character were punished. Watson witnessed violence meted out for small infractions, including beatings with a paddle with holes drilled in it. "This instrument of torture he would apply, until the slave was exhausted, on parts which the purchaser would not be likely to examine."[49]

Not fully cooperating with Denton was the chief crime. Watson recalled that the "flesh protrudes through these holes at every blow, and forms bunches and blisters the size of each hole, causing much lameness and soreness to the person receiving them." The trader paddled slaves in the mornings before buyers arrived to survey the human goods. Kidnapped free people of African descent were sold alongside slaves, but to the captives themselves there was little practical difference. Americans offered for sale did not concede the legitimacy of the slave trade, which they recalled as theft.[50]

Life on the frontier was particularly harsh for African Americans, and even contemporaries recognized the human costs of travel. In the 1840s the University of Virginia professor George Tucker argued that slaves "who had been transported from the more northern slave-holding States" to "Mississippi, Louisiana, and South Alabama" had suffered "extraordinary mortality," especially "in the first year of the term." Forced migration was deadly, he contended, and if the enslaved did not die en route to the lower South, they might die of exhaustion or disease once there. He wrote what captives like Watson had long known: "Slave labour, in the more northern of the slaveholding States, will not greatly decline in price so long as it is very profitable in the more southern." The families from which captives were taken were often old American ones, generations deep, but most forced migrants were young. If an enslaved American lived to ten years, she or he could expect to live another forty, but infant mortality and death among small children pushed life expectancy at birth down to thirty, a few years less than white Americans. In the 1810s the United States' gross national product surged, but life expectancy fell across the board.[51]

Watson was sold by one violent owner to another. He was bought by a dry goods dealer, Alexander McNeill, whom Watson recalled as "dark-complexioned, had sharp, grey eyes, a peaked nose, and compressed lips; indeed, he was a very bad-looking man." Watson would be McNeill's personal servant. Despite Watson's attempt to please him, "the first morning I was severely flogged for not placing his clothes in the proper position on the chair." The day after that he "received another severe flogging for not giving his boots as good a polish as he thought they had been accustomed to." Unflinching violence was not confined to the frontier, but there were fewer social curbs on owners' resorts to it. "Thus

he went on in cruelty," Watson shuddered to recall, "and met every new effort
of mine to please him with fresh blows from his cowhide, which he kept hung
up in his room for that purpose." The abuse continued when McNeill bought a
farm near Vicksburg, Mississippi, onto which Watson and his fellow slaves were
moved.[52] Watson would be sold again and again, lashed and beaten, until he
escaped to Boston by posing as a free sailor. There he would publish his ordeals
in 1848. His fellow bondsman James W. C. Pennington of Maryland explained
the nub of the system in which Watson found himself. "THE SIN of slavery lies in
the chattel principle, or relation." "The being of slavery," he explained, "its soul
and body, lives and moves in the chattel principle, the property principle, the
bill of sale principle; the cart-whip, starvation, and nakedness, are its inevitable
consequences to a greater or less extent, warring with the dispositions of men."[53]
The risks and costs slaves like Watson bore with his health, despair, and
unfreedom were part of the double consciousness of slavery in which his isolation and carriage were the main sources of enslavers' profits.[54]

On the long, downward road of agricultural returns in eastern Virginia, the
interstate slave trade offered a shortcut to commercial wealth. Rives and his
partners were taking advantage of a low cost for entry into a lucrative if risky
trade. Elsewhere in the Atlantic basin, enslavers who transported captives from
coastal embarkation points across bodies of water were highly capitalized and
faced a series of regulations.[55] In the United States, government oversight of the
interstate slave trade consisted of requiring a slave manifest for coastal vessels,
which complemented sporadically enforced state restrictions on transporting
black bodies across political borders. Beyond restrictions on captives transported in coastal waters, the federal government refused to regulate the interstate trade and dared not exercise its authority to tax it.[56]

There was nothing inevitable about the development of a market for enslaved
people that stretched from the banks of the Appomattox River to the Mississippi.
When Rives set out with his partners and enslaved countrymen, few envisioned
Virginia and Mississippi as part of the same region. The considerations that
framed Peyton Mason and Company's commerce in people in 1818 illustrate
the human dimensions of a process of national expansion, political consolidation, and capitalist development that boosted Americans' mobility, provided
some greater access to credit and money, and contributed to higher living standards among a broad section of the population. Captives and indigenous people
paid a high price for the development of that democratization of an American
pursuit of happiness. Each coffle of enslaved Americans who arrived for sale in
the cotton complex intensified a political strategy of white supremacy and

nonwhite servitude, which shaped the structure of the political economy of the Old Southwest.[57]

During the first two decades of the nineteenth century, slave traders tended to be marginal actors and petty capitalists. Peyton Mason and Company was an unsophisticated organization composed of neighbors who pooled resources, both tangible and intangible. Their business was a niche in a larger system of finance and trade. Rives supplied a vital component of the cotton supply chain, but he was frozen out of merchants' networks of credit. His theory of a firm was lacking in sophistication, but his competitive advantage inhered in a willingness to risk others' lives while risking his own capital, to drive bondspersons along poor roads and perilous rivers in response to a beckoning marketplace on the Mississippi River.

Strategically, Rives's firm was like a small ship trimming its sails to catch the political-economic winds rather than inventors working on new methods of propulsion. The federal government's sponsorship of roads and protection from foreign competition filled his sails. Rives's enterprise featured hundreds of practical considerations ranging from the logistics of assembling, confining, feeding, and transporting forced migrants to how to pay for and profit from the operation, including how to raise credit and what to accept as money. Yet the market rewarded slave traders' ingenuity, and slave traders' activities contributed to the development of a national market that was situated haphazardly in an Atlantic commercial network through their transport of captives to the lower South and financial instruments back to the Eastern Seaboard.[58]

Francis Everod Rives never became a professional slave trader. Rives may have served as an agent of Franklin and Armfield, the most powerful slaving firm of the 1830s, but after he and his partners marched a second coffle to the lower South in 1818, he turned to politics. Rives was elected to the Virginia House of Delegates in 1821, where he would serve ten years before joining the young Democratic Party and moving up to the state senate. Having witnessed the demand for efficient transportation and with a sense of railroads' potential to revolutionize the region's commerce, Rives went into the railroad business in the late 1820s. He became a principal in the Petersburg Railroad, which linked his home city to a strategic trading artery near the Roanoke River in North Carolina. He was known best for chicanery undertaken in the name of boosting Petersburg's commerce at the expense of railroad competitors and the rival port city of Portsmouth. Petersburg citizens rewarded Rives by electing him mayor.[59]

"THE MOST NOTORIOUS OF THE BALTIMORE NEGRO-BUYERS"

In the fall of 1815 nineteen-year-old Austin Woolfolk arrived in the city of Baltimore. Over the next fifteen years he built one of the largest slave-trading firms in the country. Like so many new arrivals, he had grand ambitions yet humble acquaintances. Six feet one inch tall, athletic and imposing, Woolfolk was beckoned by riches in the slave trade. His firm's rise is a story of the capitalist virtues of mastering the workings of a complex marketplace and developing competitive advantages. Merchant houses, wharves, taverns, and newspaper offices were his classrooms. Woolfolk's calling card was cash, but his intangible resources were golden. He quickly learned the human and market geography. Other slavers operated in Baltimore and rival Chesapeake cities, but he advertised relentlessly and cultivated Baltimore shipping merchants. He allied with kinsmen to build a supply chain. That network catapulted him from itinerant to business insider. Woolfolk worked tirelessly and thrived on the pursuits of profit and advantage. He delayed family and marriage until his early forties while building an enterprise coffle by coffle.[1]

Woolfolk initially exploited the fact that the grain economy of the Chesapeake relied less on slave labor than had its pre-Revolutionary tobacco culture, and Baltimore was a promising place for such entrepreneurship. Besides corn and wheat, it gathered scattered kernels of humanity. In 1812 the city newspaper editor Hezekiah Niles proclaimed that since the end of the American Revolution Baltimore had grown "from absolute insignificance, to a degree of commercial importance, which brought down upon it, the envy and jealousy of all the great cities of the union." Not all were so sanguine. The same year a Boston newspaper snorted that Baltimore "is in great measure made up of adventurers from other parts of this country, of foreigners, fugitives from Justices, the outcasts of society and the disgrace of it; with very little of that solid character which is the result of a great variety of moral and physical causes." Whatever the origins of its residents, the city developed amid the disorderly forces of the early republic's commerce.[2]

Approaching by water from the Chesapeake Bay, a passenger would view the city rising to the northwest above the Patapsco River, more an estuary than a flowing river. Tall ships' masts were gathered at the southeastern tip, Fell's Point. Rowboats, pilot boats, and scows carrying passengers and assorted goods flitted among merchant ships. On a workday, the buzz of saw blades and sounds of hammers punctuated the shouts of shipwrights and foremen emanating from the shipyards. Voices competed with the clatter of horse-drawn carts and rhythmic drubbing of steamboats, which appeared in 1813 to ferry passengers between Chesapeake cities. Merchants in fashionable clothing could be seen amid throngs of mariners, old salts, and green recruits working along the long wharves or climbing ships' rigging. Some workers and sailors were enslaved, some indentured. Depending on the wind, one might smell another feature of the Baltimore harbor before seeing it, and that was the Mud Machine, a dredging barge doing great damage to the layer of silt filling the harbor as it widened the harbor to accommodate larger and larger ships. The city was divided by Jones Falls, a stream powering mills, carrying waste to the river, and overflowing after rains. West of the falls stood the sturdy commercial and government buildings in the city's business center. Situated "upon very abrupt ground," remarked a visitor, Baltimore "contains many excellent streets, and fine market-houses." It was half the size of Philadelphia, a hundred miles to the north. Beyond the wharves, residences sprouted along streets that were recently paths leading into the backcountry. When Woolfolk arrived in 1815, city residents had started building a stone monument to George Washington in the respectable northwest neighborhood near the Catholic church.[3]

Woolfolk's route to Baltimore was circuitous. Born in Stokes County, North Carolina, he moved west to Tennessee as a child. Austin was one of eight children and the oldest son of William Woolfolk, a planter and landowner. According to a family history, Andrew Jackson was a neighbor and family acquaintance whom Austin met at a young age. After Austin Woolfolk's mother died and his father remarried, the teenager, fond of horseback riding and other active pursuits, fled home to protest his stepmother's behavior toward his siblings. The War of 1812 reunited father and son. At barely sixteen, Austin enrolled in the Tennessee militia and served in a regiment commanded by his father. By then, Major William Woolfolk was stationed near Wetumpka, Alabama territory, site of the Treaty of Fort Jackson. Father and son participated in the Battle of New Orleans in January 1815. Austin had risen to lieutenant and quartermaster of the Third Battalion of Tennessee militia. It is unclear what rudiments of a business education he was able to glean before relocating to Baltimore. Almost certainly, Woolfolk saw the makings of an empire of cotton, sugar, and slaves in the Deep South and witnessed up close the geopolitical tides turning in favor of Euroamerican slaveholders on the southern frontier.[4]

Woolfolk mixed in among many enterprising people in the commercial hub of the upper Chesapeake, which grew by over a third in the 1810s. Decades before the son of a Liverpool cotton merchant wrote of urban life, "The devil take the hindmost, o!" Maryland's queen city seemed to personify that ethos. During the War of 1812 and British blockade of the Chesapeake, shippers swapped bills of lading for letters of marque and reprisal. Baltimore merchants kept afloat on the plunder privateers took from the enemy. Following the war, trade quickly resumed, and the shipyards, merchant houses, and wharves hummed with activity. Besides thriving on the grain trade, Baltimore was a center of shipbuilding and other industries such as spinning and tanning. Meat, cotton, and flour were traded in its merchant houses and shipped from Baltimore's wharves. Sugar refiners prospered as well, importing raw sucrose and selling refined sugar in barrels and loaves. As trade grew, some city commission merchants became merchant bankers. By the time Woolfolk arrived, the English-born architect Benjamin Henry Latrobe was busy designing the Baltimore Exchange, which would consolidate much of the city's commercial activity under an elegant domed roof.[5] Slaves were another category of merchandise whose profit potential was ripe for exploitation.

Sellers of patent medicines pioneered advertising in newspapers and pamphlets, but Austin Woolfolk honed an advertising strategy that came to define the domestic slave trade. Between 1815 and 1831 he advertised in each month of the year, in an era before principles of advertising were formalized; he and his agents made Woolfolk into a brand name synonymous with the slave trade. In his first several years in business, he advertised intensively until buyers furnished as many enslaved people as Woolfolk calculated would make a trip to Georgia or Louisiana profitable. He paused advertising while marching or sailing a coffle of slaves out of state and resumed when reinvesting in slaves. Like other purchasers, Woolfolk used newspaper advertising to reach a wide audience and made an appeal to slaveholders to approach him with their property. But Woolfolk was hardly a pioneer.[6]

Baltimore was already home to several such merchants plying the interstate trade by 1815. Woolfolk and his kinsmen sometimes listed their address as

Augusta, Georgia. Austin owned a house there by the mid–1820s, and his uncle John was an established businessman in that town. Woolfolk's early advertisements borrowed phrasings from his brother slave traders. In January 1815 Baltimore newspapers featured ads promising that "a liberal price in cash will be given" for "A few Negroes, of different descriptions." That was not a novel appeal. An 1811 Hagerstown, Maryland, newspaper ad bellowed, "CASH WILL BE GIVEN for a few likely NEGROES." By 1815 ads promising "cash for negroes" appeared in Washington, D.C., newspapers as well.[7]

Woolfolk incorporated catchphrases as hooks to customers and sustained his appeals by repeating them. In November 1815 he began advertising with the headline "CASH FOR NEGROES," identifying himself as the buyer and beckoning interested slaveholders to a city tavern or the offices of one of the city's largest-circulating newspapers, the *Baltimore Patriot & Evening Advertiser*. The ad ran serially in November and December. By repeating the request for a number of slaves and promising cash, Woolfolk contended that he would sustain a market in slaves—a market that he imagined for readers before it existed.[8]

The appeal had some psychologically shrewd components. Woolfolk invited slaveholders to view the human beings they held in bondage in terms of the banknotes he exchanged for title to their property. Maryland slaveholders knew their bondspeople by name and often intimately. Like appeals of cash for gold or for vehicles in a later age, cash for slaves was an appeal to realize the market value in human property and to turn that property into liquid assets. Banknotes efficiently represented market value for the commodity that was being bought and sold. Woolfolk's several advertisements in the fall and winter of 1815–16 do not specify which medium he used as cash or what he sought to do with the slaves once purchased. It took him until 1821 to offer payment "in United States' money, gold or silver." But that advertisement ran for only a short time. He could not sustain its claims. By 1836 Austin Woolfolk was paying by check. By then his check was as good as cash.[9]

Woolfolk's advertising campaign harnessed the rapidly growing medium of daily and weekly newspapers, which reached tens of thousands of readers in Baltimore and beyond. Newspapers were commercial transcripts and appeals to buy a cornucopia of consumer goods, even though a growing section of readers were not themselves subscribers. Woolfolk's ad campaign reflects the power of the medium and its ability to circulate his commercial appeal. Some newspapers, like *Niles' Weekly Register*, were institutions of civil society, but Baltimore's daily newspapers were more advertising sheets than journals of democratic debate. A British visitor in the 1810s moaned that American newspapers were "extremely uninteresting, relying almost entirely for matter upon advertisements and English news." To shippers and merchants who wanted the latest marine intelligence or prices, however, newspapers were filled with interesting tidbits. The same went for those looking to buy or sell real estate or consumer products, or to find out about local events.[10]

Newspaper ads in the era were unclassified, so advertisers had to draw the attention of would-be customers from among the various other appeals. Part of the joy or frustration in reading such a newspaper was its seeming disorganization or the surprise of encountering a valuable or interesting morsel among the jumble. Some readers checked off ads with a pencil or crayon as they read them so that they would not repeat the process when picking up a newspaper after an initial skim. Woolfolk's ads were printed alongside those for foodstuffs, dry goods, medicines, surgical instruments, real estate, and legal notices. One ad ran alongside an announcement of productions of William Shakespeare's *Othello* at the Baltimore Theater.[11]

Woolfolk imagined a large and ongoing slave market, and his advertisements magnified its importance and his prominence in it. In 1815 a newly arrived and fresh-faced youth was hardly the commercial genius buyers arrived to deal with at a city tavern. But he defied naive expectations. Woolfolk claimed to want twenty or thirty bondspersons, which suggested he had thousands of dollars in cash to disburse. His claims generated interest and excitement. Woolfolk offered to buy slaves of "different descriptions," beckoning anyone with bondspersons to sell. As sellers shook his hand and sat across from him by a tavern fire, their finances could be unburdened. A glass of whiskey or cider may have lubricated the negotiations. For those startled at his youth and lack of establishment, the rustle of his banknotes was probably more reassuring than how well his coat fit, how smoothly he lit a tobacco pipe, or how confidently he talked of prices.[12]

His appeals worked. By mid-February 1816 Woolfolk had taken a coffle of enslaved people out of Baltimore. In the first few seasons Woolfolk was in business, he marched coffles along nearly six hundred miles of dirt roads leading south to Augusta, Georgia, where his uncle John Woolfolk assisted in their sales. John was fifteen years older than his nephew Austin. Besides slave trading, John sold real estate, was in the dry goods business, and knew something of supply chains and finance. He received his nephew's coffles and advertised to sell captives "low for cash or cotton."[13] Like other startups lacking investment capital, Austin had to sell one coffle of bondspeople before being able to buy another.

Austin was active at all levels of the business, and the Woolfolk caravans fit the description of a spectacle that the New Yorker James Kirke Paulding encountered in the summer of 1816 while traveling through Virginia. "The sun was shining out very hot," he recalled, "and in turning an angle of the road, we encountered the following group: First, a little cart, drawn by one horse, in which five or six half naked black children were tumbled, like pigs, together." In the uncovered cart, "they seemed to have been actually broiled to sleep." Following them "marched three black women, with head, neck, and breasts uncovered, and without shoes or stockings: next came three men, bare-headed, half naked, and chained together with an ox-chain." Driving the group was "a white man . . . on horseback, carrying his pistols in his belt, and who, as we passed him, had the impudence to look us in the face without blushing." Paulding learned that the bondspersons had been purchased in Maryland and were being driven south of Virginia for resale.[14] After returning to the city in the spring of 1816, Woolfolk appealed for "likely Young" slaves. *Likely* was code for *able*, and in the case of women, *fertile*. Distant buyers did not want the aged or very young. Woolfolk did not want bondspersons enslaved for a term of years, which prevented their sale out of state. Other ads specifically asked for "slaves for life." His message was, however, targeted to the right audience.[15]

Woolfolk was advertising to citizens who could afford the subscription price of six to ten dollars a year for the papers that Americans read with growing eagerness in the 1810s and 1820s. The rise of the penny press—cheap, widely available newspapers, hawked by newsboys and supported by advertising—was still a decade or so in the future. In 1810 there were nearly four hundred newspapers published in the United States; by 1820 there were nearly six hundred, including about sixty dailies. Many of Woolfolk's earliest advertisements appeared in the *Baltimore Patriot*, a pro–James Madison newspaper published in afternoon editions. It was a transcript of the urban emporium in which it circulated, and each issue cost daily subscribers four cents. He advertised also in the *Baltimore American and Commercial Daily Advertiser*, a six-days-a-week Democratic-Republican newspaper inaugurated against Federalists whose editor received an army commission as a reward for his political loyalty. Federalists owned slaves too, and Woolfolk's tall figure could be seen ducking into the offices of the *Federal Gazette and Baltimore Daily Advertiser* beginning in 1818. Subscribers were not merely householders and citizens but tavern and hotel keepers, and when Baltimoreans and other Americans gathered to eat and drink, they also gathered to read. The numbers of coffeehouses, taverns, hotels, libraries, reading and news rooms grew rapidly in the early republic, and their popularity can be explained in large part by the fact that newspapers were available there. Tellingly, Baltimore's City Hotel management posted a sign reading, "Five dollars reward for the discovery of *the villain who cuts or tears the newspapers!!*"[16]

Woolfolk's advertising spread with his firm. Both Austin and John Woolfolk advertised in the *Augusta Chronicle and Georgia Advertiser* in the 1810s and 1820s. Austin's younger brother Joseph B. Woolfolk moved to Easton, across the bay from Baltimore, in the early 1820s. He advertised in the Democratic-Republican *Republican Star and General Advertiser* by 1825 and the *Easton Gazette* by 1829. By 1832 Woolfolk's ads appeared in the weekly *Cambridge Chronicle* and *Princess Anne Village Herald*, also on Maryland's Eastern Shore. The *Daily National Intelligencer* carried Woolfolk's ads by that time as well. That pro–Jackson administration daily was the largest in the nation's capital. The Woolfolks did not confine their appeals to newspaper ads. The Eastern Shore native Frederick Douglass recalled that Woolfolk's "agents were sent into every town and county in Maryland, announcing their arrival through the papers, and on flaming hand-bills, headed, 'cash for negroes.'" Douglass remembered well. Handbills or sale bills were common forms of advertising in the nineteenth century, especially for public sales. They represented significant income for local printers. Sale bills with the same headings as advertisements reinforced Woolfolk's newspaper ads. He mastered what firms of a later age would call multimedia advertising. Surviving handbills from the era advertise consumables like rubberized cloth, clocks, watches, and jewelry, and appeals such as temperance. Woolfolk's message traveled far from the intended audience. Abolitionists and out-of-state newspapers reprinted the ads, usually with editorial disapproval.[17]

Woolfolk owned no copyright on ads whose language he had originally borrowed, and competitors parroted him. Isaac Franklin and John Armfield, his rival slave traders, advertised "CASH FOR NEGROES" in 1829. Some of their ads in the *Daily National Intelligencer* appeared on the same page as Woolfolk's. Slave traders seeking to stand out from the competition inflated their claims. In late May 1818 Woolfolk advertised, *"Two Hundred* NEGROES WANTED." Even during the peak of his business, Woolfolk and his agents were successful in buying two, three, or four slaves at a time, hardly the impression his advertisements give. The point was not the veracity of the claims but the interest they grabbed. Others inflated their claims substantially. In 1836 James H. Birch, the slave trader who would buy and brutalize Solomon Northup, advertised in the *Washington (D.C.) Globe*, "CASH FOR 400 NEGROES." The wads of money it would take to fulfill that claim could have capitalized a medium-sized bank. In 1842 Charles Dickens registered revulsion at such appeals. "'Cash for negroes,' 'cash for negroes,' 'cash for negroes,' is the heading of advertisements in great capitals down the long columns of the crowded journals," he complained. When Harriet Beecher Stowe supplied footnotes to *Uncle Tom's Cabin,* she reprinted one slave trader's appeal for "5000 NEGROES," which was twice the number of slaves in Delaware at the time. Slave traders were by then using P. T. Barnum–like hyperbole. Woolfolk's competitors in the early 1830s endorsed his prominence in the Chesapeake by circulating death notices. Woolfolk felt compelled to protect his brand by claiming, "he *is not dead*, as has been artfully represented by his opponents, but . . . he still lives, to give them CASH and the HIGHEST PRICES for their NEGROES."[18]

Behind the ads was a business built on a shoestring. In the first few years, Woolfolk trimmed costs by operating out of city taverns and living in boarding-houses. His enterprise was self-financed, and survival depended on lowering overhead and transportation costs. Taverns and newspaper advertising formed a nexus of Woolfolk's firm. Both were inexpensive and public and facilitated commercial ties. Innkeepers and editors were part of his network. Slaveholders from the counties surrounding Baltimore were Woolfolk's main clientele, and after reading his ads they sought him out the way a backcountry farmer or miller might seek out a merchant or shipping agent at his house near the wharves.[19]

Taverns were centers of commercial activity and temporary homes for itinerants. For those starting in business, sailors in port, or travelers, boardinghouses adjoining taverns were places to stay for weeks or months at a time. Taverns were much more than places for travelers to rest, drink, and dine on mediocre fare. They were centers of commerce, venues for entertainment, and hubs of transportation. Taverns served as stagecoach stations. City taverns had stables for horses. In western Baltimore, taverns had stockyards catering to visitors driving cattle to the market, and those near the commercial district and harbor fed and lodged merchants and sailors. Woolfolk boarded at several.[20]

Would-be sellers arriving in the city could hand their horses and carriages off to a hostler and ask the tavern keeper for the fellow who offered cash for slaves. Depending on the season, a slaveholder might arrive to find more than one resident trader offering to buy bondspersons. To distinguish himself from the competition, Woolfolk established his name as a trademark. His robust physique and assertive demeanor helped reinforce that commercial identity.[21] After an initial conversation with a seller, Woolfolk might call at the city jail to appraise the human goods for sale. The seller might enjoy a hearty supper and bed down for the night in the same boardinghouse. The enslaved found no such comforts as they were taken to market.

In the Baltimore Jail, enslaved people's miseries abounded amid the filth, noise, and rough treatment. The jail bred disease, not least from the unsanitary regime of inmates' cooking over wood fires that stained the walls with soot.

Private jails and the city jail served the same purpose, and jailers were happy to collect fees for boarding and confinement.[22] Baltimore had built a quadrangular city jail in 1802 on a six-acre lot. After an anti-Federalist mob stormed the building in 1812, the city erected an eleven-foot stone wall around it. Cells were "generally twenty feet square and well ventilated," although that was a matter of how many bodies were crammed into them. To many, the city jail was a reeking dungeon promiscuously populated by debtors, youthful offenders, hardened criminals, the wrongly accused, and the unfortunate.[23]

The enslaved people who fell into Woolfolk's possession languished along with runaway slaves confined there by the sheriff. Slave traders often visited the jail to survey runaways and buy cheaply any who might be sold either by an owner or by authorities who could not find one. Fugitives who concealed their identities or whose owners failed to claim them were sold for the benefit of the state. More than a few kidnap victims became bondspersons within its walls. Jails served more pedestrian disciplinary purposes as well. Slaveholders too squeamish to flog their bondspeople sent them to jail, where they could pay to have them whipped or incarcerated for a time. Jails were one of the few places in the early republic that were not segregated by sex or race. Males and females did not receive separate quarters in the Baltimore Jail until 1830.[24] Often those cells were the final stopover before a journey of no return.

By the end of the 1810s Woolfolk was an established trader, but expanding his firm's capabilities depended on transforming its business model. To grow, it needed a supply chain, a network of buyers and sellers, more capital, and new markets. It was an auspicious time for such a transformation.

Woolfolk's Baltimore was on the cusp of a major reorientation of Atlantic commerce. Transatlantic trade in cotton and textiles surged in the 1820s and with it a demand for slaves in the lower South. Before 1820 food was the primary American export. In broad terms, North American flour fed Caribbean slaves, who produced sugar and molasses, which New Englanders turned into rum and sold to buy British and European manufactured goods. Sugar had been the engine of the eighteenth-century transatlantic slave trade and was essential to the development of modern merchant capitalism. Those patterns were changing. Between 1817 and 1819 Britain and the United States threw up tariff barriers to American flour and British manufactured goods. Trade restrictions injured Chesapeake farmers and merchants.

Baltimore was hit hard by the sudden closure of its British West Indian flour market, and merchants scrambled to find new markets and new opportunities. Chesapeake flour began to flow to developing markets in the North American interior and South America. The explosion of cotton production in the 1820s reoriented trade to the so-called Atlantic cotton triangle, which linked commercial centers on the Eastern Seaboard of North America with southern cotton ports and overseas cotton customers. Cotton replaced sugar as the center of the transatlantic economy as English manufacturers using power looms turned out abundant varieties and quantities of cloth, much of it sold cheaply at auction. British imports of raw cotton rose at the same time as North American cotton lands expanded dramatically and planters developed higher-yielding varieties. Merchant bankers financed many of those developments. As the supply of cotton and cloth expanded, so did a web of credit. Demand for the bondspersons followed those developments. Slave prices increased sharply between 1815 and 1819, fell over the next five years, spiked in 1825, and rose again in the late 1820s, generally following cotton prices.[25]

While slavery in the Chesapeake backcountry was poised to attenuate, Baltimore was thriving on slavery's capitalism. The failures of northern Maryland farmers in the hard harvest of 1816 and financial hardships of 1819 threw thousands of enslaved people on the market. Indebted Maryland slaveholders were turning their bondspersons into liquid assets at the same time as their countrymen in the lower South were incurring a mountain of debt to buy lands and slaves. Not all cheered the slave trade that grew as a result. Baltimore's Society of Friends recoiled at the alarming rate at which their African-descended neighbors were disappearing into the holds of merchant vessels. In 1820 Quaker citizens asked the customs collector to investigate whether African-descended Marylanders were being kidnapped or smuggled.[26]

Peering into the holds of merchant ships docked at city wharves, inspectors beheld what the new market looked like. To New Orleans were being shipped enslaved people, Chesapeake flour, other processed foodstuffs, and foreign manufactures. In October 1820 a customs collector, James McCulloch, responded to a request to inspect the 389-ton *Unicorn* docked at Ramsay's Wharf and cleared to sail for New Orleans. The ship was owned by a prominent Baltimore merchant. With the shipmaster's permission, a customs inspector and a Quaker abolitionist interviewed "the Persons of Colour on board the ship." Most of the captives were in their teens, but among them were a two-year-old baby and a four-year-old child. Respondents "acknowledge[d] themselves to be slaves for life," according to the report. The *Unicorn* also carried barrels of flour, shad (a tasty local fish), coffee, and sugar. Besides barrels of refined sugar (and empty molasses barrels), the ship was freighted with five thousand sugar loaves, along with other consumables such as wine and cider royal. It carried assorted hardware and dry goods, including glass, linen, hats, kettles, iron weights, and plates. Other cargo included a pianoforte and a cart and gears. Satisfied that the shipment was legal, the inspector signed off and the *Unicorn* sailed. After landing the cargo and captives in New Orleans, the *Unicorn* was reloaded with bales of cotton and set sail for Liverpool, England. Most of the bales were delivered to William and James Brown and Company, the Liverpool branch of Baltimore's premier merchant banking firm, Alexander Brown and Sons.[27]

As the cotton economy developed, slave traders and merchant bankers used the same infrastructure. Some of Woolfolk's captives were sold to customers linked to the House of Brown through an international chain of debt. Brown extended credit to merchants in the North American interior the way English merchants extended credit to customers on the shores of Africa, South America, and the Eastern Seaboard. Because of its financial strategy, the House of Brown quickly became the second largest exchange merchant in the United States, behind the Second Bank of the United States. By 1825 it had branches in Baltimore, New York, Philadelphia, Liverpool, and London and agents in New Orleans. After several transatlantic voyages the *Unicorn* was incorporated into its fleet of ships.[28]

In 1820 Baltimore inspectors cooperating with Quaker abolitionists focused on vessels cleared for cotton ports and eyed Woolfolk's human cargoes in particular. The brigs *Emilie* and *Intelligence* were both inspected twice. Both plied a regular trade with New Orleans and carried hundreds of captives. The *Emilie* made at least seven slaving voyages between 1819 and 1821, and the *Intelligence* made eight between 1820 and 1823. Where Woolfolk's consignments went, inspectors soon followed. Three weeks after the *Unicorn* sailed, inspectors interviewed "nine Negroes" aboard a sloop bound for Charleston. All were Woolfolk's property. Two weeks after that, inspectors interviewed William and Joseph, "two persons of Colour" belonging to Woolfolk who had been packed aboard another sloop bound for Charleston. Like the *Unicorn*, that vessel was plying an Atlantic circuit that delivered cotton to Europe and finished goods to North America, taking slaves on domestic legs of international voyages.[29]

Slave traders' increasing visibility in Baltimore created a backlash. "CASH FOR BLOOD," screamed *Niles' Weekly Register* in 1821. "Advertisements headed 'cash for negroes' have been excluded from the Baltimore newspapers," its editor, Hezekiah Niles, explained, "the public feeling being in concord with that of our editors." Newspapers quietly discontinued slave traders' ads after an outcry over the surging trade. The ads would resume just as quickly after the uproar quieted. Niles charged that slave traders "have a number of dens in the suburbs of the city, wherein misery personified is groaning in chains and gagged, lest pity should enter the abodes of distress." That quip referred to Woolfolk's new Pratt Street residence and jail. Niles was an economic nationalist whose paper regularly reported the progress of American trade and industry. He knew that the slave trade was a growing business and one that was becoming essential to the global cotton economy. But he did not like the side effects.[30]

During Woolfolk's tenure in Baltimore, the maritime domestic slave trade grew from incidental to essential. Since colonial times, shippers had accepted small consignments of bondspersons to fill cargo space. Human cargo required increased security, but, like specie, bondspersons took up little space.[31] When demand rose in the 1810s, some merchant ship owners began to welcome the trade in captives and depend on the resulting revenue. As cotton and other bulk commodities rose in importance, the saltwater slave trade helped knit together business ties among Chesapeake merchants and their counterparts in New Orleans. Chesapeake shippers found a ready source of revenue on passages that connected them with southern ports.

Most merchant vessels carrying slaves from Baltimore plied a domestic trade, but the cotton triangle was actually an irregular polygon. Measured in dollars rather than in geographic space, the distance from New Orleans to Liverpool by way of New York or Baltimore was shorter than the direct route through the Gulf of Mexico and across the North Atlantic Ocean. That was because merchants and bankers in American seaboard cities extended long credit on favorable terms. Coastal trading vessels regularly departed New York, Baltimore, and Philadelphia for New Orleans and returned to those cities with cotton or tobacco for transshipment.[32]

Bondspersons fit neatly into the routes of such coastal voyages. Like most coastal trading vessels sailing from Baltimore, the *Emilie* carried typical assortments of cargo that included domestic exports and transshipments of goods, including books, brandy, wine, whiskey, glass, salmon, shad, crockery, furniture, wearing apparel, flour, plaster, paint, varnish, turpentine, rope, tobacco, and even loaf sugar. The lower Mississippi Valley was a growing market for such items. New Orleans was expanding rapidly following the War of 1812. Surging immigration and the development of effective steam-powered transport drew the Mississippi, Ohio, and Tennessee River valleys into the commercial reach of New Orleans. The city council's price controls on food and energy were removed in 1816, which threw open a local market to popular Chesapeake flour. By the fall of 1818 prices for cotton, flour, and slaves were about as high as they had been in memory. Woolfolk's Eastern Shore competitor David Anderson, for instance, speculated in flour as well as captives. On one passage of the *Emilie* he consigned 550 barrels of flour to Hector McLean and Company in New Orleans, the same firm to which he consigned slaves.[33]

Until the early 1820s, Austin Woolfolk's saltwater slaving was focused primarily on Georgia, where he was building a sales network. In 1819, for instance, he embarked fifteen bondspeople aboard a merchant vessel bound from Annapolis to Savannah. Some he sold himself. Other captives entered through the port of Charleston and were sold by his uncle John in Augusta. Beginning in 1822, John Woolfolk received saltwater consignments in New Orleans. Shifting to the Crescent City made financial sense. By the mid–1820s slave prices were 50 percent higher in New Orleans than in Charleston.[34] Profits were potentially higher. But outsiders faced pronounced difficulties in New Orleans.

The development of finance in the early republic was the key to the growth of commercial agriculture, and any sizable business selling to planters had to deal in credit. Slave traders were no exception. Some New Orleans customers paid in cash. But the primary market included sugar planters who demanded young, strong male captives and preferred to pay with bills of exchange or promissory notes. Sugar plantations were highly capital-intensive, even more so than cotton plantations. Agriculturalists who demanded bondspersons were correspondingly debt-burdened. Furnishing bound laborers to them required traders to act as bankers. But creditors had to be aware of the risks. To be successful, slave traders had to be part of the same network of bankers, notaries, and merchants whose clients included sugar and cotton planters and their agents. Until his uncle John moved to New Orleans, Austin Woolfolk hesitated to double the distance of his long-distance slave trade and multiply the financial risks.[35]

Austin Woolfolk's sea passages to Louisiana began with small consignments. In November 1818 he embarked four enslaved people aboard the brig *Temperance* for New Orleans. The 149-ton, two-masted vessel was owned by a local tobacco and general merchant. The *Temperance* sailed regularly to the German port of Bremen, touching England and carrying passengers, dry goods or textiles, iron, glassware, gin, and other items westward across the Atlantic Ocean. Perhaps the voyage to New Orleans was the shipmaster James Beard's idea. He had been skipper of the *Emilie*. Woolfolk consigned two adult men, one adult woman, and her one-year-old son to Hector McLean and Company. David Anderson shipped five young adults, also consigned to McLean. Anderson had been a lieutenant in the Kentucky Militia during the War of 1812. Like Woolfolk, he moved to Maryland following peace, setting up as a slave trader on the Eastern Shore. Like his competitor, Anderson had advertised "ready cash and liberal prices" to slaveholders in Maryland. McLean would seek the same from Louisianans.[36]

The *Temperance*'s voyage illustrates that specialists like Anderson and Woolfolk did not yet dominate the interstate slave trade. The twenty-four enslaved Marylanders held captive in the hold of the *Temperance* united the interests of some of Baltimore's leading businessmen, Louisiana planters, and interstate slave traders. Two Baltimore merchant firms consigned captives to that passage. The planter Guy Duplantier of Louisiana shipped two slaves. Like Duplantier, Stephen Watts Wikoff, a St. Landry Parish planter, traveled from Louisiana himself to buy slaves. He packed nine enslaved people aboard the *Temperance*, aged three months to twenty-five years. Each owner or shipper signed a preprinted manifest of "Negroes, Mulattos, and Persons of Color," transported on the seas "for the purpose of being sold or disposed of as Slaves, or to be held to service or Labour." Federal customs forms had required them for two years to protect against smuggling.[37] To anyone near the Fell's Point wharves in mid-December, the *Temperance* looked like any other medium-sized vessel pushing off into the harbor. Unlike transatlantic slavers, it was not fortified. Masters of vessels plying the domestic slave trade hesitated to recruit extra security personnel or arm their sailors. The captives below deck viewed the voyage quite differently.

Records of the Christmastime 1818 voyage of the *Temperance* conceal the incremental terror of the coastwise trade. Assembled over three days before the *Temperance* left port—and probably confined belowdecks until at sea—the twenty-four Marylanders spent Christmas and New Year's rolling and pitching in the frigid Atlantic Ocean. Newspapers on the East Coast reported severe weather around Christmas. Vomit and other human waste not contained in receptacles were a hazard to people confined in a dark hold from dusk to daylight. Consumer goods and barrels of flour needed no heat on the winter seas, but not so an assemblage of people torn from loved ones and thrown into a forbidding void. The hold resembled an icebox for days or weeks until the ship reached warm currents flowing from the Gulf of Mexico and thawed. The people confined in the hold over the thirty-one-day journey were probably huddled and shivering, the young children crying and suffering the most from the displacement and adversities. Passengers traveling the same route took little notice of the people transported as cargo, and on many ships citizens sailing from a port like Baltimore or Alexandria to New Orleans slept belowdecks just a few feet above the spaces in the ship in which their black countrymen languished.

Soon after the *Temperance* set sail, Anderson embarked more captives aboard another merchant vessel, the *Clio*. The *Clio* was a regular trader plying a route between Baltimore and New Orleans. In late December Anderson boarded along with his slaves. First-class passengers could expect a closetlike cabin that was semiprivate. Many had to bring bedding. Steerage passengers slept separately from but in similar fashion to sailors, on bunks or planks. As captives and passengers boarded, the ship resembled a floating barnyard, the squeals of pigs and gabbles of turkeys audible through the planking. For the monthlong passage, any meat not cured or dried was taken on board alive. One of the first-class passengers was fifty-four-year-old Benjamin Henry Latrobe, the British-born designer of the U.S. Capitol and most recently of the Baltimore Basilica and Exchange. He was traveling to New Orleans to build the city's water system, a job he would not survive.[38]

Latrobe detailed the passage to New Orleans, hinting at shipboard life for captives. After sailing from Baltimore, it took two days to reach the mouth of the Chesapeake Bay. At dawn on the third day the ship weighed anchor off Old Point Comfort, although "all hands" were by then "sick," Latrobe recorded. Five days later Latrobe was on deck, clutching the taffrail at the stern, during "the most awful sea I ever beheld or imagined." Clinging to the ship, he could see the gray sky come into full view as the ship ascended the crest of a wave. As it fell, he stared directly ahead into the cavern of the oncoming wave. The two-masted ship sped across the swells "at the rate of nine or ten knots," Latrobe reported, "skip[ping] over these mountainous waves without appearing to labor in the least." The gale could not have seemed so exhilarating to the involuntary passengers. Such excitement punctuated the tedium of oceanic travel in the age of sail.[39]

On most domestic slaving passages the forced migrants were confined belowdecks at night but were permitted on deck during daylight hours. Latrobe's journal does not hint at the kind of violent tension that characterized transatlantic slave ship passages. On Christmas Day, 1818, he recalled, the weather turned "delightful, wind gentle," and the "temperature [was] about seventy degrees" as they neared the Gulf of Mexico. The gathering of passengers was "so good-humored, from the captain to the second mate, that the day was spent very pleasantly, and the passengers remained on deck until eleven o'clock at night." The day after Christmas, Latrobe recorded "a magnificent sunset . . . inimitable by the pencil," and the following day passengers celebrated the shipmaster's birthday with "hot rolls at breakfast, a hog killed, apple pies for dinner, and a great variety of similar demonstrations of satisfaction." Latrobe explained that "all these things are important in a sea voyage, and scatter flowers over the monotonous surface of so barren an existence." Perhaps Anderson's slaves received some meat, or at least boiled tripe or offal from the slaughtered hog as a Christmas offering.[40]

Latrobe ignored the fact that sailing to New Orleans typically required more nautical skill than a transatlantic passage. The coastwise trade took ships far off the coast. After sailing out of the Chesapeake Bay's narrow shipping lanes, vessels had to clear three North Carolina capes at Hatteras, Lookout, and Fear. All had working lighthouses by the time the *Clio* sailed past them, but the shoals off the capes remained maritime graveyards. Ships set a course off the Florida peninsula rather than hugging the coastline. The least dangerous yet most direct route into the gulf was through Providence Channel and a route appropriately nicknamed "Hole-in-the-Wall," which cut through the Bahamas to the northeast of Nassau. After clearing the Bahamas, ships sailed southwest by west to approach the southern Florida coast, which in 1818 was still claimed by Spain. Gulf currents were quickest around the Florida peninsula. A nautical authority of the mid-nineteenth century counseled mariners, "The Gulf Stream, with its eddies and counter-currents, renders the navigation of the Florida pass one of the most dangerous in the world." Masters of vessels were often compelled to haul up sails and drop anchors at night or when they could not get accurate bearings, so little was the margin for error. "Those currents have strewn the Florida reefs with carcasses of ships and men," the sailing manual cautioned, "and have caused the loss of many millions worth of property." A legitimate wrecking business thrived, but profiteers put up false lights designed to lead vessels into shoals or reefs. Wreckers claimed a share of the cargo of the salvaged ships as payment. Because of the combined hazards, insurers charged up to 50 percent more to insure voyages between New York and New Orleans than transatlantic voyages between New York and Britain.[41]

On the monthlong sea voyage Latrobe ate and spoke with Anderson, whom he identified as a "notorious slave dealer." The architect noted that one of Anderson's captives, Tom, died ten days into the journey. Tom had been confined in the Baltimore Jail before his transport, where he fell ill. He died aboard the *Clio* despite being "faithfully attended by our most humane captain" and a physician on board, his body buried at sea. Latrobe was not unmoved by Tom's distress, but he conceded that citizens' property rights in slaves made it difficult for the government to suppress the "internal slave trade." The architect of the Richmond State Penitentiary was more upset that "the public jail is permitted to be a place of deposit for this sort of goods until they can be shipped." Still worse, in Latrobe's view, was the treatment Tom received from his fellow captives. Tom "had a mother and sisters on board," Latrobe contended, "who treated him with very little kindness, and he would probably have recovered had they taken better care of him." Perhaps Anderson had muttered that excuse at mealtimes, along with mentioning that "this man had cost Anderson $800 and

his passage $30 more." Tom, a "light mulatto," Anderson gave him to under-
stand, "was expected to fetch $1,000 to $1,200 in Louisiana."[42]

A lot of money was at stake. Gross profits of 25 to 50 percent were much more
than any inanimate article of cargo usually fetched, even if Anderson spent thirty
dollars on freight and another thirty jailing, clothing, and feeding Tom. Another
captive aboard, Latrobe recalled, was "half Indian, half negro, who came out of
the same depot, the public jail of Baltimore, the same time with Tom, also sick."
The man was "absolutely eaten up with vermin," maggots or worms burrowing
into his flesh. In an effort to prevent the spread of disease, the *Clio's* master "had
him stripped and wrapped in a blanket." The captive's "rags were then towed
overboard, but I doubt whether the vermin would be expelled from them."[43]

Anderson's version of that man's story circulated among the passengers. "The
other colored people on board," Latrobe recorded, "who are well clad and seem
very respectable and orderly in their way, will neither approach nor assist this poor
wretch, and had it not been for the captain's attention, he would have starved, for
they gave him nothing to eat for two days." Latrobe glimpsed the fact that not all
deportees formed a mutual bond of assistance based on their shared adversities.
To the white passengers, concern over Tom's death and his fellow captive's
miseries disappeared with the old year. Eighteen nineteen arrived aboard the
Clio with "an extraordinary exertion . . . to furnish our dinner table, and a boiled
turkey marked the day, which, like the rest, was spent in good humor."[44]

The *Clio* sailed up the Mississippi River, tacking back and forth to catch the
wind against the river's current. After a few days of sugar plantations coming
into view beyond the levees, New Orleans appeared through a fog on the riverbanks. The city had about 25,000 residents at the time, half of them nonwhite
and about a third enslaved. It had grown from 8,000 residents just fifteen years
before. By 1820 New Orleans was less than half as large as Baltimore but had
recently surpassed Charleston, South Carolina, as the fifth largest American
city. The old city (today's French Quarter) fronted the river for a mile, and
suburbs radiated from the riverbanks. From the *Clio*, farmland and scattered
dwellings appeared on the outskirts of the city behind the earthen levee, most
visible from the rigging and only intermittently in the fog. Levees were built a
foot above the high-water mark and were five to six feet wide at the base for
every foot of height, giving them large slopes inclining down to the river.
Behind the levee buildings of two and three stories were visible.[45]

The city was loud and thriving. Latrobe compared the din to "the sounds that
issue from an extensive marsh, the residence of a million or two frogs, from bull-
frogs up to whistlers." The city cathedral drew the architect's eyes, but Anderson
was probably looking for the figure of his fellow Kentuckian Hector McLean.

The captives could not disembark until a customs official certified the slave manifest on which McLean was named consignee. He had accepted Austin Woolfolk's consignment of captives a few days before, when the *Temperance* docked.[46]

Agents like McLean provided vital services to interstate slave traders. They permitted enslavers to build a supply chain in captives. McLean, along with others like the New Orleans accountant Stephen Peïllon, jailed bondspersons, negotiated prices, and represented distant owners at sale. They also held or discounted financial paper, took and released mortgages, collected debts, and remitted proceeds of sales. A great deal of trust bound agents who behaved like slave factors and their clients in the interstate trade. McLean and Anderson were both from Nelson County, Kentucky. McLean had partnered with his brother Samuel in Bardstown. They were in business in 1814 and built a house that still stands. Hector McLean moved to New Orleans and in 1817 set up as a commission merchant. He sold real estate in Faubourg Marigny, had interests in at least one steamboat, and was recognized as a *négociant*, or merchant of the city. He cultivated a distinguished clientele. In January 1821 McLean sold twenty-two-year-old Eliza to Louisiana's Governor Thomas B. Robertson. Anderson had consigned her to the regular slaver *Intelligence*.[47]

For McLean, Eliza's was one of many faces that symbolized a healthy commission. He represented several clients like Anderson, including his fellow Kentuckian Benjamin Hughes. McLean consequently gained notoriety as a slave merchant. In 1820 a West Feliciana Parish, Louisiana, owner sent eleven-year-old Charlotte to McLean with a request to sell her. Charlotte was literally sold down the river when McLean agreed to $350 from a New Orleans customer. As alliances among slave traders like Anderson and brokers like McLean tightened, planters hesitated to hazard the voyage to Baltimore or Norfolk to buy slaves themselves. Guy Duplantier, a Louisiana planter and jurist who had sailed on the *Temperance* with two slaves purchased in Maryland in 1818, became Anderson's client in 1820 when McLean sold him six captives shipped aboard the *Intelligence*. Besides saving him a trip to Baltimore, McLean extended him credit to buy slaves.[48]

The financial services McLean's firm provided removed a major financial obstacle to the interstate slave trade. Like their transatlantic counterparts, interstate traders faced the difficulty of remitting revenues from slave sales over long distances. Banknotes tended to depreciate the farther they traveled, and merchants' reputations faded with distance, too. McLean's standing as a merchant in New Orleans permitted Anderson to remedy the difficulties of distance by drawing bills of exchange payable by McLean in New Orleans.

Those bills' trajectory was the opposite of bills that paid for cotton in New Orleans and imported goods in seaboard cities. They cost Anderson a discount in Baltimore, but the advantages were considerable.[49]

Anderson's relationship with McLean and the infrastructure of the Second Bank of the United States permitted him to put some of the best bank money in the country in the hands of Maryland clients. In January 1820, for instance, Anderson drew a bill for $1,500 payable by McLean in New Orleans sixty days after sight. That sum represented the balance McLean owed him for selling slaves. Instead of sending it to New Orleans and waiting three or four months for payment to reach him in Baltimore, Anderson discounted the bill at the Baltimore branch of the Second Bank. The Second Bank either credited an account or paid in Second Bank notes. Discounting gave both Anderson and the bank distinct advantages. Anderson got paid immediately, and the bank took a small percentage as its fee. The Second Bank was the largest exchange merchant in the country and often resold bills to merchants who had bills payable in New Orleans, usually at a price over face value. Bills went from hand to hand to the drawee, paying for different transactions along the way. In times in which confidence in the banking system was high, the exchange market was strikingly efficient. In 1820 confidence was scarce. The cashier of the Baltimore branch sent Anderson's bill directly to the cashier of the New Orleans branch for payment. Not all went smoothly. McLean protested the note, saying that he did not have the money owed Anderson; he then protested another Anderson drew in April for $3,100, contending that he could not pay. In the meantime, however, McLean and his partner Robert C. Camp continued to represent Anderson and sell his bondspersons.[50] Anderson's business fell off two years later, about the time the Woolfolks expanded to the Eastern Shore. While Chesapeake-based traders sought riches in the New Orleans market, New Orleans–based slave traders were sailing to the Chesapeake and into territories covered by Anderson and Woolfolk.

Jean Baptiste Moussier was a New Orleans merchant who moved into the interstate slave trade in the late 1810s. Moussier was part of a network of Creole sugar planters and Francophone city residents. Like Woolfolk, Moussier spied a niche in the coastal trade between the Chesapeake and New Orleans and migrated from buying and selling cotton and sugar to commerce in human beings. He traded at Burgundy and Maine (now Dumaine) streets in New Orleans, in the neighborhood where he lived with his wife, Marie Elizabeth Chloé Lezongar de Lasalle. They had four children, three daughters and a son. As they grew, the Moussiers' ties to the Chesapeake were more than commercial. Their son attended St. Mary's College (now St. Mary's University) in Baltimore. His father pursued real estate and banking, to which he graduated from the slave trade. By the time of his death in 1831, Moussier was known in the city as the inventor of Louisiana property banking. At one time his real estate holdings included a plantation on Grande Terre, a barrier island between Barataria Bay and the Gulf of Mexico. In the 1810s Moussier entered the domestic slave trade as an itinerant, sailing from New Orleans to the Chesapeake, buying captives there, and shipping them back home for sale. After one such voyage in July 1819, Moussier called on a New Orleans neighbor, the lawyer and notary Hugues Lavergne, to record the sale of an enslaved twenty-four-year-old Virginian purchased in Richmond and sold to a city exchange merchant.[51]

Moussier was enterprising and affable, and by the fall of 1820 he had formed a strategic alliance with John and Philip E. Tabb of Norfolk, Virginia. The alliance gave Moussier an entrée into a Chesapeake market for Louisiana sugar and the Tabbs a sales agent in New Orleans. Such an alliance mirrored Anderson's ties with McLean. The Tabbs' main business was a direct trade in cotton and tobacco with a Liverpool merchant house, William and James Brown and Company. The Tabbs shipped Moussier a cargo of captives in the fall of 1820. On the same passage the Tabbs also shipped several hundred barrels of flour, tar, and turpentine and 40,000 bricks, consigned to another merchant.[52] The captives underwent journeys not dissimilar to those of survivors of the transatlantic Middle Passage

The coastal slave trade actually crossed thousands of miles of ocean, sailing off the coasts of islands claimed by foreign powers and disembarking captives in an unfamiliar land. Many were sold to owners who spoke a different language. John Brown was fourteen years old when Moussier appraised him in Richmond, Virginia, and bought him from a local merchant. He had probably not been to sea before and might never have left the vicinity of Richmond. In early October he boarded a boat for the journey down the James River to Norfolk, where he was put aboard a merchant ship with two tall masts and a hold full of barrels and bricks. Scores of others soon joined him, including Tom and Sarah, whom Moussier had bought in Richmond from their owner, J. Beverly Randolph. Sixty-nine African-descended Virginians and North Carolinians made up the ship's human cargo. They were assembled over six days before the ship set sail. After the three-week passage, Brown and the others arrived in New Orleans. They were transferred from the inside of a ship to the inside of a jail. Moussier sold Brown two weeks after his arrival to Pierre Chiron of St. Charles Parish. He paid with bills drawn on a St. Charles Parish neighbor. Brown underwent another dislocation as he traveled west of the city to Chiron's sugar plantation.

There he witnessed other bondspersons clearing fields for winter planting. Brown may have been relieved that he was put to domestic work instead. Moussier sold Tom and Sarah to another planter, Bernard Villars. He too paid partly on credit. Tom's and Sarah's incremental terror of shipboard transport turned to confusion and bewilderment in jail cells, at an auction site, and then on transport south of the city to Barataria on the Gulf Coast. Others were scattered west of the city. Moussier sold several of Tom's and Sarah's shipmates to a St. Bernard Parish sugar planter, François Coulon Jumonville de Villier. Moussier reinvested in slaves and eventually in a coastal trading vessel, the 240-ton brigantine *Brazillian*, which he used to transport scores of captives from Norfolk and Richmond to New Orleans in the following years.[53]

The ship eliminated reliance on others, but Moussier's main competitive advantage was his extensive knowledge of commercial New Orleans and a network of Creole customers. Among them was Francis Xavier Martin, judge of the Louisiana Supreme Court, legal historian, and former attorney general. He bought four bondspersons whom Moussier shipped on the *Brazillian* in December 1822. At Moussier's firm's apex in the early 1820s, neither Anderson nor the Woolfolks had his contacts. As Moussier expanded his slaving firm, he became something of an intranational diplomat promoting the Franco-American roots of the republic. In New York and Virginia, Moussier participated in the grand tour of the Marquis de Lafayette in the fall of 1824. The sixty-seven-year-old former ally of George Washington and champion of the American cause of independence became a sensation as he toured all twenty-four states. His abolitionism seems to have escaped Moussier's notice. At a public dinner for Lafayette in Williamsburg, Virginia, Moussier toasted, "The State of Virginia; placed on the centre of the Union, she forms the heart of it." He flattered would-be customers, declaring, "The pages of history are adorned by the names of her statesmen and heroes." Such appeals worked. Weeks later Moussier shipped a cargo of captives from Norfolk to New Orleans as an "agent for the planters of Louisiana." He formed another strategic alliance with a Richmond merchant house, Rogers and Harrison, acting as their agent in the long-distance domestic slave trade. Rogers and Harrison was an interlocking international partnership with branches in Le Havre, London, New Orleans, and New York. The French arm at one time had a monopoly contract to supply tobacco to the French government under King Louis Philippe.[54] Moussier soon graduated from slave trading to banking.

Austin Woolfolk swaggered somewhat awkwardly into the commercial world of New Orleans in which Moussier maneuvered with ease. In late June 1822 Woolfolk called at Hugues Lavergne's notary offices at 76 Chartres Street, near the center of the New Orleans slave market. The tall stranger with an Appalachian accent shook hands with the fastidious Lavergne, who exchanged greetings in French-accented English. In a legal ceremony that took just minutes, Lavergne recorded the sale of twenty-eight-year-old Silvia and her two-year-old daughter Rose to an Esplanade Avenue accountant, François Sel. Woolfolk presented a release from the Bureau des Hypothèques, or mortgage office, where he had paid a fee and the registrar had certified that the two bondspersons had no financial encumbrances. Lavergne's office was the last bureaucratic hurdle. Woolfolk gave the notary to understand that he was from Augusta, Georgia, and that the two enslaved people had been embarked aboard the brig *Hollon* from Norfolk. Silvia and Rose were among 164 bondspersons packed aboard that ship in early March and landed in New Orleans a month later. They had been jailed in the city for more than six weeks by the time Woolfolk sold them. Austin's younger brother Richard T. Woolfolk had embarked them in a coffle of forty-four, including three infants and two captives who fell seriously ill on the passage. In Lavergne's offices, Woolfolk did not need to repeat the name of the ship or its master.

Lavergne already knew about the ship's landing and the names of many of its involuntary passengers. He had certified the sales of several bondspersons disembarked from it. Besides captives, the *Hollon* carried a rogue's gallery of Virginia slave traders, including Nathaniel Rives of Lynchburg and John Isnard and Bartholomew Accinelly of Norfolk. Lavergne had also met Woolfolk's brother Samuel Martin Woolfolk, who had sold four bondspeople the day the *Hollon* landed. Austin Woolfolk signed a document drafted in French that he could not completely comprehend. His signature was nevertheless the largest. It was not the last Lavergne would see of Austin Woolfolk. Two weeks later he returned to certify the sale of twenty-five-year-old Tabby to Madame Roche of the city. On that occasion Woolfolk told Lavergne that he was from Baltimore but residing in New Orleans. But Austin Woolfolk did not leave a lasting impression. In 1824, for instance, Lavergne notarized a slave sale made by "Austin Woolfolk, Esquire, of Augusta, in the State of Virginia, now in this city," perhaps confusing him with his uncle John, who was by then resident in New Orleans. (Austin told another notary that he was from Richmond, Virginia.) But Lavergne would soon be able to tell the Woolfolks apart. John, Austin, and Austin's younger brother Samuel M. would visit Lavergne's office dozens of times over the next several years as they became the largest shippers of captives from Baltimore to New Orleans.[55] Much had changed in New Orleans since the Battle of New Orleans. The city was Americanizing, and he was one of its agents.

Austin Woolfolk's ascent to the apex of the Baltimore–New Orleans trade was assisted by kinsmen and allied traders. Employees conducted business in his absence. Someone signed his name on a manifest of seven captives shipped from

Baltimore dated May 1822, while Austin was in New Orleans. By the mid–1820s the Chesapeake branches of Woolfolk's alliance were headquartered in Baltimore and Easton, Maryland, and subsidiaries were based in Richmond and Washington, D.C. Initially, the Woolfolks transported coffles overland to Augusta, Georgia, for resale, along with the occasional shipment to Savannah or Charleston. As the Woolfolk network grew in the upper South, New Orleans became the biggest slaving port. In the lower Mississippi Valley the Woolfolks' salesmen collected captives and sold them. That permitted independence from factors like Hector McLean and Company and also allowed the Woolfolks to extend short credit to customers. The Woolfolks traded knowledge as well as slaves, and their expansive and flexible network was a key to their growth. Their propitious timing was critical, but the firm's organizational strategy permitted a sales volume of several hundred captives per year by the late 1820s. Austin Woolfolk's initial success had attracted relatives almost immediately. Austin had been in business less than a year when Augustin Woolfolk, perhaps a cousin, joined him in 1816. Both lived in and worked out of a tavern. Augustin took out ads of his own but departed soon after arriving.[56]

As Austin Woolfolk's business thrived in Baltimore, he moved into his own house, from which he welcomed customers. Business had become too brisk to run out of taverns. Like master craftsmen of the day, Woolfolk chose to work and live in the same place. His address was on Pratt Street, where he would be based from 1821 until at least the early 1840s. The city directory listed him as a "purchaser of Negroes." Woolfolk inserted a personal narrative into his ads, informing "the Slaveholders in Maryland, that he has returned from N. Orleans, and will give them CASH for SLAVES. He can be found at all hours at his residence on Pratt-street road"; he described the house as "a white frame, situate[d] a little off the road on the right when going to Washington City with trees in front." (Today it is where Martin Luther King Jr. Boulevard crosses West Pratt Street, and any remaining archaeological evidence is buried beneath a four-lane highway.) In the early 1820s Pratt Street was a residential lane quickly filling with buildings. It had become a city thoroughfare after a stone bridge was built spanning Jones Falls to the east of where Woolfolk built his house and planted his business. Visitors approaching the city from the west rode down a dusty or muddy road and could notice Woolfolk's dwelling on their left. A traveler recalled that the "pretty house in front, presented a smiling aspect," which was belied by the private jail standing in the back. "The small grated windows of his prison in the rear—the chains, fetters, and miserable objects of suffering there concealed, chilled the blood with horror," recalled the visitor. It was no crime to own a private jail. The state had not yet claimed a monopoly on violence. Woolfolk's business dwelling was little different from those of merchant traders of Luanda, Angola, at the time.[57]

Austin's younger brother Samuel Martin Woolfolk and an uncle, Austin, helped expand the Woolfolks' reach and scope in the Chesapeake. By the early 1820s his younger brother Joseph Biggers Woolfolk took up residence in Easton, across the Chesapeake Bay from Baltimore. David Anderson's business declined around the same time. Easton was central. It was the site of a yearly slave auction and also home to two newspapers. Eastern Shore slaveholders held in bondage tens of thousands of enslaved people whose market value climbed considerably in the 1820s. The tavern in which Joseph stayed was in sight of the courthouse where buyers filed bills of sale and a jail where he confined slaves at a fee of twenty-five cents a day. In 1824 he advertised, "NEGROES WANTED for West Tennessee," an unambiguous appeal to sellers wanting to dispose of slaves permanently. In 1825 he paid out nearly $23,000 to a list of sellers that included the leading families of the Eastern Shore.[58]

As the firm grew it stratified, and the Woolfolks became managers as well as owners. By the 1820s the Woolfolks employed paid agents. The Richmond slave trader William Fulcher acted as an agent for Austin in the mid–1820s. A sizable dealer himself, Fulcher subcontracted to still other agents. On the Eastern Shore, Joseph Woolfolk hired Henry N. Templeman to purchase bondspersons for his firm. After serving what amounted to an apprenticeship, Templeman opened his own slaving enterprise in Richmond and went into business with William Goodwin, the slave trader who jailed Solomon Northup in Richmond.[59]

As it grew, the Woolfolk network encompassed most of the upper Chesapeake. By the middle of the 1820s, Austin Woolfolk had partnered with the Alexandria-based trader Ira Bowman, who sent hundreds of slaves south in that decade. In 1830 two of the Woolfolks, including another of Austin's younger brothers, Richard, formed a strategic partnership on the Eastern Shore with two Virginians, Thomas W. Overley and Robert Sanders. The firm called itself Woolfolks, Sanders, and Overley. Richard Woolfolk traded in Salisbury, Maryland, a crossroads town about one hundred miles southeast of Baltimore by ferry and horse. Sanders and Overley were based in Princess Anne, a dozen miles to the south of Salisbury. The firm had an agent operating at Snow Hill, six miles to the south of Princess Anne on the Pocomoke River.[60] That network transported captives to Baltimore and other port cities, where they were embarked aboard merchant vessels.

John Woolfolk developed the firm's sales agency in New Orleans. Initially he sold captives out of city hotels and taverns, shuttling back and forth between Augusta and New Orleans. In 1825 he offered for sale his thousand-acre cotton plantation in Edgefield District, South Carolina, and moved to near the intersection of Chartres and Canal streets, New Orleans. (The New Orleans Marriott hotel stands there today.) John apparently understood French and established ties to Creole buyers, undercutting the competitive advantage enjoyed by city merchants like Moussier. In May 1825 John sold several enslaved people to Francis Xavier Martin, the French-born former Louisiana attorney general who had been Moussier's customer. The newly disembarked captives had been shipped by his nephew Austin aboard a merchant vessel called the *Lady Monroe*.[61]

John expanded his reach into the ranks of Creole sugar planters. In the spring of 1826 he sold six men in their twenties and one nineteen-year-old woman to a Jefferson Parish sugar planter, Barthélémy Macarty. Macarty was a close relative of the socialite Delphine LaLaurie and New Orleans's Mayor Augustin Macarty. LaLaurie would earn the city's ire for torturing and murdering enslaved people; Augustin Macarty had hired Latrobe to develop the city's water system. Barthélémy was apparently pleased with his initial purchases. A week later he bought five more captives from Austin Woolfolk, who was in town at the time. Austin and his brothers regularly shipped to John and, eventually, Samuel Martin Woolfolk, who also took up residence in New Orleans. Those business ties were not exclusive. Firms had not yet developed hard insider-outsider boundaries, and Austin sold captives through other agents on occasion. But John Woolfolk's services were vital. Most important was his ability to act as the firm's banker, extending credit to customers and remitting capital to his nephews in the Chesapeake. In January 1826, for instance, John sold four bondspersons to a Baton Rouge planter in exchange for commercial paper payable by a New Orleans merchant house.[62]

That business arrangement permitted the firm to grow substantially. As John became the firm's chief financial officer, he expanded sales up the Mississippi River corridor to Natchez. He advertised in 1827 that he had "just received from Maryland and Virginia, 140 to 150 LIKELY YOUNG NEGROES, of both sexes, among whom there are a large number of prime field hands, house servants, cooks, carriage drivers, seamstresses and washerwomen." He announced that "all of [them] will be sold low for cash, or on a short credit," inviting would-be buyers to call on him at his New Orleans office.[63] Demand for captives kept growing. Back in Baltimore, the Woolfolk enterprise grew in tandem with shipping merchants serving the slave trade. In the 1820s the saltwater trade was becoming dominated by several vessels that carried the lion's share of human cargoes to New Orleans. Between 1821 and 1830, surviving records indicate that each ship sailing from Baltimore with slaves averaged more than twice as many bondspersons per passage as in 1819–20, the first years for which usable data are available. In the 1820s the median number was twenty-nine per passage. Most ships leaving Baltimore with slaves carried one or two bondspersons, usually as personal servants who would return.[64]

When Woolfolk called at Fells Point shipping merchants' houses along the wharves, he got an enthusiastic response. Shipping was a tough business, and even regular traders tarried in port while owners, operators, and supercargoes scouted for goods to fill a hold. Passengers often had to wait weeks before the shipmaster filed for clearance to sail, and newspaper columns were crowded with advertisements soliciting cargoes. A prominent Baltimore merchant contended that "commerce in the shipping line is one of the most dangerous pursuits that can possibly be engaged in," adding that in his six decades in the business, "not one in fifty shipping merchants have succeeded, either in New York, Philadelphia or Baltimore."[65] In that competitive atmosphere slave traders were no outcasts. Merchants who imported West Indian sugar, Mississippi cotton, or Brazilian coffee knew that lurking somewhere down their supply chain was a group of chained laborers. Collecting princely fares to stow enslaved Marylanders in cargo holds was no large moral leap.

The Baltimore sea captain who owned the 231-ton brigantine *Arctic* was among those who warmly received slave traders. That merchant vessel made eleven passages from Baltimore to New Orleans between 1826 and 1829, embarking in four years about 7 percent of that decade's maritime traffic in slaves for which customs records survive. The ship was built in Duxbury, Massachusetts, and its master hailed from there, too. Woolfolk embarked captives on at least one of the *Arctic*'s passages. As the slave trade to New Orleans developed, shippers welcomed ever larger consignments. The 327-ton *Hibernia*, for instance, embarked 188 captives from Baltimore in early December 1826, including 130 captives consigned by Austin Woolfolk. Like so many other slavers, the *Hibernia* was a large ship plying the cotton triangle, delivering bales of cotton from New Orleans to Liverpool and returning to the Eastern Seaboard with manufactured goods.[66]

The scale of the maritime trade changed the experiences of passage. The winter passage of the *Jefferson* in December 1827 was becoming typical of voyages containing large consignments of captives. Austin Woolfolk and his brother Joseph put aboard nearly one hundred bondspersons in Baltimore between Christmas Eve and the end of December. Most were shipped as individuals. The average age was just under sixteen. Only one woman was older than thirty-nine. The youngest captives included three-week-old Lindy Berry, two-month-old Bob, and four-month-old Anna Maria. Three-year-old Harriet boarded with her mother, Sabina Snowden, who was in the final weeks of pregnancy. Conditions aboard the *Jefferson* were miserable. Weather outside was cold and fierce. Newspapers brought word to Baltimore of a shipwreck caused by it. Baltimore flour trading had halted just before Christmas because of a scarcity of available vessels. The *Jefferson* was one of the few cleared to sail. It had returned from Europe with merchandise for its operator, the same city merchant who had sponsored the *Temperance*'s passage nine years before. Collecting a few thousand dollars in fares was reason enough to cast off in a temporary lull in heavy weather. As the ship rolled, pitched, and yawed in the Atlantic Ocean, as babies puled and a mother gave birth, did the irony of the *Jefferson* heading to Louisiana with a hold full of slaves cross anyone's lips? After the vessel landed, the New Orleans customs inspector amended the slave manifest: "one child born on board." It was as much of a birth certificate as Snowden's infant would receive. The ship returned to Baltimore early the next spring with a hold full of cotton and sugar.[67]

Slave traders' collaborations with merchant shippers brought increased scrutiny and abolitionist criticism. Out of them Woolfolk eventually received public vindication. Baltimore Quakers inspecting ships and Hezekiah Niles occasionally fuming about newspaper advertisements were minor irritants. But abolitionist gadflies began to sting Woolfolk and his brethren. In 1825 Benjamin Lundy, a slight man with a steely nerve, exposed Woolfolk's business in the pages of his newspaper, the *Genius of Universal Emancipation.* That publicity would lead to violence and help launch the career of the best-known white American abolitionist, William Lloyd Garrison. Lundy was a New Jersey Quaker who had traveled extensively in the South, publicizing a moral evil. He focused on the slave trade. A coffle of slaves encountered near Wheeling, Virginia, was a sight that made "his heated blood boil in his veins." Lundy inaugurated his newspaper in Mount Pleasant, Ohio, in 1821. After pursuing an abolitionist calling in Tennessee, he moved to Maryland in 1824. In Baltimore he cofounded the Maryland Anti-Slavery Society and began agitating.[68] It was not long before he was drawn to Woolfolk.

Using a tactic that had been the hallmark of British abolitionism, Lundy investigated maritime Baltimore the way Thomas Clarkson had investigated Liverpool some three and a half decades before. The diminutive Quaker called at government offices, requested public records relating to slavery, and analyzed them. He understood the economics of the interstate trade and had investigated responses among the enslaved, including suicide. Lundy was in his mid-thirties, recently widowed, and trained as a saddler. The editor considered himself a philanthropist and a protector of his African-descended fellow Americans. Lundy was optimistic. He believed that if confronted with the sins of slavery, citizens would work to extirpate them. He worked out of an office on Calvert

Street in the commercial quarter of the city. In the summer of 1825 he published records of the springtime slaving passage of the *Lady Monroe* to which Austin and Joseph Woolfolk had consigned nearly one hundred captives. That passage included the bondspersons sold to Francis Xavier Martin.[69] Lundy drew a stark parallel for readers.

The domestic slave trade, Lundy contended, embodied the prodigious iniquities of its transatlantic counterpart, and Austin Woolfolk was at the head of it. Baltimore's wharves were like "the coast of Africa," he charged, and its slave traders resembled the "hardened freebooters and traffickers of human flesh and blood, who have so long disgraced human nature by their infamous and 'piratical' practices." *Niles' Weekly Register* reprinted Lundy's reports, and newspapers in Connecticut, New York, and even Edwardsville, Illinois, also printed parts of Lundy's exposé. Austin, Lundy argued, was responsible for over 70 percent of the slave trade in Baltimore during May, June, and July 1825. Others in the market were his brothers Joseph and Richard, along with the firm's Alexandria affiliate, Ira Bowman. If Lundy's reporting is accurate, the Woolfolk enterprise was actually responsible for 87 percent of the Baltimore slave trade during the sample period.[70] Public response was initially muted, but when an uprising occurred among captives shipped from Baltimore, reports of Woolfolk's response caused a scandal.

The 1826 rebellion aboard the *Decatur* generated the sparks Lundy hoped would ignite public hostility to the domestic slave trade. The schooner *Decatur* set sail from Baltimore that April with thirty-one or thirty-three captives. Most were Woolfolk's property. Despite the dangers of uprisings, the officers and crew aboard the *Decatur* were lightly armed. There was little security, which was not unusual. But the captives aboard were not going easily to the New Orleans slave market. Thomas Harrod, Manuel Wilson, and William Bowser were among them. The twenty-four-year-old Bowser was a native of West River, Maryland, and had tried to escape slavery once already. That had landed him in a Baltimore jail, where Woolfolk bought him for resale in New Orleans. After being transferred to Woolfolk's private jail on Pratt Street, Bowser reportedly witnessed one enslaved woman murder her child and then take her own life to avoid forced transport to the Deep South. Bowser and the other bondspersons were embarked on the *Decatur* at night. Shipmaster Walter Galloway arrived at the wharf in the morning and pushed off, but it took hours before the wind picked up enough to move the vessel out of the Patapsco River and into the Chesapeake Bay.[71]

Tensions smoldered belowdecks. Talk among Bowser, Harrod, Wilson, and perhaps others stoked discontents into a plot to overthrow the ship and sail to freedom in Haiti. Several days into the passage the *Decatur* was sailing off the

Georgia coast. A little after nine o'clock in the morning Galloway was on deck scraping mud off the anchor stock. He did not see the figures of Harrod and Wilson approach. They seized him by the legs and cast him overboard. "As the captain dropped astern," a witness later reported, "the negro men ran aft, which noise woke the mate, who was asleep in the cabin." Hearing cries, the ship's mate rushed to help, "with only his pantaloons and shirt on." He was thrown overboard as well. Chances of successfully sailing to Haiti drowned with the officers. The rebels restrained another crew member after he attempted to intervene. In control of the ship, Bowser, Harrod, and Wilson demanded that the remaining crew steer a course for Haiti and "took possession of the cabin, and as the vessel was well stocked with small stores [and] refreshments," they helped themselves to new clothes and other articles on board.[72] The rebels did not hold the ship for long.

The master of a whaling vessel returning from the Pacific and in need of supplies came alongside the *Decatur* and, after discovering the rebellion, sent armed men to capture its instigators. It was reported that one of the rebels, named Jones, "who had been to sea on a number of voyages, as a sailor, appeared to have the principal direction on board," but he was unable to navigate. The whaler took aboard about half of the *Decatur*'s captives and two sailors captured in the uprising. A second ship took fourteen of the remaining captives and designated an officer to conduct the *Decatur* back to port. When the second ship reached its home port of New York City, most of the recaptured slaves managed to escape. William Bowser was recaptured along with several others. The U.S. Circuit Court in New York City convened that November found Bowser (tried under the name William Hill) guilty—and his fellow defendants not guilty—of Galloway's murder.[73]

Austin Woolfolk featured in the trial and its aftermath. According to reports, he was the principal witness against Bowser. Lundy reported that Woolfolk attended Bowser's hanging in December on Ellis Island. The *New York Spectator* covered the trial and Woolfolk's involvement. The Baltimore trader was no stranger to the *Spectator*'s editor, who had reprinted Lundy's exposé of Woolfolk the previous year. Lundy eulogized Bowser, contending that on the eve of his death "he declared he felt a peace of mind which could not be described . . . and that he could pray even for Woolfolk his inveterate enemy, and heartily forgive all the injuries he had done him." While Bowser was led to the gallows, "he particularly addressed his discourse" to Woolfolk, repeating the sentiment of Christian love and forgiveness, to which the slave trader reportedly replied "with an oath, (not to be named,) 'that he was now going to have what he deserved, and he was glad of it,' or words to this effect!"[74] The coverage enraged Woolfolk.

He soon took revenge. On January 9, 1827, in Charles Street near the Baltimore Post Office, Woolfolk ran into Lundy. Lundy faced a man seven inches taller and as many years younger, for whom violence was an everyday part of his livelihood. Woolfolk glared into his critic's pale blue eyes and asked if he had published the offending article. Lundy answered that he had—but that he was not the author. As Woolfolk crowded him Lundy insisted that he copied the article from a New York newspaper. A throng of onlookers gathered. Lundy "drew a paper from his pocket containing the remarks," it was reported, "offered it to Woolfolk, and told him he could read them for himself." Woolfolk refused to take the paper "but immediately seized Lundy, threw him to the ground, and beat and stamped upon his head and face in a most furious and violent manner, until pulled off by bystanders." Lundy had offered no resistance and spent several days "confined to his bed" recovering from severe injuries.[75] Woolfolk was charged with assaulting and injuring his critic. The case went to trial in April.

Most white Baltimoreans were unsympathetic to abolitionists. Lundy believed he was exposing a moral evil, but the average citizen saw it differently. Commercial Baltimore knew on which side its bread was buttered. Lundy had insulted a respectable businessman and gotten rightly thumped for it. Those attitudes illustrate how thoroughly Woolfolk's business was tied into Baltimore's merchant community and how deep antiblack racism ran. In the 1820s Woolfolk was a regular customer of the city's prominent shipping merchants and a city landowner. He even sat on the board of a coal company. The *Niles' Weekly Register*, no friend of slave traders, shrugged that Woolfolk "proved" in court "that he was in Baltimore and not in New York" at the time Bowser was executed. Judge Nicholas Brice, who heard the case, "in pronouncing sentence, took occasion to observe, that he had never seen a case in which the provocation for a battery was greater than the present—that if abusive language could ever be a justification for battery, this was that case." Brice applauded Woolfolk's enterprise, contending that "Lundy had no right to reproach him in such abusive language for carrying on a lawful trade—that the trade itself was beneficial to the state, as it removed a great many rogues and vagabonds who were a nuisance in the state." The judge argued "that Lundy had received no more than a merited chastisement for his abuse of [Woolfolk], and but for the strict letter of the law, the court would not fine Woolfolk any thing." He was fined one dollar and court costs. Brice added that Woolfolk ought to sue Lundy for libel.[76] Lundy backed off.

Woolfolk's business thrived in the booming times of the late 1820s, but new threats emerged at the margins. An ambitious partnership of slave traders commenced in Alexandria in the District of Columbia. It was called Franklin and Armfield. In 1829, after a sojourn in Boston, a twenty-four-year-old native of Newburyport, Massachusetts, showed up in Baltimore and began writing for Lundy's *Genius*. William Lloyd Garrison had the pluck to risk a beating from

Woolfolk. He revived the editor's "Black List" of atrocities. In doing so he cast off decorum and spoke as a Christian indicting a towering moral evil.[77]

Garrison viewed slavery as part of a cosmic moral economy rather than a component of a capitalistic political economy. That distinguished him slightly from his mentor. Lundy was well-traveled and a largely self-taught student of politics and economics. He understood and investigated the domestic slave trade as a conflict between morality and economic interest. Garrison was raised on a Baptist theology that construed the world as a sinful clod under the weight of a righteous God's impending judgment. The crying sin of the age was slavery, which was one of a constellation of iniquities. Garrison's was a severe outlook that nevertheless carried an optimistic corollary: human beings could turn from sin, repent, and be saved. Humanity was perfectible. But the world was in urgent need of moral transformation, and the struggle was territorial. That overhaul would be completed church by church, city by city, and country by country, and only then would the prophesied millennium begin. That geographic orientation would lead Garrison to cultivate a transatlantic network of abolitionists. But it also permitted abolitionists to shade in polygonal shapes on U.S. maps corresponding to so-called slave states and thereby imagine a firm boundary between a free North and a slave South. To abolitionists political borders became moral borders. But such thinking obscured the fact that Liverpool and New York held the strongest financial links in the chain of credits and debts responsible for slavery's vitality. Ignoring such nuances, Garrison would eventually advocate disunion as a partial remedy to the national sin of slavery.[78]

Garrison's evangelical approach to abolitionism shaped his activism. He personalized the sin of slavery in an effort to shame those whom he held responsible. In the *Genius* Garrison castigated Austin Woolfolk as "the most notorious of the Baltimore Negro-buyers." He was inflammatory but not reckless in his reporting. Garrison hired African-descended informants on the city waterfront to report on slaving voyages. Suspecting that Lundy was behind the screeds, Woolfolk publicly contemplated taking him to court. In the pages of the *Genius*, Garrison chided him for confusing a "G." with an "L." and called on him to debate the merits of the slave trade at Garrison's boardinghouse. Woolfolk ignored the challenge.[79]

The incident that catalyzed Garrison's abolitionist career involved a former Newburyport neighbor, Francis Todd. Todd was the owner of the merchant vessel *Francis*. Nicholas Brown was its skipper. In October 1829 Todd's ship had been cleared to sail from Baltimore to New Orleans with cargo. At the last minute the Baltimore shipping merchant Henry Thompson accepted a consignment of slaves. Instead of sailing directly for New Orleans, Brown sailed the

Francis to Herring Bay, in northern Calvert County, Maryland, and embarked eighty-eight enslaved people. Woolfolk was said to have brokered the sale, but his involvement is unclear. None of the captives was interviewed, and Todd was hundreds of miles away. The *Francis* sailed to Annapolis to file a slave manifest and then out of the Chesapeake Bay.[80]

When news reached Garrison, he pounced on the story as a sordid bit of slaving by New Englanders who should have known better. "So much for New England principle!" he screeched in a November issue of the *Genius*. "Scarcely a vessel, perhaps, leaves this port for New Orleans," Garrison yelped, "without carrying off in chains large numbers of the unfortunate blacks." Garrison kept the story alive the following week. He set in capital letters the name of the ship's owner at the close of a paragraph excoriating him. Todd had succeeded in shipping out of a port in which others were failing, Garrison contended, because the slave trade saved him from financial ruin. That was not untrue. The *Francis* was a transient or tramp ship, which sailed wherever the owner or operator detected a hint of revenue. Earlier that year the *Francis* had returned from Lima, Peru, landing passengers and carrying specie to Thompson and others. When Todd's ship needed cargo, Thompson gave him a lucrative payload.[81]

Garrison got more attention than expected. In February 1830 a grand jury indicted him and Lundy for "a gross and malicious libel" against Francis Todd. It was an unusual charge. Todd also initiated a civil suit seeking $5,000 in damages from the *Genius*'s editors, a sum that would put the paper out of business. Sparing Lundy, the State of Maryland charged Garrison with criminal libel. The case was weak, but hearing the trial was Woolfolk's ally on the bench, Nicholas Brice. Garrison quipped that the judge possessed "all the humanitarianism of a shark." Thompson testified that he had arranged to ship slaves aboard the *Francis* and that Todd did not find out until after the ship had sailed. Garrison may have been guilty of embarrassing Todd but not of libeling him. The judge had permitted the prosecution to cast Garrison as a malicious meddler and abuser of Todd's good name. It took the jury fifteen minutes to find him guilty. Garrison was fined fifty dollars plus court costs of nearly another twenty, and, if he could not pay, he was sentenced to a six-month jail term. Garrison's attorney filed appeals, which Brice later denied.[82]

In jail Garrison was radicalized. He had been unable and unwilling to pay the fine. A new warden treated him as a naive youth and a political prisoner. Garrison ate with the warden and his wife. From a writing desk in their parlor he sharpened the quills with which he penned a flood of letters and other publicity. While Woolfolk kept an unusual distance from the jail, Garrison wrote, "power, and not justice, has convicted me." When freed he returned to

Boston to start his own abolitionist newspaper, the *Liberator*, which amplified his views.[83] Garrison had stumbled on a strategy that had profound and reaching consequences for how Americans, Britons, and Europeans understood North American chattel slavery.

That was to personalize it. Garrison's Baltimore ordeal was his first taste of that strategy's effectiveness and its peril. He was mobbed for such incendiary tactics in Boston in 1835 and nearly killed. Garrison's Massachusetts Anti-Slavery Society sponsored abolitionist orators such as Frederick Douglass and William Wells Brown and published the first editions of their autobiographies. Douglass and Brown, along with other ex-slave autobiographers, gave narrative form to abolitionists' rhetoric. They were particularly effective at capturing readers' sympathies, generating moral outrage, and directing it at enslavers. They did so by pulling readers into the texture of human bondage as they repre-sented it. Holding up enslavers as the embodiment of wickedness stirred up public reactions. Douglass was beaten and nearly killed in Indiana in 1843 on a speaking tour as an agent of Garrison's abolitionist group.[84]

But slave traders as capitalists fit awkwardly into that abolitionist script. Douglass mentioned Woolfolk by name as a bogeyman and snatcher of chil-dren. Brown wrote extensively about the slave trade in which he had been an unwilling participant. Yet they presented slavery as a social institution rather than an economic one. Ex-slave autobiographers set the tone for effective anti-slavery writing and won commercial success as well. Douglass and Brown were among the first celebrity authors who were also African-descended Americans. They took that fame abroad. White writers also published widely read anti-slavery appeals by personalizing dramas of heroic slaves and sinful slaveholders. Proslavery writers responded in kind. Instead of characterizing slavery as a system saturated with capitalistic values, the most successful pro- and antislavery novels took narrative forms that dripped with emotion. The few white southern authors whose novels featured slave traders, including the Virginian George Tucker and the Marylander John P. Kennedy, depicted them as money-grubbing itinerants and social outcasts. In contrast to planters, slave traders disrupted an organic social order founded on white benevolence and black servitude. There was no room in such imaginative literature for the sophisti-cated, rational, networked, and well-capitalized firms such as Woolfolk's.[85]

The narrative of slavery that emerged in fiction was central to how the North Atlantic world understood the institution. A tidal wave of sentimental fiction was the catalyst for turning the thorny issue of slavery into the spongy center of American melodrama. It is little wonder that the most successful American novel, *Uncle Tom's Cabin*, and indeed the genre that *Uncle Tom* represented borrowed heavily from African-descended authors' assessments of slave life. The shrewdest literary minds of the South, including William Gilmore Simms, Caroline Lee Hentz, and Caroline Gilman, ignored the slave trade and the economic system it served. In constructing a national narrative of slavery, pro- and antislavery authors, along with abolitionists, vied to characterize slavery according to its human contours, hybridizing genres of fiction and nonfiction in the process. Slavery's capitalism melted into obscurity. Britons who eventually decided against supporting the Southern Confederacy opted for the melodrama of Stowe over Simms, antislavery sentiment over proslavery sentiment.[86] In the 1830s Garrison's publicity strategy boosted his cause and made him famous. Woolfolk's expanded his business and made him rich.

Austin Woolfolk's career amounts to an early nineteenth-century business bildungsroman. Decades before readers encountered Ragged Dick or Green Henry, the flesh-and-bone Woolfolk was a teenaged runaway who walked into a metropolis friendless. There he seized his civic entitlements, accepted the values of his society, and ascended to the front ranks of American businessmen. Woolfolk harnessed the most powerful medium of democratic and commercial discourse to create an enterprise and usher a slave market into being. Not unlike evangelicals and sellers of patent medicines, Woolfolk appealed to readers as participants in a broader process. Building that business over two decades, Woolfolk created a brand name. He helped rationalize an emerging market, filling holes in his network with kinsmen and established merchants.[87]

Austin Woolfolk's business declined in Baltimore in the 1830s as his competitor Franklin and Armfield's grew. That firm seized business advantages that had eluded Woolfolk and rode the crest of an even larger economic expansion in cotton. But Austin's business continued to develop even as his market share decreased. In addition to consigning captives to merchant voyages, he advertised to charter "a good vessel, that is a fast sailer," in 1831. That fall he embarked over 180 captives, including a consignment of 32 aboard a merchant sloop, of whom 28 survived the passage. In November 1834 Austin embarked 42 captives aboard a Baltimore merchant vessel sailing to New Orleans. Some were sold there, but his attentions were increasingly focused elsewhere.[88]

By about 1840 Woolfolk was living in comfort and respectability as a planter and patriarch of a growing family. He owned a plantation in Jackson, Tennessee, of hundreds of acres that was staffed by slaves. Woolfolk had also accumulated real estate in Louisiana. He had been among the first Euroamericans to settle on Bayou Grosse Tete, in Iberville Parish, in the 1820s. By the early 1840s his holdings amounted to 5,000 acres in the area of Bayou Maringouin. He married

Emily Sparks in Baltimore in October 1839. Their children included two sons, Joseph Biggers Woolfolk, born in 1833 and named for his uncle in the slave trade, and Austin Jr., born in 1837, besides their adopted sons William and John Woolfolk. In 1840 the family moved to the Mounds or Mound Place, Austin's plantation on the west bank of Bayou Grosse Tete and Bayou Maringouin, about thirty-three miles northwest of Plaquemine. Emily gave birth to Louisiana Tennessee Woolfolk in 1840, Sarah Jane in 1842, and Samuel Richard in 1847.[89]

No abolitionists bothered Woolfolk at the Mounds. In 1840 he built an elegant one-and-a-half-story house of cypress amid the local groves of pecan and live oak. To do so he had workers level the top of an ancient Indian mound, one of three on Woolfolk's lands. "During building activities," locals later remembered, "a number of Indian relics were uncovered, among which was an earthenware pot containing the skeletons of two babies." The house built on the base of the mound still stands, nestled beside majestic trees, though the property passed out of the Woolfolk family early in the twentieth century. According to local memory, Austin and Emily Woolfolk "were extremely popular with their neighbors and kind and thoughtful masters to their slaves." Religious observance was part of the order they upheld on the plantation. African-descended residents remembered the Woolfolks differently. Emily Woolfolk "superintended the baptism of 52 Negroes," it was remembered, "and her daughter, Lou, stood as sponsor; but a few days later her interest in their spiritual welfare was somewhat dimmed when she overheard her cook exclaim: 'Law, it don't make no difference how bad us is; Miss Lou's 'sponsible for our sins.'"[90]

Austin Woolfolk died in his fiftieth year in Auburn, Macon County, Alabama, in February 1847. He was traveling from Baltimore to "home and family" at the Mounds plantation. His estate was valued at $422,828, a considerable sum at the time. Yet even death did not stop him separating members of African-descended families. His 1846 will directed the executor to "send all my slaves in Tennessee to Louisiana there to be delivered to my executors in that state to be held by them for the benefit of my said wife Emily Woolfolk and all my children." Woolfolk's father, William, who outlived him, expressed sorrow that his most successful son "had not left his sisters som[e] property." Austin's brothers Joseph Biggers, Samuel M., and Richard Woolfolk had died before him. The only brother not involved in slave-trading, William W., outlived his older brothers. His uncle John died in 1861.[91] Unlike characters in fiction, Woolfolk was never called to account for the sufferings of the captives he bought and sold.

To African-descended Americans, Austin Woolfolk's legacy was one of destruction and despair. When Alexis de Tocqueville arrived at the Baltimore almshouse in 1831, he was captivated by "a Negro whose madness is extraordinary." Although robust and physically striking, the man was terrorized to the point of insanity. The French visitor gleaned that the man imagined a slave trader who "sticks close to him day and night and snatches away bits of his flesh." He was so debilitated by the psychic trauma that he could not leave the almshouse.[92] When de Tocqueville's traveling companion, Gustave de Beaumont, inquired into the history of the "furiously demented" man's condition, he put in the mouth of a guard at the almshouse the tale of his woes. "There lived in Maryland a professional slave dealer named Wolfolk," he declared. "He made a big business of this and was, perhaps, the foremost dealer in human flesh in the United States," adding that "all the colored population knew and abhorred him." The man "had been taken by Wolfolk from Virginia to Maryland to be sold, and on the way he was subjected to such brutalities that his reason had snapped." Neither the guard nor the inmate explained the particulars of what the man experienced, but "since then," the guard reported, "one fixed idea had possessed him, never giving an instant's rest: he believed his mortal enemy was constantly at his side, awaiting the moment when he could cut out from his body strips of flesh for which he hungered." The man was delirious, inconsolable, and "took anyone he saw for Wolfolk." De Tocqueville remembered that the man "was one of the most beautiful Negroes I have ever seen, and he is in the prime of life."[93]

3

Sweet Dreams and Smuggling Schemes

John Craig Marsh was failing in the New York City dry goods business in 1817 when he decided to reinvent himself as a Louisiana sugar planter. To cut start-up costs he bought enslaved New Jerseyans cheaply and transported them to New Orleans illegally, taking along African-descended contract workers from New York. Marsh was an unlikely slave smuggler. The twenty-eight-year-old New Jersey native had left the family farm in Rahway and gone into the clothing business with a partner, Aaron Coe. They offered styles from Bordeaux, France, and South Carolina, among other places. Marsh and Coe also sold styling products such as beeswax. Political and economic developments upset the clothing business while opening new opportunities on the republic's southwestern frontier. Marsh's shift from clothing to sugar was a microcosm of that larger transformation.

The American commercial empire was growing restlessly in its political and legal framework. Americans had defended New Orleans from British capture in 1815 with the help of a range of unlikely allies, including slave smugglers. As part of a political strategy to reward such allies, authorities tolerated and even abetted slave smuggling, although that was changing by the time Marsh tried his hand at it. The federal government also cultivated Louisiana interests by protecting domestic sugar, nearly all of it grown in the southern part of the state. Related changes were apparent at Marsh's establishment on Pearl Street in the commercial heart of New York, which was nestled among countinghouses and stores close to the docks. Three-story brick buildings with high stoops and dormer windows in their roofs lined the street. Many housed residents in the upper stories, dining rooms in basements, and insurance or banking offices in parlors. To established merchants, an ill wind blew down Pearl Street, caused in part by British merchants dumping goods on the market.[1]

Marsh's failure came at a time when English merchants and British bankers revolutionized the textile and credit markets, which caused a trade war that made the business of Louisiana sugar artificially sweet. Following peace in 1815, English merchants auctioned assortments of textiles in American ports, from which they were distributed all over the republic, undercutting dry goods merchants like Marsh and Coe and the American financial houses that backed them. Because of a credit squeeze caused by the Bank of England in 1816, British merchants were willing to take steep losses on individual consignments in order to raise cash remitted as debt service. American markets were soon glutted, and many consignments sold for less than their import duty—and far less than their manufacturing cost. In the larger frame, Marsh's business suffered much as independent retailers' did in a later age of chain stores: a globalizing chain of commodities and credit was responsible for depressing labor and materials costs, manufacturing goods in massive quantities using high technology, selling them at impossibly cheap prices, and extending credit to customers. The system democratized apparel while making homespun cloth a symbol of patriotism rather than of poverty. It grew by exploiting new markets in the Atlantic basin and beyond. The commercial winds that filled the slave trader Austin Woolfolk's sails in the form of high demand for enslaved people bound to cotton fields capsized Marsh and Coe. Marsh's business sank in a sea of cheap imports. In response, American manufacturers demanded tariff protections, and New York instituted auction rules beginning in 1817 requiring that consignments be sold to the highest bidder rather than quickly for cash. The United States and Britain imposed reciprocal duties on American commodities and British goods. U.S. tariffs passed in 1816 also protected domestic sugar.[2]

If contemplating his failure from the stoop of his Pearl Street store, Marsh could look out with loathing at the hordes of New Yorkers in new English garments. Hickory wood and coal smoke accented the air as usual, but even some cart-pushing Irish coal vendors wore new calico. Young people bustling about in the streets sported shirts and dresses cut from cloth woven on Lancashire power looms. At a glance, middling women wearing muslin dresses were suddenly indistinguishable from fashionable ladies strolling in and out of perfumeries, jewelers, and hairdressers, their hair parted in the middle with ringlets over the ears. Ambitious country youths whose backs had been long chafed by coarse homespun eased about in ready-made shirting, which complemented their fashionably long side-whiskers. Short monkey jackets seemed to sprout from their chests. Class distinctions were still plain, however. Masses of New Yorkers wore simple, secondhand clothing, often a mix of homespun and manufactured cloth, dried mud and filth on the cuffs and hems. Marsh could envision the less fortunate among them laboring for him in a distant sugarcane field. One in twelve of the city's residents was African-descended. Many— regardless of color—were desperate and destitute. Sailors abounded and so did the dialects, accents, and languages spoken in the streets. Gentlemen wore long tails flapping over tight trousers, and collars bespoke status. Tailored clothing was a mark of quality, and white shirts were indicators of wealth. Some of those shirts were creditors'.[3]

One hundred seventy-five years before the phrase entered the English vernacular, Marsh had his mind on his money and his money on his mind. Through the hurried mass of humanity, he might spy the figures of fellow linen merchants or bankers to whom he was in debt. That fall Marsh's real estate was sold for their benefit. There was some cold comfort in knowing he was not alone. Arthur Tappan was a near neighbor, also in the dry goods business and specializing in silk. Tappan, one of the country's leading abolitionists by the 1830s, would himself fail in business. Failure was common in the early republic in good economic times and bad. It happened often enough not to leave a permanent stain if attributed to misfortune rather than moral failing. Marsh soon ceased sighing about his lot as a city merchant and turned his gaze fourteen hundred miles to the southeast, to a fertile patch of Louisiana known as Petite Anse Island in St. Martin Parish. There his prosperity would take root.[4]

Sugar planting seemed a lucrative business. If Marsh picked up a city newspaper as his dry goods firm went under, he read of fortunes made in the balmy climate of southern Louisiana. In the summer of 1817 an Attakapas planter reported, "The soil is very rich and produces beyond any that has yet been tried, some fields having been in cultivation for forty years in succession, without any diminution of their strength." Sugarcane yields were high in the area. "On the Mississippi a hogshead of sugar per acre is considered as a common crop," the planter contended, "but in Attakapas a hogshead and a half and two hogsheads to an acre are the common crops." If true, that amounted to fifteen hundred or two thousand pounds of salable sugar per acre per year. Labor was at a premium, the planter explained, "and of all kinds of property, the negroes are the most valuable in Louisiana." Baltimore's *Niles' Weekly Register* agreed, claiming that among all staples, sugar "is the most profitable crop to the planter," and it calculated that a slave could generate 25 percent more value in sugar per year than in cotton and over twice as much as in tobacco.[5] The message was clear: it would be foolish not to invest.

Marsh partnered with his friend William Stone and together they bought Petite Anse Island Plantation early in 1818. Petite Anse, later renamed Avery

Island (and now famous for Tabasco sauce), was not actually an island but a fertile ring surrounded by sea marshes. The lands in the area of Attakapas, where it was located, had been home to Atakapa-Ishak Indians before Acadians moved in during the last quarter of the eighteenth century. They had boiled the water to produce salt. By the time Marsh set his eyes on the area, white American citizens were streaming in with African-descended bondspeople, carving up arable lands into cane fields. New York may have been a cradle of many merchants' fortunes, but the sweet prospect of Louisiana's new frontier attracted northerners and southerners, Britons and Frenchmen alike.

Avery Island held that promise in spades. It was nearly two miles long in some places and over six miles in circumference. The most prominent feature was a salt dome, a mass of rock salt, which would generate another component of the plantation's exports, though it was not excavated until the Civil War. The dome rose nearly two hundred feet above sea level, the highest point on the flat landscape. Beneath it, a visitor later reported, "visible for miles, stretched the world of these lowlands, in concentration: thick marsh, cypress swamp, dry forest in which deer and bear can be found; hills and ravines, wide pastures for grazing, a bayou threading its way." Cypress, magnolia, gum, and live oak trees thrived, timber that would become fuel for a sugarhouse. From atop the dome, Vermillion Bay was visible to the south, beyond the prairielike expanse of wetlands. Trees along Bayou Teche could also be made out, as could other islands rising from the marshlands. White sails of ships were visible in the distance as the bay joined the Gulf of Mexico near the horizon.[6]

If the hazard of new fortunes sprouting from the earth were not enough to sway Marsh and Stone, the federal government gave sugar planters a comparative advantage over foreign producers. The United States collected three cents per pound on imported sugar beginning in 1816, half a cent more than it had before the War of 1812. The United States had taxed sugar imports since 1789, but the 1816 tariff was designed to protect planters and investors from foreign competition. To put that in perspective, the new tariff amounted to between 16 and 17 percent of the wholesale price of Cuban sugar in 1817 and nearly 19 percent in 1818, a serious impediment to foreign producers selling to U.S. customers. Inferior Louisiana sugar lived on that cost advantage. The pro-protectionist U.S. senator Henry Clay wrote in 1831 that "the effect of a repeal of the duty would compel the Louisiana planter to abandon cultivation of the sugar cane," since Louisiana sugar could not compete successfully with Caribbean sugar in a free market. Repealing the sugar tariff "would be almost as fatal to him as if Congress were to order the dykes to be razed from Point

Coupée to the Balize" near the mouth of the Mississippi River and let floodwa-
ters cover the land.[7]

In the winter of 1818 Marsh moved to Avery Island, along with his wife, Eliza,
and infant daughter, Sarah, leaving behind a son in school in New Jersey. Marsh
and Stone took planting advice from the former owner, Jesse McCall, who
wrote in the spring of 1818 with requests for money and news of "Frenchmen . . .
from all parts of the United Sates" moving into the area. He advised the new
owners on how to build a sugar mill, reported a killing frost on cotton plants in
the region, and which millstones to use.[8]

Marsh, a failed merchant with no experience planting sugar, found that his
transition from merchant in the metropolis to Louisiana planter involved
several challenges. Sugar planting required a great deal of capital, even more
than cotton. On-site processing facilities needed to be built. Even before the
introduction of steam equipment in 1822, building a sugarhouse for initial
refining was costly. Labor costs were also high. Unlike free-labor enterprises,
which paid laborers after they performed work, slave-labor enterprises required
much of the labor costs be paid upfront in the form of bound workers. Marsh
was from an old planter family in New Jersey and had some accumulated
capital, but large-scale sugar planting depended on abundant credit. In the late
1820s Louisiana property banks would emerge to serve the sugar industry. Before
that, planters depended on factors and their own resources. In 1818 Marsh economized by gathering human resources from his surroundings in New York and
New Jersey.[9]

In March 1818 Marsh and Stone returned to New York to assemble a workforce. Slaves from the Chesapeake were available, but enslaved New Jerseyans
were cheaper, if more difficult to take to Avery Island. New Jersey was home to
nearly 7,500 enslaved people, mostly in the eastern part of the state. The state
had passed gradual abolition measures, beginning with an 1804 law requiring
that any slave taken out of state be examined by two impartial officials to ascer-
tain consent. An 1812 New Jersey law reiterated that both slaves for life and
slaves for a term must consent to emigration. For enslaved people, gradual
abolition was grindingly slow, but few preferred to leave family and friends to
toil among strangers in the malarial bayous and killing canebrakes of lower
Louisiana. For owners, legal restrictions were partly responsible for keeping
slave traders at bay. Slave prices in New Jersey were lower than in Virginia and
much lower than in New Orleans. According to a contemporary observer, an
enslaved worker who sold in New Jersey for $300 might fetch $800 in New
Orleans.[10] Profit margins such as that would make an interstate slave trader
swoon. Initially, Marsh and Stone hesitated to smuggle enslaved New Jerseyans.

Instead, they devised ingenious legal ways of assembling bound workers and simultaneously deferring labor costs. In the late summer of 1818 they enrolled contract workers. Stone and Marsh took advantage of the economic distress of several free New Yorkers of African descent to bind them to multiyear contracts. Such arrangements were not unusual. Sailors on merchant or whaling voyages signed on for years, the lion's share of wages coming due at the conclusion of the voyage. It is impossible to know what Stone told the recruits that persuaded them to consent to serve future sugar masters. Likely enrollees had little real choice. Merchants like Marsh or Tappan could fail and pick themselves up again. But masses of utterly indigent, chronically ill, unskilled, or merely unfortunate people had little hope of such reversals, and many African-descended Americans shared that lot in New York City. A patchwork of private and parochial assistance organizations did not begin to meet the needs of the city's poor.[11]

The labor market was merciless and stingy, and Stone was its face. Those who agreed to leave New York for Louisiana in the waning months of 1818 would toil on Avery Island for the better part of four years if they lived that long. Their predicaments resembled indentured servitude. For thirty dollars a year, twenty-nine-year-old Ann Moore agreed to work for Stone and Marsh "as a good, honest and faithful Servant" for three years and nine months, at the end of which she would be free and entitled to her earnings. Mary Harris and Eliza Thompson, both twenty-one, agreed to identical terms the same day as Moore. Thompson was a Virginia native. Since 1806 the Commonwealth of Virginia had required freed slaves to leave the state within a year of being manumitted or else face reenslavement. New York may have had some allure initially, but Thompson was desperate. Signing on with Stone may have been the least bad option. Susan Jackson agreed to terms similar to Harris's and Thompson's. She was enrolled in late August. The twenty-year-old woman stood four feet eight inches tall. Stone and Marsh signed up Peggy Boss and Julian Jackson, both twenty-one, in early September for the same terms at the same wages.[12]

A sugar planter's assembling a workforce with so many female laborers was unusual. But Marsh and Stone were inexperienced and sought pliable workers whom they could recruit cheaply. After assembling females, Stone and Marsh sought young male workers. Stone promised to pay female workers two and a half dollars per month and male workers three and one third dollars. Twelve-hour workdays were not uncommon (enslaved sugar workers could expect to toil longer at the harvest and grinding times), and the workweek was typically six days. In addition to deferred wages, workers could expect rudimentary food, clothing, and housing no different from those of their enslaved coworkers. They could also expect violent responses to protests or requests, and passage to

Louisiana was one way. There were no vacation or sick days, save those that threatened the lives of workers, and no health care except at the pleasure of the masters. Quitting meant forfeiting wages, and even the customary Christmas holiday was not on offer in Louisiana sugar country. That was precisely the time fields were cleared for the next year's crop. Should an incapacitating injury, illness, or death occur, word might never reach loved ones in New York. It is unlikely that they knew all that.

The wolves were at the doors of Samuel Prince and others like him, and even the highest earners among Marsh and Stone's contract workforce earned far below the wage of common Euroamerican laborers. Nineteen-year-old Prince agreed to work for three years and nine months for forty dollars a year. So did thirty-year-old Samuel Peters. Working six days a week, Prince and Peters each earned less than thirteen cents per day, about one-sixth the wage of a common adult white male laborer in the south-central region of the country. Twenty-two-year-old Edward Gilbert signed up the same day as Peters. Stone advanced him thirty-eight dollars. Peters would receive the balance of $112 the day after Christmas 1822 for performing some of the most hazardous work in the country. In late October Stone promised nineteen-year-old Joseph Hendrickson fifty dollars a year for a five-year-term, which was about one-fifth the rate of common laborers' wages. Marsh and Stone were set to sail to Louisiana within days and needed to fill the ranks of their force. Twenty-one-year-old Hendrickson signed a vague contract indicating that his service was to take place "in the State of Mississippi or its vicinity." He probably had little idea where he would end up. Louisiana courts were virtually off limits if they sought remedies for breaches of the agreements. None of the contractors were able to sign their names. Instead, each made a cross as a signature.[13] While Marsh and Stone enrolled African-descended New Yorkers they were also assembling enslaved New Jerseyans. And they were not alone.

As slave prices rose to unprecedented levels in Virginia and Louisiana, some slaveholders turned an eye to New Jersey bondspersons while officials invented ways to manufacture enslaved people's consent. Charles R. Morgan's scheme to draft New Jerseyans into Louisiana slavery was the most visible and audacious. Morgan was a planter in Pointe Coupee Parish and a Louisiana state legislator. He returned to his home state of New Jersey in 1818 with $45,000 he planned to spend on slaves in Virginia. But the lower prices for slaves he found in New Jersey were too good to pass up by fair means or foul.

Morgan and his brother-in-law Jacob Van Wickle hatched a plan to evade the state's anti-exportation laws and manipulate the slave market to their advantage. The forty-eight-year-old Van Wickle was a county court judge and justice of the peace. A portrait painted years later shows a jowly, frowning man with a

George H. Durrie, *Jacob Van Wickle*, 1841 (Reproduced
in *Louisiana Portraits*, comp. Mrs. Thomas Nelson Carter
Bruns [New Orleans: National Society of the Colonial
Dames of America in the State of Louisiana, 1975], 292)

pronounced down-turning nose and deep-set blue eyes rendering a judgment
as if from the court bench. In the spring of 1818 Van Wickle trolled his network
of associations for New Jersey slaveholders willing to sell their human property
to out-of-state buyers like Morgan. New Jersey slavery was still slavery, and
owners divided families when it was in their financial interest. Morgan and his
agents bought scores of bondspersons.[14]

Van Wickle and his fellow judges helped build an underground railroad
running south. They removed restrictions on taking enslaved New Jerseyans
out of state. Acting as a judge of the Middlesex County Court of Common
Pleas, Van Wickle certified that sixty slaves for life and thirteen enslaved people
who had been promised manumission under New Jersey law had consented to
serve Morgan in Louisiana. If he interviewed the enslaved people at all, Van
Wickle promised generous wages and a sure return to New Jersey at the expira-
tion of their terms of service. Such assurances were fiction. Among those he
illegally certified were thirteen children, including a six-week-old infant. The
baby's cries were enough of an assent for Van Wickle to sentence it to a lifetime
of slavery in the lower South.[15]

Black New Jerseyans soon began arriving in New Orleans. Locals noticed. In a widely-circulated article, a New Orleans newspaper editor wryly remarked, "We are . . . much indebted to the enterprising and successful exertions of Mr. Charles Morgan, for the copiousness of the present supply" of newly arrived slaves. "Jersey negroes appear to be peculiarly adapted to this market," the editor smirked, "especially those who bear the mark of judge Vanwickle, as it is understood that they afford the best opportunity for *speculation*." The editor sneered, "We have a right to calculate on large importations in future, from the success which has hitherto attended the trade."[16] The exaggeration was not ill-founded.

Federal customs inspectors curbed some of the abuses of Morgan and Van Wickle's New Jersey slaving ring, but they had little interest in freeing the captives themselves. Morgan attracted the attentions of authorities when he arranged to transport dozens of enslaved people out of New Jersey in March 1818. The scheme had all the drama of pirate fiction. His agents loaded thirty-six souls on the fifty-eight-ton sloop *Thorn*, which sailed from Perth Amboy at night and came alongside the merchant brig *Mary Ann*, which had sailed from New York City. By prearrangement, the *Mary Ann* had anchored off Sandy Hook, a spur of land jutting north into Lower New York Bay, four days after being cleared to sail for New Orleans. A revenue cutter spotted the ships and sailed toward the suspicious meeting. As the authorities approached, the *Thorn*'s crew raised an alarm and hurried the bondspeople into its hold. It left the *Mary Ann* and sailed back into the bay. A customs officer meanwhile boarded the still-anchored *Mary Ann* and examined its manifest while his agents made a cursory inspection of the ship. One of the *Mary Ann*'s passengers heard an accusation of smuggling leveled at the ship's master. After the customs officials departed, the *Thorn* returned to its business. Again it came alongside the *Mary Ann*, and the thirty-six captives were transferred. The *Mary Ann*'s master, William Lee, later confessed to forcing at least five involuntary passengers aboard his ship. The *Thorn* then sailed back to Perth Amboy. When Lee arrived in New Orleans, authorities seized the *Mary Ann* and charged the captain with transporting slaves without a valid manifest.[17]

Customs officials had a tolerance for smuggling carried out by political clients, but the manifest Lee submitted to the Louisiana customs inspector lacked even a veneer of legitimacy. The document was an artless fig leaf, according to one report, replete with "the most evident marks of falsehood and fraud . . . it was disfigured with artful interlineations throughout, almost every word was miserably spelled, and there was left a whole blank page in the middle of the list" of African-descended Americans transported as slaves. "This paper contained only the names and ages of the negroes: the ages falsely stated in many instances." In addition to names and ages, legal manifests had to list skin color, height, and the owners, shippers, and consignees. The only seemingly valid documents Lee presented were a set of examination certificates signed by Van Wickle and another New Jersey magistrate attesting to the consent of the people taken to Louisiana as slaves. Even so, there were examination certificates for only about half of the captives. Presented with abundant evidence to convict Lee and instructed by the judge to do so, however, the jury in the case found Lee not guilty of any crime. Meanwhile, the thirty-six black New Jerseyans remained in federal custody, treated as confiscated property rather than victims of human trafficking.[18]

After Lee's trial, setbacks for Morgan and his colleagues were significant but not insurmountable. Morgan bought the *Thorn* for a slaving voyage to New Orleans. A few days before it sailed, Morgan reportedly left Van Wickle's Middlesex County estate with coffles and wagonloads of enslaved people and made for Perth Amboy. Not only was the judge producing consent forms; his brother-in-law used his estate as a slave jail. Morgan and his agents embarked the captives, but after they had sailed into the Gulf of Mexico and up the Mississippi River, U.S. inspectors discovered Morgan's scheme and seized the *Thorn*. It was later sold as a penalty for violating federal slave-trading laws. Morgan was not alone that summer. George Steer, a Baton Rouge planter, was particularly flagrant in his smuggling scheme.[19]

Like Morgan and Marsh, Steer was seeking cheap slave labor, and in an attempt to transport them out of New Jersey quickly, Steer stashed two women and seven children aboard his merchant ship *Bliss*, docked at South Amboy. In its ordinary course of business, Steer's ship was involved in the transatlantic cotton trade. After New Jersey authorities discovered the scheme, they summoned Steer to appear in a superior court in Elizabeth in late July. There the state's chancellor ordered him to post a bond of $500 for each bondsperson he intended to take out of state. The *Bliss* sailed anyway. A disgusted newspaper correspondent wrote that the ship sailed two days after the summons "at day light" and was destined for Steer's plantation north of New Orleans, its owner aboard. "Several unfortunate women and children, who were servants for a term of years, have been sold for their time," the correspondent charged, commenting that "they were totally deceived by these traders as to Louisiana, its situation and advantages; and little doubt is entertained, that those who have been sold for 4, 5 and 6 years will be slaves for life."[20]

The slave trade given cover by consent forms fabricated by the Middlesex County Court of Common Pleas caused a scandal, and a New Jersey grand jury handed down indictments that June, four months before Marsh and Stone sailed with their bound workforce. Charles R. Morgan was charged with transporting sixteen African-descended children out of state without their consent and for removing one adult by force. Two other members of his family were also indicted, as was the master of the *Thorn*. Van Wickle's son Nicholas was charged with conveying enslaved people to Morgan with the intent to sell them out of state, as was the Rahway slave trader Lewis Compton. Van Wickle had certified slaves belonging to his son Nicholas, a conflict of interest. Public outrage led to the cases, but officials bungled them.

Law was a leaky vessel. The indictments may have mollified citizens' anger, but the courts hesitated to ratify righteous indignation by convicting one of their own. More broadly, New Jersey courts were not prepared to suspend the liberty of white men for extinguishing the promise of freedom for blacks. Rather than indict the man whose court served as smugglers' headquarters, prosecutors called Van Wickle as a state witness. The proceedings must have seemed more appropriate to frontier Mississippi than Federalist New Jersey, as the judge who certified so many false consent forms gave testimony exculpating his clients and accomplices. No one was convicted of slave trading in New Jersey.[21]

Marsh may not have commenced his transition from New York merchant to Louisiana planter with slave smuggling in mind, but the culture of impunity he encountered in 1818 held out few incentives to pay higher prices for slaves in Virginia or Louisiana than he could pay in New Jersey, in addition to the added expense of a few false documents. Twenty-one-year-old Frank and twenty-two-year-old Cain found that the judges who certified their intentions to toil for the rest of their days in Louisiana sugar fields feared neither God nor public opinion. After exonerating his associates, Van Wickle continued to use his court as a reverse underground railroad. He and his fellow judge John Smith swore to having examined William Stone's latest purchases. Smith and Van Wickle both signed certificates indicating that Frank and Cain each consented to serve Stone "as a slave for life" in Louisiana.[22]

As Stone bought bondspeople, he funneled them through Van Wickle's court on their way to a compound in South Amboy. According to Peter's certificate, the fourteen-year-old "freely consented to remove and go out of this State to New Iberia in the State of Louisiana, and there to serve said William Stone for life as a Slave." Because he was a minor, New Jersey law required that Peter receive parental consent. On the form, however, Peter's new owners treated the restriction as a legal nicety, set aside with the excuse that his parents were deceased. Twenty-three-year-old Jane ostensibly agreed to toil for Stone for life in a land she had never seen half a continent away. Van Wickle swore to that consent five days after Stone had purchased her for $250 from a slave trader. Judges of the Middlesex Court were so used to documenting slaves' affirmative responses that they signed preprinted forms with "State of Louisiana" imprinted as the destination. Applicants merely had to fill in names and dates.[23]

Stone hired Compton as his agent. In late October the slave trader agreed to transport some of Marsh and Stone's bondspersons to Louisiana. Compton had already escaped punishment for buying slaves with the intention of taking them out of state. To Stone that was a bright spot on his résumé. In June Compton had purchased four enslaved New Jerseyans in Bergen County, giving sellers indications that he was to keep them in the state. The sellers were apparently suspicious enough to follow up on their inquiries and found that Compton was assembling slaves at the "grand repository at South Amboy" for transport out of state, probably working for Morgan, Steer, or Stone. Compton was called into court on a warrant, but the case was dismissed. Compton then returned the bondspersons for a refund. Slave traders' activities were hard to hide in Middlesex County. Its nonwhite population was less than 10 percent, and enslaved residents made up less than 5 percent.[24]

Renewed public concern created obstacles to a clean getaway. In late October, armed with certificates signed by Van Wickle, Compton drove a coffle of four enslaved New Jerseyans owned by Marsh and Stone from South Amboy, New Jersey, south and west, in what became a race against outraged citizens and the New Jersey legislature. In response to slave smuggling and the failure of courts to convict offenders, the legislature passed stiffer anti-exportation measures early that November. Compton's forced march was disrupted by Pennsylvania abolitionists on alert for smugglers and on the lookout for kidnappers. Meanwhile, Marsh's neighbors became worried about an African-descended woman who was apparently missing. Stone complained to Marsh that "two of the straight coat gentry"—his shorthand for abolitionists—called at the Marsh residence to inquire about her. Perhaps one of the Tappan brothers had taken an interest in Marsh's affairs. Stone indignantly responded to them "that if they ever came in again pimping for negroes . . . I would send them out faster than they came in."[25]

In Louisiana slave smuggling seemed rampant in 1818, but what appears at first as crimes abetted by corrupt officials was part of an intricate dance by which the United States asserted political control over the state. That was part of a set of compromises reached in the context of annexation, war, and economic development, one in which African-descended people held as slaves lost rights such as *coartación*, which was a bond of manumission initiated by an enslaved person. Louisiana was absorbing influences from Anglo-Americans but remained Creole in many of its tastes and textures. New Orleans had a long history of protecting local interests against distant imperial powers, and businessmen understood early that rule from Washington, D.C., was not unlike rule from Paris or Madrid. To the central government in Washington, sovereignty inhered in control over borders and trade as part of an effective federal system within a constitutional framework. To the average citizen in the East, federal measures to restrict the importation of foreign captives ought to have done just that. Federal law prohibited the importation of foreign slaves in 1808 and tasked customs inspectors with enforcing the ban. But African-descended people paid the costs of political union as architects of the federal system balanced the demands of a diverse population and tempestuous political factionalism in Louisiana.[26]

Agents of U.S. expansion sought to Americanize a political and economic culture that had been nurtured in French and Spanish imperial contexts. French Creole merchants and those who lost influence when New Orleans's Cabildo, or city council, was abolished maintained a hostile relationship to Anglo-Americans. They were hard to govern. Since the Louisiana Purchase of 1803, organization of the territories of Louisiana and Orleans in 1805, and statehood in 1812, Anglo-Americans had imposed forms of federal, territorial, and state law on a colony used to the light hand of Spanish imperial rule and used to extensive revenue raising through locally controlled legislative bodies. Resistance gave way to accommodation. The territorial constitution of 1803 banned slavery, for instance, but the restrictions were not enforced. In 1805 Congress reorganized the territory and acquiesced to protests over the ban by letting it expire. After 1805 Anglo-Americans liberalized trade under a federal legal framework that removed many locally imposed taxes. Anglo-Americans like Louisiana Governor William C. C. Claiborne sought to turn would-be adversaries into clients by asserting control and then granting exceptions. After the 1808 Abolition Act was passed, Claiborne instituted a policy of stopping ships carrying slaves at La Balize, near the mouth of the Mississippi River, and inspecting the manifests. Brazen attempts to land captives illegally were curbed, but authorities tolerated slaveholder migration from the West Indies and the introduction of foreign bondspersons. After statehood, U.S. attorney John Dick enforced federal restrictions when he prosecuted William Lee, for instance, and seized his ship and slaves. But enforcement tended to tax illegal commerce rather than to eradicate it.[27]

Hard times and war shaped the process. Federal control over Louisiana underwent serious tests during the years of the embargoes preceding the War of 1812 and the openings for smuggling and profiteering that the war made possible. British designs on Louisiana before the War of 1812 included the threat of inciting slave uprisings and filibustering, which drove slave smugglers into the arms of Uncle Sam. General Andrew Jackson had little affinity for traffickers Jean and Pierre Lafitte and their colleagues from Barataria before the Battle of New Orleans in January 1815, calling them "hellish banditti." In preparation for the defense of New Orleans against the British in late 1814, American forces under Jackson's command had sought help from a multicultural and polyglot array of unlikely allies, including Haitians, African Americans, Choctaws, Irish immigrants, and pirates. The Lafittes chose to side with the Americans. The United States had banned the importation of foreign slaves, but Britain had gone two steps further. Britain launched naval efforts to suppress the transatlantic slave trade, and British law construed seized captives essentially as kidnap victims who were owed their freedom. Under the American 1808 Abolition Act, penalties for smugglers and ships' masters were severe. But southern framers of the law insisted that the federal government possessed no power to free slaves held within a state that permitted slavery. Once a captive was landed illegally, he or she was still held in slavery. After winning the Battle of New Orleans, Jackson regarded Jean Lafitte as a brave patriot and ally.[28]

Rewarding such allies monetized the coin of loyalty. In 1815 the United States began repaying a debt owed to slave traffickers who had allied with the Americans against the British. Less than a month after the Battle of New Orleans, President James Madison granted "a free and full pardon of all offenses committed in violation of any act or acts of Congress . . . touching the revenue, trade, and navigation . . . and commerce of the United States." That was an unsubtle way of winking at violations of the 1808 Abolition Act for allies of the American cause. The proclamation was aimed at "inhabitants of New Orleans and . . . Barataria," any one of whom could obtain "a certificate in writing from the governor stating that such person has aided in the defense of New Orleans." So recognized, he would be exonerated of "all suits, indictments, prosecution, fines, penalties, and forfeitures." That was an incremental step in reifying political control over Louisiana.[29]

As foreign captives continued to arrive in Louisiana, a black market emerged, smugglers profited, and officials in Louisiana diverted revenues into their own pockets. Politically strategic exemptions spawned corruption, which proved hard to stop even when there was political will to do so. In New Orleans, foreign captives who landed in the hulls of ships sailing from Cuba, from the West Indies, or from across the Atlantic were "laundered" into the Mississippi Valley plantation complex. African captives arrived in an American Babylon, confused, humiliated, malnourished, sick, and terrorized, were sold alongside African-descended Americans landed from ports on the East Coast. One widely circulated newspaper report in 1818 explained, "It is a common practice at New-Orleans o send an agent abroad to the West-Indies, and even Africa, to purchase a cargo of slaves." As soon as a cargo of captives arrived, the "agent of the owner of the slaves" sailed "in the most expeditious manner to New-Orleans, where he gives information to the proper authority, that a certain vessel is in the Mississippi River, said to be bound to New-Orleans, and having on board a certain number of negro slaves, contrary to the law of the United States." Thus "libeled," the cargo was seized and "the slaves are sold at public vendue, and purchased cheap, by common consent, for the account of the original importer." The United States took half of the proceeds, the other half going to the informant, who treated the seizure as a tax on selling slaves in a market in which slaves sold for more than twice as much as in Cuba.[30]

The *Josefa Segunda* affair gives a glimpse of that process. In the case of the African captives seized from the ship in 1818, federal anti-importation law became a vehicle for profit. The Spanish-flagged ship sailed from Havana in July 1817 and embarked 314 captives from the Bight of Biafra and Gulf of Guinea in late 1817. After sailing across the Atlantic for Cuba, the ship was captured by a force led by Renato Beluche, a Venezuelan slave smuggler and pirate, and his motley crew. They took the *Josefa Segunda*'s crew prisoner, confiscated its cargo of captives, and sailed the ship for Louisiana, but not before selling some of the captives to Spanish buyers. When the *Josefa Segunda* arrived at La Balize on the Mississippi River in late April 1818, U.S. customs officials seized the ship and its cargo. Officials did not know it yet, but Congress had authorized just the sort of profiteering that commenced when the *Josefa Segunda* came to light. The new law "virtually acknowledged the failure of efforts to control the trade," in the words of the historian W. E. B. Du Bois, "and sought to remedy defects by pitting cupidity against cupidity, informer against thief."[31]

As news of the measure made its way slowly to Louisiana, the *Josefa Segunda* arrived with no water and scant supplies for a human cargo of 152 surviving Africans. After word reached New Orleans, Beluche's agent, the city merchant Jean Baptiste Laporte, sent provisions to the stricken vessel while customs officials wrangled over which among them might profit from the enforcement of anti–slave trading laws. Resupplied, the ship sailed to New Orleans while representatives of the Cuban enterprise that owned the *Josefa Segunda* and its cargo showed up to contest their interests.[32]

Capturing the *Josefa Segunda* was a bonanza for the officials involved. Beverly Chew, a customs collector, the naval officer Edward Lorrain, and Surveyor of the Port of New Orleans William Emerson claimed that they had captured the ship. The would-be captors had never actually seen the *Josefa Segunda* until they showed up at the New Orleans levee where it was anchored. But that was not the point. They were in a position to profit from the illegal shipment an share collateral opportunities with their friends. After seizing the vessel, the disembarked the captives and sent the survivors to a Louisiana planter and phys cian for safekeeping. The planter decided that safekeeping included force labor, a service for which authorities would receive a bill that included $1,57 for his medical care of the captives. The planter also received over $4,000 fc housing captives at 31 2/3 cents per day, a charge that was 25 percent higher tha sailors' wages. Chew received more than $1,000 "for expenses," and Laport took over $500 for the supplies he provided the captives.[33]

While Louisiana officials and their benevolent friends looked after th captives, the *Josefa Segunda*'s Cuban owners went to court to claim their prop erty. They had broken no American law, they claimed, just sought the return c their stolen property. No one asked the court to consider freeing the captives The issue became who might profit from their sale and take possession of th ship. Besides the Cuban owners, interested parties included the United States the Charity Hospital in New Orleans, who would be a partial beneficiary of an sales by the United States, and the *Josefa Segunda*'s erstwhile captors, includin Beluche. All agreed that the Africans should be sold quickly to preserve a much of the value of the cargo as remained. Captives were falling ill and dying and George Morgan, sheriff of Orleans Parish, advertised the sale of 127 captives of whom 124 were still alive by the day of sale. Since arriving, 28 captives hac died or been sold secretly. The survivors offered for sale at the end of July comprised 40 women, 29 men, 13 girls, and 42 boys. The average price realizec was $768.18.[34]

Terms of the sales ensured quick sales and speculation. Sheriff Morgan sold a man whose name was given as Banga to a Plaquemine buyer. Thirty-eight year-old Banga stood four feet nine inches tall and sold for $515. But the buyer put down just one tenth of his purchase price, the balance coming under a "special mortgage on the property until final payment." The type of payment was not specified. A city grocer bought a "very sick" nine- or ten-year-old girl named Degairy, on the same terms, paying only $18.40 down.[35] Such generous terms were highly unusual.

The legal logic of the capture was as tortured as the captives' bodies. By seizing the vessel, Beluche claimed he converted an illegal slaving voyage into a legal prize. Not so, said American officials, who claimed the prize for them selves by enforcing U.S. anti-importation laws. Beluche did not get to test his interpretation in court. While the *Josefa Segunda* affair unfolded in New Orleans, he was tried for piracy in Jamaica for swiping a fifty-dollar lifeboat and injuring its owner, a charge of which he was acquitted. Sales of the *Josefa*

Segunda's captives amounted to more than $95,000 on paper. Expenses, many of which were inflated, amounted to nearly $14,000. The net proceeds still left in excess of $81,000. Chew, Lorraine, and Emerson were awarded nearly $40,000 to divide among themselves. The Cuban owners pursued their claims to the confiscated property all the way to the U.S. Supreme Court, which affirmed the Louisiana court's ruling. The *Josefa Segunda* was sold by the government, and claimants vied for a cut. Representative John Alexander Cocke of Tennessee submitted a petition in Congress in 1827 on behalf of his kinsman and New Orleans customs collector Pleasant B. Cocke for a share of the proceeds. Meanwhile, the ship was sold to a Cuban slaving firm, which put it back into the transatlantic slave trade, embarking 288 African captives in 1824. The *Josefa Segunda* was an exceptional case but not unique. After invading Florida in 1817, General Andrew Jackson's forces in Pensacola seized one ship with eighty-four African captives aboard, along with two more vessels, all bound for U.S. ports. As the cotton and sugar market developed, however, smuggling could not begin to meet demand for bound laborers, and the United States banned the kind of profiteering that the *Josefa Segunda* case displayed.[36]

Interstate slave traders like Austin Woolfolk and David Anderson domesti-cated the slave trade. Their activities rationalized it, brought it under legal sanc-tion, and furthered the process of Americanization and a project of economic nationalism. They helped create order in the market and supplied mostly legal captives in abundance, blunting a sharp demand for illegal captives. Bondspeople sold in New Orleans were increasingly American-born English-speakers. Virginians and Louisianans came to view their complementary economic inter-ests as ties of countrymen. As the American colonization of the lower Mississippi Valley developed, the usefulness of smugglers with a history of loyalty to the United States waned. High-profile cases of slave smuggling embarrassed offi-cials, degrading confidence. Tougher federal anti-smuggling laws in the wake of such theatrical cases as the *Josefa Segunda* reflected the success of Louisiana's Americanization.[37]

Marsh and Stone sailed into that world of southern Louisiana in the fall of 1818. In late October they boarded a rickety, rented sloop called the *Schoharie*, which they loaded with a prefabricated plantation, including laborers in the form of forty-eight African Americans, enslaved and indentured. Marsh and Stone loaded nine hundred boards and planks for dwellings or a sugarhouse, eighteen grindstones, and four pumice stones. Aboard were carts, ploughs, chains, building tools, kitchen items, and household furniture, including a writing desk, cramming the *Schoharie*'s ninety-four tons of space. It was a small oceangoing vessel with a single mast and large triangular sails. It had taken many sea voyages since being launched in New York in 1806 and on those voyages carried many slave-produced products, including rice and cotton. A witness reported that Stone had "negroes in his possession at South-Amboy on board a vessel, and also on shore; saw near fifty negroes on board this vessel; saw the vessel heave anchor; [and] that Stone was on board." In a town with fewer than one thousand residents, however, the spectacle of so many black people being taken on board drew notice. That voyage, of which Marsh "was the captain of the vessel," was one of "two or three cargoes of negroes sent off that season," a witness reported. The others were Morgan's and Steer's voyages. The witness testified that "these cargoes were four or five months collecting; the last vessel sailed in October 1818."[38] Stone and Marsh evidently learned from Morgan's and Steer's shenanigans, and when they led four dozen souls to the *Schoharie* in late October 1818, they were prepared to give the voyage a sturdier veneer of legality.

For most of the enslaved and some of the indentured, the footsteps they took down to the harbor were their last on New Jersey soil. Van Wickle had certified Peter and Jane just days before the *Schoharie* set sail. They were put aboard along with Cain, Frank, and twenty- or twenty-one-year-old Hanna Johnson of Sussex County. The slave trader Compton had bought and resold her to Stone and Marsh in July. She had been warehoused for three months. Johnson stood four feet nine inches tall and was described as "black." Others had been purchased more recently, such as Jack. Compton bought him on October 15 and resold him to William Stone on October 22, less than a week before his departure for Louisiana. On board the ship the enslaved New Jerseyans mixed in with the New York contract workers.[39]

Marsh and Stone's bound workers were young people separated from family members. It was unusual, even among cargoes of coastal slaving vessels at the time, not to have young children or infants included among the involuntary passengers. The average age of the bound laborers aboard the *Schoharie* was just over twenty-one and the gender ratio was nearly even: there was one more female than male. Most aboard were men and women in their late teens and early twenties, like twenty-two-year-old Benjamin Morris, five feet one inch tall and "black." Sugar planters like Marsh and Stone valued their youth and strength. At fourteen, Peter and Fanny Thompson were the youngest. They joined fifteen-year-old Harriet Silas, sixteen-year-old Elizabeth Ann Turner, and sixteen-year-old Othello. At fifty, Caleb Groves was the oldest by twelve years. Lena was thirty-eight years old, and Susan Wilcox was thirty-six.[40]

The ship was more like a seaborne slave quarter than a floating dungeon; the plantation owners Marsh and Stone acted as master and first mate. The small ship was not fortified. Security was maintained by the stories the masters spun and the futility of revolt. Once the ship was out of the bay, hopping overboard was not an option save for suicide. Should any combination of captives rise up and seize the vessel by force, they would not be freed. New York, Newport, Rhode Island, and New Bedford, Massachusetts, contained no safe harbors. Some perhaps clung to the fictions woven by Stone or Van Wickle against the ominous words passed among more experienced passengers concerning what awaited them in the lower South. From among the thousands of slaving voyages undertaken in the coastwise trade, few forced migrants cared to remember publicly their sea passage into slavery.

Instead of sailing directly to New Orleans, the ship called at Norfolk, Virginia, which broke up the voyage and gave it legal cover. Broken voyages were old British imperial loopholes through which neutral shippers turned embargoed commodities from the French West Indies into legal cargoes for a transatlantic passage to England. That took place by sailing into and then out of an American port and redocumenting payloads. The goods never left the ship. Marsh turned an illegal New Jersey cargo into a legal Virginia cargo by similar means. Touching Norfolk permitted Marsh to file a manifest of slaves with the U.S. customs collector there. A slave manifest filed in Virginia would allay suspicion in Louisiana. His handiwork done, Stone sailed back to New York. Shipmaster Marsh sailed the *Schoharie* out of Hampton Roads in late October.[41]

Evidently Marsh navigated the New Jersey courts more smoothly than the sea route to the Mississippi River. The passage took six weeks, about one-half longer than usual. On the voyage some of the bound workers protested. Thirty-six-year-old Susan Wilcox captured the attention of New Orleans' customs collector, Beverly Chew, who detained her and another woman, Hannah, in port. It is unclear whether they returned. From the city Marsh marched his assemblage of workers overland. Even at a slave traders' quick pace of twenty miles a day, the group would have taken more than a week on foot from New Orleans to Avery Island. Carts full of lumber, furniture, and refining equipment followed. There the new arrivals would plant, tend, harvest, and mill sugarcane far from the gaze of any abolitionists. Meanwhile, Stone was making final preparations to leave New York.[42]

Stone wrote from there with prayers that his partner had enjoyed "a prosperous and pleasant passage" from Norfolk to New Orleans. He asked whether he heard "anything of the negroes that went out with Stear" and wanted to know if George Steer had made a successful getaway from his New Jersey warrant. Awaiting a response, Stone collected debts and packed his family off to Avery Island. Marsh's brother Stewart would soon follow. Stone rented out his property in Eastchester, north of New York City, and checked on the progress of Lewis Compton's coffle. Six of the African American New Jerseyans detained in Compton's attempts to spirit them out of state in the fall of 1818 were eventually taken to Avery Island.[43] Compton was not deterred and learned a valuable lesson in smuggling.

Smuggling African American New Jerseyans continued after the state passed stiffer anti-exportation laws. Lewis Compton persisted in the interstate slave trade using broken voyages, which was his competitive advantage. Compton illegally loaded enslaved people on a ship in New York or New Jersey and then filed a manifest in a southern port without either embarking or disembarking captives. In the winter of 1820, for instance, Compton sailed from New York for New Orleans and, after arriving, sold twenty-two-year-old John, a New Jersey native, to a Creole planter. That summer Compton sailed again from New York to New Orleans, touching Savannah. Somewhere between Georgia and Louisiana he sold one of the five bondspersons he put aboard. Compton was trading in goods other than slaves and shipped two casks of porter as well. The New Jersey slave trader had trouble naming his residence, listing it as Louisiana on a slave manifest and admitting that he was from New Jersey when he filed the bill of sale for twenty-two-year-old William, who was bought by a New Orleans widow. But Compton's niche closed around the same time as the Woolfolks moved to New Orleans. John C. Marsh's brother Stewart went to Louisiana but returned to New York in the 1820s and went into the dry goods business with Compton. They were trading as Marsh and Compton by 1829.[44]

The African-descended Americans shipped to New Orleans on the *Schoharie* in the fall of 1818 arrived at Marsh and Stone's plantation in time to begin clearing fields for planting. It was an alien landscape. After eight weeks in transit, a swampland symphony replaced the sounds of New York and eastern New Jersey. At dusk, the hoots of owls and rustlings of the creatures of the night joined other strange noises. A newcomer might wonder whether every thing that crept upon the earth was heard in the Louisiana darkness. By day the newcomers surveyed the coastal plain as they wielded farm implements amid the flies, mosquitoes, rodents, and snakes that inhabited the land. They might see horned cattle or black bears prowling the perimeter. Marsh was fond of shooting the latter. Migrating birds filled the air with their feathers and calls.

The predicaments into which those bound workers fell reveal a peculiar facet of the Louisiana landscape of sugar. Enslavers created a new regime of labor exploitation in the Deep South that was not simply transplanted from the Eastern Seaboard. The working lives of bound laborers on the southern

Louisiana frontier differed dramatically from the work regimes of the Mid-Atlantic and even of the cotton kingdom of the southeastern river valleys. Louisiana sugar plantations were punishing to workers because of the arduous and repetitive tasks and an often-lethal disease environment. They were mechanized factories in the fields, employing the latest technology. Federal protections for domestic sugar mirrored federal bans on imported slaves, which gave U.S. sugar producers two sets of incentives to exploit the labor of African-descended Americans.[45]

The fields Marsh and Stone had purchased earlier that year were covered with weeds and perennial grasses that competed with the prized sugarcane. In wetter areas, oyster grass, or what the locals called hog cane, grew thick alongside couch grass, goose grass, cattails, bulrushes, and razor-edged saw grass, which cut skin easily. Ditching and repairing drainage systems laid bare the ground on which workers would plant cane. Most of the newly arrived had been inured to long, hard days of manual work, but hours and days of pulling up an unfamiliar array of stubborn weeds and spiteful grasses left the hands sore, lacerated, and bleeding. Feet would be wet and backs strained, and any mistakes or miscalculations Marsh or Stone made fell most heavily on the green workers.[46]

Successful sugar masters were shrewd businessmen. Initial investments in bound workers paid off solely with brutal labor management. Profits were wrung from the sweat of the faces of the human beings forced to work in the sugar fields. Sugar estates required local processing facilities and, planters claimed, young, strong, adults to swing cane knives and operate mills. Where cotton planters looked for manual dexterity and resiliency, sugar masters wanted brawn and endurance. That partially explains the demographic profile of Marsh and Stone's force. Labor in the Louisiana sugar fields was the most regimented in agricultural North America in part because of the challenges of growing a tropical staple in a temperate zone not naturally suited to it. Southern Louisiana had a cooler climate than the West Indies, where sugar was produced in abundance, and frosts at harvest time could damage cane in the fields. Planters experimented with strains that could withstand cold. Without the ability to forecast weather, planters played a game of chance with the elements, calculating when to cut the cane. The longer the plants grew in the fields, the more juice they produced. But an early frost could ruin a crop overnight. Unlike cotton, sugar required considerable processing as soon as it was harvested. Sugar planters needed a grasp of technology that rivaled their acute sense of the market. They needed to adjust rapidly and promote efficient management.[47]

Largely because of overwork and disease, the Louisiana sugar fields were the most lethal agricultural workplaces in the nation. Milling was more arduous and dangerous than clearing and planting, and sugar workers were routinely exhausted, sick, and injured. In the 1820s an enslaved visitor, Henry Goings, interviewed New Orleans veterans of the sugar regime. "They told me that it was death to those who worked at the mill," Goings recalled, adding that "it was a rare thing if a man lived from more than 10 to 12 years of those who worked at the mill."[48]

Death seems to have visited workers on Marsh and Stone's plantation. Indirect evidence for the deadly environment comes from a receipt dated May 1, 1819, in which Stone paid the New Yorker John Lee one hundred dollars as "recompense for my black man known by the name of Molat." Sugar workers, never more than 6 percent of the total enslaved population of the United States, faced high mortality rates. Slave populations actually decreased from work, disease, and a lack of opportunities for family life. That contrasted with the natural increase that characterized nearly all other regions of the country. By the time the census taker arrived in 1820, Stone and Marsh's household contained thirty-one bondspeople, seventeen fewer souls than were taken on the *Schoharie* two years before—and that is not counting the enslaved New Jerseyans Compton spirited out of state overland. Perhaps some of the indentured servants had fled or Marsh and Stone liquidated some of the slave property in the financial panic of 1819.[49]

Attakapas may have seemed an unlikely destination for New York businessmen, but New York was a natural market for Attakapas planters. Marsh and Stone exported their sugar to the East Coast and drew credit from there as well. They were already familiar with a network of buyers and commercial agents or factors in New York City. Southern planters' business flowed through the northern metropolis.[50]

"Gotham," as Washington Irving had recently nicknamed it, was home to merchants specializing in sugar, sugar refineries, and retail as well. (Irving was another failed New York merchant at the time Marsh joined their ranks.) The merchant house of Foster and Giraud was one among many sugar merchants. Among the notable post-Revolutionary refiners was Isaac Roosevelt, patriot and great-great-grandfather of president Franklin Delano Roosevelt. Isaac established the first large-scale sugar refinery on Pearl Street in 1786, just a few blocks from where Marsh was in business in 1817. New York factors or agents sold some of the produce of Avery Island, and some went overseas. Marsh had reported to his family that he had shot a number of bears prowling the area of St. Martin. In February 1827 word reached him that some of the hides he intended to sell in London had been damaged and he owed money to the merchants to whom they were consigned. The sugar supply chain was coextensive with relationships of credit. New Orleans commission merchants endorsed Marsh and Stone's bills of exchange, although a city countinghouse protested more than $2,000 in October 1819.[51]

Bound workers responsible for Marsh and Stone's successes were nearly invisible to Americans who sweetened their coffee with Louisiana sugar or who enjoyed desserts, cakes, sweetened tobacco, or rum. Per-capita sugar consumption would not surge in the United States until the 1850s, but sugar production kept pace with a rapidly growing population. As it became cheaper and more available, more Americans craved it. Bakers and cooks, householders and workers who started their day with a sweet cake or ended it with a cordial or toddy supported enterprises like Avery Island and the cycles of unrequited toil and death it incorporated. Any American who wanted slave-free consumables had to bypass coffeehouses, forgo desserts, avoid rum, eschew tobacco, swap cotton for wool or flax garments, and perhaps shun ships with cotton sails or caulking for consistency's sake. But Americans seemed not to link their enjoyment of sugar to the circumstances of its creation. The British poet Robert Southey exclaimed, "O ye who at your ease / Sip the blood-sweeten'd beverage!" But U.S. consumers of sugar gave little thought to whether "beneath the rod / A sable brother writhes in silent woe."[52]

For some, the seemingly simple choice to buy sugar not grown with slave labor was a protest against exploitation and racism. The African-descended abolitionist David Ruggles opened a New York City grocery store selling butter, flour, sugar, and liquors in 1828. He advertised that his "fine sugars . . . are manufactured by free people, not by slaves." Ruggles allied with the Quaker-led Free Produce movement. It mobilized consumers, mainly women, who insisted that the sugar and other consumables they bought were not produced using slave labor. They recognized that consumer choices had far-reaching consequences if aggregated. But federal policies undermined such consumer movements. Nearly all U.S. sugar was the product of slave labor, and national protections for Louisiana sugar interests opposed the humanitarian efforts of Ruggles and supporters of the Free Produce movement.[53]

Marsh and Stone got away with their smuggling scheme. The enterprise saved perhaps ten thousand dollars in the start-up phase by assembling workers in New Jersey and New York and shipping them to Louisiana. But recruiting bound laborers from New York and New Jersey yielded diminishing returns in the years following 1818. From New Jersey Marsh's brother reported, "Them that are good for any thing are afraid of dying if they leave New Jersey." He could not find a blacksmith willing to sail to Louisiana. The only recruits "are not acquainted with any thing but carriage work" and were ill-suited to sugar work. Instead of more workers, Marsh's brother shipped him a horse. (By 1850 that brother owned a Louisiana plantation along with thirty-two slaves.) News followed from the East that "we have very hard times in this part of the co[untry] and don't see any prospect of there being any better." Yet the hard times after the panic of 1819 furnished a few more desperate workers. Back in New York, the day after Christmas 1822, Marsh and Stone hired two young female workers for a year each.[54]

To replace sick, injured, dead, or departed workers, Stone and Marsh turned to slave traders, first in Maryland and then in Louisiana and Mississippi. Savings from slave-buying trips conferred advantages over competitors forced to buy imported sugar workers. Prices for slaves in Louisiana remained much higher than they were in the Chesapeake. In November 1823, Stone shook hands with Austin Woolfolk in Baltimore. Stone paid "in full" $1,350 for twenty-three-year-old Perry, nineteen-year-old Joseph, thirty-five-year-old Sabery, twenty-one-year-old Henny, and her two-month-old child, Eliza. On the same visit Stone also bought nineteen-year-old Edward Coursey from a Baltimore sailmaker and eighteen-year-old Harriet from her southern Maryland owner. Sixteen-year-old Jamie Williams completed Stone's purchases. They would all get to know one another on the monthlong sea passage to Louisiana.[55]

By 1826 Marsh and Stone were again shaking hands with the Woolfolk brothers, only they did not need to travel as far as Baltimore. In April 1826 they bought twenty-two-year-old Silvia from Austin's younger brother Samuel M. Woolfolk in New Orleans. She cost $400. Short of cash, the partners bought seventeen-year-old Milley, or Millie, for another $400 on thirty days' credit. Millie had arrived a month before from Alexandria, Virginia, in a shipment of sixty-three bondspersons belonging to Austin Woolfolk and his agent, Ira Bowman. In April Stone and Marsh also bought thirty-five-year-old Terry from a liquor seller for $570 in New Orleans. In June the ravenous cane fields sent them back to New Orleans, where they bought twenty-eight-year-old Chloe from Sarah Lee for $400. Lee was listed as a "woman of color."[56]

Records leave few clues as to what became of the enslaved people who reached Avery Island in 1826. The owners sought more workers by the following year. Interstate slave traders like the Woolfolks were ready to supply replacements for those who died or became unable to perform the exhausting work. In April 1827 Marsh was buying slaves in Natchez, Mississippi, again from Austin Woolfolk and his partner Bowman. For $1,300 Marsh bought twenty-six-year-old Augustus, his nineteen-year-old wife, Anenon, and their nine-month-old daughter, Fanny, whom the sellers "guarantee free from the vices and maladies" proscribed by the state of Louisiana. Marsh's new purchases had survived a spring voyage from Norfolk aboard a notorious slaver, the *James Monroe*, where they were three of at least fifty-eight African Americans belonging to Woolfolk who were among nearly one hundred people carried as slaves and landed in New Orleans.[57]

By the late 1820s sugar production surged as a result of expanded credit and increased technology, and a developing domestic market increased demand for sugar workers. The Woolfolks and their competitors crammed ships sailing from Chesapeake ports full of captives. No longer useful American allies, smugglers focused on landing slaves farther west, in the Mexican province of Coahuila y Tejas, where a conflict pitting Anglo-American slaveholding interests against a constituted authority in Mexico was deepening over the issue of transporting black bodies across political boundaries.[58]

John Marsh and William Stone's enterprise flourished, but their ambition turned to tragedy. Marsh's older son, John C. Marsh Jr., died in Louisiana in 1820. His mother, Eliza Marsh, died in August 1826 while returning to family in the East. Marsh's youngest daughter, Helen, died at Avery Island shortly thereafter. William Stone died on the last day of September 1826. There were just twenty-eight enslaved people then left on Avery Island. Marsh married Stone's widow, Euphemia, in 1828, and she died in 1836, along with a young daughter. That was after Marsh bought what he considered healthier land on Bayou Teche. Marsh tired of plantation life and conveyed his holdings to his son George, the son he had initially left behind in New Jersey in 1818. Marsh retired to New York, but the southern landscape that made his fortune after his failure in the dry goods business claimed his life as well. He died in 1857 on a visit to Louisiana in the sixty-eighth year of his life.[59]

Despite deaths and debilitating work, the bondspeople at Avery Island nevertheless formed families, built neighborhoods, and created communities over the decades and against the odds. Eliza Thompson, who had signed up for three years and nine months' labor in New York in 1818, was still there when the U.S. Census taker arrived fifty-two years later. She was in her early seventies. The 1870 U.S. Census was the first in which most African Americans were listed by name. Thompson could have told the major life events and given epitaphs of most of the New Jerseyans and New Yorkers brought there in 1818. Millie, bought from Austin Woolfolk in 1826, was also counted in 1870. Marsh and Stone had purchased the Virginia native along with another woman, named Silvia. In 1870 Millie had a ten-year-old girl named Sylvia in her household, perhaps a granddaughter or grandniece. Millie could have told of slave ships and their unhappy cargoes. So could her neighbors. Around the Parish of New Iberia (which was formed out of parts of St. Martin and St. Mary parishes in 1868), others could relate similar stories of those who boarded the ships of slave traders. The firm Franklin and Armfield shipped Matilda Brown from Virginia to New Orleans aboard its company ship the *Uncas* in 1834. Brown was twenty when she arrived. She was in her mid-fifties and still abiding in southern Louisiana when the 1870 census taker recorded her name in federal records for at least the second time. The first had been on a slave manifest.[60] The descendants of many of Avery Island and New Iberia bondspeople are there today.

In his novel *A Confederacy of Dunces*, John Kennedy Toole noted that there is an accent "associated with downtown New Orleans, particularly with the German and Irish Third Ward, that is hard to distinguish from the accent of Hoboken, Jersey City, and Astoria, Long Island."[61] There were New Jersey accents spoken in the fields, dwellings, and sugarhouse of Avery Island long before the ones Toole evoked were heard in twentieth-century New Orleans. The African-descended victims of Marsh and Stone's smuggling schemes also anteceded many of the German and Irish immigrants who contributed to the linguistic richness of old New Jersey and New York. The longings and sufferings to which they gave utterance contributed to the fortunes and the tragedies of people stolen from relatives and hoodwinked by sharp masters, and planters lured by sweet dreams of easy wealth.

4

Bank Bonds and Bondspersons

Hugues Lavergne, a Louisiana state representative and banker, did not look like an agent of a revolution in finance as he waited for a ferry near the southeast tip of New York City in mid-July 1828. City weather had been "beyond measure oppressive" since before the Fourth of July. The thirty-four-year-old comptroller of the recently chartered Consolidated Association of the Planters of Louisiana bank was wilting in heat bothersome even to a native Louisianan. But Atlantic Ocean breezes beckoned and with them the prospect of investment that would open the bank's doors and inject credit into the Louisiana sugar industry. Lavergne had a ticket to sail to Liverpool on a ship of the Black Ball Line and from there planned to travel to the great metropolis of London. He would pitch Louisiana bank securities to Baring Brothers and Company, one of the premier financial houses in the world. Tucked in Lavergne's luggage were thousands of thin leaves of paper on which were printed the lion's share of a $2.5 million bond issue.[1]

This was a new kind of financial instrument with significant implications for the slave trade. If successful, his bank would permit slaveholders access to bank credit that would help buy thousands of enslaved people, hundreds of cotton and sugar plantations, and improvements such as refineries. It did so by leveraging plantations and bondspersons to raise investment capital. The volume of the interstate slave trade closely followed expansions and contractions of credit. In the late 1820s and early to mid–1830s, credit expansion and the financial integration of Britain and the United States helped rationalize the interstate slave trade that populated the canebrakes and cotton fields of the lower South with bound workers. Beyond merely expanding production, the Consolidated Association and banks like it gave the notoriously capital-intensive sugar industry the means to develop more efficient refining technologies and build a

95

robust supply chain. Lavergne's errand was a small part of an enormous expansion of credit.[2]

To his New Orleans associates, Lavergne was the right man to sell the bank's bonds. His entrepreneurial outlook mirrored his confidence and belief in the value the bank created for stakeholders. Lavergne felt certain that the Consolidated Association would serve as an engine of growth for the sugar industry of southern Louisiana and the merchants of New Orleans. He had been a notary in New Orleans for the better part of a decade and understood that a lack of credit to planters was the main obstacle to growth and development. He was descended from minor French nobility and an old New Orleans family. His father had sent him to France to be educated at the Ecole Polytechnique, but upon reaching Paris the young Lavergne had been betrayed and spent a year as a political detainee in the Prison de la Force. After returning to New Orleans, he served in the militia and was on General Andrew Jackson's staff during the War of 1812. Afterward he rose rapidly as a lawyer and representative of Creole business interests, which was an entrée into politics. But so far his pedigree and business acumen had mattered little in actually opening the Consolidated Association's doors.[3]

Frustrated attempts to sell bank bonds in the United States had propelled him to the New York piers and the ticket office of the transatlantic Black Ball Line. He had been traveling since April, away from his wife, Marie Adèle Villeré, and ten-year-old son, Jules. A portrait of Lavergne painted a decade later shows a man with dark features, sensitive, probing eyes, and a slightly melancholy aspect. Creole gentlemen's fashions included a silk top hat, high, tight-fitting trousers, and a high-collared coat. In the company of other passengers Lavergne would have been loath to loosen his rangy necktie or undo a jacket button. Fourteen other first-class passengers mixed with steerage passengers on the dock. Any breeze blowing from the East River was as welcome as the steamboat that would take them to their ship lying at anchor off Sandy Hook, New Jersey.[4]

Lavergne was leaving the city and two failed attempts to sell Consolidated Association bonds in the United States. The previous year, he and a fellow Creole businessman, the slave trader Jean Baptiste Moussier, traveled to New York City. But city merchants declined to invest in the bank. A group of cash-starved Creole planters converting uneven mortgages on lands and chattels into a collateral trust did not generate much confidence. Any potential investor recalling the recent cotton and financial crash caught a whiff of a foul odor in his nostrils. Early in 1825 false reports of a poor crop pushed cotton prices up dramatically in Liverpool, which led to a frenzy of speculation in London, New

York, and New Orleans. Alexander Baring, a banker and British member of Parliament, called the Royal Exchange "a gaming-House" in March 1825 as investors ploughed money into schemes to fund foreign governments, joint-stock companies, and even mining interests unconnected to cotton. The inevitable collapse arrived in Liverpool in the form of cotton-laden ships bringing news of an abundant American crop. Merchants who had hoarded cotton while prices swiftly rose rushed to sell to manufacturers who had decreased production. Cotton clogged arteries of trade. Failure at the heart of the transatlantic cotton chain had a cascading effect. Fast ships brought word back to New York and New Orleans. Baring Brothers' agent in New Orleans failed along with the overextended and unfortunate. By that winter credit froze and a wave of bankruptcies toppled confidence.[5]

Markets were recovering in 1828, but would-be investors were wary of risky schemes, especially ones billowing out of New Orleans. Ten years before, the city had seemed a den of smugglers. Now the latest financial technology was being developed in its Creole business community. That summer Lavergne returned to the East Coast to knock on the doors of Philadelphia and New York City banking and merchant houses. His July reception was as chilly as the weather was hot, and it would top 96 degrees indoors by month's end. Merchants' objections included the Consolidated Association's lack of liquid assets, lack of diversification, and lack of transparency. It leveraged lands, buildings, and slaves into credit used to buy more of the same kind of illiquid assets. Commercial lenders regularly used bales of cotton and hogsheads of sugar as collateral because they could be sold quickly. But lands and enslaved people could not. According to the bank's Louisiana charter, it permitted stockholders to borrow back half the assessed value of their mortgaged plantations, buildings, equipment, and slaves. Even ordinarily sanguine investors frowned upon learning that Consolidated Association stockholders did not actually have to pay for their shares, just hypothecate their property. Hypothecation was mortgaging without actually surrendering the title to the mortgaged property. Even to New Orleaneans the tangle of property ownership in the backcountry was far from obvious. Lavergne addressed such concerns, but investors were not willing to bet on whether the eager borrowers he represented were also the most risky. Finance was becoming more sophisticated, and banking schemes seemed ubiquitous.

The Consolidated Association was part of an explosive financial expansion then taking place in the United States. The number of banks in the republic more than doubled between 1827 and 1837, and cotton bills of exchange linked banks in New York and New Orleans to financial houses in Britain and Europe.

Though most banks lent to commercial rather than agricultural customers, agriculturalists benefited from the expansion of credit through factors acting as retail bankers. Cotton production nearly tripled between 1827 and 1837, and banking innovations were centered in the lower South as well. Lavergne laid the groundwork for the Consolidated Association in 1826 by introducing legislation appointing recorders of mortgages in Louisiana parishes. He hustled the Consolidated Association's charter through the Louisiana state legislature in 1827. To its architects the bank's plan seemed to embody a prudent and conservative approach to expanding credit. Lending was limited to stockholders. Stockholders initially became stockholders through personal networks of associations and by putting up their own property. Merchants benefited from the greater banking capacity, and, should the winds of fortune turn, the bank had a portfolio of real property to sell for the benefit of creditors.[6] But Lavergne was not able to sell confidence in the bank's bonds to his eastern countrymen, and he steamed out into New York Bay in low spirits.

To the passengers aboard the steamboat, sea air was a refreshing change from the sultry city. The boat paddled toward the merchant sailing ship *Florida*, one of the Black Ball Line's fleet of superb large sailing ships departing on schedule. Freighted primarily with cotton, it anchored on the sandbar leading from Coney Island to Sandy Hook, where passengers were embarked at the last minute before setting sail. The *Florida*'s sibling ships in the line left on the first and sixteenth of each alternating month. The company advertised heavily for passengers, but the schedule was designed to deliver commodities and business intelligence. In economic terms, packet lines facilitated market integration by remedying information asymmetry among transatlantic trading partners. The *Florida* had served as a vital messenger in the financial drama of 1825 and demonstrated that whoever controlled the fastest ships had considerable advantages. The *Florida* sailed from Liverpool to New York in April of that year with news of the cotton crash. After a quick thirty-day passage, the ship's master sent word to the Black Ball Line's New York City owner before the ship's passengers disembarked and broke the news. The owner, a textile merchant, immediately sold his position and was saved from failure. Those who read about the crash in the newspapers lacked that advantage. Packet lines boasted the quickest service across the Atlantic and would continue to do so for another decade, which is why Baring Brothers bought the line in 1834. In the summer of 1828 the *Florida* served a more modest purpose. Once all were aboard the 123-foot-long ship, sailors atop the yards unfurled the foretopsail, onto which was sewn a large black circle, the line's instantly recognizable logo. It evoked a cannonball speeding across the waves.[7]

As the three-masted ship sailed out into the ocean, Lavergne commenced a return visit to Thomas Baring, who had traveled to the United States earlier that year in search of investment opportunities. Baring was a banker, nephew of Alexander Baring, and partner in the financial firm Hope and Company of Amsterdam. He sought a partnership in the family business and scouted for investment opportunities in the United States. The Consolidated Association seemed to be dwindling when the twenty-eight-year-old financier landed in New Orleans. Baring liked what he saw in commercial New Orleans. Cotton, sugar, and other commodities were ripe for investment, and rapid agricultural growth created great demand for credit. Besides opportunities to own or finance actual commodities shipments, American state bonds were appealing. Their interest rates compared favorably to those of British and European bonds. A quarter century after financing the Louisiana Purchase, the House of Baring was poised to fulfill the promise of the Mississippi Valley slave country.[8]

But Baring was wary of the kind of swashbuckling speculation that had sunk the firm's New Orleans agent a few years earlier. While in New Orleans he struck up a friendship with the Creole financier and sugar refiner Edmond Jean Forstall. Forstall's most dulcet product was confidence. He produced it in abundance. Forstall promoted confidence in paper money and in Louisiana banks' abilities to produce wealth by it. He introduced Baring to Lavergne and the Consolidated Association. The bank's bonds were for sale at an attractive interest rate, but like any other investor, Baring sought to offload risk while reaping high returns. It became clear that his interest might deepen into investment if the state lent its faith and credit to the bank. Lavergne and the Consolidated Association then turned to Louisiana for help.[9]

The state of Louisiana saved the bank and became its principal backer. Like other areas of American finance, banking was politicized. American state-chartered banks were semiprivate, and bank charters were public policy matters. Lavergne and his allies persuaded the legislature to revise the charter so that the state would meet its bond obligations should the Consolidated Association go bankrupt. To do so would benefit planters, he argued. There was determined opposition to socializing the Consolidated Association's risk. Making citizens responsible for a scheme that the market refused to endorse seemed a violation of economic principles and of common sense. In New Orleans as everywhere else in the republic, however, the gospel of laissez-faire was proclaimed more fervently than it was practiced. The state amended the Consolidated Association's charter, appointed six directors to serve on the board, and issued $2.5 million in state bonds payable by the Consolidated Association at 5 percent interest. Louisiana's assuming a contingent liability for the bond issue complemented an industry-wide federal protection of 3 cents per pound levied on imported sugar, about a fifth of the price of a pound of Cuban sugar and nearly a third of the price of a pound of Jamaican sugar in 1828. South Carolinians howled that protectionist tariffs were abominations, but southern Louisiana planters cooed in admiration of the protectionist Henry Clay and his American System.[10]

Tariff protections and credit expansion tipped the state's agriculture toward sugar. Louisiana's 1820 sugarcane crop was valued at $2 million, and its cotton crop, $7 million. By 1829 the sugar crop was worth more than $6 million while cotton crops sank to $2 million. Sugar estates more than tripled between 1824 and 1830, and the number of enslaved people in sugar-producing southern Louisiana rose 86 percent during the decade of the 1820s. Edmond Forstall estimated that between 1827–28 and 1830 the capital invested in Louisiana's sugar industry rose from $34 million to $50 million, and the number of slaves who shouldered the burden grew from 21,000 to 36,000. Expansion complemented efficiencies. Vacuum processing saved fuel and eliminated steps, and large refiners like Forstall centralized processing that had taken place elsewhere. At the same time, British West Indian planters producing a superior product were suffering from a withering supply of enslaved workers owing to enforcement of anti–slave trading laws, eroding support in Parliament, and pressure in England toward emancipation. U.S. policy moved in the opposite direction, distorting the market in favor of slave-produced sugar. Central banking complemented tariffs, and the Second Bank of the United States under Nicholas Biddle promoted slaveholder interests.[11]

Democratic political institutions were maturing in the 1820s, but the undemocratic Second Bank laid the foundation for American economic growth and financial integration. Following the 1825–26 crash, the Second Bank crafted a policy that united sections of the U.S. economy while facilitating international trade. Responding to the fact that cotton exports represented the largest domestic interest, the Second Bank attempted to decrease the range of seasonal fluctuations in the foreign exchange market. It tried to stabilize markets by directing northeastern branches of the bank to sell bills of exchange in pounds sterling during the summer, when American merchants needed them, and directing southwestern branches to buy them during the winter, when they were plentiful. The policy boosted political integration, generated profits, and benefited regionally specialized merchants—exporters in the South and importers in the North. The Second Bank's other charter privileges included deciding which notes to accept at the U.S. Land Office, which curbed speculation, regulated banknotes, and efficiently privatized western lands.[12] Nicholas Biddle was slaveholders' best unpraised friend of the decade. Lavergne shared the Philadelphia banker's instincts for order and a commitment to growth, and the southern Louisiana sugar industry required an abundance of credit to match federal protections and probusiness federal monetary policies.

The expansion of state banking together with Second Bank policies created an efficient national framework that promoted growth in slave labor–reliant industries. In New Orleans, Lavergne worked to rationalize the credit market while expanding it. His efforts to charter the Consolidated Association grew from his knowledge of the slave and real estate markets. His Chartres Street offices were in the center of the city slave market, and notaries were the city's unofficial credit monitors. Since the Spanish and French colonial regimes, Louisiana notaries had acted as third parties to contracts, not unlike lawyers. They kept a large storehouse of information as they recorded deeds, sales, mortgages, and other transactions.[13]

They knew who was solvent and who was shaky, and above all the demand for credit. Sugar planters in particular needed external financing to build local refining facilities and replace bound workers who died or were debilitated at astoundingly high rates. A large plantation required a $20,000 investment in a sugarhouse, and bound sugar workers died in such proportions that the sugar workers' numbers were sustained by resupply rather than reproduction. Lavergne's notarial records were an index of would-be bank customers and an industry financial analysis. A bank that leveraged property needed an efficient regime of documentation. Liens, existing mortgages, and other encumbrances were less than apparent, even to local Louisianans. To improve transparency, the Consolidated Association required mortgages to be on public record. Anyone registering a slave sale in New Orleans was already required to obtain a certificate from the bureau of mortgages indicating whether the bondsperson was encumbered by a mortgage. The same now held for real property. Lavergne later bragged to Thomas Baring "that it is the first time in Louisiana that title to property were thoroughly investigated," thanks to the Consolidated Association.[14]

As he sailed eastward to promote that scheme, Lavergne practiced his salesmanship and pondered the task before him. The three-week passage to Liverpool was quicker than sailing from New York to New Orleans. But time aboard ship was a monotonous regime of constant movement. At the captain's table, where first-class passengers dined, polite conversation might touch on the ship's progress through the North Atlantic and the cook's handiwork. Over evening cups of wine gentlemen's discussion turned inevitably to Andrew Jackson's latest campaign. Instead of battling Creeks, Seminoles, Britons, and Spaniards, Jackson sought to vanquish his political opponents Henry Clay and John Quincy Adams. After winning the plurality of both popular and electoral votes

A. D. Lansot, *Compte Hugues de la Vergne,*
1838, oil on canvas (Reproduced in *Louisiana
Portraits*, comp. Mrs. Thomas Nelson Carter
Bruns [New Orleans: National Society of the
Colonial Dames of America in the State of
Louisiana, 1975], 75)

in the 1824 election and losing to Clay and Adams anyway, Jackson sought to capture the American presidency as the fall elections approached. Lavergne was polite in his correspondence, verging on unctuous. If he was the same in conversation, he would have waited until after supper to reveal that he had been General Jackson's aide-de-camp during the Battle of New Orleans thirteen years before. Lavergne was less likely to say that he had sailed to a maroon outpost on Ship Island off the Mississippi coast after the battle. There he had appealed to former slaves to return to their owners' sugar fields. That was a tougher sell than hawking bank bonds and generated the same unsuccessful results.[15] After retiring to his closetlike cabin each night, Lavergne had a chance to rehearse his sales pitch and ponder the errand on which he was embarked.

Lavergne understood intuitively that credit was the most expansive resource in human history. Credit dealt with ambition. Credit dealt with imagination. Credit dealt with the future. Financial paper such as the bonds packed in his trunk created obligations that generated capabilities. They bound borrowers' ambitions, imaginations, and expectations to future repayment, perpetual accumulation, and relationships that expanded capacities seemingly without limit. The hardest-driving planter or overseer could wring or whip but so much work out of a bondsperson in a field. Higher-yielding crop varieties could produce only so much more per acre per year. The pushiest shipmaster could take only so much advantage of winds, tides, and sails' trim. Power looms and centralized production yielded cloth by the acre, but their development was dependent on finance. The genius of credit permitted owners to leverage land and enslaved property into more while also giving customers the ability to expand production and markets. The bonds Lavergne took to England would help monetize Louisiana's economy and give a premier English investment bank—and through it, a large pool of investors—a stake in a lucrative commodity chain without risking money on particular ventures. They gave borrowers the means to build plantations up to the limits of their credit and imagination. That development was part of the integration of international financial sectors at the heart of early United States economic development.[16] Over the generations, the House of Baring had helped realize such aspirations.

Baring Brothers was an American ally, and what an ally it was. London was the center of Atlantic world finance, and Baring Brothers and Company was the center of financial London. Its assistance to the United States funded the republic's imperial expansion. Thomas Baring's uncle Alexander negotiated key parts of the Louisiana Purchase in 1803. With the allied Amsterdam banking house of Hope and Company Baring Brothers marketed the bonds the United States issued as a mortgage on the lands it acquired from France. For whittling down the price and handling the negotiations and payments to Napoleon's regime, the Barings earned a healthy $3 million in commissions. Following the War of 1812, the Barings acted as the United States' foreign banker and benefactor, extending credit to the Second Bank of the United States. Biddle used his revolving account with the Barings to enact a central banking program, and both the Barings and England benefited from commissions, commerce, and cotton. The Barings bought Erie Canal stock in 1817 but invested cautiously in American states' bond issues. The Barings sponsored the German merchant Vincent Nolte in the 1810s, which permitted him to attempt to corner the cotton market. Nolte failed in the 1825 panic, and the Barings' direct interest in the New Orleans cotton market vanished.[17]

In early August Lavergne landed in Liverpool. Before heading south to London, he called on Alexander Gordon, a cotton merchant and partner in the international interlocking partnership of Gordon, Forstall, and Company. They would travel together. Gordon's firm linked Creole New Orleans to New York, Liverpool, and other commercial cities in the North Atlantic and Gulf of Mexico. Gordon was a Scotsman who had been a shipping merchant in New Orleans. He and Lavergne could reminisce about the Crescent City. Inevitably, they would bring up their charismatic friend and fellow businessman, Edmond

Jean Forstall. Forstall was the son of a wealthy if debt-burdened Creole merchant family who had quickly worked his way into the upper echelon of New Orleans's business community. By his mid-twenties he was a director of the Louisiana State Bank and by 1826 was a managing partner in Gordon, Forstall, and Company. Forstall's network was extensive. He ran the New Orleans branch and Gordon headed the Liverpool branch. Forstall became managing partner of M. de Lizardi and Company in New Orleans, which was part of the Lizardi international banking firm that had branches in London, Paris, Liverpool, and Tampico. The Tampico branch exported silver to New Orleans, and the Lizardis invested in Louisiana real estate. Gordon, Forstall, and Company sold textiles, operated steamboats and transatlantic merchant vessels, traded in slaves, and processed sugar. By 1828 Forstall's partnership was exporting about eight thousand bales of cotton per season. His interests too traveled to London with his associates.[18]

Lavergne began warming up Thomas Baring. From Liverpool he and Gordon wrote with reassurances that the Consolidated Association's capital was to be loaned "solely on the most undoubted, productive real estate," and that stockholder-borrowers could borrow only up to half the assessed value of their cultivated lands and slaves. *Assessed* was a wiggle word. Shareholders often inflated the value of their assets, and the Consolidated Association was rare among banks in that it was willing to take on illiquid assets like real estate. But Lavergne sold those liabilities as assets. Because shareholders were the sole candidates for loans, Lavergne and Gordon assured Baring, each shareholder had "a deep personal interest in the success of the institution," and the gentlemen of property and standing who took part did so for the objective "of benefitting the country" by growing more sugar and cotton. They added that "the whole body of planters of Louisiana are remarkable for their good faith in money transactions, and . . . it would be difficult to cite an instance of pecuniary loss arising out of the default of a payment by a Louisiana planter."[19]

Baring received the pitchmen at his Bishopsgate Street offices in London. He had recently been made a junior partner at Baring Brothers. Lavergne, Gordon, and Baring talked over the deal in a commodious chamber inside a stately brick building. A portrait of Thomas Baring as a young man shows a slight figure with an affable countenance, large eyes that seem to wink solicitously, and lips on the verge of a smile. He admired Lavergne's persistence and conviction. But he cut a shrewd deal. In mid-September Baring Brothers and Company agreed to buy $1.67 million worth of Consolidated Association bonds. The firm would resell the bonds to investors ranging from foreign merchant houses to English country banks to individuals seeking security and a high rate of return.[20] To market the bonds, however, Baring made some significant demands, including exclusivity.

Lavergne's necktie must have felt like a Louisiana pine snake as he listened to Baring's terms. The bonds' 5 percent interest would be paid at the Barings' countinghouse in London rather than in New Orleans. Before Lavergne sailed down the Mississippi, the Consolidated Association's board had agreed to pay interest in New Orleans. Baring also required that the interest be paid in pounds sterling rather than dollars and fixed the exchange rate at four shillings sixpence to the dollar. It was a novel demand and the first time an American security would yield a fixed exchange rate. Paying the bonds and interest on them in pounds sterling rather than dollars saved the Barings an 8 percent exchange rate, an expense that the Consolidated Association would have to bear when its bonds matured in 1838 and 1843. On top of that, Baring agreed to buy the bonds at a 5 percent discount. Lavergne was in a bind. Communication with the board could take three months. Should he fail, Lavergne would limp back to New Orleans with a stack of unsold bonds and the bank would remain closed.[21] He agreed. The pine snake slackened.

The linchpin of a new financial scheme was in place and Baring Brothers' bills of exchange would fund slavery's expansion in Louisiana. "We have the pleasure to succeed," Lavergne chirped to the state-appointed director and Consolidated Association president Manuel Andry. He was forced to admit, however, that the "the rate of the bonds has been fixed at 95 [cents on the dollar] with interest and capital payable in England," and that "the important issue of exchange" was also settled in favor of the Barings. British capital was not cheap, but Baring Brothers gave him a number of sterling bills of exchange payable at the Bank of England in specie.[22] Lavergne and the Consolidated Association had, with the backing of Louisiana, turned lands and slaves into paper—paper that was readily convertible into gold.

Lavergne's main accomplishment was to turn bank bonds into some of the best money in the world. Baring Brothers' bills were worth more than Second Bank's notes or any other medium of exchange. They were interest-bearing notes that could form the collateral for any issue of banknotes and were accepted around the world. The Barings' sterling bills were like U.S. Treasury bills of a later age, or what central bankers of the twenty-first century call narrow money or M zero. The Consolidated Association also had the name of Baring Brothers and Company to promote its integrity. In London, Lavergne took delivery of $3.5 million worth of banknotes printed for his Louisiana bank, which he packed in a trunk along with the Barings' bills of exchange. As Lavergne sailed back to Louisiana, he had time to reflect on the negotiations that put many advantages into the hands of the Barings but which made the Consolidated Association's bonds the first American state bonds identified with and marketed by that commercial house.[23]

By the time Lavergne sailed for North America, Thomas Baring was reselling the bonds on British and European markets. European investors who bought land- and slave-backed securities from the Barings did not run the risk that American slaveholders did that an individual enslaved person might die, flee, or become incapacitated. They did not risk a poor harvest, pests, or floods. Bonds were issued in $500 and $1,000 denominations, about what an enslaved worker sold for on the market. Yet the bonds represented an immortal promise. A shrewd bondholder could count on the 5 percent state-guaranteed interest payment when the bond matured or else sell when the market rose. Lavergne returned to the United States in November, the board approved his negotiations in December, and the bank began operating early in 1829. The bank issued its own bills of exchange to American merchants. Not all were pleased. Because of Lavergne's many concessions to the Barings, Louisiana's governor replaced him with Edmond Forstall as comptroller of the Consolidated Association in 1829. Forstall's tenure was short-lived, and Lavergne would be back holding the bank's reins before long.[24]

The bank was finally open for business, and demand quickly rose for its services. Lavergne and his wife, Marie Adèle, eventually borrowed $23,000 — forty-six shares of the Consolidated Association's stock — and gave as security half of a sugar plantation in Plaquemines Parish, eighteen miles south of New Orleans. They also hypothecated half of the equity in sixty bondspeople, including mothers, their children, and "the undivided half of all the unborn infants" of the enslaved women named. In time, Lavergne and his wife used the equity in their shares to borrow more money from the association. Thanking Alexander Gordon in 1829, Lavergne wrote, "I doubt not that [Thomas Baring] is convinced that his house has made a good investment in Louisiana." The bonds sold well in England and Europe, and Baring visited Louisiana again in 1829, scouting for more high-yielding securities. Afterward Lavergne wrote to him that borrowers "will have it in their power to do much good" with the bank's money.[25]

The transatlantic market taking shape resembled a human circulatory system. Merchants and bankers in cities like Liverpool, London, and New York pumped money, manufactures, and processed goods into commercial arteries. Sailing ships acted like blood vessels. In cities like Baltimore and New Orleans, merchants pumped in slaves as well. Debt instruments, manufactures, and slaves passed like blood cells through the capillaries of the American plantation complex and other sites of production and consumption. Credit took the form of bills of exchange drawn in pounds sterling or dollars by merchants in cities like New Orleans. Through the veins of that commerce, city merchants received the cotton, sugar, and other goods that constituted the export trade. Manufacturers acted as the lungs, turning commodities into finished goods, which crossed the Atlantic to pay for commodities. Beginning in the mid–1820s the Second Bank of the United States exercised a regulatory function not unlike that of the kidneys. As the system grew, capillaries multiplied, and some of the capital exchanged for commodities bought new lands and more slaves, many of whom were shipped as captives on the same vessels transporting manufactured goods to the lower South. State banks acted as bone marrow, expanding available credit.[26] Property banks were a small but growing part of that system.

The Consolidated Association owed much to the financial ingenuity of the slave trader Jean Baptiste Moussier and his network of Creole New Orleans business associates. Moussier's association with Lavergne dated from at least 1819, about the time Moussier went into the interstate slave trade. He came up with the idea that Lavergne and Forstall refined into property banking. By leveraging real and personal property to buy more of the same through a stockholders' association, Moussier putatively solved a problem in early American banking. It was an age before bankers received customers in immaculate offices furnished with comfortable chairs and customer service was the name of the game. Banks were insider institutions, and loans were usually reserved for members of networks connected to the bank directors and stockholders. That held for the Second Bank and local banks alike. Banks faced a dilemma when it came to their credit function and their monetary function. Banks that lent liberally tended to fill their portfolios with illiquid assets such as land, which restricted their ability to redeem banknotes in gold and silver on deposit. But banks that held on to liquid assets in support of large issuances of paper money—the circulating medium on which most depended—restricted credit and frustrated borrowers. Shrewd bankers lent at short term to commercial customers on actual consignments and cleared bills of exchange along with other notes. Property banks promised to cut risk by making stockholders sole candidates for loans and expanding credit by leveraging real and personal property rather than merely lending to factors who secured loans with shipments of goods. Property banks still kept a specie reserve but dedicated themselves to serving the agricultural sector, at least in theory. Moussier claimed to be the "father" of the Consolidated Association. That innovation emerged from the New Orleans Creole business community before hostilities with Anglo-Americans resulted in the city's being split into ethnic enclaves.[27] Moussier's migration from slave trading to banking reflected a long practice of using slaves as collateral for private loans and the tight relationship between slavery and credit.

Person-to-person lending in the colonial era and early republic relied extensively on mortgaged slaves. North American slaveholders had taken out equity
mortgages on their slaves at least since the eighteenth century, and slave mortgaging had been a large portion of the mortgage market in colonial Louisiana,
Virginia, and South Carolina. Thomas Jefferson mortgaged 150 enslaved people
to a Dutch firm for the credit to build Monticello. Most small loans too were
secured with human property, and slaves were more easily salable than land.
Factors acting as retail bankers often used bondspersons as collateral for loans to
agriculturalists. Using slaves as business assets bound commercial agriculturalists ever more snugly to slavery: their workforce doubled as a means of securing
credit. In 1824 Vincent Nolte lent $48,000 to the Louisiana planter Antonio
Walsh at about 8 percent interest. One of the conditions of the loan was that
Walsh consign his cotton crop to Nolte, who would sell it in Liverpool and
return the proceeds, minus a commission (and less the costs of insurance,
freight, handling expenses, and a crowd of other fees). To secure the loan, Walsh
agreed that "from 90 to 100 head of first rate slaves will be mortgaged" to Nolte.[28]
Without their knowledge, the ninety or one hundred enslaved workers could be
sold and scattered if Walsh failed to pay or the market turned against him.
Property banking institutionalized slave mortgaging.

Some of Moussier's clients in the slave trade became customers of the
Consolidated Association. Bernard and Jean Villars purchased bondspersons
from him and bought a sugar plantation in Barataria in 1823, a transaction
Lavergne notarized. Fifteen years later Bernard Villars mortgaged over twelve
hundred acres of an East Baton Rouge plantation, along with thirty-three slaves,
for $40,000 to the Consolidated Association. That was an equity mortgage that
used fifteen females, seventeen males, and one whose gender was not disclosed.[29]

Moussier turned from bank architect to desperate customer when he got
into financial trouble. In 1828 one of Moussier's creditors in Louisiana filed suit
against his Richmond clients over nonacceptance of a bill that paid for a shipment of sugar. The Richmond firm in turn sued Moussier for a considerable
sum it loaned him through credits. By the time Moussier appealed to the
Consolidated Association's board, seventy of Moussier's slaves had been seized
on behalf of his creditors. Early in 1829 the board required that Moussier mortgage his lands and slaves as security for a $30,000 loan, and before the year was
out he was back with a request for $25,000. The Consolidated Association
complied, but Moussier's financial situation did not improve. After he died in
1831, his Grande Terre estate became the bank's property. Moussier's wife died
soon afterward. Another property bank, the Citizens' Bank of Louisiana,
bestowed a gift on his three daughters in 1836. The Citizens' Bank had not been

chartered before Moussier died. Regardless, the directors agreed that "a sum of $2500 be given to the Misses Moussier by reason of their situation and as a remembrance of the services that their father rendered the country in introducing the system of mortgage Banks."[30]

The banking network that blossomed in 1830s New Orleans was like a wheel within a wheel. Despite being designed to serve planters, the Consolidated Association got into the more lucrative and safer business of discounting and trading in bills of exchange. It also grew to serve property owners in and around New Orleans. Manuel Julián de Lizardi y Migoni mortgaged several city properties to the Consolidated Association in order to invest in more. He was a member of the international Lizardi network and a close associate of Edmond Forstall. In October 1839 Lizardi subscribed to a total of 364 shares, or $182,000, in the Consolidated Association, backed by several New Orleans properties.[31]

As the Lizardis' relationship with the Consolidated Association suggests, customers and creditors often wore the same silk hats. The London Lizardi company was part of Gordon, Forstall and Company's interlocking partnership and affiliated with M. de Lizardi Company of New Orleans and Lizardi Hermanos of Paris. In 1836 F. de Lizardi and Company marketed a second issue of the Consolidated Association's bonds on much the same terms that Baring Brothers had done eight years before. Lavergne was by then president, and he signed each of the bonds promising 5 percent interest, payable in London at an exchange rate of four shillings and sixpence to the dollar. By then Baring Brothers was exercising caution. Banking, which had always been a trade of confidence, became more of a confidence game.[32]

In the early 1830s credit demands grew and financiers' imaginations blossomed. Louisiana chartered two more property banks in 1832 and 1833, each of which raised money through East Coast and foreign investors. A river of credit flowed into New Orleans from New York, London, and Amsterdam. The three property banks chartered between 1827 and 1833 received 86 percent of the state's subsidies to banks in the dozen years after the Bank of Louisiana was chartered in 1824. Edmond Forstall moved from the Consolidated Association to the Union Bank of Louisiana. He was the most prolific Louisiana banker of the 1830s and shaped the industry for decades thereafter. A portrait painted in 1836 reveals a lively, intelligent, handsome appearance, his lips smiling faintly over a square jaw and slightly dimpled chin. His heroic forehead is crowned by a wreath of brown locks. Forstall looks as if he convinced the painter to make his dark, generous, wide-set eyes betray both tenderness and shrewdness. In a later age, Forstall might be cast as himself in a motion picture, looking every bit the

Jean-Joseph Vaudechamp, *Portrait of Edmond Jean Forstall and Desirée Forstall*, 1836 (Gift of Olga and Yvonne Tremoulet, The Historic New Orleans Collection, acc. no. 2005.0345.3)

dashing man of affairs. As credit demand rose, he "entere[ed] into correspondence" with the Barings, he wrote, and agreed to give them "such information as we think may be of interest."[33] He acted as their agent in New Orleans. In return, they had extended him credit and introductions to European financiers.

Such correspondent ties were strategic alliances designed to confer mutual benefits, including inside information on the health of merchants and the business climate. Forstall became a Baring agent, and the London house repaid him with credit. In 1830 Forstall traveled with family members to the Barings in London. He traced Lavergne's voyage of two years before, sailing to Liverpool by way of New York and traveling to Bishopsgate Street and the offices of his friend Thomas Baring. There Louisiana's most ambitious banker discussed with one of London's highest-flying financiers the possibility of the latter's buying more Louisiana bank bonds.[34] That negotiation came at a propitious time for slavery's capitalists.

The business climate was improving thanks in part to the Andrew Jackson administration's trade policies, which augmented the Second Bank's monetary policies. Early in his first term, Jackson's emissary to Britain negotiated a free trade agreement that reversed the policy of reciprocal taxes and inspections on U.S. and British merchant ships. "The arrangement," as the Jackson administration called it, provided that neither country could impose taxes or restrictions on shipping, a measure that made it much cheaper to ship American commodities to Britain from ports like New Orleans. Driving down transportation costs was more effective than the divisive protective tariff.[35] The cotton trade received a boost at the same time credit expanded, and Jackson's arrangement launched a flotilla of domestic slave ships as a consequence. New Orleans merchants and banks lent to cotton factors as well as to sugar interests, and the rising tide lifted their vessels and demands for banking facilities.

The Barings' increasing interest in U.S. debt instruments permitted foreign investors to shape important contours of American banking. The Consolidated Association and Union Bank were state-chartered, yet their reach was international. The Barings suggested in 1831 that bondholders should be able to receive interest payments at New York or London and simultaneously instructed an American agent to investigate the scheme. With the Barings' financial backing, Forstall was able to start the Union Bank of Louisiana, chartered in 1832, with eight branches, mostly in rural areas, and a state-backed bond issue of $7 million.[36]

The Union Bank was a more muscular version of the Consolidated Association. As before, the state of Louisiana amended the Union Bank charter over strenuous opposition in order to back the bank's bonds. Like the Consolidated Association's, the Union Bank's bonds' relatively high yield would be paid in pounds sterling at Baring Brothers' London firm. The Union Bank agreed to pay that interest at a rate favorable to overseas investors, four shillings sixpence to the dollar in London. Barings took a. 5 percent commission, the same as it charged its largest American client, the Second Bank. Barings also extended the Union Bank a £40,000 revolving credit line for its exchange operations, to be covered every three months. Forstall had inspired the confidence of some of the premier merchant bankers in both Britain and the United States, and Louisiana sugar producers would benefit.

By 1832 New York investors shed hesitations to buy mortgage-backed Louisiana securities. The Barings agreed to sell $5.5 million worth of Union Bank bonds, including a portion through their New York correspondents, the investment house of Prime, Ward, King, and Company. Thanks in part to the successful performance (so far) of the Consolidated Association's bonds, the Union Bank's bonds fetched a hefty premium to New York and Philadelphia investors.[37] But not all went smoothly.

A slave revolt in Virginia reminded investors that the backbone of the labor force was coerced labor. Investors were rattled at insurrection scares prompted by the Nat Turner rebellion in August 1831. In response to waning confidence among European investors, Forstall wrote to Thomas Wren Ward, the Boston correspondent for Baring Brothers and Company, reassuring him that Louisiana's 110,000 African-descended slaves were "scattered among at least an equal number of whites," who were interested "in the tranquility and prosperity of this capitol of the west," New Orleans. His numbers were an accurate reflection of the census. Whites would provide security against uprisings and, by doing so, help secure the bonds he was selling. In fact, Forstall blustered, "London and Paris have much more to dread from their rabble than Louisiana will ever have from her blacks." Forstall could have added that British emancipation in the Caribbean was a potential boon to North American sugar interests. Nat Turner's localized uprising paled in comparison to the Jamaica Rebellion of 1831, which hammered home to Britain the high costs of West Indies slave regimes. The rebellion led Parliament to propose owner-compensated emancipation.[38] While Britain curtailed chattel slavery on its imperial possessions in the Western Hemisphere, London's premier merchant house marketed Louisiana bonds that expanded credit to American slaveholders.

Lavergne, Forstall, and Gordon were among the first stockholders in the Union Bank. Spouses owned property communally in Louisiana. Hugues Lavergne and his wife, Marie Adèle, subscribed to forty shares of stock amounting to $4,000 on the mortgage of a lot on Hospital Street in New

Orleans. Transparency was desirable at the start-up phase of property banking, but the temptation to multiply mortgages was too great to resist, especially in buoyant economic times. At least one of the properties put up by Edmond Forstall and Alexander Gordon for Union Bank shares in 1832 was already encumbered by a mortgage. But they borrowed the full amount with the stipulation that the Union Bank might reduce the shares if it saw fit, at a later date, and if the board of directors decided to penalize one of its own. Erstwhile abstemious borrowers were slipping into intoxication. As property values rose, property banks permitted stockholders to claim the value of lands they mortgaged even if the actual purchase price was much lower. A buyer who paid the U.S. Land Office $1,000 for a plantation could put it up for a value of $10,000, which secured up to $5,000 in bank shares.[39] So long as property values climbed along with commodities prices, there were few reasons not to distill optimism into debt.

Sam Watts witnessed that credit expansion as a mortgagee, one of thousands who underwent similar ordeals as North American slavery financially globalized. The twenty-two-year-old enslaved Virginian was shipped to New Orleans and put to work in a Louisiana sugar refinery. The Union Bank permitted Watts's owners to leverage his market value to expand production and fund technological advances. Transactions involving him touched financial institutions in New York, Philadelphia, and London, and investors whose stomachs turned at thoughts of whips on flesh, slave ships, and shackled human beings owned an interest in Watts's body and products of his unrequited toil.

Of Sam Watts we know little beyond the financial records of his ordeals in 1831 and 1832. He was almost certainly born into legal slavery in Virginia and had family in the old Tidewater neighborhood in which he was trained as a cooper. If he was like most African-descended Americans in eastern Virginia, Watts could name American ancestors going back generations and perhaps one or two African ones. The shipping manifest on which he was inventoried lists him as standing five feet eight inches tall and having "copper"-colored skin.[40]

Watts may have been plying his barrel-making trade in the late summer of 1831 when the specter of Benjamin J. Parks appeared. Parks was a purchasing agent for the slave-trading firm Franklin and Armfield. He scoured the Tidewater region of the lower Chesapeake for individual bondspersons available at moderate prices. At the end of September Parks drove a coffle of ten enslaved purchases to Richmond, including Watts and a millwright. They were young people with old Virginia surnames, including Lightfoot, Pender, and Sprewell. Parks's employer, Rice C. Ballard, paid $460 for Watts, including Parks's $10 commission.[41]

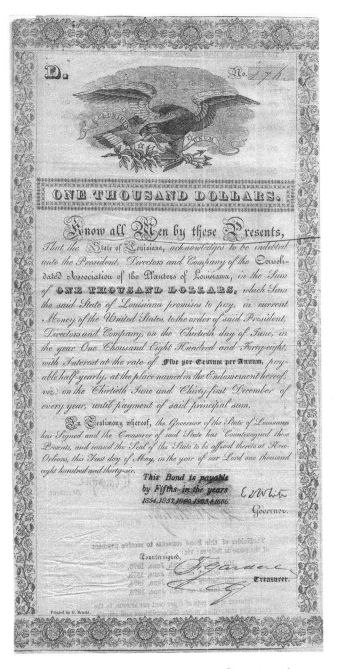

Consolidated Association of the Planters of Louisiana, $1,000
State of Louisiana bond, 1836 (Printed by G. Bruslé)

Ballard was participating in a bonanza in slaves transported from the upper South to the lower South for resale and packed Watts aboard a merchant ship bound from Norfolk to New Orleans. That trade sailed on a sea of credit and a federally protected slave market. The Andrew Jackson administration's liberalized trade policies, increasing prices for farm products, and foreign demand for commodities grown chiefly by enslaved Americans were helping fuel domestic demand for slaves. Farm product prices rose almost 51 percent between 1829 and 1836, during which time overall prices increased 18 percent. In the 1830s the slave trade surged nearly 84 percent over the previous decade. Some 285,000 bondspersons crossed state lines, compared with 155,000 in the 1820s. Perhaps two-thirds were transported in the interstate slave trade. Most would end up in cotton fields, but agents of a rapidly growing sugar industry demanded young, predominantly male slaves to perform some of the most arduous and dangerous work in North America.[42]

Watts did not languish in New Orleans. Less than two weeks after he landed, a slave trader, James Rawlings Franklin, sold him to Edmond Forstall for $950, reaping a not-unusual gross profit of over 100 percent. November was a busy month in the city and for Forstall. The legislature considered a measure banning the importation of slaves into Louisiana for sale, debated chartering the Union Bank, and protested any reduction of the sugar tariff. While working toward the Union Bank's creation, Forstall bought Watts for the Louisiana Sugar Refinery, founded earlier in 1831 and then under construction. Watts was soon transported south of New Orleans. Coopering was no light work, and if Watts did not fashion his barrels to be watertight and of specified dimensions, he might find himself tossed in among the ranks of fieldworkers on one of the surrounding sugar plantations.[43]

While Watts labored at the refinery, the Union Bank's credit infusion helped agriculturalists develop the sugar industry up and down the state. Bank credit enabled some cotton planters to shift to the more capital-intensive crop. Guy Duplantier and his wife, Azema Avart, mortgaged a cotton plantation in East Baton Rouge, the buildings on it, and thirteen slaves in exchange for $6,300 worth of Union Bank stock in 1833, the same year Duplantier was issued a U.S. patent for his sugar manufacturing equipment. He had bought bondspersons in Baltimore in 1818 and had traveled with them on the merchant ship *Temperance* over Christmastime of that year. In succeeding years Duplantier became a customer of the slave trader Austin Woolfolk. Bondspeople taken from the upper South toiled for his fortunes, but Forstall's Union Bank gave him the means to raise the stakes by planting and refining sugar. Many followed. Would-be stockholders were ravenous for Union Bank money. Its stock was oversubscribed, $12 million by New Orleans citizens and $25 million by rural borrowers as soon as the books were opened. By the end of 1832, the Union Bank reported $3,034,100 worth of property mortgaged.[44] Forstall and his relatives were among the first in line.

In late 1832 Forstall raised capital by mortgaging real and personal property to his Union Bank. In late November he and several relatives hypothecated "Sam Watts a negro man of twenty-two years," along with scores of other enslaved workers at the Louisiana Sugar Refinery. That month four Forstall brothers, their wives, Alexander Gordon, and his wife, Anne Bakewell, took out mortgages on substantial property holdings in the amount of $159,200. Among the parties to the mortgages were the New York residents François Placide Forstall and his wife, Marie Francisca de Borgia Delphine Lopez y Angullo de la Candelaria. Placide sold refined sugar. The Gordons and Forstalls hypothecated several properties in New Orleans, part of a sugar plantation in Plaquemines Parish, and a sixth of the Louisiana Sugar Refinery, including its steam-powered mill. In all, they mortgaged ninety-five bondspeople. Like Watts, nearly all were male and in their teens or twenties. The mortgages drew equity out of their bodies to reinvest in refinement technology and more enslaved workers.[45]

Beyond expanding production, bank credit funded development. Forstall's refinery collected the raw sugar of the lower delta and refined it into exportable sugar. To the Louisiana sugar industry that was like transplanting Manchester looms from the River Irwell to the cotton lands along Mississippi River. The Louisiana Sugar Refinery brought the latest French processing technologies to the center of North American sugar production. It was one of the largest industrial operations in the state in the 1830s, and while the equity drawn from Sam Watts expanded capital, his labors added value to production. The Louisiana Sugar Refinery helped make Louisiana sugar more competitive after Congress lowered the tariff on imported sugars to 2.5 cents per pound in 1832 and imposed a flat duty of 20 percent in 1833, which seriously eroded protections.

Forstall took much of the credit for the industry's success, contending that his firm, Gordon Forstall and Company, "introduced into the State the vacuo process," which resulted in "shipments of several hundred tons of sugar, refined from pure Louisiana [cane], which obtained the medal in New York." He attempted to hire the best technicians, again turning to African-descended people to realize his ambitions. Norbert Rillieux developed the multiple-effect evaporator in 1830. His younger brother Edmond Rillieux, along with Norbert Soulié, contracted with Forstall to build the Louisiana Sugar Refinery early in 1831 using similar technology. Soulié and the Rillieux brothers were free men of color. The project stalled in 1832 when Edmond Rillieux disappeared.

Forstall fought with his father, Vincent Rillieux, and the elder Rillieux died suddenly in July 1833 at his New Orleans cotton press. The family suspected that Forstall had killed him in a duel. Disagreements and death derailed Forstall's invitation to Norbert Rillieux to work for him. Soulié departed New Orleans in 1833, and, after returning from Paris, Norbert Rillieux went to work for a competitor instead.[46]

Despite Forstall's difficulties recruiting and retaining technological experts, his refinery became the premier sugar processor in the region shortly after Watts went to work there. Watts's barrels and their sweet contents crossed thousands of miles of ocean. In 1834 the Louisiana Sugar Refinery reportedly employed 130 hands producing 12 million pounds of sugar annually. "The whole process is done by steam, and it is said to be without exception, the most extensive and complete establishment of the kind in the world," crowed a widely circulated report. Much of that year's sucrose was loaded onto ships sailing for Mediterranean ports. Louisiana could now claim to compete with Cuban producers, who increased production in the late 1830s. The chain of credit that extended from London to New York to New Orleans was linked to a commodity chain that crossed the Atlantic Ocean. Bound workers were among the vital connections.[47]

Watts was at the center of a web of finance that gave competitive advantages to Louisiana sugar producers. On an international level, transactions centering on Sam Watts involved British merchant bankers and European investors buying state securities that capitalized the Union Bank and opened its doors. Bondholders in New York and Philadelphia also held interests in Forstall's leveraging the equity stored in Watts's body. His owners used that money to invest in technology and production for far-flung markets. At the level of the firm, Forstall built both a centralized processing facility and the bank that financed it. The Louisiana Sugar Refinery gave local planters the ability to refine exportable sugars, and the Union Bank extended the credit vital to doing so. Transactions centering on Sam Watts illustrate the creativity and ambition tied to slavery, along with the development of supply chains and networked interests. What became of him is unclear, but his mortgage probably outlasted his life.[48]

Debt ballooned in a market saturated with the kind of ambition and optimism Edmond Forstall exemplified. By the mid–1830s the Union Bank could not meet the demands of would-be stockholders. In 1834 Forstall took an active interest in the Citizens' Bank of Louisiana, another property bank. It was a brawnier version of the Union Bank and dwarfed the seven-year-old Consolidated Association. Chartered in April 1833, the Citizens' Bank was capitalized at $12 million and had subscriptions for $14.4 million worth of stock. Up to a third of property mortgaged could be slaves. Foreign credit animated the Citizens' Bank, as it had the Union Bank. Forstall introduced Citizens' Bank agents to Thomas Baring as they were preparing to sail for Liverpool to find buyers for its bonds. The Amsterdam merchant bankers Hope and Company agreed to sell $3 million in Citizens' Bank bonds in 1835. The Louisiana legislature agreed to back the Citizens' Bank bond issue in 1836, as it had supported the earlier ventures. Like the Union Bank's bonds, the Citizens' Bank bonds' interest was payable in Amsterdam, London, or Paris, and at the head of the bonds were printed the exchange rates for the currencies. The Citizens' Bank appointed Forstall to its board, and among his tasks was to select land on which to build the physical bank structure. In a gesture of amity, the bank's handsome edifice was built on the boundary between the French commercial section and the American quarter. After Louisiana agreed to back the bank's bonds, Forstall became its president and directed the bank's foreign business through F. de Lizardi and Company of London, of which Alexander Gordon was by then a partner.[49]

Citizens' Bank money was in great demand, and even interstate slave traders were lining up to become stockholders. Samuel M. Woolfolk sought mortgages with the Citizens' Bank for his slave jails and trading compound on Chartres Street between Esplanade and Frenchman. (As Austin Woolfolk transitioned to Grosse Tete, the Citizens' Bank permitted his neighbor Eliphalet Slack to move from cotton to sugar by becoming a stockholder; Slack's son Henry Richmond would marry Woolfolk's daughter Louisiana Tennessee.) A New Orleans real estate investor, Pleasant B. Cocke, mortgaged a Jefferson Parish plantation fronting Caminada Bay to the slave trader Isaac Franklin for $1,100 in cash and a $5,000 letter of credit, promising to pay back the loan once he mortgaged the same property to the Citizens' Bank. Cocke was a former customs officer in New Orleans and a claimant to the spoils of the *Josefa Segunda*. Cocke and Franklin agreed in 1834 "that when the Citizens Bank of Louisiana goes into operation," Cocke would use bank stock as security for the $1,100 loan from Franklin.[50]

Bankers' fever dreams conjured novel credit schemes. Among the innovations that the Citizens' Bank implemented near the height of the economic boom in 1836 was an agreement with the Huntsville branch of the Bank of the State of Alabama to accept bills of exchange that each institution drew on the other. That strategic partnership assumed that both banks' bills were sound, which was a mutual blank check. Another innovation was to allow bills drawn on up to two-thirds of the current market value of insured and warehoused cotton and sugar. That made sense so long as prices were rising steadily. Merchants and factors usually drew bills on commodities that had entered the chain. Risk was manageable since bills and commodities were both moving through commercial channels. Borrowing against warehoused cotton and sugar was a primitive futures market; it was not unlike betting on a horserace while stabled animals slept. As credit schemes proliferated, the Citizens' Bank and Forstall were increasingly subject to suspicion that the bank engaged in risky practices. While the bank distributed credit, he distributed confidence. Forstall publicly contended that the bank was being run on sound principles, including a commitment to keep one-third of the value of its banknotes as gold and silver on deposit.[51] Borrowers' habituated thirst for credit became an addiction in the flush times, and other states chartered property banks.

To expand agricultural enterprises' seemingly unbounded promises, Mississippi, Arkansas, and the Florida Territory chartered property banks. Louisiana banks were among the most heavily regulated in the country, but frontier Arkansas or territorial Florida had thinly developed financial institutions. Arkansas had no state-chartered bank until the legislature chartered the Real Estate Bank in 1836. It was a case study in venality and lent generously to stockholders with little regard to whether mortgaged property had any value. Florida planters had voracious credit appetites, which the territory struggled to serve. The Union Bank of Florida was the eighth bank chartered in that territory between 1828 and 1833 and one of thirteen chartered by 1836. Initially capitalized at $1 million, the Union Bank's capitalization was raised to $3 million by 1834. Its officers borrowed strategy from Louisiana's property banks and sought outside investors while relying on the territory to guarantee its bonds. Prime, Ward, and King of New York had marketed bonds of the Union Bank of Louisiana. They agreed to market Florida's Union Bank initial bond issue. So did Thomas Biddle and Company of Philadelphia. The Union Bank of Florida's second issue found buyers in London and Amsterdam. Florida property banking made Louisiana's loose lending practices look saintly. One director of the Union Bank of Florida secured a loan from his own bank with no money down and payments deferred for over two decades. Florida's sugar sector grew rapidly on the strength of easy credit and state guarantees.[52]

Louisiana's property banks were chartered to serve sugar planters but ended up diversifying into urban real estate and commercial lending. An 1847 accounting revealed that 70 percent of Consolidated Association mortgages had gone to sugar planters, but merchants borrowed more money. By January 1840 the Consolidated Association had loaned nearly $2 million to commercial borrowers and $1.3 million on mortgages. The Union Bank loaned $6.2 million to commercial borrowers, mainly merchants, and had $3.2 million in mortgage loans. The Citizens' Bank of Louisiana was the only one of the three property banks to have loaned more to plantation borrowers than to commercial customers. Between 1827 and 1837 Louisiana attracted over $20 million in foreign capital, mostly from England and Holland. Seven million more dollars were raised by bonds sold in the United States, primarily marketed by firms in Boston, New York, and Philadelphia, and by 1837 Louisiana's banks held an aggregate paid-in capital of more than $39 million. By 1840 Louisiana had more bank money and credit than any other state in the Union.[53]

Lower South states that imported the most bondspeople also saw the highest rates of monetization. By 1840 Louisiana, Alabama, Florida, and Mississippi had more bank money in circulation per capita than any other state or region. At over $25 for every man, woman, and child in 1840, Louisianans had more bank money circulating per capita than either Massachusetts or Rhode Island. There was three times more credit and bank money per capita circulating in Louisiana than in New York or in the states of the Seaboard South from Virginia to Georgia. Distant investors gobbled up bank bonds, but local bankers controlled the capital and how it was allocated.[54]

Financial technology surged ahead of statecraft in the 1830s. The Second Bank of the United States was reduced to a state bank in 1836, and without a central banker the sector's leadership was left to financiers like Forstall. States acted autonomously within the federal framework. There was neither a federal regulatory regime into which that fit nor even a theory of one. With no control over the blood pressure of the financial system, state banks expanded the volume of money and credit coursing through it. In 1839 Daniel Webster of Massachusetts, himself a paid agent of Baring Brothers and Company, crossed the Atlantic to proclaim that states could constitutionally act as they had for twenty years, selling state securities abroad.[55] But by that time few were buying.

In 1837 confidence brokers ran short of assurances. That spring a critic publicly charged that Forstall authorized a Citizens' Bank loan to F. de Lizardi and Company in London, the branch of the Lizardi firm that had channeled the proceeds of Citizens' Bank bonds back to Louisiana. The property bank chartered to help local planters was making international commercial loans. Forstall rebutted the accusation. He assiduously tried to retain the confidence of foreign investors and sell Citizens' Bank bonds in 1838. After a brief suspension, his bank continued to pay specie for notes.[56] Those suspicious of state subsidies to bankers howled for repudiation, and fundamentals seemed suddenly lacking in integrity. The Louisiana property banks remained open but suffered from being chartered while the sectors they served were immature.

From a post–1837 perspective, property banking made little sense, and the initial hesitations of New York investors proved correct. There was indeed speculation. For the years 1835 to 1837, money and credit expanded more swiftly than real economic capacity, and large investors such as Baring Brothers and the Bank of England lost confidence in cotton bills and U.S. monetary policies implemented in response to the expansion. An international banking system based on debt instruments connected primarily to cotton and commodities such as sugar could not be sustained. The sharp downturn in cotton and other commodity prices affected slave and land prices as well as merchants and everyone else up the supply chain. The banks had not been in business long enough to diversify or to build reputations for probity that would weather the crisis.

But the expansion of credit permitted real, sustained growth over a decade. Bank and commercial credit permitted the sugar industry to grow and develop, initially aided by federal protection. Sugar prices spiked in 1835–36 and dropped by a third between 1836–37 and 1841–42, but prices remained stable during the financial crisis of 1837 and fell in 1838–39 because of an unusually large crop. Production increased overall thereafter. The average crop produced in the 1830s was about two-thirds larger than the average crop of the 1820s, and the average crop of the 1840s was nearly two and a half times that of the average crop of the 1830s. As it turned out, Louisiana property banks were more severely affected by losses of confidence than by a crash in the sugar industry they served. The three Louisiana property banks' notes were discounted as much as 75 percent of their face value during the financial crisis, but by the end of 1844 the Consolidated Association's and Citizens' Bank's notes were trading at a 20 percent discount. Astonishingly, the Union Bank's notes were exchanged at just 1 percent below face value, which was above what most sound banks could manage during economic good times. The Union Bank of Louisiana remained solvent throughout the crisis, but Louisiana forced it into liquidation in 1844.[57]

Hard times brought Forstall financial troubles and a conversion to conservative monetary principles. In the wake of the panic, he and his brother François Placide were forced to liquidate assets. They sold several city properties to Manuel Julián de Lizardi, including the dwelling place of Edmond Durel and his wife, Clara, on Bayou Road, along with two plantations, including Jean Baptiste Moussier's old Grande Terre estate in Barataria. The Lizardis were in an advantageous position following the panic. Like Baring Brothers, they marketed Louisiana bank bonds rather than invested in them, largely avoiding the crisis. The Lizardis bought up distressed properties following 1837. In 1842 Forstall emerged from the crisis as a bank reformer by introducing state legislation that regulated specie reserves required to cover bank-issued notes. In contrast to Louisiana, New York and other states that liberalized banking laws reaped the benefits of so-called free banking following the hard times of the 1840s.[58]

As debtors sold out and creditors seized property, financial transactions converging on enslaved people like Sam Watts assumed tragic proportions. Desperate slaveholders continued to mortgage bondspersons. Creditors bore the financial risks, but enslaved people paid the costs of bad debt with shattered families and shortened lives. George McNair or McNayer was an enslaved carpenter who had been bought in the Chesapeake for $500 in 1831 by agents of the slave trading firm Franklin and Armfield. He was embarked with Sam Watts as part of a cargo of captives aboard the schooner *Industry* in the fall of 1831 and shipped to New Orleans. There the thirty-five-year-old, who stood five feet six and a half inches tall, was resold and toiled for the better part of ten years in Louisiana. He was probably the same George McNayer belonging to an Iberville Parish, Louisiana, owner who mortgaged title to his body to Forstall's Citizens' Bank of Louisiana. After hard times hit in 1840, the owner failed and the bank liquidated him. Title to his body was transferred to two men, including Abner Robinson, a Virginia slave trader turned Louisiana planter. Besides McNair, Robinson and his partner took possession of 101 other slaves mortgaged to the Citizens' Bank by the same Iberville planter.[59] Those bought in the flush times were sold in hard times.

Legislators who lent states' faith and credit bank bonds during the expansion lost their faith in the panic. Arkansas, Louisiana, Mississippi, and the Florida Territory had assumed contingent liabilities for property banks' bond issues, which were sold primarily out of state. When Mississippi banks failed, the state refused to honor its commitments. Courts that had looked the other way as enslavers brought tens of thousands of bondspersons into the state suddenly remembered constitutional injunctions against doing so when foreign and out-of-state creditors sued debtors for nonpayment in hard times. Banks closed and debtors disappeared. Paper money apostates elected antibank legislators who repudiated state debts. Only two of Mississippi's twenty-five banks operating in 1837 remained open after 1841. Despite the victory of the national Whig Party in the aftermath of the panic, "radical" antibank Democrats crafted policies that undermined banks in the 1840s. In Florida antibank Democrats forced bank closures, discouraged the formation of new banks, and in 1842 repudiated over $4 million in territorial bonds. Meanwhile, debtors fled to the Republic of Texas.[60]

Political calculations in both Florida and Mississippi were shortsighted. Officeholders reasoned that because the lion's share of bank debts were held by foreign investors rather than angry, bankrupt constituents, domestic political consequences would be light. But satisfying voters had short-term gains and long-term adverse consequences. In the wake of the financial panic of 1837, Louisiana attempted to make good on its obligations by accepting its bonds at face value as payment for state debts. The bonds were trading for far below their face value in Europe, and enterprising sellers of cotton could buy the bonds overseas and return them to the state for full credit. The plan did not, however, retire much of the $22 million in outstanding bond issues. But the legacy of state backing had profound ramifications for the future of slavery in North America. Mississippi and Florida did not count on foreign bankers' long bitter memories in 1861 when they attempted unsuccessfully to sell state bonds after seceding from the United States. Although the Confederacy raised funds by selling bonds overseas, British and European investors refused to invest in Confederate state debt and the slave system it supported.[61]

After fifteen years of intimate involvement with the Consolidated Association, failure crushed Hugues Lavergne. Following the bank's state-ordered liquidation, a cloud came upon his soul. Early one February morning in 1843, Lavergne took a ferry to the western side of the Mississippi River. He left behind Marie Adèle, his wife of nearly thirty years, and a note reportedly saying that he "found the cares and responsibilities of his position too overwhelming for him, and sought escape from them in death inflicted by his own hand." The fifty-year-old Lavergne made his way to the family cemetery in the Algiers section of the city. There was buried his father, Count Pierre de la Vergne, chevalier or knight of St. Louis, who had died thirty years before. Lavergne was his only son. A portion of Algiers had been part of the Battle of New Orleans twenty-eight years before. As he walked the sacred grounds, perhaps he recalled the sea voyage nearly fifteen years earlier and the shimmering promises embodied in the bonds he took to London. Lavergne assured survivors that his "motives will be misconstrued." In his note explaining his actions he denied personal misconduct. In the graveyard that morning, he drew a "sword cane or poniard" and stabbed himself in the chest. The wound was not immediately fatal. Discovered in distress, Lavergne was taken back to the eastern side of the city, where he died at one in the afternoon. A New Orleans obituary remembered him as "a gentleman of great amenity and elegance of manners, of distinguished connections, and in addition to the advantages of his elevated social position, he possessed the unqualified confidence and esteem of our business community." A month after the event, Londoners read the news that Lavergne had ended his financial career "by stabbing himself in the heart."[62]

"THE SLAVE-FACTORY OF FRANKLIN & ARMFIELD"

"I have always held credit above price," Isaac Franklin wrote to his Virginia partner from New Orleans in March 1834. The managing partner of Franklin and Armfield had by then built a thousand-mile supply chain in captives based on his ability to access credit, remit capital, and manage a network of agents and assets that funneled as many as a thousand enslaved Americans a year through its organization. The forty-four-year-old Tennessean and his partners, including John Armfield and Rice C. Ballard, built a business that took advantage of enormous credit expansion and market growth, generating hundreds of thousands of dollars in annual revenues. Franklin oversaw its distribution network and managed inventory and cash flow. His swagger reflected his success. Director-managers referred to their business as "the game," casting themselves and their competitors as players—"pirates"—dedicated to building wealth and prestige. The confidence of Franklin's tone, his measured, assuring cadences, punctuated by occasional outbursts at his partners, masked the landscape of social, sexual, and personal violence that turned people into commodities and flung them across a continent to toil on the far frontier of the U.S. republic. But brutal business was still business. As it expanded its capacity and increased in scale, Franklin and Armfield faced a constellation of challenges, including credit, logistics, and management, as it built a far-flung distribution network.[1]

Early in life Franklin grasped the interstate slave trade's promises. He was born in 1789 into a planter family that had settled in Sumner County, Tennessee, at the end of the Revolution. One of ten children, Franklin received primary instruction at a "country school" while working on his father's farm. At eighteen he commenced working for his older brothers transporting goods down the Mississippi River to New Orleans and returning with merchandise. He sold slaves in Natchez as early as the 1810s. Franklin served in a Tennessee cavalry company

Isaac Franklin, oil on canvas (From the Belmont Mansion
Collection, Nashville, Tennessee)

during the War of 1812 and bought land afterward. But commerce beckoned, and Franklin concentrated on long-distance trade down the Cumberland, Ohio, and Mississippi rivers.[2]

Franklin was cloudy in temperament yet shrewd in management. He had a keen social intelligence but was moody, sometimes melancholy. He worried compulsively about his personal health and obsessed over that of his firm, perpetually seeking competitive advantages yet fretting that his partners were not quite up to the task. That anxiety blended with blindness to the sufferings of the people he sold as slaves. Franklin was peripatetic, scurrying from his house in New Orleans's Faubourg Marigny to meet ships at the levee, strolling into city banks, or ducking into merchant houses with fistfuls of financial paper. During summers, he visited salubrious warm springs in the East and built gardens and elegant buildings on his Sumner County plantation. As summer waned, he supervised driving coffles of captives down to Natchez, tracing the paths blazed by Peyton Mason and Company a decade and a half earlier but superintending caravans ten times as large. In between, Franklin bought plantations in Louisiana and speculated in lands in Texas.

The cornerstones of his business principles were good credit, "good prices & good profits." On occasion, Franklin's Middle Tennessee accent could be heard echoing through the firm's private jails in Alexandria and Richmond. He nearly always had a pen within reach and at times preached like an apostle of capitalism, cramming its doctrines down the throats of his partners. "You have been long enough in the trade to know," he counseled his partner Ballard in 1831, "there is no salesman [who] can make money if the article for sale is badly layed in[;] a few negroes [well] purchased will always make more clear money than the many badly purchased." Like Ballard, he delayed marriage until he retired from active involvement in his firm in the late 1830s.[3]

Franklin learned that the cost of doing business was the main obstacle to building an interstate slave-trading firm. Buyers in the lower Mississippi Valley preferred to pay for slaves with locally circulating debt instruments, which were nearly impossible to convert into cash up the supply chain in Virginia or Maryland, where sellers demanded it. To digest such financial paper and make remittances to Chesapeake branches, Franklin and his partners cultivated relationships with merchants and bankers, integrating the interstate slave trade into an expanding credit network. The firm's money flowed in the arteries of a national and international credit system, and Franklin gave customers opportunities to incur debt to expand sales. That strategy helped Franklin and Armfield expand and undercut competitors like Austin Woolfolk.[4]

To meet growing demand for captives, Franklin and Armfield organized vertically, transporting captives from the Chesapeake to the lower Mississippi Valley on a small fleet of dedicated ships collecting captives from company jails. Isaac Franklin managed the firm's finances from New Orleans and Natchez, coordinated shipments, and delegated the firm's Mississippi sales operations to his nephew James Rawlings Franklin. The firm's Chesapeake slaving territory resembled a geometrically elegant set of converging spheres focusing on port cities and encompassing tens of thousands of square miles. In Baltimore, James Purvis, another of Isaac Franklin's nephews, managed buying in northern Maryland. Forty-five miles to the west, George Kephart and Company ran the western Maryland purchasing agency operating in Frederick. About fifty miles to the southeast of Baltimore and across the Chesapeake Bay, Thomas M. Jones bought slaves in Easton. William Hooper operated out of Annapolis. Forty-five miles south of Baltimore, Franklin's brother-in-law John Armfield ran the firm's shipping center and jail compound in Alexandria. Forty-five miles to the west of Alexandria, Jordan M. Saunders and Company ran the northern Virginia purchasing operation from Warrenton. Rice C. Ballard ran the largest purchasing agency, headquartered in Richmond. He partnered with the Fredericksburg slave trader Samuel Alsop, an old acquaintance of Franklin's. Together, Ballard and Alsop were responsible for buying and jailing captives bought in the lower Chesapeake. They embarked them overland or through the port of Norfolk, often on company ships sailing from Alexandria to New Orleans. Alsop's Fredericksburg firm was forty-five miles southeast of Alexandria. Ballard's Richmond jail was one hundred miles south of Alexandria.[5]

To his partners, Ballard was more honest than shrewd, but his purchases sustained the firm's supply chain. Ballard was born in Fredericksburg, Virginia, in 1800, and had become a prominent slave trader in Fredericksburg and Richmond. Ballard sold slaves in New Orleans and Natchez by 1828, and he soon joined Franklin and Armfield as a partner. Like other firms, the enterprise kept double-entry accounting books and felt no need for limited liability or issuing securities.[6]

Isaac Franklin had a tyrant's temperament, but the geographic remoteness of his partners tempered any strict organizational coherence he might have imposed. Because each arm or subsidiary of the business ran quasi-independently, purchasing and shipping directors had wide latitude over whom to hire and how to employ them. Some local directors were also relatives, as was common in the era, but Franklin's family ties were coextensive with business ties solely at the executive level. He held a resource-based understanding of the firm long before such theories were formalized. Franklin depended on his partners' and agents' knowledge and judgment to build a geographically vast organizational structure.[7]

As agents bought individuals at localities such as county courthouses, they severed family, community, and network ties. As Franklin and Armfield grew, the process intensified, and African-descended families bore the costs of the firm's creative destruction. Because of the high volume of captives processed through their firm, Franklin and Armfield began to categorize captives as articles of human merchandise and impose market abstractions on them. The partners became expert at erasing their histories, effacing their identities, and stamping recalcitrant human bodies with sales propaganda. In their hands, fathers and sons, sisters and cousins—people with names they also recorded—became "first rate house servants," "likely men," "field wom[e]n large & likely," and "fancy maid[s]," the last offered for sexual exploitation.[8] The captives, tightly packed aboard the firm's ships sailing to the lower South, had little cause to hope that the long arc of the moral universe bent toward justice.

Sam Watts understood that reality. It arrived like a club to the gut one late summer day in 1831. Watts was a twenty-two-year-old enslaved cooper purchased by Rice Ballard's Tidewater agent Benjamin Parks in late August. He glimpsed the financial innovations Franklin and Armfield made whenever he saw money exchanged for his body. Parks handed Watts's owner $450 and delivered him to Ballard along with several others. Watts saw the inside of Ballard's Richmond jail before being transferred to a Norfolk jail where he awaited the slave ship that took him to New Orleans. While Watts was incorporated into the firm's supply chain, the money that paid for him traveled a credit chain.

He was bought with the proceeds of slave sales remitted as bills and banknotes. Franklin had sent Ballard $10,000 in cash in June. By August 1831 Franklin in New Orleans had sent Ballard in Richmond four bills of exchange totaling $20,000. Ballard cashed the bills at his branch of the Bank of Virginia for a discount off their face value. Ballard employed several purchasing agents, and he handed Parks $5,270 in Virginia banknotes in early August along with a commission to buy young bondspersons. Those remissions of capital were the basis of "higher prices in Cash than any other purchaser who is now or may hereafter come into the market" Ballard advertised to slaveholders in Virginia.[9]

Remittances were the firm's lifeblood, and the money that bought Watts reached Ballard as debt instruments linking East Coast merchants to their New Orleans counterparts. One of the bills Franklin sent Ballard was a $2,000 bill or order to pay drawn on Bache McEvers, a New York City commission merchant, shipper, and insurer who sold Louisiana cotton and sugar. Another was drawn by the New Orleans cotton merchant Andrew Lockhart on Mackie, Lockhart and Company in New York. Mackie, Lockhart and Company was a shipper and cotton dealer trading on Broad Street. Another was payable at Foster and Giraud, also in New York City. Foster and Giraud was composed of Andrew Foster and Jacob Post Giraud; the South Street merchant firm dealt in North American cotton, sugar, and tobacco, along with Caribbean and South American commodities such as coffee. All three firms shipped southern bulk commodities to

Liverpool. Franklin bought bills in New Orleans and sent them through the Post Office to his partners.[10]

For centuries private bills had been public currency. Bills drawn on merchants such as McEvers, Mackie, and Foster were the primary interregional commercial medium. They helped integrate regions of the country, and those who used them as money endorsed the creditworthiness of the drawee. The slave trade thrived on the exchange of domestic bills, and bills that paid for commodities in New Orleans and imports in New York or Philadelphia also paid for captives in Richmond. Cotton merchants needed such intermediaries; otherwise, domestic exchange would not work and the cotton chain would break apart. Franklin assured his partner in Virginia that the bills he was sending were the best paper available. "Exchange is extremely scarce and at lower rates than I have ever known," Franklin informed Ballard in late October 1831, about the time Watts was shipped from Norfolk.[11]

The trust and confidence paper promises embodied pried captives like Watts from owners, fed and incarcerated them, set the sails on the ships in which they were transported, and generated revenues at resale. They were no less fictitious than collateral documents such as bills of sale and shipping manifests. Ballard laid out nearly $8,900 for a consignment of twenty-five bondspersons in late September 1831. He paid over $10,000 for the subsequent consignment of thirty captives two weeks later, and nearly $25,000 for the consignment of sixty-nine captives in late October, of which Watts was a part. To keep those captives coming, Franklin sent refreshers, including $10,000, which Ballard entered as cash, a $5,000 bill of exchange in early November, which he entered as "return capitol," supplemented by another $4,000 bill of exchange entered two days later.[12]

Like all promises to pay, bills and other debt instruments held value solely in relation to confidence in the issuer. Franklin and Armfield may have preferred cash sales, but banknotes made expensive remittances. While Sam Watts was in jail waiting for transport, for instance, notes from state-chartered Louisiana banks were discounted at 5 percent in New York, and even the notes of the Louisiana branch of the Second Bank of the United States were typically discounted. When accepting banknotes as remittances, Ballard had to pay what amounted to a tax on distance.[13] That same distance promised great returns on investments in bondspersons.

As Watts became part of Franklin and Armfield's supply chain, he was confined in jail, joined by scores of others. Ballard incarcerated captives until a sufficient number were assembled to make up a cargo. Jailing bondspersons was often costlier than shipping them, and more hazardous. The average bondsperson spent 117 days in jail in Norfolk, Virginia, in 1830 awaiting transport, at a cost of nearly thirty dollars. Such jails were notoriously crowded, filthy breeding grounds for infectious diseases like measles. Saltwater transport was typically less costly and less perilous, about $17 per captive between Norfolk and New Orleans in 1830. By the time Watts was packed aboard the schooner *Industry* with 134 other captives, it had been over six weeks since Parks bought him. Shipboard conditions were tight. The *Industry* had 107 tons of cargo space that accommodated 135 involuntary passengers, each allotted .79 ton, or a little less than 32 cubic feet (a shipping ton was forty cubic feet). That was roughly the equivalent of a compartment six feet long, two and a half feet wide, and two feet deep, the dimensions of a coffin.[14]

It was not uncommon to tightly pack captives aboard merchant vessels, and the *Industry* was not the sole slaver sailing at the time. In cramped quarters, amid the groans, cries, and prayers of other captives, Watts had three weeks to reflect on his misfortune, commiserate with shipmates, and dread the ordeals to come. The saltwater passage commencing in late October took twenty-three days, about two days longer than average. The *Industry* landed at New Orleans on the same November day as two other merchant vessels carrying slave cargoes from Norfolk. At the levee, James Franklin met the *Industry* and marched Watts and his fellow captives off to another set of holding cells. The younger Franklin was a business disciple of his uncle Isaac. What he lacked in his kinsman's sophistication and verve he made up for in lust and bluster. Watts set eyes on his next owner when Edmond Jean Forstall shook hands with James Franklin and agreed to buy him for $950. Hopes of somehow returning to Virginia dimmed with each mile he traveled down the Mississippi River to the Louisiana Sugar Refinery. As he commenced work, Isaac Franklin ensured that his Chesapeake purchasing managers had ample remittances to buy more like Watts. He was also hard at work amplifying the expansion of credit for which Forstall was partly responsible.[15]

Four score and seven years before General Motors incorporated a finance company to help customers buy its cars, Franklin created an in-house finance arm. In the winter of 1832 Franklin extended to qualified buyers credit at 10 percent interest. Debt-burdened buyers were eager to leverage their holdings to buy slaves. A visitor to their sales compound in Mississippi commented that "negotiable paper [was] the customary way of paying for slaves." Extending credit was some-thing small traders could not do easily. Franklin and Armfield sold captives outside Natchez. The English visitor who arrived at the firm's Forks of the Road compound sketched the scene. "A mile from Natchez we came to a cluster of rough wooden buildings, in the angle of two roads, in front of which several saddle-horses, either tied or held by servants, indicated a place of popular resort." There, out of sight of city residents, Franklin had built wooden structures to confine, process, and sell the firm's human merchandise. As the compound swelled with captives, Franklin needed a solution to the problem of buying captives with cash and selling on credit. At the same time, he instructed his Chesapeake partners to borrow to cover their operating margins, should they need to.[16]

Credit expansion was the market's magic and slavery's mainstay. The agriculturalists who typically bought Franklin and Armfield's slaves were already deeply in debt to factors and preferred to pay with what merchants called long paper: bonds, promissory notes, or bills payable in Natchez or New Orleans, maturing in ninety days or more. But the paper Franklin took as payment could not be remitted to his Chesapeake purchasing directors without punishing discounts. Promissory notes authored by indebted planters in Louisiana or Mississippi were nearly worthless in Baltimore or Richmond. Planters disdained slave traders and puffed up their own importance, accenting their managerial abilities while developing a paternalist mythology. Franklin reported that Louisiana buyers were "very savage against the traders because they have made them pay these prices this season." But they relied utterly on financial networks that linked merchants to distant buyers and banks, and their vaunted honor was their solvency in local circles.[17]

Franklin liberalized slave financing while benefiting from an expanding slave market. Initially, he attempted to economize by financing his scheme internally. Instead of immediately discounting customers' paper, Franklin acted as a bank. The firm held mortgages on the slaves they sold, releasing the mortgages when the buyer paid his debt in six, nine, twelve, or—eventually— eighteen months. It was bold and ambitious and calculated to drive competitors out of business. The problem was that Franklin failed to share his plans with his Chesapeake partners until the scheme was in place.

Ballard and the other Chesapeake directors faced challenges posed by what Franklin called "the long credit business." They needed swift and abundant remittances to keep buying and shipping bondspersons like Watts. Franklin and Armfield's business model moved like the minute hand of a clock in which planters counted only hours. Commercial agriculturalists were able to pay just once a year, when the previous season's crop sold. They needed long credit and were also particularly credit hungry. Franklin, on the other hand, needed to remit capital constantly during a selling season. Watts was bought in part with proceeds from slave sales that occurred earlier that year, and proceeds from his sale paid for more captives that winter. Demand for credit from customers and capital from purchasing managers taxed Franklin's scheme of internal financing.

He held tens of thousands of dollars' worth of illiquid debt instruments while increasing his sales volume. That winter Franklin expressed his self-satisfaction to Ballard with a sexual pun, "permit me to say I have had hard work as usual for a one eyed man," but he failed to mention what caused his flaccid remittances.[18]

But by the early months of 1832, such interruptions were beginning to starve the upper South branches while the New Orleans branch was bloated with paper salable solely at deep discounts. Franklin was forced to discount some of his best paper to feed the supply chain. In December 1831 Franklin sent Ballard the proceeds of Sam Watt's sale—and many like it—as two $5,000 bills of exchange drawn on Solomon and Moses Allen in New York, one of the largest exchange merchants in the country. Other branches in Alexandria and Baltimore also needed funds. Franklin disdained bill merchants, whom he called "shavers," but his entrepreneurial strategy then depended on them.[19]

Franklin encouraged his partners to get commercial loans to make up the shortfall. Banks regularly treated slave traders as commercial customers, and some Virginia banks thrived on the discounts they took when interstate slave traders returned with out-of-state banknotes. From Natchez in January 1832 Franklin wrote to Ballard, "Should you stand in need of friends you may borrow from your banks at 60 or ninety [days] with full confidence that the money will be returned to meet it in all our business in bills receivable." Franklin explained, "It is . . . a saving of interest to borrow from the bank instead of having our long paper discounted." That was the conventional wisdom. Franklin lent at 10 percent while his purchasing managers borrowed at 6 percent. The firm could in theory earn 4 percent while its captives sailed to market. Ballard was not sure whether Franklin was audacious or opportunistic. But there were more pressing issues.[20]

A significant part of the lower South market for slaves closed. "The game is nearly blocked on us," James Franklin screeched from New Orleans.[21] Louisiana banned out-of-state slave sales early in 1832, and Isaac Franklin had to vacate New Orleans with 270 enslaved people. In an effort to evade the new law, Franklin petitioned unsuccessfully to switch his domicile to New Orleans and claim that the shiploads of captives he imported were for personal use. Such a business shock shifted the firm's strategy and inspired a turn to external financing.

After hastily relocating, Franklin's business boomed in Natchez. Buyers were mainly Mississippi cotton planters expanding production on the strength of future expectations. Isaac Franklin accumulated a trove of bills. "I have had no time for financiering," he wrote to Ballard in January 1832, apologizing for his spare remittances. He had left New Orleans and delegated to his nephew James the duty of stewarding "upwards of two hundred thousand dollars in bills renewable," Isaac reported, "and was at a loss whether to continue the purchasing or not" until he could find another way to raise money. Franklin and Armfield had taken payment in what insiders called accommodation paper payable by city merchants. Bills were renewed when the acceptor needed more time to pay, which was common as debt ballooned. Few paid the interest in cash, and the firm faced the irony of high volume, high prices, and high paper profits, while having little capital to remit—all while paper money seemed to deluge the region.[22]

Franklin needed new ways to finance his business. The firm was selling more and more captives while loosening its credit terms to buyers, taking higher prices to cover the risk. Cotton and slave prices were on a steep upward climb. From Natchez James Franklin reported to Ballard that "all the negroes we have sold commanded fair prices" in March 1832, but he moaned that sellers "have had to take all sorts of paper in payment for negroes."[23] Natchez had its share of merchants with East Coast connections, but a newly chartered property bank was selling drafts on a New York affiliate at attractive prices.

As he concentrated on sales in Natchez, Isaac Franklin sought bank credit to make remittances. Using banks instead of bills or exchange merchants cut costs, especially if a bank had a correspondent tie with an East Coast partner. Correspondent ties were agreements between banks to exchange financial services and information, and a Mississippi bank draft payable at a partner bank in New York could be discounted in Virginia for less, potentially, than a bill of exchange and far less than Mississippi banknotes. Mississippi had chartered the Planters' Bank in 1830 in response to the same kind of credit demands that led to the Consolidated Association of the Planters of Louisiana. The Planters' Bank of Mississippi was capitalized at $3 million and issued $2 million worth of state-backed bonds, bonds marketed to foreign investors. Like property banks in Louisiana, Mississippi's property or land banks permitted stockholders to mortgage productive lands and slaves. It also made commercial loans and discounted bills. Isaac Franklin became a client of Samuel Gustin, one of its founders. Gustin had raised initial capital by selling the bank's bonds to Philadelphia and New York investors, after Mississippi guaranteed them. Some of that capital flowed into the slave trade. In May and June 1832 Franklin was able to remit Ballard three Planters' Bank drafts totaling $23,000, payable at the Phenix Bank of New York. Franklin continued to seek other financial instruments. Among the remittances Ballard recorded was a check on the Bank of America in New York on which he paid a 1 percent premium.[24] It still was not enough.

Although business was brisk for slaves, Rice Ballard howled that Franklin's financiering drove up their costs and cut into their profits. "You never informed us in what way you were managing our business or rather the sales," he wrote in

September 1832, castigating Franklin for gorging the firm on planters' bonds and bills and starving him of remittances. Ballard contended that borrowing "would be a considerable saving to us" if Franklin could remit liquid assets before Ballard's loans came due. The magic 4 percent eluded the firm. "I have been in debt ever since last fall," Ballard complained, "and at no time less than eleven thousand dollars and now upwards of twenty and was at no time able to pay my debts without stoping business."[25] A protested bill or other bad debt could spike the cost of borrowing.

Franklin sent reassurances and blamed President Andrew Jackson's veto of the Second Bank recharter bill as the reason his remittances continued to be anemic. John Armfield in Alexandria intervened, drawing four bills of exchange on Franklin and Armfield in New Orleans totaling $20,000, in September, October, and November 1832, for which his bank took a 3 percent discount. He sent the proceeds to Ballard in Richmond to cover expenses. That costly move forced Franklin to discount long paper and to seek additional commercial credit.[26] Armfield's rebuke to Franklin's financing scheme sent the firm into Edmond Forstall's financial network.

The Union Bank of Louisiana gave Franklin and Armfield an efficient means of remitting the proceeds of slave sales. It extended credit and provided financial services that permitted the firm to grow swiftly and less painfully than before. The Union Bank had a correspondent tie with the Merchants' Bank of New York, which resulted from the way its bonds were marketed by Baring Brothers and Company of London and its New York affiliate, Prime, Ward, King, and Company. The Union Bank was an attractive institution, the newest and best-capitalized bank in New Orleans. As part of its deal with Baring Brothers, the Union Bank received a £40,000 line of credit for its exchange business. Like other commercial customers, Franklin sought some of that money by discounting bills at the Union Bank and securing short-term credit. The Louisiana slave market was closed to interstate traders, but credit was unbounded. While Franklin was searching for an entrée, the Union Bank made it possible for Sam Watts's owners to draw equity out of his body. Forstall borrowed using as collateral Watts and other personal and real property. Franklin entered the Union Bank through a side door. He was a business insider but was not among New Orleans's elite. Banks were cozy hives of commercial patronage, and Franklin stood just outside Forstall's circle.

To get access to Union Bank services, Franklin cultivated a relationship with Richard L. Booker, cashier of the Bank of Louisiana. Booker acted as his financial agent, and in late December 1832 Franklin sent Ballard a Union Bank draft for $15,000, payable at the Merchants' Bank of New York, obtained by Booker.

Franklin continued to buy other financial instruments, but through Booker he cultivated the Union Bank's confidence in him. Booker, "at the request of Mr. I. Franklin," sent Ballard a $10,000 check in April 1833, issued by the Union Bank of Louisiana, again payable at the Merchants' Bank of New York. That check was signed by J. B. Perrault, a cashier, in favor of Rice Ballard, and passed through Booker's hands. Ballard cashed it to buy captives in Virginia. As Franklin became a regular customer of the Union Bank, it became his financial savior. "I can get money when no other trader can obtain a dollar," Franklin crowed during a national credit crisis the following year.[27] Money flowed again to the firm's purchasing branches, and while Franklin extended credit to buyers and integrated the firm into commercial New Orleans, John Armfield incorporated a shipping business.

The firm's large and growing sales volumes required a nimble and capacious supply chain, and John Armfield was in charge of it. Relying on existing merchant voyages was insufficient to transport hundreds of captives a month during the sales season, which ran from late summer to late spring. Armfield strove to meet that demand. Like Isaac Franklin, Armfield was a Jacksonian entrepreneur. Armfield was born in North Carolina in 1797, descended from English Quakers. The crossroads markets and riverside cities he traveled as a young man were, like Ishmael's whale ship, his college and university. He met Franklin while driving a stagecoach. Franklin introduced Armfield to his niece Martha Franklin, and the two were soon married. Armfield could be affable and charming. He disarmed a

Duplicate Union Bank of Louisiana draft, April 18, 1833, payable at the Merchants Bank of New York in the amount of $10,000 in favor of Rice C. Ballard (Subseries 1.1, folder 11, scan 5, Rice C. Ballard Papers #4850, Southern Historical Collection, Wilson Library, University of North Carolina at Chapel Hill)

New England abolitionist when the latter arrived at his smart Alexandria house and private jail in the 1830s. The visitor found him "a man of fine personal appearance, and of engaging and graceful manners." Others could scarcely understand his Appalachian twang and ridiculed his peculiar appearance. An English visitor characterized Armfield as "a queer tall animal about forty years old, with dark hair cut round as if he were a Methodist preacher, immense black whiskers, a physiognomy not without one or two tolerable features, but singularly sharp, and not a little piratical and repulsive." Armfield would have flinched at that description. For one thing, he was Episcopalian.[28]

Armfield and Franklin excelled in the practical business school of the interstate trade, learning intuitively what others would formalize as basic economic regularities: bad money drives out good money, comparative advantage derives from specialization, and economizing involves maximizing profits for a certain cost and minimizing costs for a certain profit. Armfield applied similar principles to his Alexandria purchasing and shipping agency. He ran the firm's main jail there and delved into public relations. The jail was a brick compound in the back of a dwelling house on Duke Street. Armfield or one of his agents greeted visitors with public relations bromides and a glass of free wine with which to wash them down. He invited visitors to tour the compound, segregated by sex, featuring a hospital and a tailor's shop, which supplied each captive with a suit of clothes to take to the point of sale. Armfield had an eye for detail, a virtue in the shipping business.[29]

Armfield faced a steep learning curve, but his stagecoach background served the firm well. Instead of buying spare space aboard existing merchant voyages, he chartered ships for the firm's growing human cargoes and sold unused space to competitors. Slave traders had long consigned captives to merchant voyages along coastal routes. Such ships were floating engines of slavery's capitalism, but they were insufficient to transport large consignments with the regularity that Franklin and Armfield demanded. Shippers had their own schedules, and enslavers who needed captives delivered on time lost money waiting in port while the ship operator filled available cargo space. That meant unpredictability, a weak link in the supply chain, and a potential drag on sales should a ship arrive late or not at all. At seventeen to twenty dollars per captive, that was an expensive proposition, especially if compounded by twenty-five-cent-a-day jail fees. In October 1828 Armfield hired the 155-ton coastal trading vessel *United States,* which had carried enslaved people as cargo before. It sailed from Alexandria with 149 captives. Armfield also advertised for passage aboard the ship *Jefferson* of Norfolk. It was a more capacious oceangoing ship and had delivered cotton to Liverpool. The *Jefferson* had also completed a slaving voyage. By the time it sailed, however, Armfield had few company-owned captives to send, and most involuntary passengers aboard the *Jefferson* were consigned by other enslavers.[30]

In 1830 Armfield started a packet line, inaugurating it with the most notorious slaver in the Chesapeake. That spring he chartered the *James Monroe* of Norfolk, a ship that had landed well over a thousand captives in New Orleans on dozens of passages. Captives were often more tightly packed than in the closing years of the transatlantic slave trade to North America. Armfield advertised the ship as a "packet schooner," which would sail from Alexandria instead of Norfolk on schedule. Its seasoned skipper, Walter Bush, sailed within a day of the advertised departure. In late February 1831 Franklin and Armfield again advertised the *James Monroe* as a "packet" that would depart Alexandria in early March.[31] But there were problems for the new slave shipping line.

As the *James Monroe* prepared to sail with 112 captives, Louisiana threatened to tighten restrictions on imported bondspersons. The state legislature debated curtailing slave imports by nonresidents when Franklin lobbied legislators. "I will have a petition tomorrow before the house for our relief," he wrote in February 1831. Louisiana legislators understood planters' demands for slaves but were not swayed. Franklin instructed Armfield to "be sure to have [the captives] cleared out for Natchez Mississippi [and file] your bills of lading for that place." If the market suddenly closed, Armfield had a contingency plan. Ships would be towed by steam tugs forty or fifty miles upriver past New Orleans and the captives would be transferred to steamboats bound for Natchez. Louisiana buyers could follow the coffles to Mississippi and return to Louisiana with their legal purchases.[32] Armfield was already in the business of navigating Louisiana's restrictions. Beginning in 1829 the state had required that slaves eleven years of age and older have certificates of good character signed by two freeholders or property owners of the county from which the bondsperson was taken. Enslaved persons younger than eleven were not admitted without mothers accompanying them. Penalties for noncompliance were stiff.

Armfield spied a way to evade Louisiana's certificate requirements. He printed bogus bills of sale that included boilerplate language. "Everything" on preprinted forms the firm ordered, Armfield contended, was "complete with the exception of the name of the purchaser and price of the negro which is left blank." After paying an agent to impersonate a justice of the peace and certify that the captive in question was not a criminal and possessed a good character, Armfield bribed authorities to ratify the forgery. "The clerk [of the court] certified that this man is a justice of the peace and a hell of a fellow under his hand and the seal of the clerk's office," he grinned. Armfield promised that "there will be no difficulty of getting a *load* of them made by paying those damnd rascals for making of them."[33] Armfield sulked about the trouble and expense of evading restrictions, but logistical problems grabbed his attention.

Chartered ships could not keep up with the firm's demand. Rice Ballard regularly made use of Norfolk shipping merchants, including the owners and operators of the *Industry*, which transported Sam Watts. But relying on competitors was expensive. Armfield called one allied shipping merchant "a Damnd Rascall" but conceded that the man had "good vesells that are well known in NOrleans." Ballard paid about $16.50 per person "freight" aboard that merchant's 147-ton brigantine *Ajax* in February 1832, along with other expenses. That was over $750 in revenue that the firm might have captured for themselves instead.[34] Such considerations sent them looking for their own vessel far from the Chesapeake Bay.

Anyone traveling the Connecticut River near Haddam in the spring of 1831 could witness the construction of an American slave ship. Hezekiah Child's shipyard was alive with activity. As spring trees bloomed workers laid the keel for the *Tribune* in the yard at Higganum Landing, about three miles upriver from Haddam and nearly eight miles downstream from Middletown, on the west bank of the river. Passersby could observe in a clearing a large cradle that held its skeletal structure. The shallow river limited the size of Child's ships, but the shipyard was situated strategically near abundant New England timber. The sawmills, smithies, and other collateral industries that served local shipbuilding were also nearby. The yard contained a blacksmith's shop, a steam box for bending wood, and a warehouse. The *Tribune*, perhaps an oblique reference to Andrew Jackson, who later identified himself as "a tribune of the people," was a well-built ship.[35]

Yankee workmen with generations of expertise joined the ship's ribs. If constructed like others of Child's ships, the *Tribune* was custom-built for Franklin and Armfield. Child sourced his pitch, oakum, rope, sails, anchors, castings, nails, chains, and bolts from local contractors. The air smelled of sawdust and the ground was littered with it. Workers sawed chestnut for the keel, white oak for beams, and white pine for covering and masts. As the *Tribune* reached completion, skilled caulkers pounded oakum into spaces between boards in the hull to seal it. A carpenter crafted a billet head for the bow. Child's workers fastened the bends with copper and sheathed the hull with copper as well, which protected the vessel from shipworms, small mollusks that ate holes in wood.[36]

Haddam shipbuilders had contributed ships to the domestic slave trade before. The Norfolk shipping merchant and "Rascall" to whom Armfield reluctantly consigned captives had two ships named *Ajax*. Both carried captives, and one was built in 1828 in East Haddam. The Child Shipyard had contributed at least one ship to the coastal slave trade by the time Franklin and Armfield ordered the *Tribune*. In 1815 James Kelley Child finished the 152-ton brig *Intelligence*, which was one of the most active slavers sailing from Baltimore in the 1820s.[37]

The *Tribune* was built for stability and capacity rather than for speed. Franklin and Armfield's brigantine was eighty feet long and thirty-three feet three inches wide, and its interior height was ten feet. Like all brigs, the ship launched into the Connecticut River in 1831 had two masts, square-rigged with several sails each. It had one deck and a square stern to maximize capacity. It was built to the dimensions of a coastal cargo vessel, wider and deeper than contemporary brigantines carrying the transatlantic slave trade. Unlike transatlantic slavers, it did not have to outrun British naval vessels. Child and his workers fitted the *Tribune* with modern conveniences, including gas lamps and a cookstove in the galley. Armfield outfitted it with two guns and staffed it with a crew of eight. Its most distinctive features may have been added after delivery: a bulkhead separating fore and aft compartments and shelves built to warehouse people belowdecks. This maritime architecture mirrored that of ships plying the transatlantic slave trade, where captives were packed like cordwood. The 161-ton *Tribune* was designed to hold 180 captives at about thirty-six cubic feet of space per captive, or the size of a large desk.[38]

At any given time Franklin and Armfield transported the majority of bondspersons from the Chesapeake to New Orleans. In one week in December 1831, the *Tribune* and *United States* were responsible for unloading over three-quarters of the slaves arriving in New Orleans, 291 of 371 landed. Franklin reported that in Natchez there were 400 captives on the market, including seventy company slaves landed from the *Tribune*.[39]

Armfield operated a shipping business with Yankee shrewdness, and the *Tribune* quickly paid for itself. Ballard paid Franklin and Armfield $17 per person for passage of twenty-five slaves aboard it in October 1831, about $14.50 per slave for "freight" that November, and just over $16.50 per captive in March 1832. At an average of sixteen dollars per person, Franklin and Armfield could cover the cost of the ship in two seasons, counting mariners' wages and related expenses. There were competitive advantages, too. When his rivals consigned captives, John Armfield also got an inside view of their numbers, ages, and genders, and he could tell competitors' expectations and means. Yet the firm still had to buy river transportation between New Orleans and Natchez. After Louisiana closed its slave market in 1832, Ballard paid $4.17 per captive to embark captives aboard a steamboat to Natchez.[40] Franklin's financing company and Armfield's shipping concern boosted sales volume, and the firm expanded its territory.

Armfield advanced into the northern Maryland slave market and undercut Austin Woolfolk. He reported in March 1832, "We are purchasing at Baltimore" and paying low prices, seizing a competitive advantage through the network that efficiently funneled captives out of the Chesapeake. "Woolfolk done us a great kindness when he caused us to go into that market," Armfield gloated; "we have got all the jailers and some of his agents in our employ I will go in there in a few days and establish a house (*keep dark*)[.] I intend to push the byers in that market this year his standing (Woolfolk's) is verry bad." That was Woolfolk's own fault, Armfield contended, since the trader had "rob[b]ed the people." Franklin's nephew James Purvis arrived to manage the branch. Baltimore agents marched bondspeople to Alexandria, where Armfield crammed them aboard the *Tribune* and charter vessels. In March 1832 Armfield embarked 222 souls aboard the *Tribune*, including sixteen-year-old Martha Sweart. She and the others had a tight twenty-nine cubic feet of cargo space each, the size of a twenty-first-century American washing machine. So many bodies crowded together caused body heat to rise like steam from deck hatches on a cold March night in the Atlantic Ocean. Overcrowding had unintended but foreseeable results. Measles joined the captives' miseries.[41]

James R. Franklin was largely responsible for the firm's sales venue outside Natchez and the slave production line it housed. Franklin ramped up production at the Forks of the Road, and he indulged in the fantasies the firm conjured for customers. Enslaved Americans had few if any legal protections, but in established neighborhoods many eked out informal safeguards in the persons of patrons. They built status and participated in networks, and some even murdered their abusers when the alternatives were hopeless. Slaving stripped bondspersons of even informal protections, and the young individuals Franklin and Armfield bought and sold were vulnerable, particularly females. In March 1832 Franklin awaited the captives shipped on the *Tribune* and wrote to Ballard that "only about 18 of your negroes [remain] on hand" at the Forks of the Road market. Franklin complained that prices were falling slightly and "we anticipate tolerably tough times this spring *for one eyed men*." His aggressive male sexuality was close on a continuum with market exploitation.[42]

Franklin bragged to his partner about his predation but could not separate sexual innuendo from financial imagery. "I have seen a handsome girl since I left Va that would climb higher hills & go further to accomplish her designs than any girl to the north," he crowed, "& she is not to[o] apt to leave or loose *her gold.* & the reason is because she carries her funds in her lovers purse or in Bank." Franklin equated financial intercourse with female genital penetration. His victim was eighteen-year-old Caroline Brown. She stood just over five feet tall and was labeled "nearly white" on the *Tribune's* slave manifest. Armfield was Franklin's pimp as well as his partner, and Brown had endured Franklin's rape and abuse for five months. "To my certain knowledge she has been used & that smartly by a one eyed man about my size and age, *excuse my foolishness,*" Franklin continued coyly. "In short I shall do the best with & for the fancy white maid & excellent cook that I can." Brown's reactions were not recorded. "All the negroes we have sold commanded fair prices," Franklin reported, as if buttoning his trousers and returning to other business.[43]

The captives who had reached the Forks of the Road compound early that March "appear to be in good health but very ragged & dirty," Franklin reported. "I am using all exertions to get them dressed" and suitable for sale. Much like merchants offering bales of fair versus middling or ordinary cotton, Franklin graded slaves according to his commercial imagination and sold them accordingly. "I shall open my fancy stock of Wool & Ivory early in the morning," he added, reducing captives to crude caricatures of hair and teeth.[44] Slave traders acted as amateur cosmetologists. They greased skin to make it shiny. They pulled gray hairs and dyed others. They scrubbed and scoured, all the while seeking ways to sell the bodies fatigued and injured by their ordeals. Franklin denominated top and middling grades of slave and changed their packaging to suit the type. That innovation was made possible by the volume of sales and the quotidian workings of the firm's supply chain.

The *Tribune* landed with a transatlantic-sized consignment of captives in early April, and Isaac Franklin embarked them on a steamer to Natchez. After they marched a mile from the steamboat landing to the Forks of the Road compound, James Franklin got to work processing his human wares. But Armfield's having packed the captives so tightly aboard the *Tribune* proved shortsighted. Of the ninety or so captives remaining at the Forks of the Road three weeks after the *Tribune* landed at New Orleans, James Franklin reported, "we have lost a great many sick, owing to the measles & having our negroes crowded in the Brig." One man had died, "an old diseas'd man from Alexa[ndria]," he grumbled.[45]

Franklin welcomed customers and sold slaves. In mid-May he wrote to Ballard that the firm had about sixty captives unsold, including twenty-six belonging to Ballard, and "sales [are] very slow." In the lull, Franklin returned to boasting of his sexual predations. "The *fair maid* Martha is still on hand," he wrote. "I think the chance to sell her . . . as well as our white Caroline is very bad," he added with a wink. Caroline Brown was still incarcerated there.

Perhaps she befriended her fellow captive Martha Sweart, Franklin's *"fair maid Martha."* Sweart was sixteen years old and had been purchased by Ballard's central Virginia agent, Andrew Grimm, that February. After being carted to Richmond, jailed, and transported by steamboat down the James River to Norfolk, Sweart was packed aboard the *Tribune.* She stood five feet two inches tall and was listed as yellow both in Ballard's accounts and on the slave manifest. Isaac Franklin later referred to her as Ballard's "Charlottesvill[e] maid."[46] It was a long way from that central Virginia crossroads town of fewer than one thousand residents. Ballard sized her up for sexual exploitation and shuttled her to James Franklin. Subject to violence, intimidation, emotional manipulation, hopelessness, and trauma, Sweart was confined and probably isolated while the partners enacted fantasies of domination. There were no outsiders to appeal to, and her former shipmates disappeared as they were sold or died.

Microbes were a byproduct of the firm's supply chain. Cholera joined cotton and credit as linkages among Natchez, New York, and London. In 1832 Londoners and New Yorkers suffered cholera epidemics. What Isaac Franklin termed the "Asiattick cholera . . . killed a first rate man" in December 1832 at the Forks of the Road compound. To preserve as much of the value of the other captives as he could, Franklin ordered that the bodies be disposed of secretly. Franklin confessed to Ballard, "The way we send out Dead negroes at night and keep Dark is a sin." That was about as close to a moral self-examination as Franklin submitted his enterprise to. The firm was "so hard now for money," Franklin grumbled, that he needed to keep selling. There was no inexpensive way to reorganize the supply chain to prevent outbreaks of measles or cholera, and he decided that deaths and secret burials were tolerable so long as sales were not interrupted. He demanded that Ballard send more adult bondspersons, quipping that "your little slim assed girls and boys are entirely out of the way [of] demand."[47]

To meet that growing demand, the firm expanded its fleet. In 1833 the *Tribune* was in near-constant motion, and the firm supplemented it with hired vessels. Armfield called again on the shipbuilders of Haddam, Connecticut, and bought another new vessel, the *Uncas.* The 155-ton, two-masted brig cost $7,250 and was a foot shorter and narrower than the *Tribune.* Connecticut shipwrights and sailmakers, caulkers, and carpenters had reason to applaud the assiduity of Isaac Franklin and John Armfield. The word *Uncas* was associated with the Connecticut River Valley's imagined past, and to most Americans in the 1830s the name conjured the title character in James Fenimore Cooper's immensely popular *Last of the Mohicans: A Narrative of 1757* (1826). The ship's trade carried echoes of the novel's themes, including clashes of cultures, races, and religions on the Western frontier. The *Uncas* was delivered to New York City in late

September 1833. With the fifty dollars Ballard paid him in Norfolk, the *Uncas's* master, William Smith, sailed for New Orleans in late October with nearly one hundred captives. With the *Uncas*, the firm could always have a ship sailing during the slave-selling season, and Armfield advertised his line of "PACKETS" plying slaving routes. He needed help from his partner Ballard to keep the ship- ping concern thriving. In the fall of 1833 Ballard bought a one-third interest in the *Uncas* and contributed to paying skippers of the firm's ships.[48]

Armfield's Alexandria enterprise was so successful that he robbed Baltimore shipping merchants of a majority of their business transporting captives. Between 1831 and 1840 Baltimore's saltwater slave traffic to New Orleans dropped by over half compared to that of 1821–30. It was not that Baltimore's maritime trade declined. Its domestic exports grew by over 13 percent (while foreign exports fell) during the 1830s. More ships were leaving Baltimore for domestic destinations, but they were not carrying as many slaves. Instead, Franklin and Armfield diverted slave traffic through the much smaller port of Alexandria in the District of Columbia.

Armfield inadvertently embarrassed national legislators and gave abolitionists a dramatic example of republican hypocrisy. Caravans of captives from Baltimore and elsewhere marched in front of the U.S. Capitol, which was on the main road (now U.S. Route 1) leading to the Potomac River Bridge and the road to Alexandria. Benjamin Lundy's *Genius of Universal Emancipation* reported a traffic jam in 1830 in which President Jackson and an entourage of cabinet secre- taries marched to the Capitol, encountering "another kind of procession [which] was marching the other way, and that consisted of colored human beings hand- cuffed in pairs, and driven along by what had the appearance of a man on a horse!" The national slave trade could not have had a more telling tableau. It was an age in which dirt roads passed through city centers and long before bypasses and interstate highways diverted traffic. The week before "a *drove* consisting of males and females chained in couples," Lundy reported, "starting from Robey's tavern on foot, for Alexandria, where, with others, they are to embark aboard a slave-ship in waiting to convey them to the South." Seeing so many chained Americans walking toward the Potomac River scandalized citi- zens and astonished visitors who arrived to witness the spectacle. Petitioners like Henry B. Stanton and John Greenleaf Whittier demanded that Congress halt domestic slave traffic. In 1839 Stanton argued that "the internal slave trade is the great jugular vein of slavery; and if Congress will take the same weapon with which they cut off the foreign trade, and cut this vein, slavery would die of starva- tion in the southern, and of apoplexy in the northern slave states."[49]

As it innovated in finance and transportation, Franklin and Armfield became an engine of family wreckage and social disruption. What one contemporary critic called "the Slave-Factory of Franklin & Armfield" produced captives by disarticulating families. From purchase to sale, each person processed through production units was under the authority of an agent of the firm, and the bewildering network of jails and conveyances isolated and distanced bondspeople from loved ones and former lives. Rice Ballard's paid agents included James G. Blakey, Andrew Grimm, Silas Omohundro, and Benjamin Parks. They scoured the backcountry for young, fit, able, and salable enslaved people. Ballard handed the twenty-five-year-old Omohundro $500 for slaves in 1833. Ballard forwarded the Orange County resident Blakey $33,000 from the spring of 1833 to January 1834, mostly in $1,000 increments, "to be laid out in negroes or returned on demand." The forty-year-old Blakey bought sixty-one captives at an average cost of about $465 and returned Ballard over $4,000. Ballard paid agents a fixed fee or commission of $10 per captive, which removed incentives to bid too high in order to fill coffles. Ten dollars bought thirty gallons of whiskey or eleven pounds of domestic sugar. For that sum, agents ripped captives from their families, deflecting the glares, protests, and cries of loved ones as they struggled to save their sons and daughters, husbands and wives, uncles and aunts, or cousins from strangers' clutches.[50]

Riding a meandering trail through central Virginia, Ballard's agent Andrew Grimm could at first be mistaken for a Methodist circuit rider, his solitary figure surveying and scrutinizing the human landscape. But slave traders perverted the gospel of fishing for men. Grimm's shadow fell on the front yards of courthouses where enslaved people were cried off on court days. Like most agents, Grimm had an enduring relationship with the firm and worked also for its Fredericksburg partner, Samuel Alsop. In sight of the Blue Ridge Mountains, Grimm rode along post roads and forded streams and rivers that irrigated the bountiful land. In the fall of 1832 Ballard paid Grimm twenty dollars for a new saddle. Ballard's agents bid in cash and delivered to Ballard young captives such as eighteen-year-old Matilda Graves, twenty-one-year-old Ann Harris, seventeen-year-old Martha A. Hawkins, and fourteen-year-old Peter Teagle. Grimm bought them early in 1833.[51]

Graves, Harris, Hawkins, and Teagle were probably unprepared for the thousand-mile odyssey through Franklin and Armfield's factory. The shape of their future prospects was Grimm. After he handed banknotes for title to their bodies, he tore them from family, friends, and the central Virginia landscape of tall trees, gentle foothills, fields of corn, wheat, and tobacco, and orchards of fruit. In that bucolic atmosphere, slavery's yoke was already heavy. Most enslaved people slogged through a series of social crises. If typical, each of Grimm's purchases had undergone slavery's humiliations and its hard-edged violence, awakening at a young age to psychological and spiritual slings and arrows hurled at children. Despite all, the young people he force-marched east in the winter of 1833 had learned resiliency and forged close ties with a network of family and friends, each as strong as it was unstable. All had witnessed the disappearance of loved ones into the coffles of slave traders and caravans of migrating slaveholders.[52] It was now their turn.

Graves, Harris, Hawkins, and Teagle learned one another's stories as they walked through the winter landscape and bivouacked along the roads leading to Richmond. It was bitterly cold in early March, and the hard dirt roads were lined with snow. Their furtive conversations and anguish can merely be guessed at. Grimm probably did not relish his position either. He worked on commission and served at Ballard's pleasure. In 1831 he had earned $350 and the previous year $300, a handsome wage. But lacking his own capital, Grimm could but dream of being his own boss.[53]

Entering Richmond, the captives beheld the largest city they had probably ever seen. Its smells, sights, and sounds were unfamiliar. A cloud of coal and wood smoke hovered above the rows of wooden houses, brick churches, and factories on a still winter morning. The prominent feature as one approached from the northwest was the Greek Revival capitol overlooking the James River to the southwest. The white building was already a venerable landmark after four decades of housing the legislature. Smoke blended in the streets with smells like fried bacon, baked bread, and earthy notes of manure and human waste. Carts, wagons, and carriages rutted the muddy streets, and crowds of residents passed to and fro. Over half the city's residents were nonwhite. Two in five Richmonders were enslaved. Anguished understandings of the coffle members' ordeals must have registered on some of those faces. Graves, Harris, Hawkins, and Teagle arrived on a Monday in mid-March. The town of 16,000 was bustling. A new tobacco warehouse and a grocery store had just opened, and merchants were hawking spring goods. Conversations included talk of banking and politics, the crisis converging on the Second Bank of the United States and the unfolding Nullification Crisis in South Carolina. Andrew Jackson had been re-inaugurated as president two weeks before.[54] Such murmurs probably passed over the disoriented captives as prattling irrelevancies to their immediate concerns. Their sore, cracked, and chilled feet ached for rest after marching the better part of a hundred miles through the winter.

When they reached Ballard's jail, they beheld their owner, a man with a distinct eastern Virginia accent. His appraising eyes scoured their bodies, lingering perhaps over the females. As Grimm settled his accounts with his employer, the captives were confined with scores of others in Ballard's cells. As Graves, Harris, Hawkins, and Teagle settled in for the night or two they spent in his Richmond jail, they noticed most of the eighty or so fellow inmates in Ballard's crowded cells were in their late teens and early twenties. If they could study his ledger they would learn that eighteen years was the median age of the 350 captives whose ages Ballard recorded in the early 1830s. Of 437 slave purchases he recorded, covering voyages in 1831 through 1833, the median price was $350. Buyers wanted young people and individuals rather than family groups. Like his colleague John Armfield in Alexandria, Ballard supplied captives with suits of new clothes or dresses, shoes, hats, and tinware items like cups and spoons. They ate cheap food offered in abundant portions, but the clothes were for later. Whatever rags the captives arrived wearing would have to continue to hang on their backs until they reached Natchez. Company policy also required them to be inoculated against smallpox, which was a directive Ballard had difficulty carrying out.[55]

The journey so far had been one of plodding dread, but the vessels on which they embarked were as exhilarating as they were forbidding. Driving them down to the muddy banks of the James River, Ballard embarked his eighty-five captives on a steamboat to Norfolk. The vessel Graves, Harris, Hawkins, and Teagle boarded along with the eighty-one other captives must have seemed odd, even diabolical. The 264-ton *Potomac's* hull was shaped like other sailing vessels docked below the falls of the James, but it had no masts, yards, or sails, just a long chimney thrusting up from its deck and held in place by shrouds. As gray smoke belched up the chimney, unearthly noises reverberated in the bowels of the ship. Side-wheels began to flap against the muddy water. That was the ordinary sound of business to the *Potomac's* captain and crew. The boat had steamed from Alexandria the same day the *Tribune* sailed with Armfield's captives aboard. It touched at Norfolk before steaming up the James to Richmond. It was now retracing its route down the James and up the Potomac River on its return to Alexandria by way of Norfolk.[56]

Ballard hurried his coffle to Norfolk. The *Tribune's* master, Isaac Staples, had anchored on the day Grimm delivered his captives to Richmond. When the *Potomac* reached Norfolk, Ballard disembarked his coffle and hastened them aboard the *Tribune*, which placed them in the care of another paid employee of the enterprise. Staples was an old hand at the saltwater slave trade and had weathered the wreck of the slave ship *Comet* before taking the *Tribune's* helm. The *Comet* had run aground on a reef ten miles off Abaco in the northern Bahamas in 1831. Aboard Staples's foundering brig were 164 captives, along with passengers, who were rescued and taken to Nassau. Some of the captives escaped. Authorities refused to return them, which sparked an international incident. As Graves, Harris, Hawkins, and Teagle boarded the ship, they beheld the shipmaster who would be their master for the next three weeks. Below deck they could inspect the Yankee craftsmanship of the vessel that would take them far from their homeland. On March 21 Teagle and his new shipmates sailed from Hampton Roads. Seasickness compounded the psychic strain of dislocations in a floating prison. Back in Richmond, Ballard wet his pen in ink and recorded $1,326 "freight" for the coffle of eighty-five, or $15.60 per person.[57]

If he had not been before, Teagle was separated from Graves, Harris, and Hawkins aboard the *Tribune*. Franklin and Armfield had seen that the brig contained separate areas for males and females. A visitor to the ship in Alexandria reported that "the hold is appropriated to the slaves, and is divided into two apartments." That maritime architecture was not dissimilar to that of similarly sized transatlantic slavers. "The after-hold will carry about 80 women, and the other about 100 men," the visitor reported. Armfield economized on security by fortifying parts of the ship with the most volatile captives, adult males. "On either side [of the hold]," the *Tribune*'s visitor reported, "were two platforms running the whole length, one raised a few inches, and the other about half way up to the deck." Those amounted to shelves for human merchandise, hard platforms for sleeping. "They were about 5 1/2 or 6 feet deep." "On them they lie as close as they can stow away."[58] Segregation was supposed to prevent pregnancies on the passage, but it gave shipmasters, slave traders, and officers access to women and girls unsupervised by male captives. Any spouses or brothers and sisters who had managed to avoid separation before would be out of touch belowdecks. Staples pushed the ship, which arrived in New Orleans early in April.

With a population three times the size of Richmond, New Orleans must have been correspondingly more confusing to the *Tribune*'s inmates. City residents spoke loudly in strange dialects and unfamiliar languages. The humid air intensified city smells. The dark figure whose name was uttered by their captors appeared. Isaac Franklin met the ship and disembarked the captives. An English visitor witnessing the process remarked, "I have seen more than a hundred [captives] landing from a brig, on the Levée, in New-Orleans, in fine condition, looking as lively and hearty as though a sea voyage agreed well with them."[59] It must have been some small relief to be off the ship. After a stopover in yet another jail they found themselves on another steamer.

Teagle and the others had sailed up the Mississippi River for days aboard ship, but the steamer was noisier and the atmosphere full of strange sights and smells. On a river steamer, slave traders' bondspersons were confined aboard the main deck. Poorer and rowdier passengers populated the deck along with a cornu-copia of goods in barrels and boxes. As Harris, Hawkins, and Graves stared at the shoreline, sugarcane fields gave way to cotton fields visible amid trees' new leaves. Gangs of enslaved workers could be seen preparing them for planting. Spring was in bloom, and the banks of the Mississippi must have held a strange allure as the steamboat pounded against the river current. Slaves were not merely in the fields. African-descended workers abounded on steamers, filling the lowest rungs of workers. If typical, the Virginia captives would have witnessed enslaved men gathering wood from the decks to stoke the furnace fires used to produce the steam that powered the engine. Black workers waited on white passengers, and the polyglot assortment of humanity traveling on the main deck was famously fond of cards, tobacco, alcohol, strong words, and violence.[60]

After nearly three days aboard the steamer, the captives arrived at Natchez-under-the-Hill, the steamboat landing beneath a town of just under three thou-sand residents. They stepped onto the muddy banks of another strange city. Around the time they landed, a local newspaper printed South Carolina's Senator John C. Calhoun's address to Congress advocating a constitutional theory of concurrent majority. It was an overwrought protest to Calhoun's political margin-alization and his state's imagined woes. In the pages of the *Natchez Courier* the speech and the Nullification Crisis stirred lively debate concerning the political organization of the federal union. More urgent was whether Mississippi's state office candidates stood with Calhoun or the immensely popular president, Andrew Jackson. The Agricultural Bank of Mississippi was subscribing shares and the Planters' Bank announced a 4.5 percent dividend on its capital stock for the preceding six months.[61] The credit business was blossoming creditably, and slavery was at the center of much of that activity. But if Franklin's captives heard bits of townspeople's conversations touching on those issues, it is likely they meant little to the young people forced to march a mile or so east of town to a compound straddling two roads. There they encountered James Franklin and his agents, including Samuel Johnson.

Once again, the captives were subject to the scanning squints, groping hands, and the hot breath of men assessing their bodies. As they arrived at Forks of the Road, another ordeal began. Johnson was a paid manager or overseer of the place where they would be cleaned, dressed, and compelled to participate in their sales. They were given a script in a perverse theater and forced to act the part of biddable chattel. At the Forks of the Road, the English visitor Joseph Ingraham and his companion arrived to view the spectacle. They "left [their] horses in charge of a neatly dressed yellow boy belonging to the establishment," and entered "through a wide gate into a narrow court-yard, partially enclosed by low buildings." There the visitors beheld "a line of negroes, commencing at the entrance with the tallest, who was not more than five feet eight or nine inches in height . . . down to a little fellow about ten years of age, extended in a semi-circle around the right side of the yard," about forty total. "Each was dressed in the usual uniform of slaves, when in market," Ingraham remembered, "consisting of a fashionably shaped, black fur hat, roundabout and trowsers of coarse corduroy velvet," besides "good vests, strong shoes, and white cotton shirts." The outfits, which the captives had toted from Virginia, reminded him of clothes worn by Irish immigrant laborers.[62]

The Forks of the Road sales venue embodied some of the sales principles department store chains would formalize early in the twentieth century. Customers entered a sales environment utterly manipulated to sell merchandise. The raiment was not meant to clothe or protect the captives themselves but to package them. "This dress they lay aside after they are sold, or wear out as soon as may be," Ingraham reported, because those who suffered the humiliation of sale "[dislike] to retain the indication of . . . having recently been in the market." As Ingraham observed buyers inspecting the human goods, the male captives stood "perfectly still," hats in hands, clutched by their sides, arms downward "while some gentlemen were passing from one to another examining for the purpose of buying."[63]

As they had been aboard the ships, Franklin and Armfield segregated males and females in their sales venues. "Opposite the line of males was also a line of females," Ingraham reported, "extended along the left side of the court." Twenty or so were "dressed in neat calico frocks, white aprons and capes, and fancy kerchiefs, tied in a mode peculiar to the negress, upon their heads." Ingraham called their appearance "extremely neat and 'tidy,'" but he recalled, "They could not be disciplined to the grave silence observed by the males, but were constantly laughing and chattering with each other in suppressed voices, and appeared to take, generally, a livelier interest in the transactions in which all were equally concerned."[64]

Ingraham found Isaac Franklin at the head of the business, describing him as "a bachelor, and a man of gentlemanly address, as are many of these merchants, and not the ferocious, Captain Kidd looking fellows, we Yankees have been apt to imagine them." Ingraham was a good judge of what a pirate should look like. He went on to write novels such as *Lafitte: Pirate of the Gulf* (1836) and *Captain Kyd; or, The Wizard of the Sea: A Romance* (1839). Ingraham was impressed by "the immense profit they make on their merchandise," and he commented, "If any of the worshippers of Mammon earn their gold, it is the slave-dealer." He credited Franklin as "the great southern slave-merchant . . . who, for the last fifteen years, has supplied this country with two-thirds of the slaves brought into it," and who "has amassed a fortune of more than a million dollars by this traffic alone."[65] That exaggeration hints at the scale of the operation.

The firm's sales strategy was as shrewd as its supply chain was sophisticated. Franklin and Armfield packaged and sold captives offered for field and domestic work, trades, and sexual exploitation. When purchasing captives, Ballard noted skills that would be the basis of a script attached to each captive. Jane Fry was a "first rate seamstress," William Boice was a "c[oarse] carpenter, manager, &c," and Mary Anderson "speaks French." As the captives were processed through the firm's transport and sales apparatus, agents enforced a market identity on them. In 1833 Isaac Franklin informed Ballard that customers were demanding "fancy girl[s]," or female captives sold as enslaved concubines. No such women were "on hand but your girl Minerva," Franklin explained, "and she is a caution." Minerva was not cooperating in their plans to sell her as a sex slave. "I sold your fancy girl Allice for $800," Franklin reported. Eight hundred dollars approached the price of a young, strong adult male agricultural worker. Ballard had bought Allice Sparraw for $375 and Minerva Robertson for $400 earlier that year. "There are great demand for fancy maid[s]," Franklin added, explaining "that a likely girl and a good seamstress could be sold for $1000." Franklin could scarcely mention the business of selling sex slaves without mentioning his own sexual fantasies. "I was disappointed," he smirked, "in not finding your Charlottesvill[e] maid that you promised me." Martha Sweart was being traded among firm directors but was absent from Natchez.[66] Ballard had neglected to send her to the elder Franklin, who wished to take up where his nephew had left off.

In an atmosphere charged with sexual violence, Graves, Harris, and Teagle were sold as slaves in the spring of 1833. Peter Teagle went for $425, a $100 gross profit. Matilda Graves sold for $450, which was $105 more than Grimm had given for her. Ann Harris sold for $450, nearly double what Grimm had bargained for her body in central Virginia. The twenty-one-year-old too may have been wrapped in the script and clothing of would-be customers' violent sexual fantasies. All the captives' worlds had been turned upside down. The cotton landscape in which they had arrived was vastly different from their central Virginia home. All would work relentlessly, but disease killed quicker than toil. Cholera continued to claim lives in the area. Seventeen captives Ballard had bought and sent to Natchez were buried after dying in the care of Franklin and Armfield.[67]

At times, the paths Franklin and his agents trod through the American landscape were virtually littered with dead bodies. In April 1833, soon after Graves, Harris, Hawkins, and Teagle arrived, Natchez citizens discovered a ghastly crime in the shape of "the bodies of several negroes having been found in the Bayou in the rear of the block of the city, but partially buried."[68] Several of Franklin and Armfield's captives died of cholera after contracting the disease en route to Natchez, and Johnson, the firm's overseer, had buried them in the public cemetery.

When more died, Franklin sought to avoid a loss of confidence in his human wares by secretly burying their bodies in the banks of one of the local tributaries of the Mississippi River, as he had been doing sporadically for months. "The first body found was that of a negro girl apparently from 15 to 20 years of age," a widely circulated report read, "thrown into one of the gullies leading to the bayou and but partially covered over with loose dirt." Her odyssey that began in the Virginia winter ended in a terrifying sickness, painful death, and a careless covering of yellowish brown Natchez silt loam. While the coroner convened an inquest, two other bodies were unearthed. All the bodies were "without coffins of any description, and a slight rain only, would be sufficient to bring them into view."[69]

Moonlight burials were shoddy affairs. Local outrage was ignited "on the discovery of the body of a child about eight months old, put into a hole, washed out by the rains as it run into the bayou, with its head downwards, and, which was only hid from view by a few shovels full of dirt." Slave traders were suspected, especially Isaac Franklin, whose excuses the jury of the inquest found wanting. The firm's merchandizing exposed their villainy. The jury reportedly found "that the same kind of goods or clothing is now to be seen on some of Mr. Franklin's negroes, as those found on the deceased—which were compared."[70] It did not take a forensics expert to trace the clothing to Franklin and Armfield's Chesapeake suppliers. Within two days of the bodies being discovered, over eighty citizens signed a petition demanding that slave traders be expelled from the city and that shipments of captives from New Orleans cease. Among the signatories were rival slavers who complained that Franklin's bad behavior discredited the trade.

Besides moral outrage, the petitioners complained that slave traders risked the public's health. An emergency city council meeting resulted in a law passed banning slave traders. Franklin found a scapegoat in the person of his overseer, Samuel Johnson, who conveniently died of cholera a week after the scandal broke. Johnson, a Natchez newspaper reported, was "the person who was supposed to have had the principal hand in putting the bodies of the negroes . . . into the bayou."[71] The scandal helped persuade Franklin that his firm needed a new strategy.

Franklin and Armfield reorganized late in 1833. Excesses threatened its successes. John Armfield's tightly packed ships bred disease, and Isaac Franklin's loose credit choked remittances. Rice Ballard gnashed his teeth over finances, and he and the Franklins mollified discontents by pimping for one another. The Forks of the Road yielded corpses discarded at night. Yet the slaving business was lucrative and its promises seemed unbounded. The firm was raking in revenues, edging out competitors, and maintaining a supply chain while slave prices rose along with demand. Isaac Franklin attempted to impose coherence on a hybrid corporate form.

Before the rise of integrated corporations with clear borders and formal organizational structures, Franklin and Armfield behaved like a domestic interlocking partnership of merchants. But they also resembled a factory. Branch managers supervised employees, coordinated the purchasing, transportation, and supply of captives, whom the partners referred to as "stock." Franklin managed a supply chain comprising several purchasing agencies feeding captives into a shipping business while also superintending a finance company tied to the sales venue a thousand miles from where its human merchandise was sourced. His relentless yet informal cost accounting drove him to seek external financing and other ways to feed the supply chain and lower transaction costs. But the elaborate organizational amalgam and broad geographic reach made cohesion difficult, and Franklin's managerial strategy centered on his ability to tie company purse strings to purchasing managers like leashes.[72] The problem of remittances, lack of transparency, and supply chain mismanagement strained relations.

The new organization was supposed to fix those problems. John Armfield and Isaac Franklin together paid in twenty thousand dollars. Ballard and Alsop paid in twenty thousand, and the total was to be turned into "capital stock in negro slaves." Instead of a loosely interlocking partnership, the new organization tied Ballard and Alsop into the lower South financial and sales apparatus of the company. Debits and credits were on the same set of books. Franklin promised to reside in New Orleans from November until May of each year and take "money bonds bills notes & other securities" in exchange for the captives sent him overland or by sea. The new partnership was to expire in two years. Instead of issuing stock certificates, the firm treated the bodies of its captives as shares of the enterprise, limiting investment to the partners themselves. It was a brutally simple way of denominating company assets. Ballard joined Armfield as a shipping manager. The Richmond partner bought a one-third interest in the firm's brig, the *Tribune*, which the partners gave him for a reduced price of two thousand dollars. Franklin treated it as a blandishment of the reorganization, contending that "we are aware that this is less than the value but between friends it makes but little difference."[73]

While railroads were in their infancy Franklin introduced rationalized management to the slave trade. The partners' relationships to one another and to Franklin's financial apparatus became more well defined. The firm became a joint-stock partnership of James and Isaac Franklin, Samuel Alsop, John Armfield, and Rice C. Ballard. Flour, meat, and steel companies are credited with pioneering vertically integrated large-scale industrial corporations in the nineteenth century. But the corporate structure and commodity chain Isaac Franklin envisioned differed little except that the partners' capital stock and their value-added products were enslaved Americans. The goal of vertical organization was to place more responsibility on purchasing directors for the firm's finances and hold them accountable for volumes and prices of the captives they purchased. Ballard was also bound to deal exclusively with Franklin and Armfield when selling captives in the lower South. (He had dealt on the side with a Richmond colleague, Lewis A. Collier, as a way to mitigate stingy remittances.) Franklin preserved his subsidiary-like relationships with other Chesapeake buyers, including his nephew James Purvis in Baltimore. Doing so gave rise to new tensions within the firm.[74] Franklin and Armfield reorganized at a turbulent time in the republic.

National political fights over monetary policy roiled markets. In August 1833 the Second Bank's president, Nicholas Biddle, instituted policies that contracted credit dramatically by lowering the volume of its discounts on bills of exchange, expanding specie reserves, and calling in loans. That policy seemed to confirm the Second Bank's opponents' worst suspicions. Jackson retaliated. In October the administration eroded the Second Bank's power by depleting its funds, paying government obligations out of its accounts, and depositing revenues in state banks friendly to the administration.[75]

That boosted state banks' clout and credit while curtailing the Second Bank's central banking function. Taking the popular Second Bank over his knee, Jackson positioned himself as the republic's chief paternalist paddling an effete engine of foreign intrigue and domestic corruption. Biddle, the crying victim, kept kicking, choking credit and seemingly confirming the reasons for his punishment. At the same time, the Jackson administration invented a narrative of the Second Bank as embodying imagined ills of elite privilege, a power center beyond voters' control, and unholy combinations of wealth and chimerical paper money. In good Jacksonian fashion, the Bank War shrewdly appeased hard-money advocates while subtly abetting unlimited paper money issues. The resulting monetary policy rewarded friends, gave Jackson a tenacious populist appeal, and supplied a government stimulus to state banks, which encouraged speculation. Isaac Franklin applauded Jackson and cheered his party. He knew Jackson supported businessmen like him and not some mythic democratic yeomanry.

One of Franklin's Sumner County neighbors later testified that he "was a very decided man both in politics and his friendships." A Louisiana acquaintance denied that "he ever worked much in the way of electioneering, although he expressed his opinions freely, as a strong democrat."[76] While the Bank War escalated in Washington, Franklin and Armfield tested their new strategy.

Traveling down the Mississippi River in November 1833, Isaac Franklin had completed one long journey and was embarking on another. As he steamed from Natchez to New Orleans, he surveyed the orange, red, and gold leaves falling from trees on the riverbanks and stubbly cotton plants still clinging to wisps of lint. Such fields were becoming populated by African-descended Americans who knew his name and cursed it. He, Armfield, and other agents had driven a human caravan from Alexandria to the Forks of the Road compound in late summer after hammering out the firm's reorganization. Leaving James Franklin in Natchez, Isaac was traveling to meet the *Tribune*, which was carrying scores of slaves.

Returning to the metropolis must have been exhilarating. After stepping off the steamboat in New Orleans, he probably picked up the day's newspaper, walked to the public baths by the levee, and then visited a barber's shop. Franklin sought to shed the appearance of a man who had driven hundreds of unwilling migrants along hundreds of miles of dusty roads and muddy rivers. He called at countinghouses and merchants' offices, presenting bills for acceptance and scouting for market information not printed in newspapers. His most important stop was the Union Bank of Louisiana, at the corner of Royal and Customhouse streets in the commercial heart of the city. After visiting the bank and turning proceeds from slave sales into capital, Franklin stuffed two checks into envelopes addressed to his partners in Virginia and the District of Columbia. He sent Ballard a $15,000 Union Bank draft payable in New York and a draft to Armfield for $20,000. He sketched the market as it stood: "The demand for slaves [is] considerable not so much with sugar planters as with the cotton planters." Louisiana was poised to reopen its slave trade, and prices were rising again that year. "Some say," he remarked hopefully, "that there has been some sales at $1000 a head for men but . . . sales will be very slow indeed" if traders held out for that price. Franklin stopped at the Post Office.[77]

The *Tribune* was sailing up the Mississippi River when he picked up Ballard's invoice for the shipment. Franklin opened the letter and gasped. Ballard recorded that he had paid nearly $520 each, on average, and nearly $19.50 more each for their passage. Franklin barked at his partner that prices paid were "so high that you may look out for short profits," warning that "if on the contrary they are old & unserviceable they will remain on hand until next spring & our bills & funeral expenses will take off what little we make on the right hand [of the account book]."[78] Worse, Ballard was drawing bills on Franklin, an expensive alternative to waiting for remittances. A fog of despair descended on Franklin.

Walking the levees and streets of New Orleans, the soul driver did some soul-searching. Franklin relished the game but tired of the business. He was weary of infighting among directors and mawkishly assured Ballard, "I have made a slave of myself for the benefit of others." As the *Tribune* floated the last several miles upriver, Franklin paced the levee and surveyed the shipping, miles of tall masts, steamers' smokestacks, and throngs of workers, merchants, and sailors handling the goods passing through port. Mountains of cotton bales fresh from the steam press were being loaded onto ships bound for Liverpool, New York, and other distant destinations. The grass must have seemed greener on those plantations than on his patch. Burly workers rolled barrels of flour and hogsheads of tobacco into ships' bellies. As he walked along the Mississippi River digesting the day's news, Franklin heard the din of the market vendors and city residents. On the west bank of the Mississippi he caught sight of the *Tribune*, in tow with three other ships behind the steamer *Natchez* from the English Turn, about sixteen miles downriver.[79]

Landing the ship and its cargo took hours and sometimes days. After the *Tribune*'s anchor dropped in the muddy river and the ship was tied up, a ship's officer summoned the customs inspector on duty, who matched descriptions of the captives on the manifest with the human cargo. Each had to answer to the name on the manifest and conform to the physical descriptions of height, age, and skin color. Franklin ducked inside to pen a letter to his partner. "I have just time to say that the brigg is at this time coming to anchor," he scribbled to Ballard. Most of the sixty-three bondspeople were in their late teens and early twenties. After the New Orleans customs inspector was satisfied that the cargo was legal, he signed the manifest, giving permission to land the captives. "I have seen no person from the brigg but presume alls well," Franklin penned.[80]

At the prices Ballard paid, he needed more money remitted. The day after the *Tribune* landed, Franklin forwarded to Ballard another check for five thousand dollars. "These amts I hope will keep you in operation until I have an opportunity to pay the Bills that yourself & S[amuel] A[lsop] have drawn on me," he grumbled. Franklin embarked his coffle on a steamer bound for Natchez, still under a cloud. "Uncle Isaac arrived night before last without having sold one of the lot," James reported to Ballard a week after the *Tribune* landed, "& what is worst than all [the captives] had four or five cases of *cholera* since which time have lost two of *cholera*." Franklin warned that they "have some 3 or 4 cases at

Present and several complaining." While so many captives' small intestines were being wrenched by an invisible bacterium that caused violent, painful diarrhea, vomiting, and consequent dehydration and cramps, the Franklins' stomachs were turned by prospects of weak profits. His compound now choked with bodies sick and susceptible to a contagious infection, James Franklin despaired of selling slaves. After Isaac Franklin showed his nephew Ballard's invoice, the younger man had a fit. James Franklin wet his pen and administered to Ballard a verbal flogging. "We are gone suckers at these high prices in Va[!]"[81]

Nevertheless, the slave factory stepped up production. Ballard and Armfield turned the capital Franklin remitted to them into captives. At month's end Franklin steamed back to New Orleans to meet the arrival of the *Uncas*, which landed near the end of November and was towed into port along with two other ships. In anticipation of the resumption of sales in New Orleans, Franklin leased a city lot and dwelling at the corner of Esplanade and Royal streets associated with the Canonage family. He had hired Austin Woolfolk's younger brother Samuel Martin Woolfolk as his New Orleans sales agent. Woolfolk rented the compound for one hundred dollars a month. Just blocks from the levee and river, it would serve as the firm's city jail and sales venue. In Samuel Woolfolk, Franklin had hired a slaver with extensive experience. He had been the consignee of hundreds of captives sent from the Chesapeake and owned his own sales compound and jail.[82] Woolfolk knew the business rituals and would not cringe at the blistering brutality of his duties.

Despite the reorganization, Ballard was paying high prices while heartlessly cutting costs. Captives were arriving in Natchez with smallpox as well as cholera symptoms. "Uncle Isaac arrived last evening" from New Orleans with the captives from the *Uncas*, James wrote, "with all of the negroes except 9 he sold before & that man who died of *cholera* on the steam boat." Cholera was difficult to control because its etiology was unclear. Deadly smallpox was not well understood either, but a vaccine was available. The Chesapeake partners were tasked with vaccinating captives. James Franklin endeavored to sell bodies before they succumbed to disease. In mid-December Franklin wrote that the firm had "sold about 100 negroes since they arrived & I am affraid will loose ten or twelve more this week." Fifteen were sick and suffering. The business plan now had to accommodate what would later be called, in an accounting idiom, spoilage. Families of the captives would call it murder if word ever reached them. "I am afraid," Franklin wrote, that deaths "will take off all of our profits." But he gave reassurances. "I am perhaps the busiest man you ever saw & have seen & expect to see sights."[83]

At nearly all hours James Franklin and his employees were dressing up captives for sale, showing them to buyers, haggling over prices and financing, and keeping fingers crossed that cholera's grim harvest was being gathered in somewhere other than the Forks of the Road. Other traders were moving in on a sales bonanza. "We have strong opposition & have about 550 negroes in market & we do expect to have hell this spring." Cases of cholera were reported in the vicinity. "Try to reduce the prices if possible," he harangued Ballard, "& send none but the likeliest negroes."[84]

The scents and sights of the Mississippi River fatigued Isaac Franklin as he steamed down to New Orleans yet again that fall to visit his bank and meet the *Tribune*. It was his third trip down the Mississippi in six weeks. The ship was late, and Franklin passed Christmas in the city. If Guinness Breweries had been commissioning record books, the *Tribune* would have filled the entry for swiftest back-to-back slaving voyages, departing Alexandria just two days after landing. But it took nearly a month to sail back to New Orleans, over a week longer than its previous passage. "I have had a desperate season," Franklin moaned to Ballard. The firm had "lost 3 first rate fellows with cholera since which case we have lost several others and several died after they was sold," resulting in buyers demanding refunds. "I delivered," Franklin wrote, "but there appears to be some malady attending me." He was afraid he was ill. "When I left Natchez we had several sick & very doubtful whether they will manage." Shuttling back and forth between New Orleans and Natchez "is too hard for a one eyed man," he griped. "I have had to attend to all of the shipments from this place myself." "I am running backward & forwards my health has rather failed." Nevertheless, he continued to sell captives and "made for the concerns at least $100,000" by Christmas.[85]

To salve his discontents Franklin luxuriated while the city celebrated Christmas. Ministers wrung their hands and visitors recoiled at the alacrity with which New Orleaneans participated in balls, hunts, games, feasts, and parades at Christmastime. Enjoying better health, Isaac Franklin had his own reasons for celebrating. He cheered that "the Louisiana law has been repealed and only lacks the governor['s] signature to become a law." Governor André Bienvenue Roman would sign it in January. Slaveholders in Louisiana had persuaded their representatives to repeal restrictions to save them the trouble of evading them. Franklin asked Ballard to report on his ability to buy more slaves "& also if you have any means of raising funds."[86] The *Tribune* arrived two days after Christmas, but buyers were absent. Most of the captives would spend their first weeks in Louisiana under Woolfolk's care. Franklin's activity was scarcely the managerial efficiency envisioned in the firm's reorganization.

In the lull Franklin turned his attentions to female captives. "I thought that an old robber might be satisfied with two or three maids [but] I will do the best [with one]," he winked to Ballard in January 1834, hinting that he had raped a female captive. Franklin directed his partner in Richmond to send Martha Sweart, "the Fancy Girl from Charlotte[s]ville." Money and captives seemed inseparable, and lest any hint of humanity creep into his descriptions, Franklin added, "Will you send her out or shall I charge you $1100 for her[?] say quick[!]"[87] Ballard had already embarked her on a ship to New Orleans perhaps as a way to mollify his partners' anger over finances.

The partners sent invoices for women they used for sexual entertainment. Franklin's bid was over twice what Ballard had charged him for a "girl taken by I. Franklin Esqr" on the previous summer's caravan from the Potomac River to Natchez. In a business premised on brutality it would be surprising had Franklin scrupled at sexually abusing women the firm sold as slaves. Franklin chastised Ballard for sending members of a family rather than individuals and half-jokingly suggested that "the old lady and Susan could soon pay for themselves by keeping a whore house," in Alexandria, Baltimore, or Richmond, "for the exclusive comfort of the concern & those agents" in their employ.[88] Such was Franklin's idea of company benefits.

Departing from his lascivious commentary, Franklin apologized for his lack of productive activity. "The weather has been unusually bad[;] it has rained or snowed every day since the negroes landed," he whined to his partner. "It is just two weeks since I landed the stock from the Brig Tribune & have not sold the first negroe." Winter conditions had kept buyers away. A frost reportedly killed sugarcane in the fields, and Franklin worried that sugar planters would meet debt service by selling off enslaved workers. Worse, prices for male field hands were between $700 and $800, Franklin reported, and buyers wanted "twelve months credit without interest."[89] Financial times were changing, and planters who could not get bank credit demanded it from vendors.

A national credit crunch was at the root of the firm's financial woes and was depressing the slave market. The previous winter Franklin had wrangled 10 percent interest for six months' credit. By the dawn of 1834 credit seemed like an entitlement rather than a privilege. Franklin speculated that the firm "will be hard run for cash for the next year['s] business" and suggested "that we had better curtail our business next season & by that time we will be largely in funds so as to commence the year after all the long credit business." The firm was forced to take paper that could not be discounted at terms of twelve to twenty-four months.[90] Franklin contemplated halting the supply chain, a move that would strangle the business.

Such suggestions reveal Franklin's Byronic emotional sensitivity, which complemented and confounded his clear-eyed discernment of the market. His letters display a remarkable capacity for self-pity while ignoring the human suffering he and his partners caused. "My spirits are considerably depressed," he sobbed to Ballard while contemplating a dull market for slaves in January. "Was in fine spirits, untill a short time since," he continued, when prices for slaves fell and several of the firm's captives sickened and died. But his woes were purely financial. Franklin bragged of his sexual predations during his winter torpor. "The way your old one eyed friend looked the pirate was a sin to Crocket," Franklin winked, "but he is brought up all standing."[91]

The credit climate was as chilly as the weather. Despite planters' expectations for long credit at discount rates, bank credit was scarce in the winter of 1833–34 as the panic over the future of the Second Bank spread. The firm had "no money [and] the Bank will not discount a dollar," James Franklin whined from Natchez. "My dear Rice," the younger Franklin sobbed, "I never have spent such a month as last." The competition, he claimed, was "the meanest set of pirates you ever heard of to contend with." Yet sales had picked up. "Last week I sold about 35 negroes & about $1400 apiece but was compelled to take long paper[;] we cannot receive one dollar in cash for negroes." Long paper was an encumbrance, but prices that high were unprecedented.[92] There was worse news.

Captives were dying of preventable illness. "I have had the damnd small pox to break out on two or three plantations among negroes," in the area, complained James Franklin. Locals suspected that "our negroes has that horrid disease[;] [there] are several cases in town & the citizens say it came from our negroes," Franklin exclaimed. Isaac had not emerged from New Orleans. "He was doing nothing," his nephew grumbled.[93] During a winter of frozen credit, captives could not be warehoused like cotton or folded in a wallet like a bill of exchange. Some were fatigued from long confinement in the firm's detention centers, and agents of the firm were cutting corners in caring for them.

Ballard tried to defuse tensions by sending Martha Sweart to New Orleans. When Isaac Franklin had finished with her, he embarked her to Natchez. "The old man sent me your Maid Martha," James Franklin wrote wolfishly to Ballard, "[and] she is inclined to be compliant." Imagining her trauma as a choice was part of a narrative that allowed abusers to deny their culpability. In the shadows of that statement was the woman who had sailed thousands of miles, been traded among victimizers, and all the while inhabited the dark domestic space of men who categorized her as a "fancy maid" and reveled in referring to themselves as *"one eyed men."*[94]

The Jackson administration's monetary policies brought a victory for slave traders, at least in the medium term. Nicholas Biddle had perhaps been slave traders' best ally in the 1820s, but Old Hickory won the admiration of his fellow Tennesseans Armfield and Franklin for keelhauling Biddle and sinking the Second Bank and at the same time filling their commercial sails. The fabric of confidence was composed of the diaphanous strands of commercial transactions woven into a textile called the market. The tensile strength of that fabric held the ever-increasing expectations of future prosperity and solvency. Taking one- or two-year bills in exchange for slaves would have been folly in normal commercial climates, but the magic of the new market of the mid–1830s promised to make flimsy promises into tangible assets. Slave prices surged by one-third between 1830 and 1833 and would more than double by 1836. Land sales ballooned after the Second Bank's charter regulation on what the U.S. Land Office could accept as payment disappeared. Partly as a result, the federal government sold 1.2 million acres of land in 1829, 3.9 million acres in 1833, 4.7 million acres in 1834, and 20 million acres in 1836. Much of that land was expropriated from Indians, and the numbers actually undercount the lands aggrandized by planters, speculators, and other investors. Speculators and land companies bought allotments reserved for Choctaws, Creeks, and other Indians facing removal. The Jackson administration's willingness to push nonwhite people across the landscape and tolerate fraudulent claims on their lands complemented Isaac Franklin's keenness to sell unwilling African-descended forced migrants.[95]

Isaac Franklin's financiering put the firm in a position to survive the winter of 1834 and increase its market share. In New Orleans there was a general "want of confidence in commertial transactions," Franklin reported in March, on account of troubles by "several large factors in this place." Some merchants and factors had failed. Fellow traders, Franklin contended, had it worse. "The land pirates are coming down to sell their paper," Franklin warned, "and they [will] find that when they take off the discount they will not have cash" to pay their obligations. The firm was owed over $400,000, and James Franklin in Natchez had generated between $60,000 and $70,000 in revenues since the slump at Christmas. "I have so far kept out of the hand of the shavers," or bill merchants, Isaac Franklin reported. The competition, he predicted, "will be all laid out this season [and] will have no money to purchase with." That was deeply gratifying to one so competitive.[96]

Franklin survived the winter crisis by squeezing favors out of Richard Booker, the Bank of Louisiana cashier. To Ballard he reported that Booker "will avail any thing[;] you may say to the cashier that at all times will afford me pleasure to receive his commands."[97] Creditors like Booker and the Union Bank liked what they saw in Isaac Franklin. In the civic ecology of commercial New Orleans, Franklin was a good seed, a thriving vine, and a fruitful tree. The essence of credit was one's standing in a network of endorsers. In that respect, finance capitalism of the 1830s was extraordinarily personal. There were not yet credit reporting agencies that claimed to take an objective view of one's worthiness.

While Franklin worked to retain confidence in his firm, he relished destroying it in his rivals'. Smaller firms and itinerant traders exploited niches, but Franklin and Armfield was intensely territorial and well positioned. "I assisted in skinning your friend Collier," Franklin boasted to Ballard in April, explaining that his fellow slave trader "had some good paper" amounting to more than $12,000, drawn by Natchez merchants, endorsed by other merchants, and accepted by its drawees. Lewis A. Collier was a competitor and one of Ballard's Richmond neighbors who had been in Mississippi selling slaves. He needed to cash them at close to their face value in order to pay his debts. Unlike Franklin, Collier stood outside New Orleans's bankers' networks. He could not secure bank credit and was forced into the dens of exchange or bill merchants. In response to an inquiry, Franklin gave a bill merchant inside information on the state of Collier's finances. Franklin "told him that Collier had a payment to make the next day and he must say to him he Collier must endorse the whole of the paper and discount thirty percent and the man followed my directions got the thirty [percent] disc."[98] His accepting such deep discounts signaled that his paper was subpar and his position shaky.

Thanks to Franklin, bill merchants savaged Collier, destroying his profits through ruinous discounts. "I learn that the balance of the paper he has," Franklin continued devilishly, "could not be discounted for half off and unless he can make many arrangements with you" for funds. The Richmond trader needed some assistance from his "friend" Ballard, Franklin chuckled. Ballard's credit depended on Franklin's, and after being fleeced, Collier was running to wolves for succor. Under the firm's reorganization Ballard was forbidden from providing any assistance. "He will not trouble you much this season," Franklin predicted, commenting that Collier was "making [desperate] efforts to form several concerns with other traders" in an attempt to meet obligations. He was overextended, needing loans "here to pay his bills," in New Orleans. "In addi[tio]n," Franklin laughed, "to meet his bills here he has borrowed from several of the traders and given bills on Richmond[;] should that be the case unless he has very strong bankers he must take a loosing business."[99] He was skinned after being fleeced.

A dollar was not a dollar. The reputation of the owner of commercial paper influenced how its value was negotiated and how much it was worth. Without a bank or ally like Franklin to endorse him, Collier risked the market's wrath. By telling a bill merchant that Collier was desperate, Franklin tipped that market against his fellow trader during a time in which he was vulnerable. Encouraging Ballard to spread word in Richmond of Collier's troubles, Franklin could hardly contain himself. "He looks as much like a thief as any man I have ever saw in my life," Franklin guffawed. "The [convict's] bond was hawked all about Natchez and every man I am told traded with him as they was trading with a thief & the way they will sue him and injure [him]," Franklin hooted, would cause each to become "a sinful old fellow." The behavior among Natchez merchants was like that of a pack of wolves descending on the weakest among their number, abetted by the alpha male Isaac Franklin. Collier limped back to Richmond, where he continued to run a jail.[100] Franklin soon stopped laughing.

Ballard failed to vaccinate captives, which made Armfield's ships floating infirmaries. Many arrived in New Orleans sick or fell ill soon after, and by mid-March Franklin lost his patience. After sailing the firm through a financial storm, the least his partner could do was to stop blasting holes in the ship. Franklin rebuked Ballard, addressing him in the third person, as the "Gent" who "had been advised of the risque of small pox and the necessity of vaccination it was entirely neglected until late in the season after we had lost 5 or six thousand dollars," his shorthand for the lives of bondspersons, adding that "the last shipment has arrived without more than half of the negroes being vaccinated further more after being advised of all these things he complains that his credit must suffer." Franklin loosed a torrent of criticism on his Richmond partner, and he followed with the stricture that "our success greatly depend[s] on that we must act cautiously until the times change and confidence is restored after which we may go ahead like a steam boat."[101]

After the last consignment of captives arrived at the Forks of the Road, James Franklin wound down his duties as head salesman and returned as usual to bragging about his sexual exploits. Martha Sweart remained at Forks of the Road in mid-April 1834. Franklin reported to Ballard, "I have your Charlotteville Maid Martha on hand." "She answers by the name of *Big Cuff*," he chortled, perhaps hinting that the eighteen-year-old was pregnant. "I am happy to say to you I have changed very much since I saw you," he winked at his partner. "I have become very *virtuous*." James Franklin was a feeble humorist. "I am nearly ruined," he complained, hinting at sexual overexertion. "Martha sends her best respects & says she wants to see you very much." That flattery went a ways toward mollifying Ballard and masking Martha's predicament. She may have undergone traumatic bonding in response to years of isolation and serial abuse. If not, feigning affection for one of her captors may have been a desperate way to return to central Virginia and leave the cholera-cramped and violence-saturated Forks of the Road slave market.[102]

By spring it was clear that the reorganization that streamlined Franklin and Armfield's strategy had not changed the firm's culture. It had weathered the credit crisis, and sales rose along with prices. But arrogance and mismanagement still dragged on the firm like an anchor. Ballard traveled to Natchez to patch things up with Isaac and James Franklin. Martha Sweart was there, and Ballard could lay his hands on her. She was, after all, his property. Franklin wrote to Ballard from New Orleans, "I am much dissatisfied with the way we have been compelled to do business," but he conceded that "if we do not take heavy losses in our collections we will make more money this season than we have [before]." Franklin soon made his way to Bayou Sara, Louisiana, where he had bought a plantation called Angola. Angola would later become the site of the Louisiana State Penitentiary, noted for its prison rodeos and notorious for its deplorable conditions. To Ballard he registered despair: "I feel deserted by all those I have failed to serve but don't give up the ship."[103]

The tragic drama of Franklin and Armfield's business had seasonal acts, which played out in a yearly cycle commencing each spring. It was part of the firm's annual ritual of what amounted to board meetings and the closing of one fiscal year and the opening of another. In late spring Franklin reassigned a large portion of the firm's agents to seasonal work that differed from their occupations during the times slaves were in demand in the lower South. Like a chief executive officer on a periodic tour of company factories, Isaac Franklin sailed to Virginia. He then departed for New York City. A line of credit with a New York bank would help lower transaction costs and alleviate reliance on New Orleans bankers. The *Tribune* and *Uncas* were plying different routes. In the summers, the firm sent its ships seeking cargoes other than captives. In the summer of 1832 the *Tribune* had sailed to New York with passengers before being chartered to another merchant for a voyage to the Canary Islands. The following summer the *Tribune* sailed to New York and Baltimore. While Ballard's agents were scouring the Virginia countryside for captives in 1834, the *Tribune* was hauling pork, lime, and sugar from New Orleans to Charleston before coasting to Philadelphia. Meanwhile, the *Uncas* sailed north. Armfield wrote to Ballard that September that its master, Nathaniel Boush, was "trying to get a freight for the *Uncas*" in New York City.[104] The ships would return to Alexandria in October and resume hauling human cargoes.

To plan for a further expansion, Armfield contracted for another ship, this time in Baltimore. Baltimore shipbuilders had a reputation for designing fast craft. In the 1830s they were receiving orders from transatlantic slavers seeking sleek vessels to hold human cargoes. Latin American slave traders tapped Chesapeake shipbuilders' experience building speedy ships that could outrun the British Royal Navy's Anti-Slavery Squadron and evade Spanish patrols as well.[105] Levin H. Dunkin, who constructed the *Isaac Franklin*, was one of the most productive ship's carpenters of his era.

The *Isaac Franklin* was built for speed and prestige as well as for profit. At 189 tons, it was more capacious than either the *Tribune* or the *Uncas*. The *Isaac Franklin* was longer and narrower than the *Tribune* by ten feet in length and width. Its most distinctive exterior feature was a wooden figurehead of its name-sake: Isaac Franklin's bust was affixed to the bow of the ship. Middle Atlantic sculptors had a well-earned reputation for decorative maritime sculpture. Some figureheads were female figures and others were effigies of gods or generals. Skilled artisans carved and painted intricate details that infused life into their subjects. Perhaps the sculptor captured Franklin's intense stare, which was then fixed on the forward horizon. The slave trader who boasted of his sexual incursions would carry his victims in the cavity of his eponymous vessel. As she boarded the *Isaac Franklin*, any forlorn captive who looked closely at the brig could glimpse the wooden likeness of the flesh-and-blood slave trader who met his ships at the New Orleans levee. The *Isaac Franklin* was delivered to Alexandria in September 1835. Armfield lost little time cramming the new ship with captives. On one voyage, the *Isaac Franklin* left Alexandria with 254 involuntary passengers packed in its hold, which was a tad shy of thirty cubic feet per captive, or the size of a kitchen cabinet. The ship sailed even after its namesake had removed himself from active participation.[106]

Isaac Franklin quit as managing partner, and the firm began to disintegrate. His seemingly unending stream of letters, his barbs and blandishments, and his personality and reputation had held the firm together. He relinquished control over the day-to-day operations, leaving it to others to meet ships at the New Orleans levee. By 1836 John Armfield was running shipping ads for the *Uncas* and *Isaac Franklin* under his own name even as Franklin and Armfield still advertised for captives. By the time confidence was shattered in the panic of 1837, Ballard, Franklin, and Armfield were all out of the trade. Despite its sprawling, unstable hybrid of a merchant partnership and factory, Franklin's firm nevertheless stood as an articulation of the strategic use of human resources to gain competitive advantages in a trade that, for all its human evils, relentless violence, and epic immorality, required exceptional orchestration and entrepreneurial savvy. Franklin's theory of his firm comprehended the complexities and vicissitudes of the developing commodity and credit chains using the latest technologies.[107]

As the partners retired, the firm spun off its assets. The men who would dominate the Chesapeake–to–New Orleans trade of the 1840s gobbled them up. In 1836 George Kephart, a purchasing manager from Frederick, Maryland, bought Franklin and Armfield's Alexandria jail. Kephart partnered with a New Orleans slave trader, Thomas Boudar. The pair operated the *Isaac Franklin* in the late 1830s and early 1840s. Isaac Franklin's nephew James H. Purvis continued to run his slaving firm in Baltimore, later moving into stock brokering and financial services. The Georgian Hope Hull Slatter moved to Baltimore in the late 1830s and built a slave jail on Pratt Street near the circus. Slatter bought space aboard the *Isaac Franklin* for eighty-seven captives in 1838, all bound for New Orleans. Thomas McCargo advertised for slaves in Richmond in the late 1830s, and when the railroad arrived in Richmond, that city would become the center of the lower Chesapeake slave market.[108]

The *Uncas* carried Franklin and Armfield's legacy to the shores of West Africa. The firm sold the brig to William H. Williams, a Washington, D.C.–based slave trader, and a partner. On one passage in 1840, the *Uncas* delivered at least sixty-eight captives to Williams in Mobile, shipped by his partner, Alexander Lee, in Washington, D.C., and skippered by the Franklin and Armfield veteran Nathaniel Boush. Williams sold the *Uncas* in the early 1840s, and by 1844 it was plying a transatlantic slave trade. When it was stopped off the Sherbro Coast, British officers found that the *Uncas* was already fitted out for slaving, being "equipped with the usual type of grating that slavers all carried for ventilating the hold," along with some "very large casks, which were not watertight but which the ship's cooper could easily make so." The ship was half-full of trade goods, but the shipmaster's "story was as leaky as his water-casks." A British officer strongly suspected that the *Uncas* had embarked captives in West Africa and landed them in Cuba the year before. The *Uncas* subsequently attracted the attention of the U.S. Navy. American authorities found it anchored at the mouth of the Gallinas River near the Sierra Leone–Liberia border and discovered a "notorious slave factor" known both in Cuba and in West Africa. U.S. authorities sailed the ship to Havana and then to New Orleans, arriving in April 1844, in order to try the crew for murdering the first mate (and sole American aboard) on the Atlantic crossing, a crime for which no one was convicted.[109] By then Franklin and Armfield's sole agency was bills receivable.

Armfield, Ballard, and Isaac Franklin swapped the commercial clothing of merchants for the genteel robes of planters. Rice Ballard settled in Louisville, Kentucky, around 1840 and married Louise Cabois Berthe. Over the next two decades he bought several plantations in Louisiana, Arkansas, and Mississippi. The Ballards had three daughters. Ballard partnered with a judge, Samuel S. Boyd, and his five plantations yielded about 2,500 bales of cotton a year, worth over $100,000 in annual income. He did not have to bear the Franklins' abuse and harangues and left it to factors to sell his crops. Instead of purchasing agents like Andrew Grimm, Ballard managed overseers who wrung work from bound laborers. If on his Kentucky plantation he picked up a copy of Harriet Beecher Stowe's *Uncle Tom's Cabin; or, Life among the Lowly* after it was published in 1852, Ballard could grimace and chuckle by turns at the character of the slave trader Dan Haley. Haley was more appropriate to the antislavery imagination than to the business as Ballard had shaped it. Avarice was a human characteristic not peculiar to slave traders, and he could recite an index of merchants and mariners who profited from the slave trade without fastening a shackle on another human being. But Haley was not merely a grubby version of his former self. Compared to Isaac Franklin or John Armfield, the figure who bought and sold Uncle Tom was an ill-equipped, poorly financed small operator with a surfeit of hesitation and a lack of imagination. Stowe recognized the trade's importance. But Ballard could chuckle that such a wretched character would so influentially shape public understandings of such a sophisticated business, as if Herman Melville's Captain Ahab exemplified commercial whaling or James Fenimore Cooper's Uncas faithfully represented Native Americans. Two decades before, Ballard had ruined Haley-like competitors while managing a half dozen like them. One, James G. Blakey, retired from slaving to run the Wall Street Hotel in Richmond from 1847 until his death in 1854.[110] John Armfield also migrated to the hospitality business.

Following the dissolution of the slave trading firm, Armfield returned to Tennessee and a farm called Cedar Place. He spent his spare time attempting to collect the company's accounts, assisted in that job by the merchant house of N. and J. Dick in New Orleans. In 1853 he bought property at Beersheba Springs, about ninety miles southeast of Nashville, and developed it into one of the South's premier resorts. He and his wife called it home. With "chefs and musicians" lured from New Orleans, contends a historian, "Beersheba Springs attracted wealthy visitors from across the South and enjoyed lively social seasons until the Civil War." In 1859 Armfield wrote to Ballard, "I think it probable that I added several years to my life by cominge to this place," beckoning Ballard to "come over and bringe your family with you." Ballard died the following year. Armfield was a principal benefactor of the University of the South in Sewanee, Tennessee. He outlived his partners by many years, dying in 1871.[111]

By the time Isaac Franklin quit managing the firm, he had been building his sumptuous Fairvue plantation in Sumner County, Tennessee, for years. His "splendid large brick mansion," a neighbor estimated, "must have [cost] some $8000 or $10,000," and was "finished in most splendid and costly style." Irish marble mantelpieces were said to cost $500 each. The compound reflected Franklin's prestige. He built "a large and extensive garden" with brick walls bordering it. Long gravel walkways, imported plants, and a greenhouse aped English garden architecture. In addition to the main buildings, Franklin built brick barns, slave quarters, a carpentry shop, an icehouse, and a blacksmith shop. His brick greenhouse had steam heat. Fairvue was staffed by scores of enslaved workers selected from among thousands Franklin's firm bought and sold. Andrew Jackson may have been the most famous Tennessean alive, but Isaac Franklin was among the wealthiest. Fairvue was "a place more finely embellished than any I have seen in the State of Tennessee," according to a nearby resident. His vehicles consisted of carriages, buggies, and wagons, which complemented stables of thoroughbred horses. A neighbor estimated that "the furniture belonging to the house, would cost at least ten thousand dollars, and probably a good deal more." Besides Fairvue, Franklin owned several plantations in Louisiana by the time of his retirement, amounting to 8,500 acres and 550 slaves.[112]

In his fiftieth year, Franklin's transition to agricultural gentility was completed through his marriage to Adelicia Hayes, the daughter of a wealthy Nashville planter family. Implicitly contrasting Franklin's behavior before marriage, a neighbor testified, "I believe him to have (been) a virtuous man after his marriage, and conducted himself with great propriety." Children arrived soon after, and Franklin turned his attentions to domestic concerns and building a school for posterity. He died after a brief stomach complaint in late April 1846 on one of his Louisiana plantations. Armfield had Franklin's body preserved in whiskey for the journey home to Tennessee.[113]

Isaac Franklin was a business innovator who built a firm incorporating his strategic understanding of money and markets and held together by shrewd leadership. Obituaries published soon after his death ignored the substance of his business, commenting instead on his "tact, address, firmness and intelligence, which his multifarious dealings so often called into plan, and fully developed; he acquired a reputation for the due management of business, which placed him in a position to realize a rapid fortune." Franklin was credited with "keeping steadily in his view the bright vision of some grand benevolence to his kind." Franklin and Armfield took advantage of a booming slave market, but the convulsive economic growth of the 1830s strained the business model. The firm's culture of excess mirrored the market, but it grew too quickly to sustain its strategy. Franklin failed to institutionalize the managerial practices that held the various branches together even in the flush times. As if to save the partners from a tragic epilogue to a corporate culture of titanic hubris, the panic fell on their successors. There was no cost accounting for epochal miseries that agents and partners of the firm produced as by-products of "the game" from which they retired with hundreds of thousands of dollars' profit.[114]

The seeming lifelessness of money and business contrasts with the particular voice, inflection, and set of values that Franklin's enterprise embodied as it disarticulated families and devastated social worlds. The dryness of paper that passed among traders, bankers, planters, and merchants conceals the calamities that befell the people traded: odors of blood and sweat, bacteria and infections, the cries and wails of flesh-and-bone victims, and the unmarked graves of those traded as slaves.

6

CHAINS OF VIOLENCE

Violence was enslavers' great economizer. The hard brutality of the slave trader Theophilus Freeman's supply chain illustrates the human costs of a mechanical market taking shape in the 1840s. Solomon Northup witnessed Freeman's string of allied firms as a chained commodity in a blasted succession of bolted souls, a pitiable procession of wrecked humanity. Slavers' profit margins grew in proportion to the violence, and kidnap victims like him offered great potential. Northup was born free in New York, and his family was part of Saratoga Springs's braided history of people of European and African descent. His skin color was described as "yellow," and he stood five feet seven inches tall. In late winter 1841 the thirty-three-year-old was living near Lake Saratoga on a railroad route, with his wife, Anne, née Hampton, and three children, Margaret, Elizabeth, and Alonzo. Like so many African-descended Americans, he worked at a variety of jobs. Northup labored on the Champlain and Erie canals, visiting Canada and Great Lakes cities, including Rochester and Buffalo. Northup was a small entrepreneur. After helping build improvements near Glens Falls, New York, he built a small business rafting timber down the Champlain Canal. Rafting required a constellation of skills, including leadership, carpentry, and mechanics. No stranger to a culture of drinking and fighting, he got in trouble with employers and ran afoul of the law. In consequence, he had some trouble keeping his business afloat.[1]

Despite his rough edges, Solomon Northup had a talent for the violin and an eye for opportunity. Two strangers calling themselves Merrill Brown and Abram Hamilton lured him to Washington, D.C., with the promise of a job as a violin player in a traveling entertainment show. Those were aliases for Alexander Merrill and Joseph Russell. Locals warned Northup not to leave town with them, but he had worked with whites before and shrugged off the suspicion.

Anne and their children were out of town when he left. She had taken a temporary job twenty miles away. En route Northup took part in Merrill and Russell's "feats of ventriloquism and legerdemain"; there was little warning that he would be the subject of their next trick.[2] In Washington, D.C., Merrill and Russell lodged in Gadsby's Hotel at Pennsylvania Avenue and Sixth Street Northwest, about half a mile's stroll from the jail of the slave trader William H. Williams.

Gadsby's was a posh place and curious lodgings for a low-rent company of entertainers. President-elect William Henry Harrison had stayed there before the inaugural. In late March, however, Harrison was dying and with him the Whig Party's plans for reversing the course of Democratic policies. As the Whig nominee, Harrison had won the presidency in 1840 on a platform of measures to pull the country out of hard times, including robust federal reforms. On March 4 the sixty-eight-year-old former general and U.S. senator from Ohio gave a long-winded inaugural address on federalism, finance, and freedom, and he participated in the festivities hatless. He developed a lung infection that became pneumonia and died on April 4, replaced by John Tyler of Virginia. The states'-rights Tyler would undermine his predecessor's legislative agenda, alienate his backers, and unsuccessfully attempt to annex a new constituency in the Texas republic.[3] As Northup and his employers took rooms in the hotel, political turbulence swirled about the national capital.

After the public procession accompanying Harrison's state funeral, Merrill and Russell invited Northup along on an evening of convivial drinking. Northup joined his companions as they bought rounds of whiskey at city saloons. Someone slipped a draught into his glass. Northup returned to his lodgings but suffered severe aches and thirst, slipping in and out of consciousness. As Merrill and Russell dragged him from Gadsby's, across the National Mall, and into the bowels of a slave trader's compound, they muttered that they were taking their employee to a physician. For the cost of railroading Northup to Washington, D.C., the hotel bill, and a few bits' worth of whiskey and poison, his captors sold him to a slave trader. James H. Birch paid $650. Merrill and Russell left town, one clutching an ivory cane and displaying a gold watch and chain. Both had new clothes and haircuts.[4] As they made their way back to New York, they could chuckle that Northup ought to have been more wary in the prevailing lean times. Unless he could escape or prove otherwise, he was now a piece of property in a particularly unforgiving market.

By the dawn of the 1840s the heady wine of the previous decade's credit expansion had caused an economic headache. Social relations of capital became increasingly impersonal. In the recovering market interstate slave-trading firms fractured into alliances among geographically specialized agents and partners. Birch's New Orleans associate Theophilus Freeman was among the most successful of the early 1840s. But businessmen who had feasted at the table of confidence now competed for scraps in an era of suspicion and fragmentation. Freeman's firm hungered for credit but subsisted on transportation efficiencies instead. A banking system reliant on cotton bills of exchange survived the 1830s, but New Orleans began its decline as a financial center while New York City rose to preeminence in North America.

Reconfigured finance propelled America's transportation revolution as the republic's population grew by more than a third in the 1840s. In that decade the population of enslaved people grew from 2.5 million to 3.2 million as the United States' empire expanded across the continent. Even so, distances among market actors seemed to shrink. Steam engines coughed, hissed, and panted along rails and on rivers bringing buyers and sellers closer together. Slave traders took full advantage, serving a slave-commodity chain that linked finance and transportation. Cotton bales secured bills at the center of banking, and banks joined insurance, trust, and investment companies to fund railroads, which changed the republic's social and commercial landscape.[5]

Slavery steamed ahead on that nexus of investment and emerging technologies, yet enslaved people bore many of the social costs. Enslavers continued a pattern of intergenerational theft, selecting young bondspersons from old families and sending them to urban slave markets. Captives like Northup saw the mechanical market up close before most of their fellow Americans when they were passed among agents of allied firms and packed aboard steamboats like cotton sacks, corralled into railroad cars like cattle, and plunked in the holds of ships like barrels. Enslaved African-descended Americans were scattered fifteen hundred miles from the head of the Chesapeake Bay to the bottomlands of the Brazos River in the debtors' republic of Texas. Demands for slave labor came from new places in between, which filled in as Americans cleared lands of natural obstructions and Native Americans. Slaving frontiers widened. Even free African-descended New Yorkers were terrorized by kidnappers and con men prowling the region for people whose ancestry marked them for enslavement.[6]

Theophilus Freeman was an architect of the post-panic interstate slave trade. Northup described him as "a tall, thin-faced man, with light complexion and a little bent"; his success resulted from strategic alliances with other slaving firms and financiers.[7] They were the slave trade's trunk lines. The pursuit of money was the hardpan of his character, as it was for Isaac Franklin. Originally from Prince William County, Virginia, Freeman set out to build an interregional

Slave Auction, 1832 (The Historic New Orleans Collection, acc. no. 1941.3)

commodity chain in captives. In the 1830s he competed directly with Franklin and Armfield. In contrast to Austin Woolfolk and Franklin, Freeman enrolled partners of similar status rather than kinsmen. He did so in strategic areas such as Halifax, North Carolina, and Washington, D.C., allying with former agents of the Woolfolks and Franklin and Armfield. To receive and sell captives sent from the upper South, Freeman took up residence in New Orleans and plied the Mississippi River corridor between there and Natchez.

As Freeman built his supply chain, local partnerships blossomed into regional alliances. They rode on the back of technological development and what amounts to a theory of the firm emphasizing network ties and resources gathered through alliances rather than family connections or vertical organization. Freeman initially partnered with Walter H. Finnall of Stafford County, Virginia. Finnall was in the transportation business and had a contract to carry mail between Washington, D.C., and Richmond. On occasion he sold captives in Natchez. Their "copartnership, for the period of three years, in the purchase and sale of negroes" commenced in 1834, and the firm advertised for slaves in Fredericksburg, Virginia, where Finnall built a jail.[8]

Finnall's operation showed the hard-edged brutalities that John Armfield sought to conceal. E. A. Andrews, a New England abolitionist, visited his jail and found it smaller, less secure, and filthier than Armfield's Alexandria compound. Finnall's dungeon windows "were grated with iron, in the same manner as Mr. Armfield's," he contended. Unlike Armfield's compound, Finnall's had no corporate script or guided tour. Andrews surveyed the compound from the Fredericksburg city streets. "As we turned the corner of the yard, I observed two or three negro women, from without, conversing through the fence with some who were confined in the yard, but apparently cheerful and happy." Finnall "is said to have about one hundred and fifty on hand at this time, whom he is soon to send off, over land, I believe, to New Orleans." Andrews heard a report that Finnall had "sen[t] off a number of mothers without their little children, whom he had purchased with them." Rumors abounded in the neighborhood concerning the horrors concealed behind the sixteen-foot-tall walls of a jail one neighbor labeled "the Bastille."[9]

Freeman's management was more like that of the lead in an improvised musical act than that of an orchestral conductor. He relied on a transportation network that he did not own and focused on managing that supply chain of captives and information. He did so through correspondence that accompanied remittances of the proceeds of sales. As transportation became a commodity, it made little sense to buy ships, and the company's upper South distribution network centered on the rail hub and port of Richmond. Freeman orchestrated credit relationships that linked his operation in the lower Mississippi Valley to merchants and bankers in Philadelphia and Baltimore. Freeman's leadership capacity was coextensive with his ability to remit money and information to his partners. He lacked Franklin's force of personality and strong ties of family. But weak ties mattered. Banks, steamboats, railroads, and county jails also featured in Freeman's far-flung slaving network.[10]

As Freeman's business grew, its tentacles reached into collateral businesses of cotton and banking. In the lower Mississippi Valley, he partnered with John Goodin and Company, led by two cotton merchants, John Goodin and his brother, William F. Goodin. John resided in New Orleans and William in Vicksburg. William was cashier of the Planters Bank in Port Gibson, Mississippi. Bank money was scarcer after one quarter of American banks failed or faced forced closures and the volume of money shrunk by a third between 1837 and 1843. Despite that financial contraction, the republic's economy did not undergo structural change. Planters still imported credit and exported cotton. When the former became more difficult to obtain, planters ratcheted up violence against workers, expanded acreage, and experimented with new varieties to seek competitive advantages. In

the 1840s cotton production rose dramatically. As was true in the 1830s, the cotton
chain linking East Coast merchants to lower Mississippi Valley counterparts also
linked to the slave trade. Agents of John Goodin and Company sold captives from
the Forks of the Road, where Franklin and Armfield had established their slave
sales venue. Freeman supplied the operation. In payment he took cotton bills for
slaves, and debt obligations that originated in Britain and Europe entered the
bloodstream of Freeman's slaving firm.[11]

Freeman built merchants' confidence as a way to lower transaction costs. To
remit proceeds of sales, he relied on financiers like the Chesapeake merchants
R. and I. Smith. The Smiths acted as local bankers in a climate in which bankers
were widely regarded as the moral equivalent of counterfeiters. In February 1840
Freeman sent the Smiths a check payable at the Girard Bank of Philadelphia,
one of the Jackson administration's pet banks that had survived the financial
crisis. In turn, the Smiths handed his firm two $2,500 bills of exchange, which
they sent to Freeman's Eastern Shore buyers. The Smiths took a percentage, but
their bills brought a lower discount than Freeman's Louisiana check. That
capital went to Thomas W. Overley and Robert Sanders. They discounted the
bills in exchange for local banknotes and purchased captives much as Woolfolk's
or Rice C. Ballard's agents had in the 1820s and 1830s. In 1840 the Smiths used
Freeman's network as an entrée to the New Orleans market. "You named in
your letter that our House was not known in New-Orleans," they wrote, "and
therefore could not use a draft on us." They encouraged Freeman to spread
word. "If our name is any service, it is at your command, either in New-Orleans
or Richmond—the latter place, you can always use us to advantage."[12]

Like Franklin and Armfield's, Freeman's suppliers in the upper South were
located strategically throughout the Chesapeake and eastern North Carolina,
each operating independently but cooperating in shipping, incarceration, and
information sharing. Overley and Sanders did business from a Princess Anne
tavern on the Eastern Shore. They advertised, "CASH FOR NEGROES," and
demanded captives, "including both sexes, from 12 to 25 years of age." They
were old hands at the interstate slave trade. Overley was a Virginian, and both
he and Sanders had been associated with the Woolfolk brothers. Freeman
instructed them: "I want you to buy nothing but No. 1 negroes, as you will find
plenty of them for sale before you can get money. Don't pay a dollar for an old
negro, unless you get it very low, nor don't buy *families*." Such language reflected
a market in which captives were abstract commodities, graded by number.
Freeman's using "it" rather than a gendered pronoun testified to his outlook.[13]

Freeman's supply network on the western shore of the Chesapeake Bay
included thousands of square miles. Besides ties to Freeman, suppliers shared ad

copy. James Birch in Washington, D.C., advertised, "CASH FOR 200 NEGROES, Including both sexes, from 12 to 25 years of age," in 1835. Birch operated out of a city tavern. Instead of sending captives from Alexandria, Birch funneled them to William Goodwin, Freeman's ally in Richmond.[14] George W. Barnes was Birch's counterpart in Halifax, North Carolina, about ninety miles south of Richmond.

Barnes's enterprise relied on Freeman's remittances and a cluster of agents who scoured coastal North Carolina for bondspersons. In late October 1839 Barnes bought captives in the neighborhood of New Bern, at the coastal confluence of the Trent and Neuse rivers. New Bern was among the oldest Euroamerican settlements in North Carolina and the home of generations of African-descended people held as slaves. Barnes dispatched an agent to Onslow County, about forty-five miles to the southwest. He and his agents assembled captives in Halifax, near the Virginia border. From there captives were marched, carted, or railroaded another hundred miles north to Richmond. By the time Barnes's coffles reached Richmond jails, they had already been transported two hundred miles at the hands of strangers.[15] Because of Freeman's supply-chain configuration, Carolina captives went north before heading south. After passing through a Richmond jail, they were packed in a coastal trading vessel and shipped to Freeman in New Orleans.

Freeman's agent James Birch was assembling another coffle in the nation's capital in April 1841 when he bought Solomon Northup. In Williams's Washington City jail, Northup awoke from a drug-induced delirium to a nightmare. The jail, he recalled, contained "one small window, crossed with great iron bars, with an outside shutter, securely fastened." Birch and one of his agents, Ebenezer Radburn, greeted him as their slave. After Northup protested that he was a free man from New York, Birch and Radburn humiliated and tortured their captive, stripping his clothes off, shackling him to a floor, flogging him with a cat-o'-nine-tails and beating his naked body with a wooden paddle until the hated instrument broke. Violence, incarceration, and geographic isolation turned him from a free citizen into incarnate capital. The technology of race, or racist pseudoscience applied to enterprise, aided that transformation. The captors lashed and humiliated Northup until he stopped insisting that he was free.[16]

In that "dungeon" Northup learned how a slave was made. Most enslaved people endured incremental violence that marked bondage's boundaries. Northup's captors needed him to play the biddable chattel and delivered the blows all at once. That he was kidnapped did not categorically distinguish him from other captives sold in the U.S. slave trade. Isolation and the brutality that accompanied it was the moral equivalent of kidnapping. Northup's captors thrashed him into a commodity they would designate as "Plat Hamilton," a credit to the alias of one of the men who had lured him to the city.[17] In the jail he met several others whose fortunes fell at Birch's hands.

Eliza's world was shattering. Her children, seven-year-old Emily and ten-year-old Randall, were, like their mother, sold and jailed. Eliza had been enslaved in Maryland and had made a choiceless choice to live as a concubine with her owner, the Prince George's County planter Elisha Berry. Berry's behavior mocked his marriage and alienated his wife and her family. While Northup was being kidnapped, Berry's son-in-law took Eliza to Washington, D.C., with a promise of her instant manumission. It soon became clear that her deed of manumission was actually a bill of sale. When Northup met her in jail, she was still wearing the fine dress and jewelry she thought would adorn her as a free woman.[18] Under cover of night, Northup was led out of the jail in chains. Eliza, her children, and a Georgetown resident, Clemens Ray, made up the rest of the small coffle. The captives' troubles multiplied as Birch moved them. Handcuffed and marched through Washington City in the darkest hours of night, Northup, Eliza, her children, and Ray were put aboard a steamboat.

Steamboat travel was becoming part of the ritual of slavery's isolation, and the machine's mechanical cadences accented the disorientation each captive suffered. Northup recalled, "We were quickly hustled into the hold, among barrels and boxes of freight." In that stuffy space, dread settled over them. "A colored servant brought a light, the bell rung, and soon the vessel started down the Potomac, carrying us we knew not where."[19] To rhythmic sounds of the wheezing of steam and motion of pistons, the captives endured the several-hour ride down the Potomac River. After dawn the boat landed at Aquia Creek, and Birch paid a stagecoach driver to transport them to the rail depot in Fredericksburg for the ride to Richmond. There another gleaming artifact of the new landscape awaited them.

Virginia railroads embodied capitalism's slavery as they reoriented the economic geography. With little hesitation, architects of the most advanced transportation technology harnessed bound labor, incrementally changing the political economy of slavery in the process. By the time Northup boarded it, the Richmond, Fredericksburg and Potomac Railroad (RFPRR) included sixty miles of track connecting Richmond and Fredericksburg. Several more miles of track linked a railhead a dozen miles from the Potomac River. It was the sixth road chartered in Virginia and just the third to operate with steam engines. (Some roads used horses drawing stagecoach-like cars, and experimental railroads ran on wind and even dog power.) The RFPRR was also a public-private partnership. After chartering it, the railroad issued bonds and the Commonwealth of Virginia bought nearly two-fifths of the capital stock.

The road competed for the business of slave traders, and roads like it made Richmond the principal Chesapeake slaving port of the 1840s. "Servants half price," beckoned an RFPRR fare schedule in 1837. The half-price seats were in the baggage car. Some railroads sold space for bondspersons in smoking cars, which were essentially roving saloons in which passengers who could not afford first-class fares had to put up with riders puffing cigars, spitting tobacco juice, and swigging whiskey. Whatever the atmosphere, selling carriage to slave traders was part of the logic of capital. A railroad traveling a major artery of the slave trade could ill afford not to compete for slave traders' business even if the tickets they bought were one-way. Children under three rode for free, and those twelve and under, half price.[20]

The RFPRR was a Virginia corporation, but the road itself was a transatlantic construction. The knowledge, the capital, and much of the equipment, including the iron rails and locomotive, were imported from England. A Virginia native, Moncure Robinson, the chief engineer of the RFPRR, had risen to become one of the United States' pioneering railroad engineers while still in his twenties. As a young engineer who had already worked on the James River and Kanawha Canal, Robinson sojourned in Europe and Britain, where he studied civil engineering. In 1827 the twenty-five-year-old civil engineer returned to the United States as one of an elite group capable of engineering railroads. He worked on the Pottsville and Danville Railroad in Pennsylvania and the Chesterfield Railroad in Virginia, which connected Richmond to the coal pits of Chesterfield County. By 1829 bondspeople were building the means to transport bituminous coal thirteen miles to Richmond via horse-powered cars. Robinson engineered the Petersburg and Roanoke and the Richmond and Petersburg railroads, two of the first passenger and freight roads to use steam locomotives.

As the chief architect of Virginia's roads, Robinson helped reorient the commercial geography of the commonwealth to Richmond. That development was spectacularly announced in 1832 by the 2,844-foot wooden bridge carrying cars of the Richmond and Petersburg Railroad sixty feet above the James River and into the depot at the Basin, the terminus of the James River and Kanawha Canal (where boats turned around). In 1834 Robinson commenced work on Pennsylvania's premier coal railroad, the Philadelphia and Reading. While working on the extension of that road, he won a charter to extend the RFPRR to Aquia Creek, where Northup and his comrades landed.

To extend the road, Robinson looked for capital across the Atlantic Ocean. In 1837 he traveled to London to negotiate the sale of RFPRR bonds through the investment bankers Gowan and Marx. The firm agreed to market nearly $100,000 worth of the bonds, sold on terms resembling those of Louisiana property banks.

Robinson turned the promise of Virginia railroads into a £20,000 sterling bill of exchange. As Robinson built the RFPRR, he also invested heavily in its stock and graduated from engineer to capitalist. As homage to his English backers, Robinson named a prototype of a four-driving-wheel locomotive the *Gowan and Marx*. At the end of the 1830s the RFPRR sold its 6 percent bonds to Philadelphia investors. As in the slave trade, outside investors supplied southern railroad capital, which traveled through northern commercial banks.[21] Capitalists' modern marvels were constructed with slave labor.

A portion of railroad capital raised from bond issues went into the pockets of slave traders and hiring agents. Virginia slaveholders found new ways to profit from the institution by renting bondspeople to the RFPRR and other railroad companies. Gangs of African-descended railroad workers cut wood, hewed sleepers, piled up ballast, and laid track. They worked in the chill of winter and the swelter of summer. In 1836 the road paid one hundred dollars for a year's rent for an adult male worker and promised to return him "at the end of the year well clothed, also with a hat and Blanket." Teams of enslaved men had built the road on which African-descended captives, including friends and neighbors, rode to market. Virginia railroads expanded steadily in the 1840s from 147 miles of track in 1840 to 481 in 1850. The process would intensify in the 1850s as railroad construction boomed. Virginia had 1,731 miles of track by 1860. Should any bound worker tire of the arrangement, an owner or overseer could threaten that if he did not swallow his discontents and get back to work, he would be packed aboard a baggage car and sold in the Richmond slave market. To bondspersons the railroad was an ominous technology.[22] Customers too found it less than user-friendly.

Revolutionary conveyances at first seemed like revolting annoyances. Riders sought convenience but contended with filth, noise, tedium, and danger. Customer service was scarce. Visitors traveling long distances south of the Ohio River or Delaware Bay griped that they had to exit railroad cars at termini like Richmond or Weldon, North Carolina, buy new tickets from tobacco-stained yokels, lug their trunks to the next train, and then repeat the ritual at the end of each short line. Cars were drafty and smoky, the seats hard and light dim at night. There was no food service, no sleeping berths. Train toilets were nonexistent. Buckled wooden rails called snake heads sometimes broke through the wooden carriage floors, on occasion impaling passengers. Yet a lack of comforts obscures the fact that southern railroads grew to connect a greater proportion of residents to markets than those north of Delaware. Southerners' barriers of time and space eroded more quickly than those of their countrymen.[23]

That was a process scarcely visible to Northup and the others who climbed aboard baggage cars at the Fredericksburg depot. About the time he was kidnapped, the legislature was contemplating funding the completion of the road to the steamboat landing. As they had in the steamboat, Northup, Eliza, and her children rode with passengers' trunks and bags of mail along the sixty miles of track to Richmond. Northup and the others arrived there before night-fall. From there, he recalled, "we were taken from the cars, and driven through the street to a slave pen, between the railroad depot and the river." Birch bought his bondspersons confinement in William Goodwin's jail.[24]

By the time Northup entered Richmond, it was becoming the largest slave market in the upper South. Steamboat lines and railroads drew in networks of traders and their agents in the hinterland, reaching down into North Carolina, up into the southern counties of Maryland, and out into the Virginia piedmont and even as far as southwestern Virginia. Traders carted, marched, floated, or railroaded enslaved people to Richmond for resale, and rarely did an enslaved person destined for the market enter Richmond without a stopover in a slave jail.

Such detention centers were, according to Northup, "a very common estab-lishment, it appears, in the cities of the South." Birch's coffle stepped off the railroad cars on the northwest side of town, at Broad Street and Seventh. They marched southeast along the city's unpaved streets a dozen blocks down Broad Street, behind the stately capitol, past the First African Baptist Church, and downhill, over Shockoe Creek and by the jail of Lewis A. Collier. It had been a wet spring, which resulted in abundant greenery and also streets rutted with gullies carved by rainwater. William Goodwin's slave jail was located on the corner of what later became a parking lot at East Broad and North 16th streets. There Northup and his traveling companions were confined in an open-air yard surrounded by high walls. He recalled that the compound included "two small houses standing at opposite corners within the yard." "These houses are usually found within slave yards," he explained, "being used as rooms for the examination of human chattels by purchasers before concluding a bargain."[25]

Goodwin's compound was a captive distribution center joined to a sales venue. Its architecture was fashioned to the purpose. The jail opened on auction rooms. "Quite a number of slaves," Northup recalled, "as many as thirty I should say, were moving about, or sitting on benches under the shed." As in Washington, D.C., the inmates were fed a rudimentary diet of pork and bread. The mood inside the compound mirrored the poor food. His fellow captives, Northup recalled, "were all cleanly dressed—the men with hats, the women with handkerchiefs tied about their heads." The costumes were packaging meant to create the appearance of a uniform commodity.[26] As Northup met Goodwin he admitted he was from New York, after which Birch threatened more torture should he forget to adhere to his script. Once they were delivered, Birch washed his hands of Eliza, Northup, and the others, returning to Washington City and assembling other captives while awaiting payment in the post.

Goodwin had no direct financial interest in caring for captives, and so long as they left his jail alive he could collect his fees from Birch when the trader next stepped off the railroad cars. Goodwin's jail compound was large and chaotic, and captives mixed and talked. There was little segregation by gender, and Northup reported that inmates had some latitude as to where to sleep and with whom to speak. Because so many traders' human property moved through it, Goodwin had no incentive to institute an Isaac Franklin–style health regime or vaccinate captives against smallpox. A variety of regional accents could be heard in the din. The small coffle Birch transported mixed in with George Barnes's new purchases from North Carolina. There Northup learned that his own abduction and the brutality to which he was subject was part of a business strategy.

Kidnapping had long been part of North American slavery, but agents of Freeman's firm did not hesitate to traffic in freeborn African-descended Americans they could pound into chattels. It was a way to cut purchasing costs. As Northup and the other captives set about "learning the history of each other's wretchedness," he was handcuffed to a kidnap victim from Ohio named Robert, a "large yellow man, quite stout and fleshy, with a countenance expressive of the utmost melancholy." In a ship's slave manifest he was identified as Robert Jones, perhaps an alias. "He was a man of intelligence and information," Northup recalled, and "it was not long before we became acquainted with each other's history."[27]

The man's kidnapping had been strikingly similar to Northup's. Jones left two children and a wife in Cincinnati with the promise of employment in Virginia. An opportunity in the country's largest slave state was not an ideal option, but African-descended Americans faced tough prospects even in good times. Jones's Cincinnati family was left with the dread of not knowing where he had disappeared. He was probably betrayed into Finnall's hands. Northup recalled that he was "placed in confinement" in Fredericksburg, "and beaten until he had learned, as I had, the necessity and the policy of silence." Identifying the process as company policy was astute. Jones had been confined three weeks already. The two "became much attached." "We could sympathize with, and understand each other," Northup recalled.[28] In the space between those words lay hours of listening and telling, recognizing and affirming their humanity and hard times, bonding in friendship while chained to each other as bondsmen.

Captives seized opportunities to exchange information and provide one another support but lacked a unified script for the ordeal they were experiencing. Some persevered and preserved tatters of their social worlds. Northup met a married couple, David Singleton and Caroline Parnell, both in their early twenties, who feared losing each other. Singleton was one of two dozen Singletons embarked with Northup on the ship to New Orleans. Their fragile unity was probably the result of a slaveholder's bankruptcy, and Barnes bought them in North Carolina despite Freeman's warning against buying families. Not all had Parnell's or Singleton's courage. Mary Singleton was paralyzed with fear and shock. Northup described her as "a tall, lithe girl, of a most jetty black, [who] was listless and apparently indifferent." About twelve years old, she was being uprooted and seemed terrorized.[29] Others responded with anger.

Lethe Shelton voiced fury at her captors. Northup recalled her "long, straight hair" and features that conjured Native American ancestry. With "sharp and spiteful eyes," Shelton "continually gave utterance to the language of hatred and revenge." Having lost her husband to sale, she seemed indifferent to her surroundings and future, guarding her dignity with indignation. "Pointing to the scars upon her face," Northup remembered, "the desperate creature wished that she might see the day when she could wipe them off in some man's blood!" Each experienced separations and dislocations in intensely personal ways. One of the captives with whom Northup had traveled on boat and train, Clemens Ray, got a reprieve and returned to Georgetown. Northup later learned that he had escaped to Canada.[30] The constellation of responses Northup witnessed were consequences of an inherently destructive trade, yet the thuggish business culture was part of a strategy.

Freeman's upper South allies were accustomed to using violence to manage business risk rather than to invest in infrastructure and formulate or implement rational supply-chain management. One reason was the firm's loose and improvised vertical division of authority. Theophilus Freeman and his allies lacked Franklin and Armfield's capital and integrated supply chain. Instead of transporting captives through an unremitting sequence of secure and largely segregated spaces leading from purchase to sale, Freeman and his associates funneled captives through a series of hired intermediaries, none of whom had much interest in accounting for what later firms would call spoilage. Birch beat Northup into submission at the commencement of his odyssey, and Freeman would threaten the same at the point of sale. In between, captives seized opportunities to plot and plan, talk and offer mutual support.

While Northup was in Goodwin's jail, news of the wreck of the slave ship *Hermosa* and its captives' liberation was whispered like a good omen in some dark corners of Richmond. Word stoked the imaginations of some captives held for saltwater transport. The *Hermosa* had sailed from Richmond, bound for New Orleans, the previous fall. It wrecked off one of the Abaco Islands in the Bahamas, and British authorities freed the thirty-eight captives aboard. Like marine insurers, however, enslaved people understood the odds were long against such outcomes.[31]

Three weeks after being kidnapped, Northup and some forty others were embarked on yet another conveyance belonging to a third party. On a pleasant afternoon in late April, Goodwin ordered Northup and his companions to fall in and march to the city dock with their blankets and belongings. There they beheld the brigantine *Orleans*, tugging gently at its moorings. It was loading for a passage to New Orleans. In Richmond the James River tide rose and fell three feet, and the dock held oceangoing ships at high-tide level. "She was a vessel of respectable size," Northup recalled, "full rigged, and freighted principally with tobacco." The *Orleans* had about as much cargo space as two semitrailers in a later age of American commercial trucking. The Baltimore-built ship had been sailing for nearly three years and was a regular slaver.[32]

The commercial logic of the shipping company that owned the *Orleans* was as hard as that of the railroad. Selling passage to slave traders was good business. Hauling captives was woven into the fabric of coastal maritime commerce from Chesapeake ports. Freeman paid over $2,300 in shipping expenses on an 1839 passage in which the *Orleans* carried 135 involuntary passengers. If typical, the *Orleans*'s owners, Richard O. Haskins and Luther Libby, charged Freeman twenty dollars per captive for adults and ten dollars for children. As they did on the railroad, children rode for half price. Freeman gave a gratuity to the ship-master for their safe arrival. He also paid the bill for barrels of drinking water and meal to feed the captives.[33] The *Orleans* was nearly indistinguishable from the other oceangoing vessels that frequented the port.

Northup's captors, customs officials, and members of the shipping company were authors of a commercial transcript in which captives were simply slaves, listed by name in neat rows with descriptions of gender, age, height, and skin color and the names of the consigner and consignee. In the hours before the ship sailed, the ship's owner Luther Libby, the customs collector Thomas Nelson, and the *Orleans*'s master, William Wickham, signed a preprinted "Manifest of Slaves," which indicated that the named items of human cargo were "bound from the Port of Richmond, State of Virginia, for the Port of New Orleans, in the State of Louisiana." The falsehoods they created were not merely lies but lies they were willing to swear to under penalty of law. Northup was listed as "Plat Hamilton." He would not hear the name Plat until reaching

New Orleans. Eliza's identity was obscured by the name "Drady Cooper." She was listed as twenty-two years old; her height, five feet five inches tall; and her skin, "black." Birch reduced her age as enslavers often did, like a twentieth-century used-car salesman altering a car's odometer. "Her children" were enumerated but not named. The other kidnapping victim, Robert, was not listed on the manifest in Richmond. Libby, Nelson, and Wickham "solemnly [swore], to the best of [their] knowledge and belief, that the abovementioned Slave[s] were not imported or brought into the United States from and after the first day of January, one thousand eight hundred and eight, and that under the laws of the State they are held to service or labor. SO HELP us GOD."[34] The *Orleans* had regularly concealed such lies below its wooden decks.

The ship's owners put it into the coastal slave trade immediately after its launch in 1838. By 1843 the *Orleans* was being operated as part of Haskins and Libby's "Line of Packets, between Richmond and New Orleans," which included other slave ships. Besides William Goodwin, consigners of captives aboard previous voyages of the *Orleans* included Bacon Tait and Henry Davis, two of Richmond's most active traders in the 1840s. Henry Davis sent his human wares to Mark Davis in New Orleans. In 1840 the Davis brothers were responsible for 8.4 percent of saltwater slave imports into New Orleans. Theophilus Freeman was responsible for 15 percent. Over the decade, the Davis brothers increased their market share to 15 percent. On at least one occasion the *Orleans* sailed from Baltimore with captives belonging to Isaac Franklin's nephew James F. Purvis, who shipped captives to his former rival, Thomas McCargo in New Orleans. Like other slaving vessels in the coastwise trade, the *Orleans* plied a diverse trade. Besides the tobacco Northup witnessed, the ship carried foodstuffs such as butter along with passengers and assortments of goods to several merchants in Baltimore, Richmond, and New Orleans.[35]

To the captives locked belowdecks as the *Orleans* sailed down the James River, the ship was a place of confinement rather than a node on a commercial network or a floating firm. The temperate behavior of the captain and crew disarmed Northup. Shipmaster William Wickham was among the few managers in Freeman's supply chain who used guile to enforce discipline, even though the prerogative to flog insubordinates supported his shipboard authority. Northup recalled Wickham as "a small, genteel man, erect and prompt, with a proud bearing, and looked the personification of courage." His assessment may reflect traumatic bonding. Whatever the cause, Northup's characterization is scarcely reminiscent of eighteenth-century transatlantic slave shipmasters, whose well-deserved reputations as demons and sadists were legendary.

Wickham must have seemed a gentle soul compared to Birch and his partners. Yet such a shipmaster was willing to participate in slaving and kidnapping in the regular course of business.[36]

After sailing down the James River, Wickham anchored the *Orleans* in Hampton Roads, and several more captives were put aboard, including at least one more beaten and confused kidnap victim. At every stop Northup's coffle picked up another American robbed of legal freedom, a reflection of the terror that radiated through nearly all African-descended neighborhoods and families. The Norfolk trader George Apperson embarked Arthur Curtis, a Norfolk resident, his swollen face "covered with wounds and bruises, and, indeed, one side of it was a complete raw sore," Northup recalled. Curtis was still defiant as he was forced down into the ship's hold but "sank into a gloomy and thoughtful mood, and appeared to be counseling with himself," his face desperate yet determined. The second slave manifest signed in Norfolk lists Curtis as standing five feet ten inches tall and having dark skin. Northup discovered that Curtis had been assaulted and overpowered by several men in a Norfolk city street. Afterward "he was gagged and bound with ropes, and beaten, until he became insensible." Isolation followed. "For several days they secreted him in the slave pen at Norfolk," before they forced him to board the ship. His story was startlingly familiar. In Norfolk seven more souls were added to the official record of the *Orleans*'s human cargo, including Northup's friend and fellow captive Robert Jones. As it had in Richmond, the radical dislocation affected each differently. Curtis's attitude contrasted with that of Maria, embarked at the same time.[37]

Maria McCoy, or Mary McCoy, as she was listed on the manifest, must not have seen the sores on Curtis's face. She was sauntering into a sea of perils seemingly unaware. Northup recalled that she was "a rather genteel looking colored girl, with a faultless form, but ignorant and extremely vain." The sixteen-year-old stood five feet one inch tall. "The idea of going to New-Orleans was pleasing to her . . . [and] she declared to her companions, that immediately on our arrival in New-Orleans, she had no doubt, some wealthy single gentleman of good taste would purchase her at once!" In the ensuing weeks aboard ship Eliza may have counseled her against that risky strategy and to watch out for the lustful glances and lingering eyes of male buyers.[38]

The occurrence of sexual violence was not limited to land. The *Creole* uprising that occurred later in 1841 was touched off by enslavers' arrogance and sexual assaults on female captives. The *Creole* was similar to the *Orleans* in build and size, and it too plied a route between Richmond and New Orleans. On its autumn voyage, males and females were segregated belowdecks, but males were permitted on deck at any time. Yet they were forbidden access to females' compartments. In the *Creole*'s cabins, officers and traveling slave traders isolated six female captives in spaces accessible to themselves. Thomas McCargo was among the traders aboard. On that passage he took along his young son Theophilus as part of his apprenticeship in the slave trade. (That son was named after Theophilus Freeman, whom McCargo deemed a mentor.) Until the ship reached the Caribbean, the passage was uneventful. But a visit by a captive, Madison Washington, to the women's quarters precipitated the uprising. Washington and his fellow rebels killed one slave trader and held the rest of the crew and officers captive. The *Creole* landed in Nassau, where all but four of the rebels were later freed.[39]

Well before the *Creole* uprising, rapes of captives aboard domestic vessels attracted abolitionists' attentions. One report of "a cargo of slaves [taken] from some port in Virginia, round by sea, to N. Orleans," in the early 1830s hints at the sexual abuses to which captives were subject. "Once on the passage, in consequence of alarm, they kept them in the hold the whole period of four days and nights, and none were brought on deck during that time but a few females — and they, for purposes which I will not name." Domination was part of maritime culture. It was an age in which law and custom sanctioned corporal abuse and punishment as part of sailors' working conditions. It took a confident maritime manager to enforce discipline without such victimization. Young and green sailors, and especially sailors of African descent, were routinely exposed to harsh treatment, and in that atmosphere captives were vulnerable to a variety of abuses. A witness to the slaving passage "said the owners and sailors treated them most unmercifully — beating them, and in some instances literally knocking them down upon the deck."[40] Aboard some ships the brutal regime was unremitting.

As the *Orleans* sailed out of the Chesapeake Bay, Shipmaster Wickham deployed an alternative strategy that used ritual and maritime tradition, which reflected a crafty understanding of human political psychology. The ship had a crew of six, besides a cook, a mate, and Wickham. Without tight security, nearly fifty captives could overwhelm that force. Instead of segregation and physical abuse, the master and mate elevated some captives above others, putting them to work while granting small privileges. If this approach was done right, they could get captives to guard or police other captives. Northup recalled that "the hand-cuffs were taken off, and during the day we were allowed to remain on deck." That gave fifty captives about 1,800 square feet of deck on which to wander, not counting the space taken up by rigging, masts, and other gear. It was a crowded place. Wickham made Robert wait on him and the crew and designated Northup a ship's steward. Three others, Jim, Cuffee Singleton, and

Jenny were placed under Northup, preparing food and a "scorched" corn concoction that the cook called coffee. The captives took meals of boiled bacon and hoe cakes together, eating with fingers and drinking out of tin cups that each had carried from Richmond. Northup observed that Jim and Cuffee were "somewhat inflated with their situation as second cooks," and two would-be rebels were mollified.[41]

Food and eating were regimented, meals commencing at ten in the morning and five in the evening. During the day they were permitted on deck, and at night "we were driven into the hold, and securely fastened down."[42] Most had never been to sea and reacted accordingly. During a "violent storm," the ship "rolled and plunged," Northup recalled. Some became ill, and "others [were] on their knees praying, while some were fast holding to each other, paralyzed with fear." Vomit made the hold "loathsome and disgusting," and viewing the circumstances that would befall him and his fellow captives, Northup mused that it might have "saved the agony of many hundred lashes, and miserable deaths at last" had the vessel simply sunk.[43] Wickham's management strategy began to unravel when calm weather slowed the passage.

In the narrow shipping lane through the Bahamas, the *Orleans* stalled and a plot developed. Northup and his fellow kidnap victim Arthur Curtis talked of overthrowing the ship and sailing north. Neither knew how to sail, but they planned to head to New York City, a thousand miles to the north, rather than the Bahamas, which were practically in sight, trusting a "lucky wind" to carry the vessel there. News of the *Hermosa* rescue had apparently eluded them. The security aboard Wickham's ship would make a transatlantic slaving captain tremble and sweat. Similar conditions had permitted the rebellion aboard the *Decatur* in 1826, which exposed Austin Woolfolk to scrutiny. The *Decatur*'s master, Galloway, regretted his strategy to treat captives like passengers the moment he was tossed overboard to drown. Most coastal shipmasters were wary of such plots and locked captives belowdecks when the ship approached the Bahamas. William Grose, a Virginia native, had been snatched from his family, enslaved, and embarked on a ship from Baltimore to New Orleans among seventy others. "Nothing especial occurred except on one occasion," he recalled of the sea passage, "when, after some thick weather, the ship came near an English island: the captain then hurried us all below and closed the hatches. After passing the island, we had liberty to come up again."[44]

Northup and his coconspirators hit on a plan to surprise their captors. They tested out a hiding place under a lifeboat, where Northup spent a truant night on deck. Robert Jones, who had been designated a waiter, was allowed into the cabins. There he observed where the crew slept and how they were armed.

Northup and Curtis were to seize pistols and a cutlass and kill Wickham and his mate. Curtis was a strong man. A mason by trade, he was to wield a club to "beat back the sailors." Northup would use his canal boat experience to pilot the ship. Planners lost their nerve when Jones fell ill with smallpox and died four days later. All were "panic-stricken by the appearance of the small-pox."[45] A crew member sewed Jones's lifeless body into his blanket along with a ballast stone. After a perfunctory prayer it disappeared into the blue Caribbean, far from loved ones in Cincinnati.

The plot died along with Robert Jones, but Northup found an unlikely salve for his anger and anguish in John Manning, an English sailor. He "was a tall, well-built man, about twenty-four years old, with a face somewhat pock-marked, but full of benevolent expression," who had spent some time in Boston. He agreed to help Northup after learning that he was a kidnap victim. Such a security lapse was an unintended consequence of Freeman's business model. Wickham thought himself a merchant shipmaster and not a seaborne prison warden. He was not the *Orleans*'s regular skipper. Wickham staffed his ship with sailors picked for their seamanship rather than their thuggery. Transatlantic slavers were notorious for violence against crewmembers as well as captives; shipmasters' unremitting threats or uses of force were necessary to keep ships on course. In consequence, slave ship sailors were typically recruited by force or mischief. In contrast, crews of coastwise American vessels were recruited with high wages. American seaports were haunts of crimps and runners, to be sure, but the crews of American coastwise slavers signed on for a relatively short passage that included jailing duties. Hauling kidnap victims, however, was more than sailors like Manning had bargained for.[46]

As the ship sailed into the Mississippi River, Northup dictated a letter to his father, which Manning wrote by candlelight. It explained his predicament and called for help. Manning would post it from Louisiana. The letter led to an abortive attempt to rescue him, but since Northup's captors had smuggled him under an alias, there was little hope of locating him. By the time Manning finished Northup's note, the ship had reached La Balize, near the river's mouth, where a customs officer ratified the lies in official records. The customs officer "examined [the slave manifests] and found [them] Correct with the exception of Robert Jones," who Wickham testified "died on the passage." The ship sailed upriver to New Orleans, and after its arrival authorities freed Arthur Curtis. Word had reached the city that he had been kidnapped. He would return to Norfolk aboard the *Orleans*, listed again on a slave manifest. Nevertheless, Northup recalled, he "was almost crazy with delight."[47] His mood contrasted with those of his erstwhile shipmates.

There at the levee Northup, Eliza, Lethe Shelton, and the others met the man who claimed to own them. Theophilus Freeman expected each to play the part of a cooperative slave. He appeared on the *Orleans* and seized Birch's "gang." "Reading from his paper, he called, 'Platt,'" Northup recalled. He did not answer. He had never heard the name. "The name was called again and again," he recalled, "but still there was no reply." At last, Freeman identified Northup by his physical description on the manifest. After inquiring who shipped him, Wickham replied that Birch had. Wickham had simply called him Steward, the office he had held aboard ship. Freeman insisted on calling him Plat, the designation of slavery "forwarded by Burch to his consignee."[48] Freeman disembarked him at the levee.

As he emerged from the ship, Northup beheld a city about a third the size of New York City but five times larger than the one from which he had departed. In contrast to Richmond, the ground was flat and the built environment commanded the landscape. A generation before, visitors' eyes had focused on the three towers and spires of St. Louis Cathedral, which rose from the beige multistory buildings behind the levee. The focus of the landscape in 1841 was the 185-foot-tall St. Charles Hotel, known as the Exchange. Its gray-white dome and cupola rose prominently, an architectural symbol of the city's commercial progress. Men of affairs crowded its interior rooms talking prices, concluding deals, and auctioning slaves. At the levee, Northup spied scores of steamboats' smokestacks like black chutes rising out of decks, crammed in next to one another. In places the smokestacks were more numerous than the masts of sailing ships. The river air stank of wood smoke, decay, and excrement.[49]

From the levee he and the other *Orleans* captives were herded a short distance to Freeman's compound on Chartres Street, part of the city's business center. Northup and his companions trudged through streets paved solely with shells, planks, or ballast stones sunk in mud. Horses clomped alongside them, pulling drays and hacks. People speaking in regional dialects crowded them. Along the streets were low-slung cottages and multitiered buildings, some with elaborate exterior ironwork. After a short walk, Northup found himself confined in another slave jail. Freeman's compound was in a notorious section of the city through which much of the slave traffic moved. It reeked of commercial aspirations. Despair and misery, debauchery and victimization thrived in its shadows. If Henry David Thoreau had sought inspiration on Chartres Street in New Orleans instead of Walden Pond near Concord, Massachusetts, he might have written that the mass of men lead lives of strident desperation, their clamorous disputes and protestations silenced solely by the grave. The city's slave market was the biggest in the nation and also the most conspicuous. A Virginian visiting in 1836 remarked that the slave auction was "a scene of tumultuous confusion, in which all the business and professional men of the City engage. It seems to be the Soul of New Orleans."⁵⁰

That soul had many dark chambers. Confined in a cell invisible from the street, Northup may have shared the visitor's appraisal that the city was a "great Southern Babylon—the mighty receptacle of wealth, depravity and misery." Freeman's jail and auction rooms were located on what is now the 1400 block of Chartres Street between Esplanade Avenue and Kerlerec Street. Two-story brick buildings stood next to slate-roofed cottages with yellow walls and green doors and shutters. Neighboring traders included Thomas Boudar, who part-nered with Bacon Tait of Richmond and Mark and Benjamin Davis, also in the Richmond slave trade. Another resident, B. M. Campbell, imported captives from Baltimore, and John Hagan plied a trade between Charleston and New Orleans. Hagan had jails in both cities. Northup recalled that Freeman's compound resembled the two other jails in which he had been held, "except the yard was enclosed by plank, standing upright, with ends sharpened, instead of brick walls."⁵¹

Inside that stockade Freeman finished the work of making captives into slaves. All the violence, the isolation, the hands and chains of captors were rehearsals for the performance Freeman orchestrated on Chartres Street. Early one morning, Northup sardonically recalled, "the very amiable, pious-hearted Mr. Theophilus Freeman, partner or consignee of James H. Burch, and keeper of the slave pen in New-Orleans, was out among his animals." Northup captured the irony of his captor's given name (a translation of the Greek Theophilus is God lover, referenced in the Gospel of Luke and Acts). Freeman whipped and kicked his captives awake, which was a prelude to their being "properly trained" in how to act at his auction.⁵² Until then, there had been no gender segregation.

But males and females had separate parts to play in Freeman's theater. Customers demanded it. "The men were arranged on one side of the room, the women on the other," Northup recalled. Angular forms of the adult men formed one end of the line, while the thin frames of boys formed the other. "The tallest was placed at the head of the row," Northup recalled, "then the next tallest, and so on in the order of their respective heights." Clothed to accentuate characteristics customers valued, women were similarly arranged. The smallest, Eliza's daughter, Emily, "was at the foot of the line of women." Choreographing with blasphemy on his lips and a whip in his hand, Freeman "charged us to remember our places; exhorted us to appear smart and lively,— sometimes threatening, and again, holding out various inducements." He "exercised us in the art of 'looking smart,'" Northup recalled, "and of moving to our places with exact precision."[53] An assistant was sawing away at a fiddle in an awkward attempt at theme music.

Seizing an opportunity to play once again—and exit the procession—Northup took a turn at the instrument, and in a short time the performance began. Freeman "would make us hold up our heads," he recalled, "walk briskly back and forth, while customers would feel of our hands and arms and bodies, turn us about, ask us what we could do, make us open our mouths and show our teeth, precisely as a jockey examines a horse which he is about to barter for or purchase." Humiliation bled into abuse. "Sometimes a man or woman was taken back to the small house in the yard, stripped, and inspected more minutely," he remarked euphemistically. "Scars upon a slave's back were considered evidence of a rebellious or unruly spirit, and hurt his sale." Nearly all the traders paraded their human wares in lines or rows accenting gender and height, and the processions of slaves for sale converged on the St. Louis and St. Charles hotels. So much commercial activity took place below the eighty-eight-foot rotunda of the St. Louis Hotel that locals called it, like its sibling the St. Charles, the Exchange. The St. Louis had burned in February 1840, but it was being rebuilt by the time Freeman offered Northup for sale.[54]

In Freeman's auction, customers commenced buying. He asked fifteen hundred dollars for Northup, unsuccessfully. The commercial tune played in 1841 New Orleans remained the same as it had at the market's height five years before. But the tempo had slowed. Allegretto became adagio. The volume of captives was lower in response to slack demand. Prices had dropped in half since the peak year of 1836, but the same sorts of transactions were carried out. Cash-poor buyers haggled with traders over prices and financing, and after accepting financial paper, traders looked to bankers and merchants for trans-portable money to remit to distant suppliers. Among Northup's fellow captives on the *Orleans*, Maria McCoy was sold to William Theophilus Raynal of Jefferson Parish, who bought her for his son Louis.[55]

Some spouses survived the market ordeal together. David Singleton and Caroline Parnell were purchased by the same Natchez planter, but Eliza's family was disarticulated. Freeman sold Randall to a Baton Rouge planter who also bought Lethe Shelton, the woman venting rage when Northup met her in Richmond. Eliza's pleadings to buy her and prevent the separations led to little but Freeman's violent response and a mother's trauma and humiliation, "her tears falling in the boy's face like rain." Not realizing the ramifications, Randall assured his mother, "'Don't cry, mama. I will be a good boy. Don't cry.'" "What has become of the lad, God knows," sighed Northup twelve years later. His mother would never embrace him again, but Randall did live to adulthood. His

Baton Rouge neighbors would know him as Randall Berryman in 1870, a laborer who had grown up in bondage and been deprived of an education.[56] Back in Freeman's jail, the outlook worsened.

Freeman may have had Isaac Franklin's foresight concerning preventable disease, but he chose risk over the piddling cost of vaccinations. Some captives paid with their lives. About two weeks after Robert Jones died of smallpox aboard the *Orleans*, Northup began suffering symptoms, including severe head and back pains. Eliza and Emily developed them too, as did forty-year-old Harry Hyman, another captive disembarked from the *Orleans*. New Orleans was experiencing an epidemic, and enslaved people were suspected as vectors. Northup contracted hemorrhagic smallpox, a strain that is nearly always fatal, and went blind for three days. In the hospital, Hyman and Northup were housed together and lingered near death. After anticipating eternal release, both recovered and returned to Freeman's hell.[57]

Smallpox ravaged captives' bodies and savaged Freeman's profits. After convalescing, Eliza and Emily rejoined Northup and Hyman. Since Northup and Eliza had met in a Washington, D.C., jail, they had been in the slave market nearly three months and showed signs of sickness and fatigue. In late June Freeman sold all three adults to William Ford, a Baptist minister and planter. He paid one thousand dollars for Northup, seven hundred for Eliza, and nine hundred for Hyman. Northup supposed that "small-pox had depreciated our value." The trader kept Emily despite Ford's offer to buy her.[58]

Sexual exploitation was an integral part of the market. A visitor remarked on the practice of city gentleman keeping light-skinned concubines "for [their] exclusive use." On the main commercial thoroughfare, Freeman's "Chartres Street is also the promenade of the fashionable Prostitute, who flaunts along in her gaudy trappings, the subjects of gaze and remark of all who resort to this famous Street."[59] Calling attention to the woman herself obscured the brutalization she endured as an unwilling sex worker and the business culture that supported the trade.

Sexualized violence was part of Freeman's brand, and he explained that Emily would generate high returns as she grew. "There were heaps and piles of money to be made of her, he said, when she was a few years older." Northup could sympathize with Eliza; he had a daughter Emily's age. Like his Chartres Street neighbors, Freeman was a pimp as well as a trader. Slave trading and pimping were not exclusive pursuits, and one contemporary source characterizes traders' purchasing agents as "pimps." "There were men enough in New-Orleans who would give five thousand dollars," Northup recalled Freeman saying, "for such an extra, handsome, fancy piece as Emily would be, rather than not get her."[60] Emily was the daughter of a white planter and a woman with European and African ancestry. Freeman had a particular eye for such victims. His more theatrical displays corroborate Northup's recollections.

Freeman made sexuality into a calling card. Two decades before Ivan Goncharov's *Ilya Ilyitch Oblomov* satirized Russian aristocracy by receiving visitors in bed, Freeman presented himself as a spectacle of carnality by doing the same. Unlike the impotent Oblomov, Freeman reposed with his formerly enslaved concubine Sarah Connor. It was an eroticized advertisement of his market penetration. Freeman succeeded in generating publicity, but his tableau was an arrogant disaster from another perspective. James and Isaac Franklin victimized and violated female captives, though they also charmed and culti-vated New Orleans merchants and bankers. They had built credit and standing, but Freeman blithely confirmed suspicions of abolitionists and travelers who considered New Orleans "a second Sodom."[61] Whatever cachet such displays brought him on Chartres Street, they did not endear him to the financial estab-lishment, especially in the lean times of the early 1840s. While Freeman cocked his hat and sneered at convention, Connor used her sexuality defensively.

In part for publicly endorsing Freeman's potency, Connor demanded and received her manumission from the slave trader. A newspaper contended that by 1850 Connor had "been living with Freeman, as his wife, for a number of years" in an arrangement not unlike that in similar households of slave traders in Richmond, such as Corinna and Silas Omohundro. Connor actively partici-pated in splintering so many families, if only to preserve and extend ties supported by her domestic partnership with Freeman. She too faced a desperate series of non-choices. She must have witnessed scenes like the one Northup narrated of Emily and Eliza being parted in 1841. As Emily cried for her mother, Freeman tore Eliza from her. The grieving mother went with her new owner, Ford, along with Hyman and Northup.[62] At the levee all boarded a steamer bound for the cotton frontier.

The geoeconomic transformation of Louisiana's Red River region was part of an unbroken chain of violence that uprooted forests and disarticulated families to make cotton country. The ordeal of Northup's capture and sale was a preface to his forced labor transforming the landscape onto which he was tossed. He, Eliza, and others would shoulder the burdens of hewing wood and carrying water for cotton planters and sugar masters. The journey to William Ford's Avoyelles Parish estate in Louisiana's piney woods began with a river passage aboard the 150-ton *Rodolph*, another conveyance that sped goods to market and captives to sites of production. The Indiana-built side-wheel steamer had been based in Cincinnati before being put into service connecting the Red River port of Alexandria, Louisiana, with New Orleans.[63]

River steamers were perilous and inefficient by the measure of future generations, but boats like the *Rodolph* were keys to the cotton kingdom. Steamboats were third behind land and slaves as investments in the Mississippi Valley after the 1820s, and their mechanical rhythms were the musical embodiments of capitalist development. Despite the danger of boilers exploding from operators' furor for speed, hulls ripped by snags or submerged debris, prohibitively low water levels in summers and droughts, and hazardous currents after winter storms, steamboat carriage drew vast territories of the interior South into the transatlantic commodity chain. They powered slavery too.[64]

Steamboats made bondspersons more valuable, raised productivity on plantations, and gave any landowner near a river with timber to cut into firewood a ready source of income. By the time Northup and Eliza were steaming upriver, there were thousands of landings on rivers like the Mississippi and the Red, many invisible except to experienced boaters. Riverfront plantations frequently had landings on which would-be fuel vendors, passengers, and cargo consigners waved hats or handkerchiefs to flag down passing boats. River steamers connected port cities to places isolated by distance and previously served by flimsy and dangerous flatboats. Packed to the guards, the *Rodolph* could transport 1,200 bales of cotton down the Red River and into the Mississippi River. It also carried news back and forth between Alexandria and New Orleans. In late June 1841 it landed in New Orleans, and Ford took his recently purchased bondspeople aboard.[65] From the deck Northup could survey the large muddy river against whose currents the steamboat struggled. The Mississippi made the James River look like a stream and the Champlain Canal a ditch.

On its shores Northup witnessed the rich natural tapestry being reworked from woodlands into long furrows of cotton and fields of sugar. Acres of knee-high corn broke on groves of tall trees. His journey of two hundred miles between New Orleans and Alexandria included a turn into the muddy Red River. Northup described it as "a sluggish, winding stream, flowing through a vast region of primitive forests and impenetrable swamps, almost wholly destitute of inhabitants."[66] The *Rodolph* landed several times to embark and disembark passengers and goods and to load wood that the boat's furnace devoured. Northup and his traveling companions disembarked in Alexandria. The village of a few hundred residents had grown up as a Spanish trading hub and part of an old overland trading route to Texas and Mexico.

Steam transport continued inland, the hissing and pounding announcing the extent to which Euroamerican development penetrated the piney woods.

As they had been in Virginia, Northup and Eliza were taken from steamer to railroad. In their formative stages, railroads connected steamboat landings to one another. Ford's bondspeople boarded the Alexandria and Cheneyville Railroad, one of several state-sponsored internal improvements. Louisiana had chartered the Alexandria and Cheneyville in 1835. Capitalized at $500,000, it was to connect the two river port towns, one on the Red River and the other on Bayou Boeuf. It was the tenth railroad Louisiana had chartered but the first that terminated on a river other than the Mississippi. The road "is coming on quite briskly," a report from New Orleans chirped in 1838. "Two steam cars have lately arrived, one of which has been put on the track," which then stretched for two miles. Locals were riding back and forth for pleasure. Six miles had been built by 1839 and ten more would be completed. The road was not insignificant. Louisiana had just forty miles of roads operating in 1840, and many if not most of the state's railroads used slave labor. As in Virginia, several Louisiana railroad companies held slaves simultaneously as laborers and assets.[67] That was a variation on a theme played in several registers.

The land through which Northup and his companions traveled was being transformed from a trading route to Texas into a highway for cotton and sugar going to market in New Orleans. Settlers streamed into Texas, flowing in the opposite direction of the cotton they smuggled to New Orleans for sale. By 1845 one ferry operator was advertising "The Great Texas Crossing" at the Red River's mouth, which funneled travelers to a route over "a new road having been cut from Tunica Hills, passing through Isaac Franklin's Plantation to the Mississippi, by which all swamp is avoided." Franklin's estate was making piles of money selling wood to steamboat operators, and bondspersons were cutting timber on the spot that would later become the Louisiana State Penitentiary at Angola.[68] Travelers fleeing obligations and seeking fortunes swarmed the landscape.

Like planters, southern railroad companies consumed credit as voraciously as steam engines consumed wood. Railroads incurred up-front costs for labor in the form of buying enslaved workers. Because of that, they needed large amounts of capital at the start-up phase of development. Once construction began, companies employing slaves had to borrow more money to keep on track, in effect financing their labor costs before the labor was performed and long before the results of the labor generated revenues. Railroads that employed wage workers and even hired slaves paid labor costs after the labor was complete. In such schemes, workers and slaveholders financed industrial employers, whose capital investments consisted of building materials, real estate, equipment, and debt-servicing payments. Hard times set back the process. The panic of 1837 hobbled railroad expansion, and the bank failures of the early 1840s left Louisiana legislators reluctant to sponsor further construction. Foreign investment declined with the market's confidence. Miles of track in Louisiana doubled in the 1840s, but they doubled to just eighty miles by 1850. The state preferred to rely on its abundant waterways rather than to invest in railroad building. In contrast to banks and railroads, steamers were lightly regulated private investments, although both state and federal authorities worked to improve river navigation.[69]

Slave traders also promoted railroads. The Pointe Coupee planter and erstwhile slave smuggler Charles R. Morgan—brother-in-law of Judge Jacob Charles Van Wickle—became a commissioner of the Atchafalaya Railroad and Banking Company when it was incorporated in 1835. Like other hybrids of common carriers or utilities and banks, railroad banks were incorporated to finance construction and operation of the road simultaneously. According to a contemporary source, railroad banks were supposed "to ensure the construction of the Road, the *Means*, are to give the Stockholders of the Road the privilege of Banking, to such an extent as will yield interest on their investments from the beginning." Recognizing that finance fertilized technology, the railroad bank "will hold out a temptation to extend the Road as far as possible, by expanding the capital of the Bank with the extension of the Road." Not coincidentally, Morgan's Pointe Coupee plantation served as the Atchafalaya Railroad and Banking Company's Mississippi River terminus, which raised its value considerably.[70]

Euroamerican migrants envisioned cotton and sugar as the main staples of Avoyelles and Rapides parishes, but the woodlands ecosystem that covered those lands yielded a rich initial harvest. The Red River Valley of Louisiana consisted of dense forests and varied habitats along the abundant waterways. The tall old-growth woodlands seemed inexhaustible. A traveler passing through to Texas in the 1830s remarked, "To ride a short distance in them, is not unpleasant; but to continue on, day after day, is monotonous—there is no change of scenery." Thick groves greeted Ford and his new purchases as they exited the train at its terminus at Bayou Lamourie and walked the dozen miles down the Old Texas Road. Northup was impressed by the low, marshy landscape, forested with white oak, chinquapin, gum, sycamore, cypress, and tall straight yellow pines. Roving beneath them were native longhorn cattle. Americans were already sending them northeast to Tennessee, Kentucky, Illinois, and Ohio. Mississippi River steamboat passengers complained of the foul-smelling hoofed cargoes, and migrants arriving on the eastern Texas grasslands found the range thick with longhorns. While cattle roamed the Louisiana forests, wetlands were crawling with alligators and swamps with moccasins, and flies and mosquitoes "swarmed the air." Northup recalled that the insects "penetrated the porches of the ear, the nose, the eyes, the mouth"; he shuddered, remembering mosquitoes' proboscises sinking into his skin, threatening to "devour us—carry us away piecemeal, in their small tormenting mouths." Bears, cougars, and jaguars also inhabited the area, but their roaming grounds were under assault. Mosquitoes and flies thrived in the new environment, but larger predators did not. Steamers hungry for fuel and settlers demanding building materials made deforestation and drainage pay.[71] Ax men felled the tall trees, and entrepreneurs like Ford built steam-powered sawmills. As they did in other areas of the cotton frontier, new landowners assembled enslaved Americans to shoulder labor burdens while pressuring Indians to leave.

The piney woods landscape was not empty of indigenous people, but as Native Americans' homeland disappeared, newly arrived captives' troubles were compounded. Choctaws had moved into the area decades before, pressuring the Adais, members of the Caddo Confederacy of northwestern Louisiana, western Arkansas, and East Texas. (The Sabine River had been previously known as the Rio de los Adais.) Northup recalled in detail Indian inhabitants who hunted and traded in the neighborhood. Indians too used the land to their benefit, but a thousand years of human habitation had not changed the Red River Valley as much as thirty years of American redevelopment.

That capitalist engine used human as well as wooden fuel. For Eliza, dislocations and losing her children intensified her woes and sped her decline into utter despair. "When we left Washington Eliza's form was round and plump," Northup recalled, "and in her silks and jewels, [she] presented a picture of graceful strength and elegance." Eliza became "a thin shadow of her former self" on Ford's cotton plantation. "Her face had become ghastly haggard, and the once straight and active form was bowed down, as if bearing the weight of a hundred years." Losing her children disabled her, and after she became "useless in the cotton-field, she was bartered for a trifle" to a planter named Peter Compton. "Grief had gnawed remorselessly at her heart," Northup lamented, and debilitated her "until her strength was gone." On Compton's farm Eliza died grieving for her children.[72] The indifferent landscape consumed thousands like Eliza as people like her owner clamored for improvements that sped the region's transformation.

The government responded and hired a force to remove the main natural obstacle to developing the Red River, which was a vast logjam. The Great Raft on the Red River northwest of Natchitoches was an ancient impediment to navigation. Shifting clusters of rotting logs and debris obstructed the river for miles at a time for a distance of 150 miles. In the early nineteenth century it blocked steamboat travel and settlement. Because of the raft, Natchitoches had

been the transit point for Stephen F. Austin's migrating group to Coahuila y
Tejas and Euroamerican adventurers following them, such as Davy Crockett,
Sam Houston, and the Louisiana planter and slave smuggler James Bowie.
Northup and the others trod part of the way to Ford's plantation in their footsteps. To open the Red River north of Natchitoches, the U.S. government
funded major navigation improvements projects. Even before Americans negotiated the cession of northwestern Louisiana from the Caddo Confederacy, the
War Department gave the steamboat captain Henry Miller Shreve a contract to
clear the raft.[73]

Shreve exemplified a capitalist imagination captivated by wealth-creating
possibilities and the transformative potential of human ingenuity. Shreve was
the apotheosis of a steamboat entrepreneur and the Jacksonian exemplar of
humanity against nature. The New Jersey native shaped the architecture of
southeastern riverboats with shallower drafts and wider beams than eastern
steamers, and he developed the iconic two-decked, twin-smokestack design that
made steamboats look like great layer cakes. Shreve theatrically steamed the
Enterprise to New Orleans in 1814 to assist General Andrew Jackson's forces in
the city's defense. Long a fierce competitor in the Mississippi River steamboat
business, Shreve cut in on Robert Fulton and Robert R. Livingston's federal
steamboat monopoly on the Mississippi River. He migrated into government
contracting, clearing obstructions on the Ohio, Mississippi, and Arkansas rivers.

Northup's enslavement owed much to Shreve's efforts to straighten rivers
and improve navigation. Improvers' coordinated efforts were rivaled only by
their hubris. Shreve and others advocated clear-cutting along riverbanks to
prevent fallen logs from snagging riverboats and then contracted to clear the
cave-ins caused by the consequent erosion. Shreve heroically cut channels to
shorten distances taken up by meanders on the Mississippi River.

Northup witnessed the results of Shreve's 1831 attempt to right nature's
imperfections. Before then the Mississippi River flowed in a meandering arc
called Turnbull's Bend that intersected with the Red River, which flowed into
it, and the Atchafalaya River, which flowed out of it. Shreve put steam-powered
digging machines and 159 men to work cutting a channel that lopped off eighteen miles of the Mississippi at the bend's neck. At the same time it lengthened
the Red River and made it the source of the Atchafalaya. Within days of the
Mississippi's flooding Shreve's ditch, the river widened in that spot to half a
mile and deepened to the upriver depth. Shreve sought to straighten other parts
of the river, but the Army Corps of Engineers stopped him. Improvements put
increased pressure on the levees downriver and threatened more erosion.
Shreve went to work instead clearing the Red River's Great Raft. In 1833 his

force started hacking away at it with the help of a two-hulled snag boat, the *Archimedes*. By the spring of 1837 steamers like the 139-ton *Nicholas Biddle* could reach Shreve Town, later Shreveport, and by 1838 steamboats could reach East Texas from New Orleans or Saint Louis. Twenty years after Shreve's crew began attacking the Great Raft, railroad construction linking Shreveport to Texas and points west was under way. The steamers delivered a world of consumer goods and construction materials, including railroad ties and nails. Hopeful planters like William Ford bought lands in the valley and sent cotton, hides, and other commodities back to New Orleans.[74]

Clearing the Great Raft opened the Red River region to ranching and raising cotton and sugar. It also opened it to slavery. Enslavers put people like Northup to work realizing their ambitions. Using his knowledge of wood and water, Northup became involved in efforts to annihilate distances between raw materials and their markets. Ford owned a lumber mill on Indian Creek, a tributary of Bayou Boeuf. To build some social capital with Ford, Northup constructed a canal from his owner's sawmill on Indian Creek via Bayou Boeuf to Bayou Lamourie, where Ford's customers wanted their lumber delivered. Ford's foreman at the mill took a dim view of Northup's internal improvement project, but Northup was determined not to be confounded.

He engaged with the spirit of the age. Though enslaved, Northup oversaw a small workforce of at least three other men. Using his canal experience, his workforce cleared Indian Creek of obstructions, principally fallen trees. Northup's workers then built four parallelogram-shaped cribs from squared-off logs. Cribs were superstructures on which logs were fastened. "One hand could manage three cribs," Northup recalled. "I took charge of the forward three, and commenced poling down the creek," the raft of twelve cribs proceeding downriver laden with lumber. "In due time we entered [Bayou Boeuf] . . . and finally reached our destination in a shorter period of time than I had anticipated." "The arrival of the raft at Lamourie created a sensation, while Mr. Ford loaded me with commendation." A chorus of grudging praise greeted Northup's ingenuity. "On all sides I heard Ford's Platt pronounced the 'smartest nigger in the Pine Woods'—in fact I was the Fulton of Indian Creek."[75] The improvement buoyed Ford's fortunes and paid dividends on his investment in Northup. Viewing his future in slavery, Northup set his face like a flint and refused to be ashamed.

James Birch had pounded Northup into a slave, Theophilus Freeman had orchestrated his transfer to the cotton kingdom, and William Ford stole the fruits of his labor during his most productive years. Ford knew little and cared less for the businesses run by the traders Freeman and Birch, jailor William Goodwin, shipmaster William Wickham, and the steamboat and railroad companies deep in their supply chain. But that chain furnished workers who turned old forests into new fields, sawing the timber into lumber, and expanding an empire for slavery in the process. As projects such as those on which Northup toiled transformed forests into fuel and buildings, cleared land for fields, and improved transportation, waves of planters like Ford moved in and demanded bound laborers to grow cotton. Traders like Freeman, Goodwin, and Birch fed the demand. On Ford's plantation, Northup met Sam, who "had worked on a farm near Georgetown," Washington, D.C., before being shipped to New Orleans for sale. "Sam knew Burch," Northup recalled wryly. The men talked of their similar ordeals on the journey from Washington. Northup grimaced, "It was remarkable how well we agreed upon the subject of his superlative rascality." Yet Northup had just commenced working for a succession of owners in a constellation of enterprises, including toiling on cotton and sugar plantations.[76]

Solomon Northup's odyssey shows a less organic and more mechanical market than the one Isaac Franklin had mastered. Theophilus Freeman's slaving business appears as a sequence of horror chambers opening on a growing landscape of fantastic creativity matched only by its capacity for ferocious violence. And yet Northup traveled through a vital center of a geoeconomic order that was becoming more highly elaborated, complex, and robust. The prevailing social relations of capital jarred critics who identified the cash nexus as one of capitalism's mortal sins. Thomas Carlyle warned of a "Mechanical Age" that destroyed individual freedom and dignity, and Karl Marx contended that reducing humans to specialized workers and their production to monetary exchanges extinguished community. Carlyle and Marx analyzed upheavals at the eastern ends of the great chain linking American bondspersons to the workers of Britain, Ireland, and Europe.[77]

Carlyle and Marx had yawningly different premises, theories, and remedies, but they both cried that industrial capitalism rotted organic social relations, fattening property holders and starving workers and their families of bread and dignity. While Northup toiled in Louisiana, Marx grasped some of the economic linkages that connected alluvial lands and aboriginal forests in the North American southeast to industries that extended Britain's economic clout. "Without slavery you have no cotton, without cotton you have no modern industry," he wrote in 1846. Sans chattel slavery, Marx contended, "North America, the most progressive country, would be transformed into a primitive country." Yet he and other political economists tended to historically layer slavery beneath an emerging capitalist order, ignoring the experiences of those like Northup. Marx focused on horizontal divisions of labor that distinguished supposed wage slaves from the African-descended bondspersons who gave workers in old and New England fibers to spin and weave and crystals to sweeten their coffee and tea.[78]

Northup's enslavement was a consequence of capitalist development rather than a drag on it. He glimpsed the vast market geography on which that drama played out. Yet it remained hidden to most reformers. Northup's depictions of a chain of power and violence in his commercially successful autobiography *Twelve Years a Slave* (1853) rebuked but did not appreciably change the prevailing narrative. The focus of that narrative partially explains why slavery's violence appeared personal rather than systemic. Antislavery writings focused on the human dramas of owners and enslaved people. Mastery and slavery form the primary themes in *Twelve Years a Slave*, but Northup narrates the capitalist linkages submerged in the sentimentality of competing characterizations like those in Harriet Beecher Stowe's *Uncle Tom's Cabin*. Carlyle was seduced by such novelistic characterizations of American slavery and the racist caricatures of African-descended people in which they were often wrapped. He contended that bondspersons were excluded from "the poisonous taproot of all mischief," the free market. Carlyle did not see Freeman's supply chain, but Northup's testimony is a sterling argument against racism.[79]

The same racial technology that permitted Northup's captors to sell him into slavery also construed wage labor as white and slave labor as black. Instead of linking North American captives like Northup with workers in the English northwest through chains of credit and commodities, critics' and writers' racial imaginations accentuated differences that fused human phenotypes with socioeconomic categories. Geographic borders like the Ohio River, featured as ideological boundaries, were reflected in geospatial designations of free and slave states. Such fractured thinking helped both antislavery activists and proslavery polemicists like George Fitzhugh obscure connections and emphasize differences between capitalist labor organization in Britain, Europe, and elsewhere and chattel slavery in the United States. The resulting sociopolitical narrative of a house divided was tenacious, however belied by flows of money and goods.[80]

At the heart of the process Northup endured was the fact that enslaved workers were both human resources and capital investments. Violence paid their dividends. The diversifying market put renewed stresses on the family lives of the enslaved. In places from which captives were taken, transportation, extractive, and commercial processing enterprises used slave labor extensively. Throughout the country internal improvement projects expanded navigation and in the southeast brought the cotton complex farther up rivers like the Red in Louisiana. Changes in the land altered the ecology, and the acres cleared of timber and brought under cultivation intensified the demand for bound laborers, expanded an interest in slavery in the United States, and added to the lands that supported the commercial and imperial rise of Great Britain. Those acres grew along with demand for carbon fuel, which accelerated deforestation and caused ecological disasters. Planters in Texas were expanding slavery's frontier in the trans-Mississippi West. Slave traders reaped newfound profits in the resulting bonanza, and their business practices reflected capitalist development in a mechanical age.[81]

After toiling for twelve years in sugar and cotton fields, Solomon Northup was rescued by allies who came for him from New York. They had a difficult time locating him, and Northup's reentry into his old life was troubled. The world to which he returned from bondage had even fewer legal protections than in 1841. The Fugitive Slave Act of 1850 outlawed many of the means African-descended Americans had used to defend themselves and loved ones against kidnapping, and anyone accused of being a fugitive also bore the burden of proving he or she was not. Northup's journey home in 1853 solemnly retraced the links in a slave supply chain that continued to furnish thousands upon thousands of captives to the lower South. Its complexion had changed, but the slave market was robust and growing. In New Orleans Northup ran into Theophilus Freeman. "I did not think it worth while to renew acquaintance with him," Northup remarked bitterly. Freeman had tumbled from successful businessman to "low, miserable rowdy—a broken-down, disreputable man." His ambitions had turned to tragedy. After building a fortune out of the miseries and deaths of African-descended Americans, Freeman failed in 1842. By then he held assets of nearly $138,000 and debts approaching $187,000, and creditors and courts hounded him until at least 1861.[82]

While he suffered bankruptcy, Sarah Connor paid a steep price for Freeman's theatrics of sexual liberation, race rebellion, and sharp dealing. In the mid–1840s Freeman was struggling to collect the debts of the failed John Goodin and Company and was involved in a suit to collect debts owed his North Carolina partner, George Barnes. During that time he was sued by the Bank of Kentucky. It claimed that Freeman owed money and that he had hidden assets by transferring them to Sarah Connor, his former slave and concubine, now his wife—assets concealed by her manumission. The bank demanded that Connor's freedom be revoked and that Freeman forfeit her as an asset, along with her property. Perhaps Freeman glimpsed the irony of a distant entity snatching away his wife after he had broken up so many marriages in the slave trade. Connor was not sold for his creditors' benefit, but the episode embarrassed the friendless Freeman.[83] Freeman's failure caused no more than a ripple in the slave market.

Other traders simply took over his business. His strategic alliances disintegrated while his allies reformed a supply chain focused on rival sales agents.

Nathaniel Orr, depiction of Northup's arrival home,
meeting with his wife and children (From Solomon
Northup, *Twelve Years a Slave: Narrative of Solomon
Northup, a Citizen of New-York, Kidnapped in
Washington City in 1841, and Rescued in 1853*
[Auburn, N.Y.: Derby and Miller, 1853], 320)

Freeman's sexual theatrics with an African-descended woman gave critics the
theme with which they dishonored him. The "celebrated negro-trader," a
Mississippi newspaper sneered, "who once fixed his head quarters or African
harem at the forks of the road, Natchez," was charged in a perjury case. Connor
had accused a man of kidnapping a slave. The accused was acquitted but
"gratified his revenge by prosecuting the woman for perjury," for which she was
convicted, a conviction sustained on appeal. The alleged slave stealer prosecuted Freeman for suborning perjury, "inducing the woman to swear falsely."
It was a way of retaliating against a woman of color who dared cross a white
man and a smack at Freeman's honor and integrity. Connor was ordered jailed
in New Orleans during the proceedings. Freeman, the report speculated, "has
a large fortune, a fortune safely concealed—and the lawyers will enjoy the

benefits of it."[84] There was no justice for Northup in Freeman and Connor's humiliation and failure.

Northup returned to the East Coast sites of the crimes against him. He entered the city of Richmond, "where I caught a glimpse of Goodin's pen." It was strategically located near the rail depots and had grown along with the city slave market. Goodwin was still in business, and in the early 1850s he partnered with the Woolfolk veteran Henry N. Templeman. By then Templeman and Goodwin were receiving captives railroaded from the hinterland. The railroad ran all the way from Richmond to Washington, D.C., and any passenger seeking passage back to New York merely needed to change trains several times at city depots in Maryland, Pennsylvania, New Jersey, and New York. Northup's rescuers and allies sought vengeance, but his captors escaped justice. Birch was tried in Washington, D.C., but acquitted. The two men who kidnapped him were tried in New York but never convicted.[85]

Twelve years after his disappearance from Saratoga Springs, Northup returned home. The family had moved to Glens Falls, where his wife, Anne, got a job in a hotel. His mother had died but a grandson had been born. He was named Solomon Northup Stanton. Northup's daughter Margaret, he recalled, "did not recognize me." "When I left her, she was but seven years old, a little prattling girl, playing with her toys." Twelve years later, "she was grown to womanhood—was married, with a bright-eyed boy standing by her side." "When told who I was, she was overcome with emotion, and unable to speak." His daughter Elizabeth appeared, and his wife "Anne came running from the hotel" where she worked in the kitchen. Northup's son Alonzo was just five when his father was abducted. Alonzo would eventually wear a United States uniform during the Civil War and participate in the 1864 Battle of Bloody Bridge in South Carolina. "They embraced me," Northup said of his family, "and with tears flowing down their cheeks, hung upon my neck." Northup hesitated to remember more for his readers. "I draw a veil over a scene which can better be imagined than described."[86]

MACHINES OF EMPIRE

On any particular evening in the 1850s the steamship merchant Charles Morgan could be seen exiting his New York City offices at 5 Bowling Green. In his mid-fifties, Morgan gazed out on a city that knew him as Commodore Morgan, a captain of a growing industry. His steamships burned coal, but his firm was powered by federal largesse and the republic's expansion in the American Southwest. Army contracts during the U.S.–Mexican War gave him a commanding advantage over competitors, and a flood of westbound slave-holders sustained it. They permitted the firm to grow to such proportions that it projected private power in foreign affairs. Morgan embodied the tycoon just as the word entered the English lexicon and owed more than a little of his rising fortunes to the Gulf Coast slave trade. Casting an eye leftward up Broadway, he could spy the front stoop of his competitor Cornelius Vanderbilt's offices. Beyond it rose the spires of Trinity Church, beneath which carriages and carts rattled up and down Broadway. Looking southward, Morgan glimpsed the Battery and steamers on New York Bay. In front of him was the elegant fountain in Bowling Green Park and the carriage that took him home to a stylish mansion in Madison Square. Six feet tall, strong, and clean-shaven, Morgan had widely spaced eyes, a prominent nose, thick, graying, sandy hair, and traces of a Connecticut accent. He was quiet, shrewd, and self-confident. As his carriage lumbered uptown, he could contemplate a business that reached thousands of miles from the metropolis.[1] With strokes of a pen rather than strokes of a lash, his New York–based partnership profited from slaving and the enlargement of the cotton complex.

Morgan's line dominated steamship travel on the Gulf Coast and was one of the largest shippers of enslaved people in the 1850s United States. Morgan's firm served the slavery business like an oilfield-services company in the petroleum age. Steamship technology changed the interstate slave trade as it grew to serve a strikingly dynamic zone of commercial agriculture. But Morgan owed his successes to strategy and not merely technology. During its rise in the 1840s his firm was in many ways a traditional shipping merchant enterprise. Morgan was an owner-manager who preferred an agile private venture to a cooperative public one and staffed key management positions with male family members. The corporate culture was like one of his ships, with him at the helm, charging into a gale at full speed. Morgan took few steps to limit liability at a time in which steamship companies were flexing their corporate muscles to do so. His enterprise sought advantages through government subsidies and by buying out or ruining competitors rather than by competing in quality and creating value for customers. Morgan's firm embodied the James K. Polk administration's imperial ambitions and matched the swagger of the Texans on whose business it depended. On most workdays Morgan rode to and from Madison Square, but he kept a desk at branch offices in New Orleans and Galveston.

On the distant wharves of Louisiana and Texas, the great machines he owned took on goods and passengers, offering efficiencies to travelers. On some passages one of Morgan's ships carried nearly as many bondspersons as sailing ships like the *Isaac Franklin* in the heyday of the domestic saltwater trade. But Morgan's New York–built steamships were capacious enough to combine that traffic within a thriving passenger and cargo trade. Some 99,000 bondspeople entered Texas in the 1850s, about two-fifths of the enslaved people moved across U.S. state lines in that decade. They took many routes, some on wagons and others on steamboats through Louisiana's Red River region, passing cotton bales hauled in the opposite direction. Along the Gulf Coast the forced migration of thousands of bondspersons took place within a company that achieved an economy of scale rare among contemporary enterprises.[2]

The 1,043-ton *Mexico* was among the line's workhorses. That side-wheel steamer was constructed in New York City in 1851, its machinery built at the Morgan Iron Works. The *Mexico* had two decks, three masts, a round tuck, and a prominent chimney venting coal smoke. It was the length of a modern Airbus A330–300 transoceanic jetliner and about twice as wide as the airliner's fuselage. Its coal bunker, boilers, and other machinery took up about 18,500 cubic feet. Available cargo capacity was 577 tons, or about 23,000 cubic feet, about five and a half times the capacity of a 53-foot semitrailer in the age of U.S. commercial trucking. Few who encountered the ship at the New Orleans levee would mistake the *Mexico* for a riverboat. Besides its distinctive shape, the *Mexico* had over three and one-third times more cargo capacity than the steamboat that took Solomon Northup up the Red River in 1841. The largest river steamers would

U.S.S. *General Bragg*, ca. 1862–63 (formerly the
Mexico) (Photo 46642, Naval History and Heritage
Command, Washington, D.C.)

reach its size only by the end of the 1850s. Enslaved cargoes of transatlantic
proportions were concealed in its wooden hull. In early January 1853 the *Mexico*
departed New Orleans with at least 155 enslaved people aboard; they belonged to
eighteen different citizens or firms in seven southern states. A Matagorda newspaper editor cheered the large consignments of African-descended bondspersons
disembarked in Texas from nearly every steamship arriving from New Orleans.[3]

Morgan's fleet of steamers did not look like slave ships, at least compared to
the "floating dungeons" of the Atlantic trade. Instead of being confined to
coffin-sized shelves fitted with shackles for captives, bondspeople were plunged
into baggage or freight compartments alongside merchandise and bags of mail.
Instead of weeks or months at sea, passage between New Orleans and the Texas
coast took just days. Much of the interior of the *Mexico* was crammed with
machinery and fuel. Iron straps reinforced the hull to bear up against the
pounding of the engine and rotation of the side-wheels. In January 1854 the
Mexico's operators advertised that the three-year-old "new and magnificent
steamship" would depart New Orleans for Galveston, Indianola, Port Lavaca,
and Matagorda Bay, the principal coastal entry points into Texas. Customers
interested in "freight or passage" were directed to the line's New Orleans office
near the wharves at the foot of Julia Street.[4]

Slaveholders showed up in droves. On one passage from New Orleans in
February 1854, the *Mexico* carried at least 238 bondspersons belonging to sixteen
different owners. The ship was loaded over several days before firemen kindled
a blaze in its furnace. Five days before departure, a Kentuckian embarked two

young bondspersons; the next day a Texan bought passage for two more. A Mississippian signed a slave manifest of twenty souls, including two infants. Two days before departure, an Alabamian consigned two more bondspersons. The same day they were joined by ten enslaved people belonging to a Georgian. Another migrating Georgia slaveholder embarked forty-eight bondspersons. A shipping agent embarked scores more who belonged to several owners from Texas and Tennessee. Enslaved people who were tumbled into the *Mexico*'s cargo areas met fellow bondspersons whose homes were hundreds of miles apart, making the slave jails of Richmond look like local gatherings. The enslaved had differing accents and ancestries, though they were briefly united in an ordeal of dislocation and disorientation.[5]

The ship carrying despairing captives also carried the bright aspirations of Texas fortune seekers. The day before departure the *Mexico*'s shipmaster signed a manifest of forty-six enslaved people belonging to an Alabama resident, John Drisdale. Among them were twenty-two-year-old Virginia and twenty-eight-year-old Stephen, along with enslaved people as old as sixty and as young as nursing infants. While Virginia, Stephen, and their fellow bondspersons gathered themselves in baggage compartments, their owners opened the doors to cabins or staterooms. The Drisdales were leaving what had been a cotton frontier in Alabama a generation before for a new one in Texas. They were moving to Fayette County, 150 miles west of Galveston. There their bondspersons would plant cotton on the prairie. Relatives would join, and the Drisdales' assemblages of bound laborers would grow to over sixty by decade's end. The enslaved people whose ordeals included steamship passage would also re-form families, however tenuous. In 1860 the Drisdales would claim to own at least fourteen souls born in Texas.[6] While the Drisdales settled in for the *Mexico*'s passage, slave traders filled the balance of available space.

The *Mexico* served several slave supply chains linking the bustling slave markets of the Texas coast to New Orleans and its economic hinterland. The same day the Drisdales loaded their bondspersons, one of Texas's biggest slave traders, R. A. Layton, embarked fifty souls to sell in his Houston auction. Most were in their teens and twenties, but ages ranged from infancy to forty. Some of Layton's captives had been sold down the Mississippi River from Missouri. Sea passage to Texas was part of a bewildering and terrifying odyssey for those who had commenced their journey in a St. Louis auction room or at a Kentucky courthouse door. Most bondspersons whom Layton or his agents bought would face another assemblage of hungry-eyed white faces after disembarking from the steamship. In 1854 Layton advertised the sale of "fifty young likely Negroes" on Houston's Market Square off Congress Avenue.[7]

The Morgan line offered true packet service to the Texas coast, and instead of leaving at intervals of weeks or months, the *Mexico*'s sibling ships departed every few days. As it pushed off from the New Orleans wharf, the *Mexico*'s machinery ground into motion. But anyone who missed the boat had merely to inquire at the next wharf. While the *Mexico* steamed downriver, its sibling ship the 1,056-ton *Louisiana* was loading. It had just returned from Texas. The New York–built *Louisiana* was scheduled to depart a week later for Galveston and other Texas ports. Eight slaveholders from Virginia, Kentucky, Georgia, Louisiana, and Texas embarked twenty-one bondspeople aboard it. While the *Louisiana* was preparing to sail, Morgan's 827-ton *Perseverance* arrived. It, too, had been constructed in New York City and plied the Texas route. Its master oversaw the loading of sixty-seven bondspeople belonging to nine owners from Alabama, Arkansas, Kentucky, Louisiana, North Carolina, Tennessee, and Texas. As the *Perseverance* steamed down the Mississippi River, it passed the brand-new 1,215-ton *Charles Morgan*, which was on its initial passage from New York City to New Orleans. The *Charles Morgan* also served Texas routes, building capacity. Eleven days after the *Mexico* departed, thirty-three bondspeople were loaded into its hold. By then the *Mexico* had returned to port. While the *Charles Morgan* loaded, twenty-six bondspeople, belonging to six owners from Florida, Georgia, Louisiana, Mississippi, Texas, and Tennessee, were embarked on the *Mexico*. It departed on Valentine's Day, along with another Morgan ship, the 1,151-ton *Texas*, bound to Veracruz, Mexico. That fleet consisted of New York–built vessels gathering the multitudes suffering from Texas fever.[8]

How Charles Morgan built that line is a tale of good fortune, propitious timing, and shrewd business instincts. Empire City merchants had long been drawn to opportunities in the American South. Morgan's headquarters at 5 Bowling Green had once been occupied by Robert R. Livingston, a pioneer of steam navigation. Livingston was a signer of the Declaration of Independence, an abolitionist, and a negotiator of the Louisiana Purchase, and he helped establish both the Hudson River and Mississippi River steamboat trade. Morgan was his legatee. Both Livingston and Morgan shared an enthusiasm for steam navigation and a keen eye to connections between New York City and the trans-Mississippi West, Livingston within the searching vision of Jeffersonian imperial republicanism and Morgan in the thundering furor of the Polk administration's proslavery imperialism. Capitalists like him supported an expansionist vision articulated by partisans such as John L. O'Sullivan, who helped craft a narrative that linked the founding of the republic to an imperial entitlement. O'Sullivan's *United States Magazine and Democratic Review* contended in 1839 that "our national birth was the beginning of a new history, the formation and progress of an untried political system, which separates us from the past and connects us with the future only." The United States was exceptional, he wrote, and "destined to be *the great nation* of futurity." Morgan's line was a vehicle of that vision even as it became part of a business culture of ruthless competition in a globe-striding sector.[9]

By the 1840s many New Yorkers were involved in financing the slave economy that supported such visions. New York credit boosted cotton production, and city merchants took commissions, insurance premiums, and loan interest from the agricultural export trade to Britain and Europe. Like so many of his neighbors, Morgan planted his fortunes in the South. Many New York merchants were morally opposed to slavery and would weep or gnash teeth at the sight of a slave auction. But the logic of capital gave them compelling reasons to dry their eyes, set their jaws, and invest in the southern economy.[10] Morgan's investments in technology provided a rich linkage between his entrepreneurial ambitions and technological capabilities.

Morgan's journey to Bowling Green was the stuff of American legends of self-reliance. He was born in 1795 to a middling family from Killingsworth, now Clinton, Connecticut, about halfway between New Haven and New London. At fourteen years old he moved to New York City, where he worked as a grocery clerk. By twenty-one he owned his own maritime provisioning shop and chandlery in Peck Slip on the East River. He began importing fruit from southern locales and investing in sailing vessels plying the West Indies trade. Unlike those portrayed in coming-of-age fiction, Morgan's rise was a combination of geoeconomic good timing, grit, and market savvy rather than pluck, charm, and shrewd social navigation.[11]

By the 1830s Morgan had linked his fortunes with the political economy of the lower South and Gulf Coast. Morgan awoke early to the business potential of steam technology in saltwater navigation, advancing it through strategic investments in ships designed for the Cotton South and eventually the Gulf Coast trade. He bought an interest in the first regular steam trader between New York and Charleston. It was launched in 1834 and made weekly voyages between the cotton port and New York City in half the time sailing packets took. Morgan and his partners added another steamer to the route the following year. Merchants could sell cotton more quickly, and market news arrived ahead of competitors using sailing ships. Morgan partnered with other investors to build the Southern Steam Packet Company and then bought out his partners.

The Second Seminole War gave Morgan's line a critical boost. By 1837 the Southern Steam Packet Company had three vessels in operation, including the

745-ton coal-fired *Neptune*. Besides goods and passengers, the line transported troops the War Department sent to fight Seminoles in Florida. Morgan cashed in on the war, but federal military contracts did not support sustainable growth. The Post Office did. The federal government awarded Morgan's line the lucrative contract to carry the U.S. Mail between New York City and Charleston. Post Office contracts indirectly subsidized the new technology and simultaneously made the postal system more efficient. But not all went smoothly. Steam technology combined the hazards of mechanical propulsion with the perils of sea passages. Operators' fascination with speed also threatened safety. In 1838 the company instructed the *Neptune's* shipmaster "that he is prohibited, under a penalty . . . from racing with other steam boats, under any circumstances."[12]

Morgan was enticed by the possibilities emerging on the Gulf Coast. As part of a policy that uprooted Seminoles, the United States removed other southeastern nations and confederacies, and commercial agriculturalists poured in. As the cotton frontier pushed westward, its agents pressured and extirpated Native Americans, and by the early 1840s Texas loomed as the next chunk of North America to be incorporated into the federal republic. Morgan and his partners envisioned a shipping network that delivered packet service to that undeveloped route. They attempted linking one of the newest outposts of the cotton complex to New Orleans and New York.

Texas was alluring to any businessman. It had a vast hinterland that was rapidly becoming cattle and cotton country, several fine ports, and rivers up which steamboats could travel. With oceangoing vessels linking the ports, merchants and factors in New Orleans and New York could tax Texas produce as they taxed the produce of the Mississippi River Valley, at the same time extending credit to outposts like Victoria and Waco. Through those connections New York merchants and financiers' networks stretched deep into the heart of Texas, and Liverpool merchants would grade and trade Texas cotton (much of it initially smuggled to New Orleans) just as they did cotton from across the globe. Texans sought access to credit and the cornucopia of goods that it bought, including enslaved people.[13]

Proslavery expansionists argued that Texas was part of a sectional contest over the geoeconomics of the U.S. republic. Texas was indeed a Pandora's box of causes of the American Civil War, but Morgan's line illustrates hidden linkages cutting through ideological contests that beggared national political discourse. The New Orleans publisher J. D. B. DeBow helped inflate the claim that Texas was a landscape of strategic competition, which boosted an increasingly strident sectionalism. He contended in 1847 that "a contest has been going on between the North and South, not limited to slavery or no slavery . . .

[but is] a contest for the wealth and commerce of the great valley of the Mississippi"; the question was whether "the growing commerce of the great West, shall be thrown upon New Orleans, or given to the Atlantic cities." Texas annexation and the U.S.–Mexican War accelerated the pace of that imagined competition. Like so many ostensible contrasts between "North and South," however, viewing sectional antagonisms as existential threats ignored the financial and federal support that belied such claims. The produce of the "great West" did increasingly flow easterly rather than through the port of New Orleans, but credit and capitalist technology did not stumble over the geographic borders DeBow imagined for his readers. Even his pro-filibustering New Orleans neighbors sought federal sponsorship for their plans to annex Cuba and enlisted New York City steamship and sugar interests. The Texas slave country joined New Orleans's commercial hinterland because it was served by steamships whose advantages resulted from New York City's financial and mechanical capacities.[14] Morgan could see beyond such sectional antagonisms and adapted technology to serve the Texas market.

The economic geography of the Gulf Coast was as promising as the physical and political geography was forbidding. The Texas coast had some superior ports, but sandbars at the mouths of rivers and bays could ground a ship at low tide. More dangerous were northerly winds that blew at gale force. Heavy merchant vessels foundered on the sandbars in Matagorda and Galveston bays, and the wrecks of some of Morgan's vessels still haunt the depths. Morgan's 533-ton *Palmetto* sank in Matagorda Bay in 1851. The 1,376-ton *Independence* and the 542-ton *Meteor* went down there the following year. After eleven months in service, the 276-ton *Cincinnati* sank off Brazos Santiago in 1852. The following year the 249-ton *Yacht* foundered on the Brazos Bar. It had run aground on sandbars many times before, but the nine-year-old ship finally splintered and sank. Besides perilous waters, docks and wharves were often primitive landings, and in places hundreds of people exiting ships often had to travel for miles to hotels, stagecoaches, and steamboat lines. And that was after paying fifteen dollars for steerage passage or thirty dollars for a small cabin. Yet maritime steam travel had considerable advantages. It was swift, and ships could depart in inclement weather. Travel between New Orleans and Galveston could take thirty-five to forty hours rather than a week. Political circumstances shifted like coastal sandbars and were every bit as dangerous.[15]

Texas port cities were at the edges of states, empires, and confederations in conflict. Between 1836 and 1848 Mexico claimed that Texas was a breakaway state. Indian confederacies were in firm control of the southern Great Plains, including much of the territory Texans claimed and through which they traveled.

By the time Morgan's ships began to serve Galveston, Texans were waging war against Native American inhabitants, and Comanches and Kiowas had confederated against them. Following Texans' massacre of Comanche negotiators and their family members in San Antonio in 1840, Comanches and allied Indians fought Anglo-Texans, including a conflict at an entrepôt on Matagorda Bay. The Gulf Coast was a site of imperial competition as well. British and European interests in Latin America were wary of growing U.S. power in the region. No shipping entrepreneur could ignore those developments.[16]

Yet revenues from the Texas slave country seemed worth the risks. To launch the Texas–New Orleans line in 1837, Morgan partnered with the New Orleans shipping merchant James Reed, part owner of the *Neptune* and several other vessels. Reed was also in the slavery business as a consignee of captives shipped from Norfolk, Virginia. The *Neptune*'s speed-obsessed skipper, James Pennoyer, also invested in the venture. Morgan and Reed's ships began scheduled voyages between New Orleans, Galveston, and Velasco on the Brazos River. They combined capacious cargo space with promises of luxury travel. Finely decorated accommodations beckoned the well-to-do. First-class passengers could enjoy meals at the captain's table prepared by a French cook. The table settings appeared to be silver and ivory, and the food was served by white waiters. Staterooms included white linen sheets and were kept by well-mannered chambermaids. To attract all comers, the line offered three levels of service. First-class or cabin passengers had semiprivate rooms and uniformed servants. Steerage passengers had bunkhouse-like curtained berths for sleeping. Deck passengers slept under awnings and included both the rowdiest and poorest classes of passenger. Often enslaved people shared deck space with them or mingled with baggage and cargo belowdecks.[17] On eastbound passages, cattle were herded aboard, and the stench of the terrified animals' excrement was difficult to clear. Morgan struggled to build his Gulf Coast line in the early 1840s, using New Orleans merchant shippers and local skippers to coordinate the voyages and sell tickets.

The line paddled ahead haltingly. Steamers possessed technological advantages over sailing vessels, but they were more capital-intensive and required carbon fuel sourced far from port. The plumes of sooty smoke left in the wake of Morgan's steamers could be measured in dollars. Besides New York credit, Morgan's line relied on coal from producers far from the coast, in Illinois, Missouri, Pennsylvania, and Ohio. Steamers needed steady supplies at good prices, and New Orleans coal merchants acquired their domestic coal from as far away as Pittsburgh. Oceangoing sailing ships from Britain transported coal cheaply as ballast. Morgan and his partners sold the efficiency and predictability of steam transport at a premium in part to cover operating costs. But human resources were also precious and less reliable than coal. Oceangoing steamships needed officers with considerable maritime expertise as well as an understanding of the propulsion technology. In turn, they had to staff ships billed as luxury liners while meeting a demanding schedule. But old salts were not naturals in the hospitality business. Taking care of equipment posed perhaps the biggest challenge.

Technology propelled returns but compounded risks and costs. Engines added to stresses on ships' structures by ocean waves, winds, and the chafing ordinarily transferred to hulls through sails and masts. Steam engines making fifteen or twenty-five revolutions per minute also transferred destructive vibrations to the hull. Iron-hulled ships were a cost-saving technology, but most American steamers and all Morgan's ships on the Gulf Coast line before the Civil War were wood-hulled. In Morgan's early ships, machinery had not yet been seamlessly incorporated into maritime architecture. Heavy side-lever engines and the boilers that powered them were planted in the center of long, narrow hulls. Ships jarred and agitated goods, animals, and people as they moved them. By the early 1840s some of Morgan's ships used screw-propulsion technology, but side-lever engines powering side-wheels were standard. Like so many of their operators, steamships lived fast and died young.[18]

New Orleans had long been the principal landing zone for captives, but by the mid–1840s the slave market was being transformed. The city was declining from dominance as the great southern entrepôt and commercial hub, and the turning tide of the slave market marked that transition. The cotton frontier was moving west, and after Texans declared independence from Mexico, the New Orleans levee saw the flow of captives up the Mississippi River began to turn downriver as ships carried enslaved people out into the gulf by the coffle. In December 1843 Reed and Pennoyer's 200-horsepower *Neptune*, along with a merchant sailing ship, disembarked some seventy enslaved people in Galveston. In addition, the *Neptune* disembarked "a large number of passengers," including the newly married soldier Albert Sidney Johnston, who was heading to a new plantation home in Brazoria County. Johnston was part of a surge of Euroamericans into that region and fought fiercely for the interests that carried him there. He rose to the rank of general in the Texas Army, the U.S. Army, and the Confederate Army before being killed at the Battle of Shiloh nineteen years later. Besides the Johnstons, the *Neptune* also carried 1,600 barrels of freight, newspapers, and diplomatic correspondence from the United States.[19]

As the line grew, Morgan tried snatching the Texas trade from his erstwhile allies. In the process he brought an interest in slavery's expansion to factories on

New York's East River. Initial cooperation among owners of the Southern Steam Packet Company dissolved into competition when Reed and Pennoyer tried to undercut their partner's ships by accepting Texas banknotes and exchequer bills at fifty cents on the dollar. Morgan had insisted on specie or New Orleans banknotes. Texas paper money was fiat currency that fluctuated wildly, but once eastbound customers were able to exchange them for tickets, Morgan was forced to accept them too. It was a shortsighted scheme. Texas notes depreciated into worthlessness following statehood. But Morgan did manage to squeeze Reed and Pennoyer by seizing advantages available in the Empire City.

Morgan rationalized the steamship business to the Texas coast by sponsoring specialized ships and adding vessels to the line. To create those linkages he helped establish T. F. Secor and Company in New York City, a factory building ships' machinery. Shipwrights incorporated engine technology into vessels with shallow drafts, which were needed for Gulf Coast navigation. As Morgan's Gulf Coast line began to flourish in the 1840s, he also invested in a line of steamers linking New York and New Orleans. Such a service would connect Texas planters and ranchers more directly to creditors and markets in New York City. Packet sailing ships had served the southern route well for a generation, and shippers in the cotton trade were happy to sail vessels to the Texas coast. To counter them Morgan promised the same kind of mechanization that had made the Charleston–New York line attractive to cotton merchants. The proposed line faltered after gold was discovered in California. Morgan briefly turned his attentions to serving the newest El Dorado of the West, but the Empire City line was an example of New York capital invested in developing the southern market. Even without a line of steamers linking Texas to New York City via New Orleans, the backcountry of the newest cotton frontier was becoming an economic suburb of the Empire City.[20]

Like banking, the steamship business thrived on New York's resources, which New Orleans lacked until after the Civil War. Access to credit was paramount, but New York's industrial infrastructure also conferred advantages. In the 1840s and 1850s Morgan's steamers were refitted in New York City rather than in New Orleans. In an age before standardized machinery, the T. F. Secor ironworks could furnish parts or rebuild steamship engines. A federal framework benefited Morgan's enterprise as well. Morgan avoided the high personal property tax rates that property owners residing in southern states paid, and lawsuits against Morgan or his company would have to have been heard in federal rather than southern state courts, or else be initiated in New York. Yet the Morgan line also took advantage of its having a stake in Louisiana and Texas. Morgan's firm was a slaveholder. Its agents filed records in New Orleans of purchases or sales of sixty-six bondspeople between 1846 and 1862, including males and females ranging in age from infancy to forty-five. Many were company slaves working for company agents or aboard ships.[21]

Morgan consolidated those advantages in the Gulf Coast line. In 1845 he put into service two side-wheel steamships, the *Galveston* and the *New York*. Customers could depart twice weekly from New Orleans to Texas. The line's Galveston agents, the firm of McKinney and Williams, beckoned would-be passengers to inspect a diagram of a "highly finished and fast running boat" at its countinghouse, which could accommodate two hundred passengers and six hundred barrels of freight, steaming between the Mississippi and Galveston in as little as thirty hours. They claimed that "her accommodations are of the first order, and for speed she is unequalled on the southern waters." The republic of Texas had given Texas-owned vessels a cost advantage that amounted to 10 percent, but when the republic became a state in 1845, that protection disappeared. When the U.S. Post Office merged with the Texas postal system, Morgan sought additional advantages. Like his New York steamship competitor George "Live Oak" Law, who founded the steamship lobby famous for its ties to expansionist Democrats like Stephen Douglas, Morgan too sought government patronage. Morgan's line won U.S. Mail contracts between New Orleans and the Texas coast. That arrangement faltered when his steamship *New York* sank in September 1846 with the Texas postmaster aboard.[22] But as it generated federal revenues, the line became incorporated into expansionist policies.

Charles Morgan's steamships became instruments of American imperialism. After the Polk administration provoked war with Mexico in 1846, the War Department chartered both of Morgan's Gulf Coast steamers to transport troops and supplies. Morgan had a history of army contracting and took no public stance against the U.S.–Mexican War. That separated him from New York steamship operators such as his Wall Street competitor William H. Aspinwall, later president of the Pacific Mail Steamship Company. Morgan aimed to please the army and immediately interrupted passenger and mail service to carry soldiers and supplies.[23] War contracting was a windfall for the company. Morgan's services made his firm $400,000 between August 1845 and June 1848. Morgan added five ships to his Gulf Coast fleet in 1847, each ferrying soldiers and supplies from New Orleans to the Texas coast. With that expanded capacity he reinstated and expanded passenger service between New Orleans and Texas, including forty-one nongovernment voyages in 1847, up from six in 1846.

Government contracting propelled his company from a Gulf Coast competitor to a quasi monopoly. Ships got bigger and more capacious. Among the new members of Morgan's Gulf Coast fleet was the 869-ton *New Orleans*, built by the New York shipbuilder William H. Brown and powered by a 700-horsepower engine built by the T. F. Secor ironworks. The 225-foot-long side-wheel steamer cost $120,000, and Morgan collected $33,000 from the War Department in its first three months of service, steaming troops and supplies into Texas. He then sold it to the Quartermaster Department for $125,000, taking a patriotically small 4 percent profit on the used vessel. He added the New York–built *Palmetto* to the Gulf Coast fleet in 1847. Three months of the *Palmetto*'s service brought Morgan's company $27,000 from the government during wartime, after which it hauled bondspersons, passengers, and goods to Texas. The War Department paid handsomely, but the military advantages of steaming rather than sailing troops were substantial. The U.S. Army got a boost that its Mexican counterpart lacked. No more could stalled sailing vessels delay the arrival of soldiers or supplies to port.[24]

As the shipping line grew, Morgan incorporated a subsidiary in charge of running an enterprise of scale. In 1848 Morgan's son-in-law Israel C. Harris and son Henry R. Morgan took over management in New Orleans. Charles Morgan retained a controlling interest, but the new line began operating as Harris and Morgan. Previously, Charles Morgan had permitted shipmasters like Pennoyer and New Orleans merchants like Reed to run the routes on a profit-sharing basis. After the war his relatives took charge of the business operations and ran a New Orleans commission house buying and selling goods the line brought to market. Shipmasters could buy shares of the vessels they commanded. Within that business organization, coastwise slaving was a stream of revenue that paid investors dividends.[25]

Wartime demand for Morgan's ships generated business for his partners, and Polk's war for empire showered New York machinists with equipment orders. During the U.S.–Mexican War, Morgan's partnership with T. F. Secor and Company flourished. The engine factory and ironworks were expanded into a plant employing seven hundred workers and occupying nearly two blocks on the East River between Eighth and Tenth Streets. From 1847 to 1849 it turned out engines for ships as capacious as 2,727 tons. Workers could cheer Manifest Destiny and the Polk administration's aggression. As in other areas, Morgan bought controlling interests in profit centers and drove out partners. He appointed a son-in-law as financial director of T. F. Secor and Company and bought a controlling interest in 1850, renaming it the Morgan Iron Works. With a brief interruption, Morgan would control the firm until 1867.[26]

The end of War Department contracts following the U.S.–Mexican War threatened the Harris and Morgan line with overcapacity. Wartime expansion of the fleet could not be sustained by its routes from New Orleans to Galveston and Velasco, so the line expanded to Lavaca and Brazos Santiago. The Post Office eased that transition. By July 1850 the line had secured a $15,000-per-year U.S. Mail contract on the Brazos Santiago route, 550 miles from New Orleans. Morgan received a U.S. Mail contract to deliver the mail to Galveston and Indianola at $12,000 per year. That was a gift, since the Brazos Santiago, Indianola, and Galveston routes overlapped. Mail arrived more quickly, but other services were lacking.

Harris and Morgan seemed intent on serving investors and Uncle Sam at ticketed customers' expense. Lavaca-bound passengers complained bitterly that Harris and Morgan advertised carriage there but landed a few miles south of the port and discharged passengers who either had to hire local water transportation or secure carriage overland. After two nights being shaken to the sounds of mechanical noise and another day of the same, passengers were in no mood to lug trunks and other belongings on dirt paths to a small town or else pay local water taxis. Many bondspersons' first experience of Texas was as the equivalent of pack animals, lugging heavy loads to a town perched on a bluff twenty-five feet above the bay. While doing so they passed herds of cattle driven down to the waiting steamer. Harris and Morgan reluctantly responded, building a wharf near Powderhorn Lake, several miles to the southwest of Lavaca. That was as much to steer clear of local taxes and dockage fees as to avoid the hazards of a shallow port. The town that grew out from that wharf became Indianola, which was destroyed by hurricanes later in the century.[27]

Once insulated from serious competition, Harris and Morgan enjoyed rising returns from Texas's rapid growth. Vessels laden with passengers, lumber, and manufactured goods unloaded in Galveston and other ports and were reloaded with cotton, sugar, specie, and cattle. Texas cotton production mushroomed in the late 1840s, from just under 40,000 bales in 1848 to over 62,000 in 1852, a jump of 55 percent. By 1856 cotton had surged another 85 percent to just over 116,000 bales, and by 1860 Texas exported nearly 194,000 bales, another 67 percent jump, or nearly five times the 1848 total. Much of the lint went directly to market on sailing ships, but Morgan's line captured much of the collateral commercial traffic between Texas and New Orleans, along with revenues from passenger service. In the 1850s Morgan's fleet of steamers would grow to over a dozen ships registered in New Orleans and plying routes from that hub of operations. Besides commodities, all steamers on domestic routes in the Gulf South carried enslaved people.[28] Through its war and postal contracts, the federal government bolstered a corporate interest in slaving.

Marie Adrien Persac, *Port and City of New Orleans*, 1858 (The Historic New Orleans Collection, acquisition made possible through the Clarisse Claiborne Grima Fund, acc. no. 1988.9)

For thousands of enslaved Americans, the journey west to Texas took place inside one of Morgan's vast machines. Mariah Robinson was one of the forced migrants. She had been born into slavery in Georgia. In about 1857 eight- or nine-year-old Robinson was taken from her home in Monroe, Georgia, by her new mistress, Josephine Young. Robinson had been made a wedding gift to Young and her husband. In the process she was removed from her mother and eleven siblings. The Youngs were heading west. Robinson sailed to New Orleans with her uncle and aunt, who were also enslaved. After arriving, she recalled, they were "[ar]rested and put in de trader's office." Their owner, Robert B. Young, had "left Georgia without payin' a cotton debt," she remembered, and creditors caught up with him in the Crescent City. For Young the allure of the Lone Star State was cattle. Robinson recalled that at the time of her passage, her uncle Johns and aunt Lonnie were children as well, confined with her in the slave trader's jail. Young eventually appeared, "walkin' down de street with he goldheaded walkin' cane," Robinson recalled, and ransomed the captives.[29]

They then walked to the New Orleans levee and the waiting steamships. If the river was at low tide, it reeked of garbage and decay. Jefferson Parish and

Algiers slaughterhouses processing Texas longhorn cattle dumped offal and even carcasses into the Mississippi, which floated downriver and created nuisances, public health hazards for residents, and feasts for vultures and other scavengers. As Robinson boarded the ship, she may have detected lingering odors of dung. Overhead, perhaps her eye caught a blue pennant flying from the mast. Like other shipping lines, Charles Morgan's flew a company flag. On the fluttering blue field was a white five-pointed star enclosing a red monogram, "M," for the owner. The levee and river were soon out of sight as the captives were stowed with the baggage. In the bowels of the ship they were tossed in among trunks and sacks, furniture and merchandise. Moldering wood and the faint scent of vomit replaced outside odors of rot and feces.[30]

When customers booked passage with Harris and Morgan, they bought efficiency but not necessarily value or comfort. Government contracting conferred a competitive advantage that demoted customer service on a hierarchy of concerns. Harris and Morgan "have already made money enough off our people," complained a Texas correspondent in 1850, "and while they enjoy the monopoly they now do, they should at least give us good, safe, sea-going vessels." Unlike state and federal monopolies granted to innovators like Livingston to protect investments in emerging technologies, the advantages Harris and Morgan enjoyed evolved into an anticompetitive strategy. A defender of the company admitted that company ships "have been declared, in printed articles, *old rotten hulks, unseaworthy, unsafe, miserable old crafts*," and that Texans suspected the company of "extortion, monopoly, fraud, knavery, chicanery, meanness, villainy, robbery," and other sins. Morgan and his agents took so many consignments of captives that they were occasionally suspected of slave smuggling.[31]

Leaving New Orleans, bondspersons like Mariah Robinson were embarked on a third middle passage. In each generation, enslaved people of African descent suffered separations and dislocations, which tore at the social fabric and destroyed what little social capital ancestors accumulated and passed down. Robinson's African ancestors had been shackled aboard merchant sailing ships plying transatlantic routes. In the early nineteenth century, their descendants had undergone enforced relocations from the Eastern Seaboard to the interior South, some funneled through Austin Woolfolk or Isaac Franklin's supply chains. That demographic catastrophe had a sequel in the 1850s, when thousands of children and family members of Robinson's generation were dislocated again as the United States expanded to the trans-Mississippi West. Those who rode in the lower reaches of Texas-bound steamers were re-isolated, away from their neighborhoods and networks. Because of that isolation, they were left intensely reliant on enslavers' contexts rather than the wisdom of ancestors and a community of African-descended Americans. Punctuating that violent dislocation was the mechanized means of transport. The incremental terror of transatlantic or coastwise navigation was replaced by a jarring and quick passage that was frightening even to their captors.

The English traveler Matilda C. F. Houstoun embarked on a passage from New Orleans to Galveston expecting a swift passage in company-advertised comfort. She was disappointed. Houstoun glimpsed a veneer of value on the route Mariah Robinson also took, recalling that the Morgan steamer she boarded "was a very fine boat to look at, particularly inside; but she was long, narrow, and shallow, and much better suited to the navigation of rivers, than to encounter the fierce 'northers' of the Gulf of Mexico."[32] Mariners in the age of sail had cultivated a respect for the elements that eluded steamship operators.

Morgan's ships were frighteningly top-heavy, which was partly a consequence of the technology. The ship Houstoun boarded was the New York–built *Galveston*, nearly 195 feet long, 26 feet wide, and nearly 7 feet deep at the waterline. On each side of the ship a large wheelhouse enclosed a side-wheel that propelled the ship, but it also had two masts, fore and aft, and sails for supplementary wind power. Inside the cabin, the vessel "was fitted up with the choicest woods, birds'-eye maple and rose, and the decorations of the saloon were really beautiful; there was, however, (as we soon found) a great deal too *much above* water, and far too little below, for either safety or comfort." Steamships of the day took the design of an oceangoing sailing vessel and then crammed an engine in the center of the hull, making it difficult to balance the ship despite the side-lever engines' low center of gravity. "The steamer literally consisted of three stories, one more than the ordinary river boats," Houstoun recalled.[33]

Another first-class passenger on the same route complained in 1851 that the Morgan steamer she boarded was "an old disabled shell that had already been condemned as unsafe." Teresa Griffin Vielé recalled a first-class passage that deteriorated into terror. While contemplating her fear and shock, she also recorded the ordeals of those forced to ride on top of others' luggage. "Our sail down the Mississippi from New Orleans was spent on deck, and was rather pleasant," she wrote, "but towards night, when we got into the Gulf, the ship began to toss among the short sharp waves, and I was shown to the 'ladies' cabin,' where a shelf a foot wide was pointed out as *my bed*." The ride got worse. "I closed my eyes to shut out the scene of dreadful squalor and confusion around, which sickened the very soul." In the lower reaches of the vessel, Vielé recalled, "families of emigrants lay about on piles of trunks and boxes, all blessed with numerous young children, who cried, screamed, and were sea-sick incessantly."³⁴ Vomit on passengers' luggage could be listed among customers' complaints.

Some of those "emigrants" were enslaved people belonging to "an old Virginia planter, who had sold his plantation in his native state, and with his sons and sons' sons, and their united families, slaves, and household property." Vielé was fortunate to have disembarked on dry land. On its next passage the ship disintegrated and sank in sight of Brazos Santiago. The Virginian whom Vielé encountered was headed to the Brazos River region. He was taken aback when he learned that Vielé was a New York native. "'It's an awful sinful place,' he groaned out."³⁵ Charles Morgan might have chuckled at that quip while glancing at the slave carriage revenues recorded on the right hand of his ledger. The Virginian failed to grasp the Empire City's connection to the decrepit vessel that wheezed and convulsed its way to Texas.

Once aboard Morgan's steamers, Texas-bound passengers could not get there fast enough. Mariah Robinson must have shared the fear caused by mechanical agitation and a rough ride. Houstoun recalled that on the open sea, "the good ship 'Galveston' rode by no means easily in heavy weather." She shared Vielé's experience of cabin passage. "I never heard a vessel make such a noise as she did through that remarkably disagreeable night, for the wind, from having been southerly, turned suddenly into a 'norther,' and continued to freshen, so that before morning there was more than half a gale of wind." Houstoun noted, "Every timber and bulk-head creaked, and complained in a most painful manner; the motion, too, was most disagreeable, and the sense of insecurity very great, owing as much to the above causes as to the drunkenness of the captain, who was in a state of intoxication the whole time we were on board." The consolation of a short passage did little to cheer passengers. "At length, day dawned upon our miseries . . . and it was such a bright, joyous looking sunrise, that it made us all look still more cross and frightful than we should perhaps otherwise have done."³⁶

Multitudes of the enslaved could recall their first sight of the Texas coast from the deck of such a steamship. Mariah Robinson recalled "comin' down de Mississippi 'cross de Gulf," and seeing "no land for days and days" as they traveled "through de Gulf of Mexico and lands at de port, Galveston."³⁷ Sightings of the coast came with the sensation of the humid, salty air carrying coal smoke that rumbled up and billowed out of the stacks of the low-pressure boiler. As the marshy dunes of Galveston Island came into the view of those on deck, those beneath it perceived a slowing in the throbbing rhythm of the ship's machinery, which reverberated through the wooden superstructure as strange mechanical music. Its base notes were octaves below what a church organ could play back in Alabama, Georgia, or Kentucky. Steam whistled through the escape valves as pressure dropped, the resulting mechanical diminuendo announcing entry into port.

Steamers disembarking captives passed sailing ships landing goods and loading cotton. As the city of Galveston came into view, Houstoun recalled that "a great many merchant-vessels" were anchored "outside the bar, the captains or supercargoes preferring to unload their freight there, to running the hazard of crossing the formidable impediment at the mouth of the harbor." Another visitor who arrived around the same time as Mariah Robinson recalled Galveston's cityscape as "low and destitute of anything that may deserve the name of a tree." The city's "wharves present quite a business-like appearance — a few foreign ships — three or four bay steamers that ply between this port and Houston, the Brazos and the Trinity — one or two sea steamers — the packets and cotton ships from New York and Boston — and a host of smaller craft." Each year brought more trade. *DeBow's Review* reported that three times as much cotton left Galveston in 1854 compared to 1850; the average annual increase was nearly 14,500 bales. Sugar and molasses exports doubled during the same time, as did those of longhorn cattle. In 1854 seventy-one steamship arrivals captured much of that traffic, as did 156 coastal sailing vessels and seventeen three-masted ships. Eighty percent of cotton exports in 1854 went to domestic entrepôts such as New Orleans, New York, and Philadelphia, while the balance was shipped directly across the Atlantic Ocean. In the 1850s, according to the census, Galveston's population grew by three-quarters, from just under 4,200 in 1850 to over 7,300 in 1860. Six percent were enslaved, but they were unusually visible. Bondspersons ported goods, labored in the city's brickworks, dug ditches, undertook road repair, serviced ships, and performed domestic work.[38]

Galveston was a polyglot mix of aspiration and desperation. About half the free population was foreign-born, mostly German and Irish. The Irish famine of the mid–1840s and the 1848 revolutions in Europe pushed many to American shores, and Texas beckoned migrants with opportunities, even if Anglo-Texans were suspicious of Irish and Germans. In that ferment Galveston was a city of transients. Its businesslike daytime atmosphere turned rowdy at night. After dusk brothels opened that catered primarily to sailors. Legally enslaved prostitutes serviced customers alongside nominally free girls and women who had little real choice.[39] Daylight hid those social relations.

In the 1850s Galveston became a petite New Orleans. Wrought-iron fronts were added to buildings, sidewalks were constructed, and main thoroughfares were paved with oyster shells. A traveler noted that "the regular streets are of dazzling and solid white sand — the houses new and nearly all painted white — the dwellings built in that easy, sans-souci style peculiar to the French and Spanish cottage; and all of them surrounded and embowered with the shrubbery of the tropics—the several varieties of fig, the orange, the lemon . . . and great numbers of flowering plants."[40] Mariah Robinson passed through that landscape after exiting the steamship.

Rumbling over rutted roads in a wagon, she made the 275-mile journey to the central Texas town of Waco. There the former "cotton buyer" Young reinvented himself as a "stock raiser," contributing to longhorn exports at the coast. Robinson's memories of loved ones back in Georgia faded on the gently rolling landscape of fields, farms, herds of cattle, and pretensions to refinement on the banks of the Brazos River. There the Young family grew, but ranching turned out to be less lucrative than they had hoped, and by 1860, Robinson, Johns, and Lonnie were their sole bondspersons. Many more bound laborers from Georgia followed them, disembarking at the town's landing.[41]

As in New Orleans, captives landed on the coast were regularly embarked on steamboats. After arriving in Galveston on another visit to Texas, Matilda Houstoun took a steamboat journey up Buffalo Bayou, which emptied into Galveston Bay. Houstoun was impressed by the landscape. "It cannot be denied, that as a field for settlers, Texas has considerable advantages over almost every other country," she wrote in the early 1840s. "Its climate, except in the lowlands, is excellent, and the settler has to encounter neither the extreme cold of the winter season, nor the scorching summer heat of the more northern states of America and Canada." Local wisdom held that in the low-lying areas along the Brazos, "the production of this part of Texas can be brought forth by slave or black labour alone."[42]

Aboard the Buffalo Bayou steamer, Houstoun traveled deep into the newest part of slave country, its development a variation on a theme that had transformed the Mississippi and Tennessee River valleys in the previous generations. River steamers, she recorded, "have the appearance of wooden houses, built upon a large raft; there is a balcony or verandah, and on the roof is what is called the hurricane deck, where *gentlemen* passengers walk and smoke."[43] She was importuned by such a figure who asked if she drank liquor and offered "a tumbler of *egg-noggy*, which seemed in great request." Manners of Texans were blunt, and their ambitions were as large as the portions of meat consumed at every meal. Supper aboard the boat "consisted of alternate dishes of boiled oysters, and beef steaks, of which there was plenty, and the latter disappeared in marvelously quick time between the strong jaws of the Texan gentlemen." The beef was fresh, too fresh even for the Englishwoman's taste. "On one occasion our dinner was delayed for some time, while the cook went on shore and 'shot a beef.'" The lands upriver "seemed one vast shrubbery" of magnolias and "a great number and variety of evergreens, laurel, bay, and firs, rhododendrons, cistus, and arbutus."[44]

The tenor of men's interactions hinted at the society Texans were building. "Cards and drinking constituted no inconsiderable part of the pleasures of the evening," Houstoun recalled, "but with all the excitement of talk, tobacco chewing, and brandy, I never heard people more orderly and reasonable." A sense of purpose animated men used to social intercourse mediated with tobacco juice and ardent spirits. "Their talk as usual was of dollars: politics, indeed, occasionally took their turn," Houston contended, "but the subjects ceased to become interesting, when the pockets of the company could no longer be affected by the turn of affairs." The main theme was money. "There was no private scandal, no wit, no literature, no small talk; all was hard, dry, calculating business."[45] On the decks of such riverboats were gathered the African-descended people whose labor realized those ambitions.

As Euroamericans pushed the slaving frontier into the Texas interior, they encountered other slaveries, each with its own logic of capital. Southern plains Indians had a long history of captive-taking and slave trading. Native Americans' slaving strategies differed from Texans', even if both operated by market principles and within imperial frameworks. Slavery among the Comanches was exploitative and "economically driven," an artifact of the Comanche empire. Markets mattered in Indian contexts just as they mattered in the development of Texas and the region Americans called the New Mexico territory. Slaving was violent but served both local political and social strategies and distant markets. Mexican political weakness and Indians' raiding and trading patterns had created openings for Euroamericans like Moses Austin to settle as Mexican citizens, soon planting cotton in the fertile river valleys of eastern Texas. Cotton and hides linked Texans to a global system of capital and markets just as Euroamerican trade goods linked Comanche, Kiowa, Cheyenne, and Arapaho polities into broader trade networks. Raiding in the northern Mexican border-lands resulted from a pattern Mexicans and Texans understood primarily through a cultural lens rather than as a geopolitical strategy. On Mexico's northern borderlands, Mexican settlements succumbed to such raids.[46]

Even in those borderlands, capital and trade connections to New York City were important to development. Trade in goods such as weapons, ammunition, copper, blankets, tobacco, and even groceries flourished. The Torrey Trading Company opened houses in Houston, Austin, San Antonio, New Braunfels, Fredericksburg, and other locations on the Brazos River. It was Texas's first chain store, and captives were among the items sold and ransomed. The houses mediated trading relationships among Comanches and other Indians who sold bison hides, furs, deer skins, and specie. Sam Houston spied the Torrey Trading Company's strategic importance in 1843 and used its stores as sites of trading diplomacy with Indians. The company acted as a bank and the hub of a credit network. Deposits at one store could be credited at another. The New York firm of Grant and Barton auctioned merchandise that passed through Torrey's houses.

Morgan's steamers were an available conduit for their business and facilitated an economic linkage between Euroamerican markets and the Native American network of the southern Great Plains. The Torrey Trading Company houses attracted Comanches from as far away as Taos and Caddos from the Red River who arrived to trade and politick. As diplomacy degraded into confrontation in the 1840s, however, the trading centers declined into country stores. Grant and Barton nevertheless remained active in the region, winning government contracts to supply the Bureau of Indian affairs with "blankets and dry goods" in the late 1840s and early 1850s, and the Morgan line continued to serve as an instrument of imperial expansion. It won army contracts to transport soldiers and officers to the Texas coast late in the 1850s.[47]

In that context, chattel slavery in Texas was axiomatic to most Euroamericans' economic calculations, and like New Orleans, Galveston and Houston sprouted slave markets and attracted slave traders. After Texas joined the United States, Houston's Long Row hummed with business. In 1848 Fred Scranton offered his services as an agent to the markets of Houston, Galveston, and New Orleans, charging consigners an auctioneer's commission. The commission merchant in his early forties exploited a niche transporting enslaved people from the New Orleans slave market for sale in Houston. In August 1850, under the banner of "The Old Texian," the Connecticut native advertised that he had "just returned from New Orleans with a lot of Negroes, 4 men, 6 women, 4 girls and 3 children, to sell for cash" and added that he had dry goods, including "Negro Shoes," along with flour, coffee, and sugar, all of which were delivered by steamship. Scranton frequently shipped captives, embarking at least five consignments aboard four of Harris and Morgan's ships between 1850 and 1853. In February 1853 he paid passage for a dozen souls from New Orleans to Galveston aboard the Morgan steamer *Texas*. Their age profile resembled those in New Orleans traders' coffles: all were between the ages of sixteen and thirty-five.[48]

The Harris and Morgan line also powered John S. Sydnor's slave-trading firm. After moving from Richmond to Galveston in 1838, the Virginia native became the largest North American slave auctioneer west of New Orleans. Sydnor shipped his enslaved property on Morgan's ships beginning in at least 1846 and advertised his services as a "Broker and Auctioneer." Like so many slave traders seeking growth, Sydnor acted as a private banker. Responding to the need for local infrastructure in Galveston, he branched into the hospitality business. Sydnor's notable failure was his Powhatan Hotel, built too far out of town for the comfort of visitors. He was more successful at selling human beings. In the spring of 1852 he advertised, "I have on hand 10 negroes, consisting of men, women, boys and gals and shall have in a few days 15 more, among them some mechanics."[49]

Sydnor was elected mayor from 1846 to 1847 and promoted Texas development by building a warehouse and wharf in the 1850s and dredging the harbor. By 1860 he was a long-established merchant fighting upstarts and competitors who also used Morgan's line. Forced to lower his fees, Sydnor also competed by hiring out slaves in the city for a short time before offering them for sale in a building adjoining his store. He ran a slave auction in Houston even into the Civil War. It was on Congress Avenue between Fannin and Main streets, now the site of the Harris County Attorney's Office. A witness to his auctions recalled, "He was an expert as an orator in the description he gave of the qualities and abilities of the slaves offered for sale; and often attracted large crowds at his place by his eloquence and voice."[50]

The number of Houston slave traders doubled in the 1850s in response to surging demand. Shaben and Brother held auctions every day and by candlelight at night. They advertised their business as a perpetual clearing house for enslaved people and other movable property. Morgan's steamships landed captives at points connecting other supply chains reaching the East Coast. The merchant Thomas S. Gresham received a coffle of fifty captives, between the ages of ten and twenty-five, who sailed from the Chesapeake. Morgan's competitors also disembarked captives. Thomas B. Chubb, master of the Philadelphia-built steamship *William Penn*, plied a trade serving planters and merchants of the Trinity River Valley. A Galvestonian with a local reputation for "strict integrity" when it came to confronting riverboat gamblers, Chubb nevertheless shanghaied African-descended sailors and enslaved them. A visitor recalled that Chubb "hired a colored crew at Boston, and then cooly [sold] them at Galveston." He was later tried for an unrelated charge of slave stealing and acquitted.[51]

Texas embodied a contradiction that made enslavers intensely reliant on chains of supply and credit linking the plantation interior with merchants and bankers in other U.S. cities. Vast promises of wealth from cotton and ranching relied on capitalist advances in credit, industry, and transportation, but many Texans were refugees from debt. They needed credit but were hostile to bankers. Texas's 1845 constitution prevented the state from chartering banks, and the resulting financial infrastructure contrasted with those in states such as New York, Massachusetts, and even Virginia, which still promoted banking after the panic of 1837 and enjoyed the economic expansion to which so-called free banking and expansive chartering gave rise. Creditors had good reasons to be wary of Texas. In Louisiana and Mississippi so many deadbeats had gone to Texas across the Sabine River following 1837 that sheriffs executing collection writs simply marked "G.T.T." on them. Fleeing debtors would chalk the acronym on the front gates of their delinquent estates as a warning not to attempt collection.[52]

Because Texans cultivated reputations for ducking obligations, Galveston and Houston merchants had few connections with banking houses on the East Coast or across the Atlantic. It was not until the late 1850s, for instance, that the House of Brown contemplated sending an agent to Galveston, and that plan was abandoned in 1859. Galveston's largest private banker was the merchant firm of McKinney and Williams, which not coincidentally served as the Harris and Morgan line's Galveston agent. Thomas F. McKinney was one of the first Anglo-American settlers to arrive under Moses Austin's colonization scheme. Initially he traded goods between New Orleans and Chihuahua via San Antonio and plied a lumber business in eastern Texas. Before Williams arrived in Texas, the Rhode Island native had served an apprenticeship to his uncle, a Baltimore commission merchant, training that included traveling to Buenos Aires as a supercargo. On the Baltimore–Buenos Aires route he mastered Spanish and Latin American trade. He moved to New Orleans in time for the panic of 1819 and failed in business. Like so many other debtors, he fled to the colony of Coahuila y Tejas in 1822 and became Stephen F. Austin's secretary and, later, partner. McKinney and Williams formed a partnership in Brazoria County in 1834 and were dealing in cotton and slaves even before Texas's independence from Mexico. Williams became Texas's foremost merchant banker before the Civil War. McKinney and Williams was later Lynn and Williams, which was connected through family ties to banking, shipping, and insurance merchants in Baltimore. Texans relied on such long chains of credit but refused to permit an efficient allocation within the state's political borders, which worked against specialization and efficiency since merchants tended to be cotton factors, private bankers, and slave traders.[53]

Steamships brought movable capital in the form of bondspersons, who served as collateral for Texas's constellation of small, unchartered banks and merchants who served commercial agriculturalists' credit needs. In that credit climate enslaved people became circulating media alongside private notes. Texas slaveholders and their agents in the cotton business frequently used bondspersons as money disbursed to planters as payment for the previous year's crop, and in turn planters commissioned merchants to buy enslaved people and charged them to their accounts. As in New Orleans before the rise of slave traders like the Woolfolks and Franklin and Armfield, Texas planters relied on factors to purchase their bondspersons. In cases where planters owed money to factors, the factor might have to take a bondsperson as payment and transfer her or him to another planter to satisfy an obligation.[54] It was a form of commoditization that Louisiana property banking made look primitive, but it suited credit-thirsty Texans.

As in other such schemes, enslaved people bore the costs of being traded like bills of exchange. Bondspersons disembarked from steamers and sold in Galveston or Houston were shuttled about among temporary owners. In the 1850s Frederick Law Olmsted, traveling in Texas, caught sight of a coffle of "slaves consigned to some planter in the interior, probably by his factor in New Orleans, as part of the proceeds of his crop." Tolls on the bondspersons were palpable. "They were much fagged, and sullen with their day's walk," he recalled. "The prospect before them was a boundless flat prairie, with a cold north wind, and rain threatening. They were evidently intending to camp upon the open prairie, as for eight miles we had passed no house." The "gang" Olmstead encountered consisted of "three men, two women, and two boys, under guard of a white man and a very large yellow mastiff." In a scene evocative of overland marches from the interior of West Africa to the coast, each captive had to carry trade goods, "one an axe, another a rifle, another a kettle, a fourth led a horse to whose saddle were attached a ham, a coffee-pot, and a buffalo robe," which Olmstead guessed was "the white man's covering at night, the negroes having no extra clothing." They were delivering themselves along with trade goods. Everything in the procession except the dog, the trader, and his gear was part of a credit chain reaching New Orleans. "Before midnight, a severe rain-storm did, in fact, commence," Olmstead reported disgustedly.[55] In a lean year the melancholy procession marched in the opposite direction, back to the Galveston or Houston slave market, or a waiting steamship. The merchant or factor serving the planter might find himself with enslaved property he needed to convert back into paper money.

The Texas trade paid Charles Morgan's firms steady returns by the early 1850s, but the titanically profitable steamship trade to California captured his imagination. The slavery business propelled his firm to a size that allowed it to intervene in foreign affairs as part of a competitive strategy. During the Gold Rush the neighborhood housing New York City's shipping district saw rivalries and betrayals that would scandalize a Gilded Age muckraker. Fiercely competitive and highly capitalized, steamship lines slipped the moorings of state control, in the process graduating from capitalists to nonstate actors exercising international power and reach. Morgan's main object was an isthmian route between the Caribbean and the Pacific Ocean and a portion of the gold that traversed it. Linkages between the West and East coasts ostensibly strengthened the federal republic and connected Empire City merchants with the westernmost outpost of the American continental empire. But Morgan and his competitors like Cornelius Vanderbilt quickly realized that steamships, unlike railroads, were largely out of government control and free to serve private interests even when they conflicted with public ones and ran afoul of international law.

Steamship entrepreneurs were impatient with the pace of the United States' march into Latin America. Because of a British preponderance of power, the Monroe Doctrine of European noninterference in American affairs had the effect of an eagle screeching at a lion. Meanwhile, the federal government refused to create substantial alliances with other independent American republics, clothing that policy with pretensions to racial, religious, and cultural superiority. In that atmosphere private companies moved on Latin America, shipping tycoons steaming ahead of American diplomats, supporting private military ventures, perturbing British and European powers, and meddling in Latin American internal affairs. New York steamship magnates had a natural affinity to proslavery expansionists who demanded that the republic annex Caribbean and Latin American territories. But as they provoked British and local resistance, they tended to undermine American diplomacy and strategic U.S. interests. The Morgan line, built on federal largesse and the Texas trade, was poised to graduate to an imperial aggressor.[56]

Steamship lines warred with one another while seeking to annihilate distances between the West Coast and East Coast. Theirs was a rapidly growing sector. Tonnage of U.S. vessels plying a domestic or coastal trade grew by 40 percent between 1850 and 1855, and shipping tonnage of U.S. vessels plying an international trade grew by over 60 percent in the same period. They added routes and served a rapidly growing global trade. Freights to California, Australia, and Asia brought windfalls to shipping merchants capable of building economies of scale. Shippers on early routes to California charged between forty and fifty dollars per ton at a time when fifteen dollars a ton would have yielded a healthy profit. Between 1849 and 1852 westbound passenger traffic from New York to

San Francisco via the Isthmus of Panama grew by over 450 percent. The Nicaragua route between New York and San Francisco was surging in importance as well. Westbound traffic rose more than tenfold between 1851 and 1854. Ferocious competition turned into filibustering and a frenzy of political influence in Washington, D.C. Morgan had staked his claim on the Gulf Coast, but its profit potential paled in comparison to those of the New York–San Francisco routes.[57]

In good steamship fashion, the leading contenders sought federal sponsorship and protections. Early to the California trade, the New York steamship merchants William Aspinwall and George Law won federal contracts—some through bribery—to carry the U.S. Mail between New York and San Francisco via the Isthmus of Panama. Aspinwall and Law reached an agreement with Columbian authorities to build a transisthmian railroad connecting New York steamships landing from the Caribbean Sea with San Francisco–bound steamers on the Pacific Ocean side. Part of the deal included suppressing Panamanian freedom fighters, a policy that the United States supported with military force based on the fishy premise that what was good for Law and Aspinwall was good for Uncle Sam. Besides $2 million, the scheme cost about four thousand lives, mostly Chinese and West Indian workers whose circumstances amounted to slavery. Aspinwall and Law combined their ventures into the U.S. Mail Steamship Company.[58]

Cornelius Vanderbilt spied a shorter transisthmian route through Nicaragua that was potentially more lucrative, and he partnered with Morgan, who diverted steamers such as the *Mexico* from their New Orleans–Texas routes to connect New York and Nicaragua. Vanderbilt reached an agreement with Nicaraguan authorities to build a canal linking Caribbean and Pacific steamship ports, promising fees and shares of the profit. The canal scheme was grandiose and improbable but provided cover for another Vanderbilt plan to build a transisthmian route linking the Caribbean port at San Juan de Nicaragua to the Pacific at San Juan del Sur. Steamboats and eventually a railroad would traverse the isthmus. Vanderbilt called it the Accessory Transit Company. British officials were not amused. Britain colonized Honduras (now Belize) and claimed the Mosquito Coast. Royal Navy warships harassed American shipping and even shelled one of Vanderbilt's steamers in San Juan de Nicaragua harbor for refusing to pay a port fee. Other steamers sank, and Wall Street stockbrokers nicknamed the Accessory Transit Company "sick Transit." A federal government that supported steamship interests lent military assistance and negotiated the Clayton-Bulwer Treaty of 1850. It refused further colonization or fortifications and pledged Anglo-American cooperation in transisthmian routes to the

Pacific. But steamship tycoons like Vanderbilt ignored or misinterpreted it as protecting their strategies. By the mid–1850s it was difficult to tell whether New York City steamship companies were furthering U.S. interests or whether the U.S. was pandering to a group of rogue imperialists.[59]

Onto the Nicaraguan scene loped the former New Orleans newspaper editor and filibuster William Walker, the proslavery "Grey-Eyed Man of Destiny." In his early thirties, Walker viewed himself as the fulfillment of prophecies of Latin American liberation. His motley army of Euroamericans intervened in a Nicaraguan civil conflict in which Walker emerged as the country's dictator. Sensing an opportunity to wrest the Accessory Transit Company from Vanderbilt, Morgan backed Walker, lending his government money and sending supplies and settlers. In turn, Walker repaid Morgan for his assistance by handing over the transit concession, which was the linchpin of any New York–San Francisco route through Nicaragua. Together with a San Francisco partner, Morgan swiped the route from his erstwhile partner while Vanderbilt was vacationing and consolidated the line at 5 Bowling Green. At its peak the Accessory Transit Company carried two thousand passengers a year and millions of dollars' worth of gold as freight. Yet Morgan and his partners undermined a cooperative attempt to compete with the U.S. Mail Steamship Company, saddled Vanderbilt with company debt, and manipulated Accessory Transit stock prices on Wall Street. Vanderbilt was furious at the betrayal. In a letter that came to light after Vanderbilt died a quarter century later, he threatened Morgan and his partners: "Gentlemen: You have undertaken to cheat me. I won't sue you for the law is too slow. I'll ruin you." Over the next two years, Vanderbilt sued his former partners and sold Accessory Transit stock in large blocks to force Morgan to buy to maintain his claim on the isthmian concession. Vanderbilt supported rival filibusters who assisted Costa Rican forces in toppling Walker's regime. Walker surrendered to the U.S. Navy in 1857. Despite the promise of securing Nicaragua for Euroamerican interests, Walker's military adventure disrupted the development of the Nicaragua route and strengthened Vanderbilt's and Morgan's competitors Aspinwall and Law, operating the Panama route. Vanderbilt next tried driving Morgan out of the Gulf Coast steamship business.[60] Morgan returned his attention to the Texas–New Orleans line and the revenues from slaving and stock hauling.

Because of his failure in Nicaragua, Morgan suddenly needed the infusion of capital available from a joint-stock company. He graduated from private ownership and in 1856 reorganized his Gulf Coast line as the Southern Steamship Company of New Orleans. The new company was incorporated separately from Morgan's other enterprises, which included a San Francisco bank and the Morgan Iron Works. The old Harris and Morgan line was depleted by the Nicaraguan intrigues, dilapidated, and in desperate need of reorganization. That gave New York investors a new and tradable stake in the Gulf Coast slave trade and expansion of the cotton economy.

Morgan "dominated" the new company, in the words of his biographer, despite not holding the presidency. He was sympathetic to Southerners and even sought to mollify proslavery chauvinists like DeBow. In part to show trans-sectional solidarity, the Southern Steamship Company's charter required that profits be invested locally in real estate in Orleans and Jefferson parishes and in Louisiana stocks and bonds. In 1856 the company bought four Harris and Morgan ships already on the line, the *Charles Morgan, Louisiana, Mexico*, and *Perseverance*. The company also bought "eight negroes" to help staff the line and purchased more enslaved people later in the decade. Supporting illegal filibustering schemes had not extinguished federal support, notwithstanding hot competition. The line won expanded contracts to carry the U.S. Mail to and from Texas.[61] As Morgan sought to rehabilitate his Gulf Coast line, Vanderbilt sought to make good on his threat to ruin his Bowling Green neighbor.

Before the Nicaragua adventure, Morgan's Gulf Coast line thrived on a lack of rivals, but competition suddenly materialized in Vanderbilt's fury for revenge. Late in what newspapers called the Transit War, two New York tycoons struggled to build a more efficient transportation route between New Orleans and Texas, which would shorten the time and distance between urban slave markets. Vanderbilt tried driving Morgan off his New Orleans–Texas steamship routes through an ambitious plan to make the Mississippi River downstream from New Orleans irrelevant to travel between New Orleans and Texas. The eighty-mile New Orleans, Opelousas, and Great Western Railroad Company (NOOGWRC) was under construction in 1856 and would open in April 1858, connecting the New Orleans suburb of Algiers to a seaport on Berwick Bay on the lower Atchafalaya River. The transit point at Berwick Bay was known as Tiger Island, and the port town called Brashear City after a local sugar planter. It was an ambitious project but an unglamorous bypass. A traveler moaned that the railroad journey took one through "crocodile or alligator swamp," which was "covered with water and heavy timber, and a thick undergrowth of cane, Spanish daggers, and dwarf palm."[62] Despite the route's being subject to prolonged impassability on account of floods, boosters planned to use it as part of a road linking New Orleans to the Pacific Coast.

Unexpectedly high construction costs left the NOOGWRC in debt and unable to generate revenue until Morgan approached it with a sharp deal. The terminus at Berwick Bay went nowhere without steamships, which the railroad company could ill afford. Morgan offered to carry freight over the NOOGWRC at a one-third discount plus a flat fee for hauling the U.S. Mail, which would be transferred to Southern Steamship Company vessels. He also demanded the privilege of lowering rates if he saw fit. Such a strategy ensured bankruptcy and a path to Morgan's buying the road. He also reserved the right to land steamers at the Sabine Pass on the way to Galveston, which would interrupt direct service to Galveston and delay passengers who paid extra for the railroad route from New Orleans. NOOGWRC directors felt compelled to accept the Faustian bargain until Vanderbilt appeared with a better one.

Seeking to flog Morgan for his Nicaraguan betrayal, Vanderbilt offered the NOOGWRC a marginally better deal in September 1856. That began a bitter competition for what was known as the railroad route to Texas. (No railroads actually crossed the Sabine River until after the Civil War.) If connected by steamships, the railroad route cut 160 miles from the distance between the Texas coast and New Orleans. Vanderbilt contracted with the road to set up a steamship line linking Berwick Bay to Galveston. Locals were happy to see Vanderbilt turn his attentions to the cattle, cotton, slave, and provisioning trade. "This is the beginning of an excellent enterprise," a New Orleans newspaper contended, "and as competition is the life of trade it will doubtless redound greatly to the interest of the people of Texas and New Orleans."[63] In January 1857 Vanderbilt diverted the 1,035-ton *Daniel Webster* from its Nicaragua route to staff the new line. The ship would steam down the Mississippi River since the railroad was not yet open.

With the *Daniel Webster* another New York tycoon captured revenues from slaving on the Gulf Coast. On one passage to Texas in 1857, two Georgia slaveholders embarked thirty-two bondspeople. They joined two enslaved people shipped by a Kentuckian and ten embarked by an army officer. When the railroad opened to Berwick Bay, Vanderbilt replaced the *Daniel Webster* with four ships on the railroad route to Texas and another on the Mississippi River route, which competed directly with Morgan's Southern Steamship Company. Vanderbilt's partnership with the NOOGWRC gave passengers twenty-four-hour service from New Orleans to Galveston. Both Vanderbilt and Morgan competed for the U.S. Mail contracts that would widen profit margins for the successful carrier. With his new line, Vanderbilt threatened the heart of Morgan's enterprise. Morgan sought a settlement that would remove it.[64]

The Transit War ended with an armistice. Morgan and his partners sold their remaining interests in the Nicaragua route to Vanderbilt, and Vanderbilt sold his Gulf Coast interests to Morgan's Southern Steamship Company.

Having jolted Morgan's line with stiff competition, Vanderbilt was glad to exit the Gulf Coast trade. Vanderbilt had suffered setbacks on the railroad route, including two of his ships colliding in late 1857. Morgan's company bought the four remaining ships. Morgan invested in port development at Brashear City, and his cash deal with Vanderbilt was sealed with Morgan's promise to stay out of Nicaragua. Political economists theorized a free market made healthy through competition, but Morgan and Vanderbilt each understood that anti-competitive strategies helped widen margins of profit and advantage.[65]

With the Southern Steamship Company free of Vanderbilt competition, the commercial steamship transport of enslaved people to Texas was again dominated by one company. But it was not smooth sailing. Two ships sank in the first year of its incorporation. The *Perseverance* caught fire off Indianola in October 1856, which gutted the ship and burned hundreds of bales of cotton and cattle hides. The *Louisiana* sank in May 1857 in Galveston Bay. Two of its three life-boats burned, and thirty-five people perished as the vessel burned to the water-line.[66] The all-too-frequent disasters were casualties of the furious pace of development and a business strategy that failed at managing risk.

Expanded transportation led to a slave market that behaved like a stock exchange. Prices for enslaved people became unmoored from agricultural prices as steam transportation revolutionized travel within the United States. Instead of lowering prices, as new efficiencies should have done, they coincided with unprecedented economic expansion and generated a market psychology in the lower South that reflected increasing perceptions of bond-spersons as tradable commodities. Cotton and slave prices were generally correlated until about 1850. Slave prices climbed between 1850 and 1854, dipped at mid-decade, then surged in 1858, reaching unheard-of prices. Price gaps widened too between the upper and lower South. A Mississippi correspondent was alarmed in 1859 that reports "from all parts of the South and West, are teeming with notices of the extraordinary high prices at which slaves are now held." Guessing at the cause, the correspondent discounted connections between a booming cotton market and slave prices. Price and earnings ratios were out of line: "a return in the value of the product, sufficient to justify a purchase, at the prices now ruling, cannot be the cause," he argued, "and all reasoning based on the proposition, proves ephemeral, for the influx of slaves this season into the cotton and sugar growing States is enormous." Reports from Augusta, Georgia, held that slave "shipments South and West by the trains, average 200 daily, while the tide of emigration by way of other points is proportionally as great."[67]

Buyers behaved like speculators when they bought bondspersons for an expected return on investment rather than as workers. Slaveholders had always treated bondspersons as investments, but expectations of returns based on resale had been secondary to the actual work that enslaved people performed. Even in the flush times of the 1830s agricultural prices rose faster than land and slave prices, making cotton and sugar production objects of a thriving domestic slave trade. By 1854 slave prices in New Orleans were over 50 percent higher than in 1850. Even accounting for dollar inflation, slave prices nearly doubled in New Orleans in the decade of the 1850s. On the eve of the panic of 1857, a New Orleans correspondent noticed "exorbitant prices" paid for slaves in Avoyelles Parish, including thirty-one-year-old Lewis, an agricultural worker, selling for $2,360 and sixteen-year-old Laura selling for $2,020.[68]

Enslavers were paying higher prices in a market that seemed to reward such investments. In Marshall, Texas, in late 1854 adult male agricultural workers were selling for between $1,500 and $1,800, and females from $1,000 to $1,200, prices redolent of the boom years two decades before. In the 1830s, however, the town had not existed. Marshall was fifty miles west of Shreveport and about fifteen miles south of the major steamboat terminus at Jefferson, Texas. By the early 1850s hundreds of steamers plied routes west of Shreveport on the Red River complex, making that once-isolated forest a haven for cotton planters and cattle ranchers. Price rises were good for owners but bad for those hiring bound laborers. During the winter 1854 hiring season, male workers were hired out for as much as $312 per year and females for as much as $170, prices that were unprecedented even for skilled tobacco and iron workers in Richmond, Virginia, a thousand miles to the east.[69]

The Southern Steamship Company was part of an ever-thickening network of steam transportation that ushered into being a superregional slave market. Telegraphic communications and newspapers distributed by train and steamer flashed market information across space with astonishing speed. "Look around you at the world," roared a Mississippi newspaper correspondent in 1852, "all going on the wings of lightning and the power of steam, at the rate of thirty miles per hour by the latter, and a rate of thousands of miles per second by the former." Those developments sent Transcendentalists like Henry David Thoreau running to the woods and wringing their hands about a mechanical civilization grinding away humanity. The same advances set slaveholders atwitter at the mountains of money they expected would repay their frenetic speculations. By 1860 railroads made it possible for buyers to travel from Alabama to Richmond in mere days, take their pick of the enslaved people offered for sale, and return with their purchases. Slave traders in Richmond

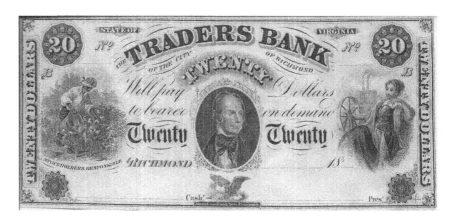

Unissued twenty-dollar banknote, Traders Bank, Richmond, Virginia

found the need to incorporate a bank serving the sector, and the auctioneer Hector Davis opened the Traders Bank in 1859, serving as its president. As if to emphasize the trade on which the bank depended, its twenty-dollar notes featured an enslaved man picking cotton and fifty-dollar notes another bondsman toting a basket of lint. (Like so many commercial connections to slavery, the notes were printed by the American Banknote Company of New York.) In faraway Texas, rail lines linked Galveston to Houston, Beaumont, Millican, Brenham, and Hempstead. Another railroad linked the port of Indianola to Victoria, Texas, and bondspersons disembarking from steamers would find themselves packed aboard railroad cars in what had recently been the cotton frontier.[70]

Two decades after Solomon Northup was steamed up the Red River in 1841, there were no obstacles to steam transportation from the Mississippi River to East Texas. Shreveport, which had been in existence just twenty-four years by 1860, was a thriving river depot. A Texas newspaper correspondent commented, "The steamboats coming and going, the immense piles of freight, merchandise, produce, cotton, stock, &c., the large warehouses and stores, etc., [were] filled to overflowing." The Southern Pacific Railroad connected ports on Caddo Lake to Marshall, Texas, by 1860, and a report that January contended that "more slaves had been cleared this year from the custom house at Mobile destined for Texas, than for five preceding years, as large as the emigration has been during that period." All over Texas, it seemed, "the prospects are indeed flattering" for slaveholders. The rise was unsustainable, but few slave investors were ready to sell out just yet. "The demand for laborers is good," a Mississippi newspaper reported late in 1859, "but we do not think it justified the exorbitant and high rates which prevail, although the South was never more solvent than now."[71]

By January 1860 one Georgia newspaper warned of "The Negro Fever" infecting buyers. "There is a perfect fever raging in Georgia now on the subject of buying negroes," the correspondent wailed. The specter of overconfidence and overbuying was taking shape. "Men are borrowing money to-day at exorbitant rates of interest to buy negroes at exorbitant prices," he warned. Higher and higher prices paid by planters demanding bondspeople seemed to justify investing in slaves even if they would not be used. "The speculation will not sustain the speculators," he predicted, "and in a short time we shall see many negroes and much land offered under the sheriff's hammer, with few buyers for cash, and then this kind of property will descend to its real value." It seemed like 1836 again, and slaveholders' judgments became unhinged from the inevitable consequences of ever-rising expectations. The correspondent cautioned that the prices of slaves, once pegged at the price of cotton, no longer had a firm basis. "Negroes are twenty-five per cent. higher now with cotton at ten and a half cents, than they were two or three years ago, when it was worth fifteen and sixteen cents." He threw up his hands. "Men are demented on the subject. A reverse will surely come!" Critics had screeched, Cassandra-like, at the threshold of every economic panic, but buyers kept bidding. Slave price rises upset the calculations of industries that relied on slave labor, such as tobacco factories and ironworks in Richmond, Virginia. The fever dreams of lower South slaveholders ready to sever national political ties in 1860 over an imagined threat to their prerogatives to buy and sell African-descended Americans like company stock could not have conjured the nightmare of the resulting Civil War.[72]

Capitalists like Charles Morgan collected a toll on Manifest Destiny and imperial expansion. He and other steamship magnates sold efficiencies that deepened slaveholding interests and sustained geoeconomic connections between the East and West coasts. American expansion in turn changed the landscape of capitalism. Morgan reinvested proceeds taken from the growth of the cotton kingdom and slave country and briefly built a company with hemispheric reach and the ability to project private economic power abroad. Propelled by coal, credit, and the march of empire, steamship lines grew to serve world markets and the magnates who owned them. In the process capitalists intervened in or provoked foreign civil conflicts, supported filibusters, and undermined national interests, all while propelling unheard-of economic growth.

Ships like the *Mexico* were machines of empire when used to land armies in Florida, disembark captives in Texas, or connect New York City to San Juan de

Nicaragua. Morgan's steamships sped enslaved people to far-off destinations while linking ports on schedules that were predictable, however perilous the routes. They sustained credit relationships often mediated by those bondspersons and carried the produce of the Texas interior to entrepôts serving world markets. They delivered civilization in bags of mail and tied outposts of empire into a federal republic headquartered in Washington, D.C. For forced migrants like Mariah Robinson, they were forbidding voids of mechanized misery clanging and chugging against hostile winds and tides, disgorging captives on strange sandy lowlands.[73]

Within Morgan's business strategy was a means of realizing the aspirations of American imperialists at midcentury. Morgan's steamships did more to promote the expansion of U.S. slavery than his fellow New Yorker John L. O'Sullivan's slogans or J. D. B. DeBow's political economics. William Walker relied on Morgan's ships, supplies, and loans. His regime fell because of the intrigues of two Bowling Green shipping merchants. Shortly before Walker faced a Honduran firing squad for attempting another Latin American coup, he yelped that Morgan and his allies' scheme revealed "as much folly as timidity, and jeopardized their reputation of skilful merchants fully as much as it damaged their character for honesty and integrity." But Walker's arrogance blinded him to his erstwhile allies' motives. Morgan did not buy into his pennywhistle ideology but instead used him as part of a dollar strategy. Though it failed, Morgan's support for Walker fit a pattern similar to the imperial drama that unfolded in Cuba involving American filibusters supported by steamship companies and other private interests. Unlike Walker, O'Sullivan, or DeBow, Morgan sought realization of profits rather than fulfillment of prophecies from westward expansion and the advance of the U.S. empire. Morgan's line was oriented to the Gulf Coast market, but it was not constrained by an imagined line between North and South, clouded by proslavery impudence, or constructed within a political narrative of U.S. democracy spreading across the Americas.[74]

When civil war came, Morgan's southern fleet served another slaveholding interest, the Confederate States of America. The Confederate War Department conscripted the steamship *Texas* in 1862. The Confederate States Navy also put the *Charles Morgan* into service as a gunship and renamed it the *Governor Moore* after Louisiana's governor, the Red River planter Thomas Overton Moore. The ship was burned on the Mississippi River in 1862 to avoid capture. The *Mexico* was refitted and launched as the Confederate *General Bragg*. U.S. forces captured it on the Mississippi River in 1862, and the vessel was reflagged as the U.S.S. *General Bragg*. It survived the war, and afterward Morgan continued to develop steam transportation in Texas and Louisiana while building his substantial fortune. New Orleans got its version of the Morgan Iron Works, and Brashear City on Berwick Bay was renamed Morgan City. The New Orleans, Opelousas, and Great Western Railroad Company and the shipping line linking it to Texas became the Morgan's Louisiana and Texas Railroad and Steamship Company. His portrait was featured on stock certificates.[75]

CONCLUSION

The slavery business was a deep entrepreneurial well, and slavery's capitalism was shaped by innovators who used advances in technology as part of business strategies, their 'nimbleness a necessity when serving a rapidly transforming zone of commercial agriculture and industries reliant on slavery. Enslavers overcame a constellation of challenges as they transported captives across American land- and seascapes, entered networks of credit, and situated their businesses in the larger commercial environment. The business of slavery benefited largely from a federal framework and policies designed to give enslavers advantages. When Francis E. Rives drove bound Americans across the Blue Ridge Mountains, through the Tennessee Valley, and into a Mississippi River slave market in 1818, he relied on federal protections from foreign competition. The War Department and Post Office eased the passage by establishing roads, however rude and rutted, the former pressuring and removing Native Americans who stood in the way. Rives's enterprise was a thin thread linking upper South slaveholders' interests to lower South buyers', making investments in bondspersons in one end of the republic and reaping returns in the other.

Austin Woolfolk created an economy of scale through an expansive organization and built a brand by relentlessly broadcasting the fruits of his commercial imagination to slaveholders thirsty for the liquid assets he offered. Woolfolk's strategy took advantage of the reorientation of mid-Atlantic domestic maritime trade to the lower Mississippi Valley. He used a wealth of human resources in the persons of three brothers and an uncle heading allied firms, employing agents, and sharing knowledge. As Woolfolk's business grew, Baltimore's elite treated him as one of their own. They defended him when dewy-eyed abolitionists called him to account for his trade's social destruction. City shipping merchants were glad to have his custom. Together Rives, Woolfolk, and their partners helped develop an interregional slave market in which captives were movable if fragile investments, which showered clients in the transportation and incarceration businesses with revenues. Woolfolk mastered the economic geography of a republic that construed a national economy as containing the slave market, drawing advantages from the democratic advancements of newspapers, thickening interregional commercial ties, and seizing the efficiencies offered by paper money.

John C. Marsh's smuggling scheme shows that in the post–War of 1812 economic expansion, the economic imperatives of an expanding slave market exceeded the legal framework regulating slavery. Domestic slave smugglers had little to fear regarding the loss of their own freedom, and returns on enslaved investments were the fruits of illegal competitive strategies. Marsh's trajectory was set by an abrupt turn in Anglo-American trade and monetary policies, which stitched him out of the textile business while Uncle Sam clothed domestic sugar with tariff protections. Smuggling cut Marsh and his partner's start-up costs in a capital-intensive industry, ostensibly revealing ravels in federal and state laws regulating slavery. But Marsh was part of a larger ring that formed a domestic counterpart to foreign smuggling of African-descended captives.

Slave smuggling was part of New Orleans's Americanization, and the slave trade was in that sense a political paste. Federal authorities excused and abetted smuggling to reward allies, in the process propitiating Louisiana planters' interests and incorporating what had been a notoriously hard-to-govern commercial center into the U.S. federal republic. In Marsh's time and place it cemented interests among New Jerseyans, New Yorkers, and Louisianans seeking to savor sugar's returns. After the 1819 financial panic interstate slave traders like the Woolfolks domesticated the slave trade by legally supplying the captives whom sugar planters and their cotton-growing countrymen consumed in abundance. The ability to buy those captives removed an obstacle to growth.

As sugar replaced cotton as Louisiana's main crop, some of the most creative financiers in New Orleans developed schemes to expand credit and banking facilities using enslaved people as a basis of growth. Hugues Lavergne, Edmond Forstall, and the slave trader Jean Baptiste Moussier developed property banks that attracted investors from Britain and Europe, who partnered with New York bankers to expand Louisiana's money supply. Other lower South states and territories followed suit, governments accepting a contingent liability. Leveraging slave property or abstracting bondspersons' value and reexpressing it as debt instruments gave foreign investors whose moral sympathies tilted toward American bondspersons a tangible stake in slavery, much like investors today who happen to be vegetarians for ethical reasons but who may fail to connect their convictions to the shares they hold in agribusinesses operating factory farms, feedlots, and slaughterhouses. The expansion of slavery was utterly reliant on investors, bankers, and merchants in states and countries where citizens were prohibited from owning slave property, and cities like New York offered technological and commercial resources unavailable in New Orleans or Natchez. Britons, Europeans, and northerners bought an interest in the expansion of slavery and, in turn, brightened the business of interstate dealers like Woolfolk and his competitors Franklin and Armfield.

State and federal banking policies also made slavery pay, whether in the Second Bank of the United States' foreign exchange business of the 1820s or in the expansive chartering of state banks in the following decade. Those policies complemented liberalized trade that lowered transportation costs for cotton and finished goods to and from Britain. Louisiana briefly became the most credit-laden, most monetized state in the nation thanks to banking expansion, trade liberalization, and the credit elasticity provided by the bodies of enslaved people disembarked in New Orleans by the hundreds, along with the lands they cultivated. But Lavergne, Forstall, and Moussier did not merely fill the purses of their fellow Creole planters and merchants with banknotes or tie their ambitions, expectations, and imaginations to fulfilling investors' expectations. Expansion of credit also improved production technology and advanced commercial development. It added to the agricultural lands on which Great Britain depended for its rise among the powers of the earth.[1] As slavery's bankers made flesh-and-blood bondspersons into immortal promises, Franklin and Armfield served the resulting expansion of southern commercial agriculture.

Isaac Franklin realized that credit and the movement of money were keys to success in the interstate slave trade. As his firm grew, he tapped into New Orleans's commercial network and became a client of Forstall's Union Bank. Cotton bills of exchange and Union Bank drafts decreased the tax on geographic distance that had diminished the returns of small operators like Rives. The chain of credit that linked the Union Bank and New Orleans merchants to New York merchants, bankers, and overseas investors gave Franklin and Armfield competitive advantages when it lowered transaction costs. Lines of credit from property banks in Louisiana and Mississippi also permitted Franklin to extend retail credit to customers, and his firm's size allowed him to accept lower South buyers' bills and other financial paper while offering local banknotes to slaveholders in the Chesapeake. His career illustrates that trust, imagination, and nerve were virtues in the slavery business.

Franklin and Armfield built a thousand-mile slave-supply chain that funneled a thousand or so bondspersons per year from Alexandria, Richmond, and Norfolk to New Orleans and Natchez. Most were embarked on New England–built company ships, which were custom-made for the firm. Hundreds of other captives were marched overland each year between the firm's regional headquarters and passed among company agents. By 1834 Franklin and Armfield was run on railroad-like management principles and behaved like a vertically integrated organization. There were few contemporary industries that required such agile entrepreneurship. Railroads were then in their infancy, and no steamboat line in the country had Franklin and Armfield's geographic reach. Yet even Franklin's forceful leadership could not keep control over the growth that splintered the firm in 1836, the peak year of the interstate slave trade.

The slavery business of the 1840s exemplified the cash nexus that capitalism's radical and conservative critics argued eroded sociality and erased human dignity. But in an irony not lost on captives like Solomon Northup, commercial technology that threatened to sever human ties of community and grind down individual creativity delivered Theophilus Freeman's firm competitive advantages. Freeman partnered with non-relatives, using weak ties of status and geographic advantage to build a supply chain in a mechanical market. Like most innovators, he used technology as part of a business strategy, and the landscape of competition in the early 1840s discouraged vertical organization or the formation of a Franklin-and-Armfield-like interlocking partnership. Freeman's firm relied on railroads and steamboats, and it heartlessly cut costs by kidnapping captives and refusing to spend money mitigating risks to their lives and health.

By the 1850s slavery's capitalism developed into proslavery imperialism, and market efficiencies provided by steam locomotion helped unmoor slave prices from commodity prices. Charles Morgan used transportation technologies as part of an aggressive business strategy to dominate the Gulf Coast steamship trade between New Orleans and the Texas coast, becoming one of the largest shippers of enslaved people in the 1850s United States. Transportation advances annihilated distances among market centers, and steamship merchants were the quintessential capitalists of an era of rampant U.S. expansion and development. The cotton kingdom's dynamism propelled an enterprise in which slavery's expansion fit seamlessly with the disorderly forces of American imperialism. With the proceeds of the Texas trade Morgan built a company capable of exercising power as a nonstate actor when developing the Nicaragua route. Though he lost the Transit War to Cornelius Vanderbilt, Morgan's Nicaragua scheme was part of a geoeconomic process in which private firms' strategies influenced and even undermined U.S. geopolitical interests.

In the bowels of Morgan's steamships slavery's capitalism appears more like the capitalists' slavery, in which the commercial transport of captives and the consequent maintenance of Texas slave traders' supply chains was a revenue-generating component of a globe-striding enterprise. While the slavery business steamed ahead in great machines operated over vast distances, its linkages became invisible to Americans who argued over slavery's character and future. Much like credit chains connecting slavery's bankers to New York, London, or Amsterdam, Morgan's steamship line's economy of scale and titanic geographic reach concealed northern interests in slavery's expansion and obscured the subjects of abolitionists' concern. William Lloyd Garrison had embarrassed a New England shipping merchant in 1830 when he accused him of accepting a consignment of captives said to belong to Woolfolk on a passage from the Chesapeake to New Orleans. Garrison's subsequent trial and imprisonment steeled the young abolitionist and propelled his career as the country's chief social gadfly. Two decades later Morgan, another New England native, built a shipping empire that embarked captives on near-daily passages from New Orleans to Texas, sometimes by the hundred. Yet that traffic in bondspersons was unremarkable to locals and invisible to abolitionists. Morgan's enterprise is a variant of the aphorism that "if a man can steal an empire, he becomes, not a thief, but an emperor. If a pirate captures a large enough prize, he may be transformed into a statesman."[2] Morgan's slave ships embodied the republic's imperial aspirations when they transported soldiers and bags of mail, generating revenues from Manifest Destiny that made him a tycoon. One result was that enslaved people whose ancestors were marched along rough roads over lonely mountain ridges were fully commoditized by the close of the 1850s, roughly on a par with shares of steamship company stock.

Strategy and technology complemented each other, and rather than acting independently, firms tended to develop more numerous network ties and richer linkages to collateral industries as the slavery business developed. There were still small traders plying dirt trails with small coffles even during the early 1860s, their fettered human wares purchased with local debt instruments and sold for the same. There are today local retailers, restaurants, and artisans who thrive in niches not served or ill-served by chain stores and mass-manufactured products. But in general the slavery business developed along with the available technologies harnessed to entrepreneurial ways of deploying them. Slavery's finance progressed from itinerant Virginia traders departing Natchez with wads of assorted financial paper and a few coins to mortgage-backed securities on arable lands and personal property including bondspersons, sold on British and European markets by leading investment houses. Enslavers' transportation progressed from wagons and carts traversing nearly impassible trails to coal-powered thousand-ton steamships making scheduled departures. Routes that were essential to one set of enslavers became obsolete to their posterity, and by the close of the 1850s the railroad route between New Orleans and Texas made unnecessary a portion of the great highway of the slave trade, the Mississippi River downstream from the Crescent City. Yet as they created efficiencies, enslavers raised costs kept off their ledgers.

Ancient Greek tragedians and their Elizabethan English counterparts could scarcely have imagined the tragedy of ambition that was the American slavery business of the nineteenth century. As is the case in modern tragedy, the protagonists were common people whose social ascent and wealth accumulation were predicated on the miseries of others. The tragic form takes on added significance through narratives of national origins and destinies under construction in the early republic. Democrats who envisioned an empire for liberty in the West and spoke honeyed phrases concerning equality and the blessings of representative government helped craft a narrative of sacred national purposes and lofty republican ideals. Political economists who theorized a self-regulating competitive market as a tide that raised all craft invigorated that narrative with the triumphal optimism that prosperity for all was just over the horizon if the ship stayed on course. Cultural, religious, and racial chauvinists joined in singing a national anthem reflecting a sunny self-confidence. They scaled the rhetorical and theoretical heights and articulated a hopeful narrative from which slavery's architects took a moral fall, even as they supported the realization of the United States as a great commercial republic. Democratic development, material accumulation, human creativity, organizational sophistication, and technological improvements mastering time and space did not necessarily chart humanitarian progress. The personal costs of the slavery business align with what an American philosopher calls "the nightside of the precocious American democratic experiment."[3]

As they developed strategies, enslavers became increasingly adept at dislocating, disorienting, and disappearing captives, immiserating them by disinheriting children and young people, cutting them off from community, family, and ancestors' social capital. As enslavers delivered a portable human commodity, they made African descent a marker of noncandidacy for the opportunities and entitlements of those who held property in other people. Slave traders delivered to buyers young, fit, and fertile bondspersons, in the process leaving a trail of human wreckage. Each generation of that commerce was a prolonged episode of social violence in which enslavers took captives from their homes, families, and neighborhoods and transferred them to intensive sites of toil. Slaving and slavery had cascading effects on successive generations of African-descended

Americans. Waves of resettlement sweeping from tidewater to piedmont, piedmont to interior South, and interior South to trans-Mississippi West, tore generation from generation in enslaved families as the political union through which they were moved grew westward. The Chesapeake and Carolina Lowcountry, among the few places in the Americas where the enslaved population had reproduced in abundance, were also the places where they were prevented from maintaining family ties and with them cultural continuity. The Atlantic seaboard became a landscape of intergenerational theft as slavers separated young workers from their families.[4] The slavery business expedited that process.

Misery, trauma, death, and social destruction were the great human externalities of slavery's capitalism. Taken from his Virginia home about the time Francis Rives entered the slave trade, Henry Watson suffered the cold, hunger, and ill-usage of the long, hard slog from eastern Virginia to Natchez and the walking paths that led to riches for interstate traders. Watson followed his mother, who had disappeared into the slave market's terrifying oblivion. That was one in a succession of disorienting and jarring movements that culminated in his sale in a town fronting the Mississippi River. He was sold five times before he escaped and eventually published an account of his ordeals, lending texture to appeals to stop the trade and with it the innovations made by entrepreneurs like Rives.[5]

Others responded to adversity with violence, fear, and trembling. William Bowser struck back at his enslavers, including Austin Woolfolk, when he took a slave ship's master by the boots and tipped him into the Atlantic Ocean. That small rebellion reached its conclusion at the end of a rope in New York City, as his erstwhile enslaver reportedly looked on fiendishly. Bowser might not have forgiven Woolfolk on his walk to the gallows had he known the extent of his successes or notoriety. Frederick Douglass never met Woolfolk but recalled him as a bogeyman who carried off children or any other bondsperson who stepped out of line. "In the deep, still darkness of midnight, I have been often aroused by the dead, heavy footsteps and the piteous cries of the chained gangs that passed our door," Douglass recalled of the echoes of Woolfolk's processions he witnessed as a child in 1820s Baltimore.[6] Others suffered untold traumas. The man encountered at the Baltimore Almshouse by Alexis de Tocqueville and Gustave de Beaumont showed symptoms of what modern physicians call post-traumatic stress disorder. He had been taken from his Virginia family by Woolfolk or one of his agents and jailed, awaiting transport. His shock was so severe that he could not stop imagining Woolfolk's constant torment as cannibalism. In the deep recesses of a house of misery he had no contact with a family from whom he had disappeared at the hands of slave traders, cared for solely by poorly paid social workers who lacked medical training or a theory of his illness.

Most captives survived their passages and rebuilt networks, neighborhoods, and families, however constrained by burdensome bondage and grinding poverty. Millie encountered Austin Woolfolk as a stranger who bought, jailed, and sold her to John Marsh and his partner in 1826. She underwent transport from the Chesapeake to a distant marshy corner of Louisiana sugar country. There Millie met New Jersey natives whose bodies were racked by disease and wore out quickly in the canebrakes, which resounded with oaths and curses uttered against those who engineered a reverse Underground Railroad to Avery Island. Eliza Thompson too could tell of the betrayals that befell her and other indentured servants whose furtive passage from New Jersey in 1818 would never be reversed. Knowing the strategies that lay under slaveholders' schemes might have added to the flood of tears Millie and Thompson shed over their bitter four decades of toil in Louisiana. Those like them who survived slavery were never repaid for their toils.

The enduring promises of Louisiana property bank's bonds were ultimately backed by the capital stored in the perishable bodies of enslaved people like Sam Watts. The lifelessness of financial paper contrasts with the humanity of Watts, who took a forlorn glance back at Virginia as he was hustled aboard a Norfolk slave ship in 1831. If Watts could somehow have escaped his fetters and chased the debt instruments exchanged for the banknotes that bought him or were remitted as the proceeds of his sale, he would have breathed the free air of New York City, where the cotton bills of exchange given for Franklin and Armfield's captives were paid. After a harrowing sea passage to New Orleans, Watts met James Franklin, who sold him to Edmond Forstall. Watts was soon put to work in the Louisiana Sugar Refinery and mortgaged to the Union Bank of Louisiana. Enslavers not only kept what he earned by his sweat but made his continued servitude part of a credit obligation. If Watts could somehow have abstracted himself from the refinery and followed the Union Bank bond that represented his mortgaged value, he might have popped up in the English or Dutch countryside, perhaps in the vault of a provincial bank or the cabinet of a widow or innkeeper whose financial security was tied to the bond's interest. Watts's mortgage, however, probably outlasted his life.

Martha Sweart may have prayed for death's eternal release from her torment. Beginning at age sixteen, she was flung far from her native Charlottesville, Virginia, and underwent many middle passages, thrust about as an object of sexual violence and fantasies of domination. James and Isaac Franklin, along with her owner, Rice Ballard, bragged of their exploits to one another while insisting she play the part of a willing partner and domestic servant. Sweart's travels aboard company ships and years of confinement in slaveholders' rape rooms made a mockery of their resource-based theory of the firm, their exalted standing in a system of social trust, and their good credit. Some of Sweart's fellow captives died after agonizing cases of cholera, their lives vanishing in a sales compound in the company of other stricken souls. Ballard graduated from a merchant in misery to a dealer in death when he failed to vaccinate captives against smallpox before packing them in the firm's vessels like cordwood. The families of those whose bodies Franklin and his overseers buried in the Mississippi moonlight along Natchez bayous never found out what happened to their sisters or sons. Yet even Franklin and Armfield's lusty entrepreneurship could seem marginally less inhumane than that of their successors like Theophilus Freeman.

Solomon Northup found that out when he regained consciousness in a jail in sight of the U.S. Capitol in 1841 in the stare of James H. Birch and a henchman. Through Northup's ordeal of kidnapping and sale to men who beat him until he acted the willing chattel, he learned that slavery's violence was the key to its profitability. The mechanical market appeared to Northup as a series of thugs delivering heavy blows in a succession of horror chambers, a near-fatal case of smallpox, and sale into twelve years of unrequited toil. Such were the artifacts of Freeman's strategy to master a fragmented market and build a slave supply chain that reached from the Potomac River to the Red River, where the brutality of captives' ordeals was joined to the region's ecological transformation in the service of enlarging the cotton kingdom.

Most bewildered perhaps were children like Mariah Robinson, forced to relocate nearly nine hundred miles, from the north Georgia hills to the banks of the Brazos River in Texas in the late 1850s. Probably jostled about inside of one of Charles Morgan's steamships, Robinson could hardly comprehend the march of empire of which she, the ship, and the New York–based firm that owned the ship were a part. Slave markets that acted like securities markets were also beyond the comprehension of children who witnessed their families disarticulated. Yet captives' resiliency was both an asset to slaveholders and a cornerstone of the ability of young people to survive and even thrive under adversity. Robinson called the Civil War the "freedom war," during which she married a local preacher and fiddler, Peter Robinson, who was elected a state representative during Reconstruction. In Texas the Robinsons made a home and a life together, founded a church, welcomed into the world ten children, and struggled as they rose to be small landowners in Meridian. By the time a federal interviewer arrived to record Robinson's story, she had lived in Texas for eighty years.[7] She was still a young woman when enslavers' hubris turned into their fatal flaw.

Even as slaveholders enjoyed power out of proportion to their representation, their ambitions metastasized into an aggressive arrogance combined with alarm at the imagined threats of abolitionists and other non-slaveholding countrymen. A robust proslavery imperial vision of the 1850s provoked reactions among politicians in the northern and western regions of the country. But contests over the future of slavery in the republic turned on arguments over lands in the Great West absent of bondspersons and schemes to annex Caribbean territories or overrun Latin America. The Republican leader Abraham Lincoln had no beef with the slavery business in 1860. Lincoln sought to protect northern freedom rather than to oppose southern slavery, and his was a conservative response to the jolting growth of the republic since Texas's annexation and the U.S.–Mexican War he had opposed in the 1840s. Lincoln and other Republicans sought safeguards for the liberties of the 22 million Americans who lived north of Maryland rather than freedom for the 4 million Americans held in slavery. Civil war would change that, but in the 1850s Republicans sought to check proslavery Southerners' resurgent expansionism if only to ensure that American expansion served the millions west of the Ohio River Valley for whom the West promised opportunities for generations unborn. But that did not matter to southern partisans who interpreted the Republican Party as a threat to their interests.[8]

When lower South slaveholding interests severed ties with their countrymen in 1860 and 1861, they began destroying the relationships of credit, commercial connections, and networks of transportation that supported slavery. In doing so they invented an idea of the South that had not been fully present before, a proto-nation made up of a region that was united by slaveholding interests and opposed to the seeming threat of the Republican Party. But the country they formed in violent opposition to Lincoln's party was one without critical features of the commercial infrastructure on which they relied. Southern slavery's downfall began with secession and not war, much less Confederate defeat.

Secessionists strained and broke the supply chains that sustained their fortunes and spurned a federal republic that had supported their interests for seven decades. Notwithstanding their business acumen, they ignored the fact that cotton fortunes ran through banks and warehouses in places like New York City when they staked their fortunes and sacred honor on a bankrupt rhetoric of the rightness of their cause and the indispensability of their snowy lint. The South's self-sufficient localism was a fiction belied by connections forged in the slavery business. The interstate slave trade suffered disruptions as planter-capitalists split with northern capitalists in 1861. Old slave traders could have predicted that. Francis E. Rives resisted his state's exit from the Union and was among Petersburg Democrats whom the secessionist Edmund Ruffin decried as "demagogues" and adherents of "blind unionism" during the secession winter of 1861, the year Rives died. Virginians followed their lower South countrymen out of the Union over a contest of interests that ostensibly hinged on slavery's future. But slave traders like Rives and Armfield had succeeded so well in tying Virginia's interests to the lower South and delivering to commercial agriculturalists the bound laborers who supported their strident proslavery schemes that planters forgot that the federal union had secured the blessings of slavery for them and their predecessors, and that Lincoln and his party promised not to interfere with slavery where it existed. The retired slave trader and shipping merchant John Armfield quipped that the Southern Confederacy was "the worst shipwreck I have ever seen."[9]

When war came, northern capitalists were largely unable to extend to Confederates the resources needed to make good on their slaveholding republic. War severed the chains of the slavery business. Expansionist Democrats in New York City briefly considered following their debt-ridden clients out of the United States (and out of New York State) in 1861, but the war effort and not troubled investments in the Confederacy spurred the creativity of northern capitalists during the war. Capitalism's agility and entrepreneurs' dexterity quickly led to a pivot when Uncle Sam invested in war-making capabilities and reshuffled economic incentives according to the new political landscape. Longitudinal economic linkages thickened along with political ones as the non-seceding states became a nation at war. Despite clandestine trading between belligerent nations, some of which was tolerated by the Abraham Lincoln and Jefferson Davis administrations, commercial ties attenuated. Military campaigns and the resulting harvest of death and destruction unsettled southern markets and made it difficult for even sympathetic northern merchants to invest or do business in the Confederacy.[10] In forming a country free of vocal critics, Confederates also formed one that was nearly free of viable creditors.

Foreign investment withered. Baring Brothers and Company spurned a Confederate loan request, and the British government declined to aid the Confederacy until it won independence. Old memories of states' reneging on property bank bonds did not generate much of an interest in Confederate state bonds among British bankers. To the extent that secessionists considered the economic ramifications of disunion, they tended to look down their supply chains, betting their experiment on the marketability of slave-produced crops abroad, contending that they could yank Great Britain into supporting them against the United States. They all but ignored the fact that southern imperialists had persistently antagonized British and European powers through strident proslavery expansionism into Cuba and Nicaragua and in debates over reopening the transatlantic slave trade. The Confederacy did secure a substantial loan from the Erlanger banking firm in Paris in 1863, and by then millions of dollars worth of its treasury bonds and cotton certificates were traded on European exchanges. But France was hardly an ally. It was building an empire in Mexico, which threatened Texas and Louisiana and, if successful, might have impeded Confederate expansion into Central America. There were other problems for Confederate recognition. Confederate strategies to deprive British factories of North American cotton and force their intervention failed to produce the desired results. British factories took the opportunity to use a huge backlog of cotton imported on the eve of disunion, reduce labor costs, and upgrade manufacturing facilities. American cotton exports to Britain plummeted from 3.1 million bales in 1861–62 to 11,000 in 1863–64. British imports of cotton dropped in half between 1861–62 and 1862–63, then rose as northwest England manufacturers acquired their lint from elsewhere. The interstate slave trade would never revive, but those engaged in the slavery business had already fatally undermined Confederate foreign diplomacy through the conspicuous brutality of their business strategies.[11]

A different military strategy might have secured independence for the Confederate States, but the horrors of the slavery business ultimately helped end slavery. A capitalist empire of print had for decades featured contests over slavery's narrative, featuring plantation romances by southern regionalists who argued with persistent and shattering depictions of the interstate slave trade by ex-slave autobiographers. Henry Watson, Frederick Douglass, Solomon Northup, and so many other formerly enslaved witnesses had testified to the violence and epochal miseries authored by agents of the slavery business. Novels, plays, songs, histories, and poetry had rehearsed that narrative contest. Antislavery fiction writers won great commercial success arguing that enslavers took unfair advantage of African-descended people, citing the slave trade as the pinnacle of immorality. That version of slavery's narrative captivated many Britons' imaginations and captured their moral allegiances.

Business ties submerged an Anglo-American discourse on slavery, however much abolitionists agitated on the issue. It broke into the open when the British government deliberated in 1861 and 1862 over whether to openly aid the Confederate States. It was then that Uncle Tom did his most effective work. Harriet Beecher Stowe's slave trader, Dan Haley, may have been a pale shade of the late Isaac Franklin, but the human costs of the slave trade *Uncle Tom's Cabin* romantically represented helped shutter the slavery business. Against such understandings of enslaved people, plantation romancers' stilted sentimentality did not compare, much less the proslavery manifestos manufactured and sold to a domestic audience of slaveholders. A Confederacy built on the rock of a proslavery narrative could not be ignored, which was the subtext of the Preliminary Emancipation Proclamation of 1862. By then the proslavery narrative was as shaky as the country it depicted, even if proslavery authors had for generations cashed in on novels featuring contented bondspersons cared for by doting maters. Lincoln may have exaggerated when he credited Stowe with starting the Civil War, but the social violence she, along with Northup and so many others, stylized was an obstacle to Confederates' attracting allies. So were the military defeats at Gettysburg and Vicksburg in 1863, which shattered confidence in Confederate securities. With no cotton, no confidence, and a decades-long slave trade exemplifying the screaming sin of the age, British capitalists and their American counterparts had nothing left to invest in.

NOTES

Abbreviations Used in the Notes

DU   Perkins Library, Duke University, Durham, North Carolina
NARA   National Archives and Records Administration, Washington, D.C.
NARA-MA   National Archives and Records Administration, Mid-Atlantic Region, Philadelphia
NARA-SW   National Archives and Records Administration, Southwest Region, Fort Worth, Texas
NONA   New Orleans Notarial Archive, New Orleans
RASP   Records of the Ante-Bellum Southern Plantations from the Revolution to the Civil War (microfilm)
UNC   Wilson Library, University of North Carolina at Chapel Hill

INTRODUCTION

1. Tom Wolfe, *The Bonfire of the Vanities* (New York: Farrar, Straus and Giroux, 1987), 53 (quotation).
2. Peter Temin, *The Roman Market Economy* (Princeton: Princeton University Press, 2012); Fernand Braudel, *Capitalism and Material Life, 1400–1800*, trans. Miriam Kochan (New York: Harper and Row, 1973); Immanuel Wallerstein, *Capitalist Agriculture and the Origins of the European World-Economy in the Sixteenth Century* (New York: Academic Press, 1974); Eric Williams, *Capitalism and Slavery* (Chapel Hill: University of North Carolina Press, 1944); Walter Johnson, *River of Dark Dreams: Slavery and Empire in the Cotton Kingdom* (Cambridge: Harvard University Press, 2013); Walter Johnson, "The Pedestal and the Veil: Rethinking the Capitalism/Slavery Question," *Journal of the Early Republic* 24.2 (Summer 2004): 299–308; Robin Blackburn, *The Making of New World Slavery: From the Baroque to the Modern, 1492–1800* (London: Verso, 1996); Marcus Rediker, *Between the Devil and the Deep Blue Sea: Merchant Seamen, Pirates, and the Anglo-American Maritime World, 1700–1750* (New York: Cambridge University Press, 1987); Joseph C. Miller, "Investing in Poverty

in Africa—Financial Aspects of the Global Historical Dynamics of Commercialization," paper presented at Understanding African Poverty over the Longue Durée, International Institute for the Advanced Study of Cultures, Institutions and Economic Enterprise, Accra, Ghana, July 15–17, 2010; Joseph C. Miller, "Credit, Captives, Collateral and Currencies: Debt, Slavery and the Financing of the Atlantic World," in *Debt and Slavery in the Mediterranean and Atlantic Worlds*, ed. Gwyn C. Campbell and Alessandro Stanziani (London: Pickering and Chatto, 2013), 105–22.

3. Joseph C. Miller, *Way of Death: Merchant Capitalism and the Angolan Slave Trade* (Madison: University of Wisconsin Press, 1988), 657 (quotation); Sven Beckert, *The Empire of Cotton: A Global History* (New York: Knopf, 2014); Robert Harms, *The Diligent: A Voyage through the Worlds of the Slave Trade* (New York: Basic Books, 2002); Marcus Rediker, *The Slave Ship: A Human History* (New York: Viking, 2007); Ian Baucom, *Specters of the Atlantic: Finance Capital, Slavery, and the Philosophy of History* (Durham: Duke University Press, 2005); Daniel Carey and Christopher Finlay, eds., *Empire of Credit: The Financial Revolution in the British Atlantic World, 1688–1815* (Dublin: Irish Academic Press, 2011); S. D. Smith, *Slavery, Family, and Gentry Capitalism in the British Atlantic: The World of the Lascelles, 1648–1834* (Cambridge: Cambridge University Press, 2006).

4. Edward E. Baptist, *The Half Has Never Been Told: Slavery and the Making of American Capitalism* (New York: Basic Books, 2014).

5. Steven Deyle, *Carry Me Back: The Domestic Slave Trade in American Life* (New York: Oxford University Press, 2005); Michael Tadman, *Speculators and Slaves: Masters, Traders, and Slaves in the Old South* (Madison: University of Wisconsin Press, 1996); Walter Johnson, *Soul by Soul: Life inside the Antebellum Slave Market* (Cambridge: Harvard University Press, 1999); Robert H. Gudmestad, *A Troublesome Commerce: The Transformation of the Interstate Slave Trade* (Baton Rouge: Louisiana State University Press, 2003); Ira Berlin, *The Making of African America: The Four Great Migrations* (New York: Viking, 2010), chap. 3; Ira Berlin, *Generations of Captivity: A History of African-American Slaves* (Cambridge: Harvard University Press, 2003); Robert William Fogel, *Without Consent or Contract: The Rise and Fall of American Slavery*, vol. 1 (New York: W. W. Norton, 1989), chaps. 1–6; Charles G. Sellers, *The Market Revolution: Jacksonian America, 1815–1846* (New York: Oxford University Press, 1991); James Oakes, *Slavery and Freedom: An Interpretation of the Old South* (New York: Knopf, 1990); Wilma A. Dunaway, *The First American Frontier: Transition to Capitalism in Southern Appalachia, 1700–1860* (Chapel Hill: University of North Carolina Press, 1996); Gavin Wright, *Slavery and American Economic Development* (Baton Rouge: Louisiana State University Press, 2006); Brian Schoen, *The Fragile Fabric of Union: Cotton, Federal Politics, and the Global Origins of the Civil War* (Baltimore: Johns Hopkins University Press, 2009); Adam Rothman, *Slave Country: American Expansion and the Origins of the Deep South* (Cambridge: Harvard University Press, 2005); Martijn Konings, *The Development of American Finance* (New York: Cambridge University Press, 2011), chaps. 1–3; Howard Bodenhorn, *A History of Banking in Antebellum America: Financial Markets and Economic Development in an Era of Nation-Building* (New York: Cambridge University Press, 2000); Scott Reynolds

Nelson, *A Nation of Deadbeats: An Uncommon History of America's Financial Disasters* (New York: Knopf, 2012); Richard Follett, *The Sugar Masters: Planters and Slaves in Louisiana's Cane World, 1820–1860* (Baton Rouge: Louisiana State University Press, 2005); Edward E. Baptist, *Creating an Old South: Middle Florida's Plantation Frontier before the Civil War* (Chapel Hill: University of North Carolina Press, 2001).

6. David Waldstreicher, *Slavery's Constitution: From Revolution to Ratification* (New York: Hill and Wang, 2009); George William Van Cleve, *A Slaveholders' Union: Slavery, Politics, and the Constitution in the Early American Republic* (Chicago: University of Chicago Press, 2010); David F. Ericson, *Slavery in the American Republic: Developing the Federal Government, 1791–1861* (Lawrence: University Press of Kansas, 2011); Gautham Rao, *At the Water's Edge: Customhouses, Politics, Governance and the Origins of the Early American State* (Chicago: University of Chicago Press, forthcoming); Walter Johnson, "White Lies: Human Property and Domestic Slavery aboard the Slave Ship *Creole*," *Atlantic Studies* 5.2 (August 2008): 237–63.

7. Hans-Georg Gadamer, *Truth and Method*, trans. Garrett Barden and John Cumming (New York: Continuum, 1975); Edward L. Ayers, *In the Presence of Mine Enemies: War in the Heart of America, 1859–1863* (New York: W. W. Norton, 2003), xix–xx, 335–61; Ben Schiller, "US Slavery's Diaspora: Black Atlantic History at the Crossroads of 'Race,' Enslavement, and Colonisation," *Slavery and Abolition* 32.2 (July 2011): 199–212; Annette Gordon-Reed, *The Hemingses of Monticello: An American Family* (New York: W. W. Norton, 2008), chap. 4; Saidiya V. Hartman, *Scenes of Subjection: Terror, Slavery, and Self-Making in Nineteenth-Century America* (New York: Oxford University Press, 1997).

8. Ronald S. Burt, *Neighbor Networks: Competitive Advantage Local and Personal* (New York: Oxford University Press, 2010); David J. Teece, *Dynamic Capabilities and Strategic Management: Organizing for Innovation and Growth* (New York: Oxford University Press, 2009); John F. Padgett and Walter W. Powell, *The Emergence of Organizations and Markets* (Princeton: Princeton University Press, 2012); Trevor J. Barnes, *Logics of Dislocation: Models, Metaphors, and Meanings of Economic Space* (New York: Guilford Press, 1995); Adam Tickell, Eric Sheppard, Jaime A. Peck, and Trevor J. Barnes, eds., *Politics and Practice in Economic Geography* (London: Sage Publications, 2007); Peter J. Burke and Jan E. Stets, *Identity Theory* (New York: Oxford University Press, 2009).

9. Edward E. Baptist, "'Stol' and Fetched Here': Enslaved Migration, Ex-Slave Narratives, and Vernacular History," in *New Studies in the History of American Slavery*, ed. Edward E. Baptist and Stephanie M. H. Camp (Athens: University of Georgia Press, 2006), 243–74.

CHAPTER 1. SOUL DRIVERS, MARKET MAKERS

1. Ledger, Francis E. Rives Papers, DU; Historical Census Browser, Geospatial and Statistical Data Center, University of Virginia Library, http://mapserver.lib.virginia.edu/index.html (accessed February 18, 2012); Saidiya V. Hartman, *Scenes of Subjection: Terror, Slavery, and Self-Making in Nineteenth-Century America* (New York: Oxford

University Press, 1997), 32–42; Vincent Brown, *The Reaper's Garden: Death and Power in the World of Atlantic Slavery* (Cambridge: Harvard University Press, 2008), 25–43; Ira Berlin, *Generations of Captivity: A History of African-American Slaves* (Cambridge: Harvard University Press, 2003), chap. 4; Joseph C. Miller, *Way of Death: Merchant Capitalism and the Angolan Slave Trade, 1730–1830* (Madison: University of Wisconsin Press, 1988), chaps. 1–9.

2. Ledger, Francis E. Rives Papers, DU; Alan Taylor, *The Internal Enemy: Slavery and War in Virginia, 1772–1832* (New York: W. W. Norton, 2013); Joseph C. Miller, *The Problem of Slavery as History: A Global Approach* (New Haven: Yale University Press, 2012), chap. 4; Margaret A. Peteraf, "The Cornerstones of Competitive Advantage: A Resource-Based View," *Strategic Management Journal* 14.3 (March 1993): 179–91; Robert M. Grant, "The Knowledge-Based View of the Firm," in *The Strategic Management of Intellectual Capital and Organizational Knowledge*, ed. Chun Wei Choo and Nick Bontis (New York: Oxford University Press, 2002), 133–48; Steven Deyle, "Rethinking the Slave Trade: Slave Traders and the Market Revolution in the South," in *The Old South's Modern Worlds: Slavery, Region, and Nation in the Age of Progress*, ed. L. Diane Barnes, Brian Schoen, and Frank Towers (New York: Oxford University Press, 2011), 104–19; L. Diane Barnes, *Artisan Workers in the Upper South: Petersburg, Virginia, 1820–1865* (Baton Rouge: Louisiana State University Press, 2008); Jacob M. Price, *Capital and Credit in British Overseas Trade: The View from the Chesapeake, 1700–1776* (Cambridge: Harvard University Press, 1980); A. Glenn Crothers, "Banks and Economic Development in Post-Revolutionary Northern Virginia, 1790–1812," *Business History Review* 73.1 (Spring 1999): 1–39; A. Glenn Crothers, "Commercial Risk and Capital Formation in Early America: Virginia Merchants and the Rise of American Marine Insurance, 1750–1815," *Business History Review* 78.4 (Winter 2004): 607–33; Gordon S. Wood, *The Idea of America: Reflections on the Birth of the United States* (New York: Penguin Press, 2011), chap. 4; Robert W. Fogel, *Without Consent or Contract: The Rise and Fall of American Slavery* (New York: W. W. Norton, 1991), chap. 1.

3. David J. Teece, Gary Pisano, and Amy Shuen, "Dynamic Capabilities and Strategic Management," *Strategic Management Journal* 18.7 (August 1997): 509–33.

4. Philip D. Curtin, "Location in History: Argentina and South Africa in the Nineteenth Century," *Journal of World History* 10.1 (Spring 1999): 41–92; Michael Tadman, *Speculators and Slaves: Masters, Traders, and Slaves in the Old South* (Madison: University of Wisconsin Press, 1996), chap. 2; Ulrich B. Phillips, *Life and Labor in the Old South* (1929; repr., Columbia: University of South Carolina Press, 2007), chap. 10.

5. Ledger, Francis E. Rives Papers, DU (quotation); Robert H. Gudmestad, *A Troublesome Commerce: The Transformation of the Interstate Slave Trade* (Baton Rouge: Louisiana State University Press, 2003), chap. 2; Wilma Dunaway, *Slavery in the American Mountain South* (New York: Cambridge University Press, 2003), chap. 3.

6. John Owen, "John Owen's Journal of His Removal from Virginia to Alabama in 1818," *Publications of the Southern History Association* 1.2 (April 1897): 91 (quotations); Richard R. John, *Spreading the News: The American Postal System from Franklin to Morse* (Cambridge: Harvard University Press, 1995).

7. John Randolph to Harmanus Bleecker, October 10, 1818, Papers of John Randolph of Roanoke, Small Special Collections Library, University of Virginia, cited in George William Van Cleve, *A Slaveholders' Union: Slavery, Politics, and the Constitution in the Early American Republic* (Chicago: University of Chicago Press, 2010), 228 (quotations); Gudmestad, *A Troublesome Commerce*, chap. 2; Angela Pulley Hudson, *Creek Paths and Federal Roads: Indians, Settlers, and Slaves in the Making of the American South* (Chapel Hill: University of North Carolina Press, 2010), chap. 5; Henry DeLeon Southerland and Jerry Elijah Brown, *The Federal Road through Georgia, the Creek Nation, and Alabama, 1806–1836* (Tuscaloosa: University of Alabama Press, 1989).

8. *Niles' Weekly Register*, October 24, 1818, 133 (quotation); Timothy Pitkin, *A Statistical View of the Commerce of the United States of America* (New Haven: Durrie & Peck, 1835), 328; John, *Spreading the News*; William Bergmann, "Delivering a Nation through the Mail," *Ohio Valley History: The Journal of the Cincinnati Historical Society* 8.3 (Fall 2008): 1–18; Hudson, *Creek Paths and Federal Roads*, chaps. 2, 5; Karl Raitz and Nancy O'Malley, "The Nineteenth-Century Evolution of Local-Scale Roads in Kentucky's Bluegrass," *Geographical Review* 94.4 (October 2004): 415–39.

9. Ledger, Francis E. Rives Papers, DU (first quotation); James F. Brooks, *Captives and Cousins: Slavery, Kinship, and Community in the Southwest Borderlands* (Chapel Hill: University of North Carolina Press, 2001), 363 (second quotation); "Disease: Cysticercosis," in *Atlas of Human Infectious Diseases*, ed. Heiman Wertheim, Peter Horby, and John P. Woodall (Chichester, U.K.: Wiley Blackwell, 2012), 136–37.

10. *Carolina Federal Republican*, March 14, 1818, 2; Albert Matthews, "The Term Indian Summer," *Monthly Weather Review* 30.1 (January 1902): 24.

11. Christina Snyder, *Slavery in Indian Country: The Changing Face of Captivity in Early America* (Cambridge: Harvard University Press, 2010); Van Cleve, *A Slaveholders' Union*; Edward E. Baptist, *The Half Has Never Been Told: Slavery and the Making of American Capitalism* (New York: Basic Books, 2014); Hudson, *Creek Paths and Federal Roads*, chaps. 3–4; Dunaway, *Slavery in the American Mountain South*, chap. 3; Claudio Saunt, "Taking Account of Property: Stratification among the Creek Indians in the Early Nineteenth Century," *William and Mary Quarterly* 57.4 (October 2000): 733–60.

12. John C. Calhoun to unknown recipient, in *The Papers of John C. Calhoun*, ed. Robert L. Meriwether, vol. 1 (Columbia: University of South Carolina Press, 1959), 401, quoted in Adam Rothman, *Slave Country: American Expansion and the Origins of the Deep South* (Cambridge: Harvard University Press, 2005), 172.

13. John C. Calhoun, quoted in Robert G. Angevine, *The Railroad and the State: War, Politics, and Technology in Nineteenth-Century America* (Stanford: Stanford University Press, 2004), 16.

14. Richard Barnes Mason to his brother [?], March 1, 1819, Camp Covington, Alabama Territory, Mason Papers, American Antiquarian Society, Worcester, Mass. (quotation); Yancey M. Quinn, "Jackson's Military Road," *Journal of Mississippi History* 41 (November 1979): 335–50; Rothman, *Slave Country*; John Lauritz Larson, *Internal Improvement: National Public Works and the Promise of Popular Government in the Early United States* (Chapel Hill: University of North Carolina Press, 2001).

15. Renatus Enys to Secretary Bennett, November 1, 1663, quoted in W. E. B. Du Bois, *The Suppression of the African Slave-Trade to the United States of America, 1638–1870* (New York: Longmans Green, 1904), 4 (quotation); James D. Drake, *The Nation's Nature: How Continental Presumptions Gave Rise to the United States of America* (Charlottesville: University of Virginia Press, 2011), chaps. 2, 7; Douglas Bradburn, *The Citizenship Revolution: Politics and the Creation of the American Union* (Charlottesville: University of Virginia Press, 2009); Joshua D. Rothman, *Flush Times and Fever Dreams: A Story of Capitalism and Slavery in the Age of Jackson* (Athens: University of Georgia Press, 2012); Jane Burbank and Frederick Cooper, *Empires in World History: Power and the Politics of Difference* (Princeton: Princeton University Press, 2010), chap. 9; Herfried Münkler, *Empires: the Logic of World Domination from Ancient Rome to the United States* (Cambridge: Polity Press, 2007), chap. 4; Steven Deyle, "The Domestic Slave Trade in America: The Lifeblood of the Southern Slave System," in *The Chattel Principle: Internal Slave Trade in the Americas*, ed. Walter Johnson (New Haven: Yale University Press, 2004), 91–116; Robin L. Einhorn, "Institutional Reality in the Age of Slavery: Taxation and Democracy in the States," in *Ruling Passions: Political Economy in Nineteenth-Century America*, ed. Richard R. John (State College: Pennsylvania State University Press, 2006), 21–43; Gavin Wright, *The Political Economy of the Cotton South: Households, Markets, and Wealth in the Nineteenth Century* (New York: W. W. Norton, 1978).

16. Robert H. Gudmestad, *Steamboats and the Rise of the Cotton Kingdom* (Baton Rouge: Louisiana State University Press, 2011), 12 (quotation); Scott Reynolds Nelson, *A Nation of Deadbeats: An Uncommon History of America's Financial Disasters* (New York: Knopf, 2012), chap. 3; Carol A. Smith, "Economics of Marketing Systems: Models from Economic Geography," *Annual Review of Anthropology* 3 (1974): 167–201; Trevor J. Barnes, "Place, Space, and Theories of Economic Value: Contextualism and Essentialism in Economic Geography," *Transactions of the Institute of British Geographers* 14.3 (1989): 299–316; Carol Sheriff, *The Erie Canal and the Paradox of Progress, 1817–1862* (New York: Hill and Wang, 1996), chap. 1; David S. Landes, *The Unbound Prometheus: Technical Change and Industrial Development in Western Europe from 1750 to the Present* (1969; repr., New York: Cambridge University Press, 2003).

17. Ledger, Francis E. Rives Papers, DU; Gudmestad, *Steamboats and the Rise of the Cotton Kingdom*, chap. 1; John C. Hudson, *Across This Land: A Regional Geography of the United States and Canada* (Baltimore: Johns Hopkins University Press, 2002), chaps. 7–12; Rothman, *Slave Country*; Federal Writers' Project, *Tennessee: A Guide to the State* (New York: Viking, 1939), 91–97.

18. Anthony F. C. Wallace, *Jefferson and the Indians: The Tragic Fate of the First Americans* (Cambridge: Harvard University Press, 1999); Joyce Chaplin, *Capitalism and a New Social Order: The Republican Vision of the 1790s* (New York: New York University Press, 1984); Peter J. Kastor, "The Many Wests of Thomas Jefferson," in *Seeing Jefferson Anew: In His Time and Ours*, ed. John B. Boles and Randal L. Hall (Charlottesville: University of Virginia Press, 2010), 66–102; J. C. A. Stagg, *The War of 1812: Conflict for a Continent* (New York: Cambridge University Press, 2012); Kenneth

J. Hagan and Ian J. Bickerton, *Unintended Consequences: The United States at War* (London: Reaktion Books, 2007), chap. 2.

19. Katherine M. B. Osburn, *Choctaw Resurgence in Mississippi: Race, Class, and Nation Building in the Jim Crow South, 1830–1977* (Lincoln: University of Nebraska Press, 2014), chap. 1; Brett Rushforth, *Bonds of Alliance: Indigenous and Atlantic Slaveries in New France* (Chapel Hill: University of North Carolina Press, 2012); Susan Schulten, *Mapping the Nation: History and Cartography in Nineteenth-Century America* (Chicago: University of Chicago Press, 2012), chap. 4; Ian Tyrell, "Making Nations/ Making States: American Historians in the Context of Empire," *Journal of American History* 86.3 (December 1999): 1015–44; Stanley Harrold, *Border War: Fighting over Slavery before the Civil War* (Chapel Hill: University of North Carolina Press, 2010); Franklin Evan Nooe, "Result of This Great Conquest: How the Southern Indians Made the Old South, 1811–1842" (PhD diss., University of Mississippi, 2012); Pekka Hämäläinen, *The Comanche Empire* (New Haven: Yale University Press, 2008), introduction; Robbie Ethridge, *From Chicaza to Chickasaw: The European Invasion and the Transformation of the Mississippian World, 1540–1715* (Chapel Hill: University of North Carolina Press, 2010), chaps. 4, 7; Eric Bowne, *The Westo Indians: Slave Traders of the Early Colonial South* (Tuscaloosa: University of Alabama Press, 2005); Claudio Saunt, *A New Order of Things: Property, Power, and the Transformation of the Creek Indians, 1783–1816* (New York: Cambridge University Press, 1999); Amanda L. Paige, Fuller L. Bumpers, and Daniel F. Littlefield Jr., *Chickasaw Removal* (Ada, Ok.: Chickasaw Press, 2010); Anthony F. C. Wallace, *The Long, Bitter Trail: Andrew Jackson and the Indians* (New York: Hill and Wang, 1993), introduction.

20. A. J. Langguth, *Union 1812: The Americans Who Fought the Second War of Independence* (New York: Simon and Schuster, 2007); David L. Lightner, *Slavery and the Commerce Power: How the Struggle against the Interstate Slave Trade Led to the Civil War* (New Haven: Yale University Press, 2006); Rothman, *Slave Country*.

21. Nicholas Onuf and Peter S. Onuf, *Nations, Markets, and War: Modern History and the American Civil War* (Charlottesville: University of Virginia Press, 2006), 280 (quotation); Patrick Luck, "Creating a Deep South: Making the Sugar and Cotton Revolutions in the Lower Mississippi Valley, 1790–1825" (PhD diss., Johns Hopkins University, 2012).

22. Daniel Walker Howe, *What Hath God Wrought: The Transformation of America, 1815–1848* (New York: Oxford University Press, 2007), 360 (quotation); Gudmestad, *Steamboats and the Rise of the Cotton Kingdom*, chaps. 6–7; William G. Thomas III, *The Iron Way: Railroads, the Civil War, and the Making of Modern America* (New Haven: Yale University Press, 2011), chap. 1; Onuf and Onuf, *Nations, Markets, and War*, chaps. 8, 10; Douglas I. Irwin, "Antebellum Tariff Politics: Regional Coalitions and Shifting Economic Interests," *Journal of Law and Economics* 51.4 (November 2008): 715–41; John Mark Hansen, "Taxation and the Political Economy of the Tariff," *International Organization* 44.4 (Autumn 1990): 527–51; W. Elliot Brownlee, *Federal Taxation in America: A Short History*, 2nd ed. (New York: Cambridge University Press, 2004), chap. 1.

23. Henry B. Fearon, *Sketches of America: A Narrative of a Journey of Five Thousand Miles through the Eastern and Western States of America* (London, 1818), 267–71.

24. William Darby, *Darby's Edition of Brooks' Universal Gazetteer; or, A New Geographical Dictionary* (Philadelphia: Benjamin Warner, 1823), 682 (quotations).
25. D. Clayton James, *Antebellum Natchez* (Baton Rouge: Louisiana State University Press, 1968), chap. 4; Timothy Ryan Buckner, "Constructing Identities on the Frontier of Slavery: Natchez, Mississippi, 1760–1860" (PhD diss., University of Texas, Austin, 2005); John Craig Hammond, *Slavery, Freedom, and Expansion in the Early American West* (Charlottesville: University of Virginia Press, 2007), chap. 2; Michael M. Edwards, *The Growth of the British Cotton Trade, 1780–1815* (Manchester: Manchester University Press, 1967), chap. 5; Ariela J. Gross, *Double Character: Slavery and Mastery in the Antebellum Southern Courtroom* (Princeton: Princeton University Press, 2000), chap. 1; Harold D. Woodman, *King Cotton and His Retainers: Financing & Marketing the Cotton Crop of the South, 1800–1925* (Lexington: University of Kentucky Press, 1968), chap. 1; Daniel H. Unser Jr., "The Frontier Exchange Economy of the Lower Mississippi Valley in the Eighteenth Century," *William and Mary Quarterly* 44.2 (April 1987): 165–92; Dale L. Flesher and Michael G. Schumacher, "A Natchez Doctor's Ledger as a Source of History, 1804–1809," *Journal of Mississippi History* 58.2 (June 1996): 177–92.
26. Fearon, *Sketches of America*, 269–273 (quotations); Darby, *Darby's Edition of Brooks' Universal Gazetteer*, 682–83; Jim Barnett and H. Clark Burkett, "The Forks of the Road Slave Market at Natchez," *Journal of Mississippi History* 63.3 (September 2001): 168–87.
27. Georg Borgstrom, *The Hungry Planet: The Modern World at the Edge of Famine* (New York: Macmillan, 1965), 70 (quotation); Kenneth Pomeranz, *The Great Divergence: China, Europe, and the Making of the Modern World Economy* (Princeton: Princeton University Press, 2000); Rowena Olegario, *A Culture of Credit: Embedding Trust and Transparency in American Business* (Cambridge: Harvard University Press, 2006); R. C. Nash, "The Organization of Trade and Finance in the British Atlantic Economy, 1600–1830," in *The Atlantic Economy during the Seventeenth and Eighteenth Centuries: Organization, Operation, Practice, and Personnel*, ed. Peter A. Coclanis (Columbia: University of South Carolina Press, 2005), 95–151; Martijn Konings, *The Development of American Finance* (New York: Cambridge University Press, 2011), chaps. 1–4; Richard E. Ellis, *Aggressive Nationalism: McCulloch v. Maryland and the Foundation of Federal Authority in the Young Republic* (New York: Oxford University Press, 2007), chap. 4; Ian Baucom, *Specters of the Atlantic: Finance Capital, Slavery, and the Philosophy of History* (Durham: Duke University Press, 2005); Robert E. Wright, *The Wealth of Nations Rediscovered: Integration and Expansion of American Financial Markets, 1780–1850* (Cambridge: Cambridge University Press, 2002); Richard Sylla, "Financial Systems and Economic Modernization," *Journal of Economic History* 62.2 (June 2002): 277–92; Peter L. Rousseau and Richard Sylla, "Emerging Financial Markets and Early U.S. Growth," *Explorations in Economic History* 42.1 (January 2005): 1–26; Howard Bodenhorn, *A History of Banking in Antebellum America: Financial Markets and Economic Development in an Era of Nation-Building* (Cambridge: Cambridge University Press, 2000).
28. Philip McMichael, "Bringing Circulation Back into Agricultural Political Economy: Analyzing the Antebellum Plantation in its World Context," *Rural Sociology* 52.2 (Summer 1987): 242–63; John R. Killick, "The Cotton Operations of Alexander Brown

and Sons in the Deep South, 1820–1860," *Journal of Southern History* 43.2 (May 1977): 169–94; Leland Hamilton Jenks, *The Migration of British Capital to 1875* (New York: Knopf, 1927); Edwin J. Perkins, *Anglo-American Trade: The House of Brown, 1800–1880* (Cambridge: Harvard University Press, 1975); Woodman, *King Cotton and His Retainers.*

29. James, *Antebellum Natchez*, 36.

30. Barnett and Burkett, "The Forks of the Road Slave Trade at Natchez"; James, *Antebellum Natchez*, 45–46, 87–88.

31. Estwick Evans, *A Pedestrious Tour of Four Thousand Miles, through the Western States and Territories during the Winter and Spring of 1818* (Concord, N.H.: Joseph C. Spear, 1819), 213–14 (quotations); Christian Pinnen, "Slavery and Empire: The Development of Slavery in the Natchez District, 1720–1820" (PhD diss., University of Southern Mississippi, 2012), chaps. 5–6; Gudmestad, *A Troublesome Commerce*, 23–26.

32. *Mississippi State Gazette*, October 24, 1818, 1.

33. Gudmestad, *A Troublesome Commerce*, 148–52; Andrew Burstein, *The Passions of Andrew Jackson* (New York: Knopf, 2003), chap. 5; Harold D. Moser and Sharon Macpherson, eds., *The Papers of Andrew Jackson*, vol. 2, *1804–1813* (Knoxville: University of Tennessee Press, 1984), 261–63, 293.

34. Nelson, *A Nation of Deadbeats*, chap. 3; Amanda Reece Mushal, "'My Word Is My Bond': Honor, Commerce, and Status in the Antebellum South" (PhD diss., University of Virginia, 2010); J. S. Gibbons, *The Banks of New-York, Their Dealers, the Clearing House, and the Panic of 1857* (New York: D. Appleton, 1859), chap. 2; Robert V. Remini, *Andrew Jackson: The Course of American Empire, 1767–1821*, vol. 1 (1977; repr., Baltimore: Johns Hopkins University Press, 1998), chaps. 7–9.

35. Ledger, Francis E. Rives Papers, DU (quotations); *Mississippi State Gazette*, December 12, 1818, 3; December 2, 1820, 1; May 12, 1821, 4; January 1, 1825, 1; James, *Antebellum Natchez*, 138; Christoph Antweiler, "Local Knowledge and Local Knowing: An Anthropological Analysis of 'Cultural Products' in the Context of Development," *Anthropos* 93.4/6 (1998): 469–94.

36. Michael O'Malley, *Face Value: The Entwined Histories of Money and Race in America* (Chicago: University of Chicago Press, 2012), chaps. 1–2; Joseph C. Miller, "Credit, Captives, Collateral and Currencies: Debt, Slavery and the Financing of the Atlantic World," in *Debt and Slavery in the Mediterranean and Atlantic Worlds*, ed. Gwyn C. Campbell and Alessandro Stanziani (London: Pickering and Chatto, 2013), 105–22; Stephen Mihm, *A Nation of Counterfeiters: Capitalists, Con Men, and the Making of the United States* (Cambridge: Harvard University Press, 2007), chaps. 4–5; Walter Johnson, *Soul by Soul: Life inside the Antebellum Slave Market* (Cambridge: Harvard University Press, 1999).

37. Ledger, Francis E. Rives Papers, DU.

38. Howard Bodenhorn, *State Banking in Early America: A New Economic History* (New York: Oxford University Press, 2003), chap. 3; Caitlin Clare Rosenthal, "From Memory to Mastery: Accounting for Control in America, 1750–1880" (PhD diss., Harvard University, 2012).

39. Jessica M. Lepler, *The Many Panics of 1837: People, Politics, and the Creation of a Transatlantic Financial Crisis* (New York: Cambridge University Press, 2013), 132

(quotation); Rikard Larsson, Lars Bengtsson, Kristina Henriksson, and Judith Sparks, "The International Learning Dilemma: Collective Knowledge Development in Strategic Alliances," *Organization Science* 9.3 (May–June 1998): 285–305; Gordon S. Wood, *Empire of Liberty: A History of the Early Republic, 1789–1815* (New York: Oxford University Press, 2009), chap. 13; John Lauritz Larson, *The Market Revolution in America: Liberty, Ambition, and the Eclipse of the Common Good* (New York: Cambridge University Press, 2010), chap. 1; John Kenneth Galbraith, *Money, Whence It Came, Where It Went* (Boston: Houghton Mifflin, 1975), 75–77; Jerry L. Mashaw, "Reluctant Nationalists: Federal Administration and Administrative Law in the Republican Era, 1801–1829," *Yale Law Journal* 116.8 (June 2007): 1636–1740; Peter S. Onuf, "Federalism, Republicanism, and the Origins of American Sectionalism," in *All Over the Map: Rethinking American Regions,* ed. Edward L. Ayers, Patricia Nelson Limerick, Stephen Nissenbaum, and Peter S. Onuf (Baltimore: Johns Hopkins University Press, 1996), 11–37; Donald H. Kagin, "Monetary Aspects of the Treasury Notes of the War of 1812," *Journal of Economic History* 44.1 (March 1984): 69–88; Richard S. Yeoman, *A Guide Book of United States Coins, Forty-fifth Edition,* ed. Kenneth Bressett (Racine, Wisc.: Whitman Publishing, 1992), 136, 154, 201; Murray N. Rothbard, *The Panic of 1819: Reactions and Policies* (1962; repr., Auburn, Ala.: Mises Institute, 2007), chap. 1.

40. Bodenhorn, *A History of Banking in Antebellum America,* chap. 2; George D. Green, *Finance and Economic Development in the Old South: Louisiana Banking, 1804–1861* (Stanford: Stanford University Press, 1972); H. C. Carey, *The Credit System in France, Great Britain, and the United States* (Philadelphia: Carey, Lea, and Blanchard, 1838).

41. *Mississippi State Gazette,* September 5, 1818, 3; Konings, *The Development of American Finance,* chap. 3; Nelson, *A Nation of Deadbeats,* chap. 4.

42. Nelson, *A Nation of Deadbeats,* 58 (quotation); *Grotjan's Philadelphia Public Sale Report,* March 30, 1818, 379; September 28, 1818, 171.

43. *Baltimore American and Commercial Daily Advertiser,* October 21, 1818 (quotations); Jane Kamensky, *The Exchange Artist: A Tale of High-Flying Speculation and America's First Banking Collapse* (New York: Viking, 2008), chap. 3.

44. Ledger, Francis E. Rives Papers, DU (quotations); Bray Hammond, *Banks and Politics in America from the Revolution to the Civil War* (1957; repr., Princeton: Princeton University Press, 1991), 178–96.

45. Henry Watson, *Narrative of Henry Watson, a Fugitive Slave* (Boston: Bela Marsh, 1848), 6, http://docsouth.unc.edu/neh/watson/watson.html (accessed October 12, 2011).

46. Susan Eva O'Donovan, "The Politics of Slaves: Mobility, Messages, and Power in Antebellum America," paper presented at the Newberry Seminar in Early American History and Culture, Chicago, April 2010; Calvin Schermerhorn, *Money over Mastery, Family over Freedom: Slavery in the Antebellum Upper South* (Baltimore: Johns Hopkins University Press, 2011).

47. Watson, *Narrative of Henry Watson,* 6–9.

48. Ibid., 9–10 (quotations); Marcus Rediker, *The Slave Ship: A Human History* (New York: Viking, 2007), 9–10.

49. Watson, *Narrative of Henry Watson*, 12.

50. Ibid. (quotations); Todd A. Herring, "Kidnapped and Sold in Natchez: The Ordeal of Aaron Cooper, a Free Black Man," *Journal of Mississippi History* 60.4 (December 1998): 341–53; Edward E. Baptist, "'Stol' and Fetched Here': Enslaved Migration, Ex-Slave Narratives, and Vernacular History," in *New Studies in the History of American Slavery*, ed. Edward E. Baptist and Stephanie M. H. Camp (Athens: University of Georgia Press, 2006), 243–74.

51. George Tucker, *Progress of the United States in Population and Wealth, as Exhibited by the Decennial Census* (Boston: Little and Brown, 1843), 94–95 (quotations); Susan Eva O'Donovan, "Traded Babies: Enslaved Children in America's Domestic Migrations, 1820–1860," in *Children in Slavery through the Ages*, ed. Gwyn Campbell, Suzanne Miers, and Joseph C. Miller (Athens: Ohio University Press, 2009), 88–102; Herbert S. Klein, *A Population History of the United States* (New York: Cambridge University Press, 2004), chaps. 3–4.

52. Watson, *Narrative of Henry Watson*, 12–14 (quotations); *Courrier de la Louisiane*, July 30, 1821, 2.

53. James W. C. Pennington, *The Fugitive Blacksmith; or, Events in the History of James W. C. Pennington, Pastor of a Presbyterian Church, New York, Formerly a Slave in the State of Maryland, United States* (London: Charles Gilpin, 1849), iv–v, http://doc-south.unc.edu/neh/penning49/penning49.html (accessed February 11, 2012).

54. W. E. B. Du Bois, *The Souls of Black Folk*, ed. Henry Louis Gates Jr. and Terri Hume Oliver (1903; repr., New York: W. W. Norton, 1999), chap. 1; Johnson, *Soul by Soul*, 163.

55. Miller, *Way of Death*, chaps. 6–9, 12–15.

56. Tadman, *Speculators and Slaves*, chap. 4; Lightner, *Slavery and the Commerce Power*.

57. David Libby, *Slavery and Frontier Mississippi, 1720–1835* (Jackson: University of Mississippi Press, 2004); Nicholas Guyatt, "'The Outskirts of Our Happiness': Race and the Lure of Colonization in the Early Republic," *Journal of American History* 95.4 (March 2009): 986–1011; Daniel F. Littlefield Jr., *Africans and Creeks: From the Colonial Period to the Civil War* (Westport, Conn.: Greenwood Press, 1979); Quintard Taylor, *In Search of the Racial Frontier: African Americans in the West, 1528–1990* (New York: W. W. Norton, 1998), chap. 2; Gary Zellar, *African Creeks: Estelvste and the Creek Nation* (Norman: University of Oklahoma Press, 2007); Tiya Miles, *The House on Diamond Hill: A Cherokee Plantation Story* (Chapel Hill: University of North Carolina Press, 2010); John Craig Hammond, "'Uncontrollable Necessity': The Local Politics, Geopolitics, and Sectional Politics of Slavery Expansion," and Brian Schoen, "Positive Goods and Necessary Evils, Commerce, Security, and Slavery in the Lower South, 1787–1837," in *Contesting Slavery: The Politics of Bondage and Freedom in the New American Nation*, ed. John Craig Hammond and Matthew Mason (Charlottesville: University of Virginia Press, 2011), 138–82.

58. Tomoko Yagyu, "Slave Traders and Planters in the Expanding South: Entrepreneurial Strategies, Business Networks, and Western Migration in the Atlantic World, 1787–1859" (PhD diss., University of North Carolina, Chapel Hill, 2006), 89; James G. March, "Exploration and Exploitation in Organizational Learning," *Organization Science* 2.1 (1991): 71–87.

59. James C. Burke, *The Wilmington & Raleigh Railroad Company, 1833–1854* (Jefferson, N.C.: McFarland, 2011), 130–37; Tadman, *Speculators and Slaves*, 196–97.

CHAPTER 2. "THE MOST NOTORIOUS OF THE BALTIMORE
NEGRO-BUYERS"

1. Elizabeth Carrow-Woolfolk, *Pioneers, Patriots and Planters: A Historic Narrative of a Woolfolk Family* (Houston: Wynnton Publishing, 2004), 212; Christopher Phillips, *Freedom's Port: The African American Community of Baltimore, 1790–1860* (Urbana: University of Illinois Press, 1997), 27; Michael Tadman, *Speculators and Slaves: Masters, Traders, and Slaves in the Old South* (Madison: University of Wisconsin Press, 1996), chaps. 2–4; William Calderhead, "The Role of the Professional Slave Trader in a Slave Economy: Austin Woolfolk, A Case Study," *Civil War History* 23 (September 1977): 195–211; Ronald S. Burt, *Neighbor Networks: Competitive Advantage Local and Personal* (New York: Oxford University Press, 2010).

2. *Niles' Weekly Register*, September 19, 1812, 45 (first quotation); *Boston Repertory*, August 28, 1812, 2 (second quotation); Seth Rockman, "Mobtown U.S.A.: Baltimore," *Common-Place* 3.4 (July 2003), www.common-place.org/vol-03/no-04/baltimore/ (accessed November 19, 2011); Charles G. Steffen, *The Mechanics of Baltimore: Workers and Politics in the Age of Revolution, 1763–1812* (Urbana: University of Illinois Press, 1984).

3. Edward Thomas Coke, *A Subaltern's Furlough: Descriptive Scenes in the United States, Upper and Lower Canada, New Brunswick, and Nova Scotia* (London: Saunders and Otley, 1833), 78 (quotation); Edward Matchett, *The Baltimore Directory and Register for 1816* (Baltimore: Wanderer Office, 1816); Thomas W. Griffith, *Sketches of the Early History of Maryland* (Baltimore: Frederick G. Schaeffer, 1824), 101; Seth Rockman, *Scraping By: Wage Labor, Slavery, and Survival in Early Baltimore* (Baltimore: Johns Hopkins University Press, 2009), chap. 3.

4. Carrow-Woolfolk, *Pioneers, Patriots and Planters*, 224–31; Allen D. Candler and Clement A. Evans, eds., *Georgia: Comprising Sketches of Counties, Towns, Events, Institutions, and Persons, Arranged in Cyclopedic Form*, vol. 3 (Atlanta: State Historical Association, 1906), 297; Judy Riffel, *Iberville Parish Cemeteries* (Baton Rouge: Comité des Archives de la Louisiane, 1989), 207, 212; Adam Rothman, *Slave Country: American Expansion and the Origins of the Deep South* (Cambridge: Harvard University Press, 2005); Ernest Obadele-Starks, *Freebooters and Smugglers: The Foreign Slave Trade in the United States after 1808* (Fayetteville: University of Arkansas Press, 2007), chaps. 1–2.

5. Arthur Hugh Clough, *Arthur Hugh Clough: Selected Poems*, ed. Shirley Chew (New York: Routledge, 2003), 51–52 (quotation); Jerome R. Garitee, *The Republic's Private Navy: The American Privateering Business as Practiced by Baltimore during the War of 1812* (Middletown, Conn.: Wesleyan University Press, 1977).

6. Steven Deyle, *Carry Me Back: The Domestic Slave Trade in American Life* (New York: Oxford University Press, 2005), 63; Robert H. Gudmestad, *A Troublesome Commerce: The Transformation of the Interstate Slave Trade* (Baton Rouge: Louisiana State

University Press, 2003), 73; Ira Berlin, *The Making of African America: The Four Great Migrations* (New York: Viking, 2010).

7. *Baltimore American and Commercial Daily Advertiser*, January 10, 1815, 3; January 12, 1815, 1 (first and second quotations); May 5, 1815, 4; May 6, 1815, 4; *Hagers-Town (Md.) Gazette*, April 23, 1811, 1 (third quotation); *Federal Republican*, November 7, 1815, 1 (fourth quotation).

8. *Baltimore Patriot*, November 17, 1815, 3 (quotation).

9. *Republican Star*, January 2, 9, and 23, 1821; February 20, 1821; March 20, 1821; April 10, 1821, 3 (quotation); Frederic Bancroft, *Slave-Trading in the Old South* (Baltimore: J. H. Furst, 1931), 40–42.

10. Henry Bradshaw Fearon, *Sketches of America: A Narrative of a Journey of Five Thousand Miles through the Eastern and Western States of America* (London: Longman, Hurst, Rees, Orme, and Brown, 1818), 232 (quotation); Edd Applegate, *The Rise of Advertising in the United States: A History of Innovation to 1960* (Lanham, Md.: Scarecrow Press, 2012), chap. 2; Charles G. Steffen, "Newspapers for Free: The Economies of Newspaper Circulation in the Early Republic," *Journal of the Early Republic* 23.3 (Autumn 2003): 383; T. J. Jackson Lears, *Fables of Abundance: A Cultural History of Advertising in America* (New York: Basic Books, 1995); Richard L. Bushman, "Shopping and Advertising in Colonial America," in *Of Consuming Interests: The Style of Life in the Eighteenth Century*, ed. Peter J. Albert, Ronald Hoffman, and Cary Carson (Charlottesville: University Press of Virginia, 1994), 233–51; Michael Schudson, *Discovering the News: A Social History of American Newspapers* (New York: Basic Books, 1981), chap. 1.

11. *Baltimore Patriot*, November 17, 21, 22, 28, and 29, 1815; December 6, 13, and 27, 1815.

12. Seth Rockman, "An Artist of Baltimore," in *New Eyes on America: The Genius of Richard Caton Woodville*, ed. Joy Peterson Heyrman (New Haven: Yale University Press, 2013), 25–36; Walter Friedman, *Birth of a Salesman: The Transformation of Selling in America* (Cambridge: Harvard University Press, 2004), chap. 1.

13. *Augusta Chronicle and Georgia Gazette*, November 17, 1819, 1 (quotation); June 30, 1810, 1; August 13, 1825, 4.

14. James Kirke Paulding, *Letters from the South, Written during an Excursion in the Summer of 1816* (New York: James Eastburn, 1817), 128.

15. *Baltimore American and Commercial Daily Advertiser*, May 21, 1816, supp., 1 (first quotation); May 31, 1816, 3 (second quotation); Tadman, *Speculators and Slaves*, chap. 5; Deyle, *Carry Me Back*, 97–99.

16. Coke, *A Subaltern's Furlough*, 79 (quotation; emphasis in original); *Federal Gazette and Baltimore Daily Advertiser*, November 18, 1818, 2–3; Clarence Saunders Bingham, "Bibliography of American Newspapers, Part III," *Proceedings of the American Antiquarian Society*, n.s. 25 (April 1915): 137–41; Thomas C. Leonard, *News for All: America's Coming-of-Age with the Press* (New York: Oxford University Press, 1995).

17. *Augusta Chronicle and Georgia Advertiser*, November 17, 1819, 1; September 27, 1823, 3; *Easton (Md.) Republican Star*, April 12, 1825; *Easton (Md.) Gazette*, September 26, 1829, 1; *Daily National Intelligencer*, June 30, 1832, 4; *Liberator*, February 2, 1831, 22; Bancroft, *Slave-Trading in the Old South*, 40–42; J. Thomas Scharf, *History of*

Baltimore City and County, from the Earliest Period to the Present Day (Philadelphia: Louis J. Everts, 1881), 612; Frederick Douglass, *My Bondage and My Freedom* (New York: Miller, Orton, and Mulligan, 1855), 447–48; Mac E. Barrick, "The Salebill," *Pennsylvania Folklife* 25.3 (1976): 24–31; Nathaniel Manley Hayward, "India Rubber Cloth" (handbill, Woburn, Mass., 1838); C. Leavitt, "Clocks, Watches, & Jewelry," (handbill, Rockville, Conn., 1842); Paul T. Carcieri, "A History of Temperance and Prohibition in Rhode Island, 1820–1916" (PhD diss., Providence College, 2007), 232, 234, 236; Jeffrey L. Pasley, *"The Tyranny of Printers": Newspaper Politics in the Early American Republic* (Charlottesville: University Press of Virginia, 2001), 233, 297, 402–5; Schudson, *Discovering the News*, 14–42; Steffen, "Newspapers for Free," 387; Henry Mayer, *All on Fire: William Lloyd Garrison and the Abolition of Slavery* (New York: St. Martin's, 2000), chap. 5; Jason Rhodes, *Somerset County, Maryland: A Brief History* (Charleston, S.C.: History Press, 2007), 47–52.

18. *United States Telegraph*, September 18, 1829, 4 (first quotation); *Daily National Intelligencer*, June 30, 1832, 4; *Baltimore Patriot*, May 29, 1818, 1 (second quotation; emphasis in original); *Washington (D.C.) Globe*, August 28, 1836; November 12, 1836, 3 (third quotation); Charles Dickens, *American Notes for General Circulation [1842] and Pictures from Italy [1846]* (New York: Charles Scribner's Sons, 1910), 277 (fourth quotation); Harriet Beecher Stowe, *A Key to Uncle Tom's Cabin* (Boston: John P. Jewett, 1853), 141–42 (fifth quotation); *Baltimore Republican*, October 1832, quoted in Bancroft, *Slave-Trading in the Old South*, 40 (sixth quotation; emphasis in original); Arthur H. Saxon, *P. T. Barnum: The Legend and the Man* (New York: Columbia University Press, 1995), chap. 6.

19. Matchett, *The Baltimore Directory and Register for 1816*, 104; *Baltimore American and Commercial Daily Advertiser*, May 4, 1815, 3; July 27, 1815, 4; February 16, 1816, 3; May 8, 1816, 3.

20. Scharf, *History of Baltimore City and County*, 513.

21. *Baltimore Patriot*, June 27, 1818, 4; *Baltimore American and Commercial Daily Advertiser*, May 8, 1816, 3; June 15, 1816, 4; October 26, 1815, 1; Rockman, *Scraping By*, chap. 1.

22. Calderhead, "The Role of the Professional Slave Trader in a Slave Economy," 199; Rockman, *Scraping By*, chap. 2.

23. Scharf, *History of Baltimore City and County*, 201 (quotation); Mayer, *All on Fire*, chap. 5.

24. Susan Eva O'Donovan, "Universities of Social and Political Change: Slaves in Jail in Antebellum America," in *Buried Lives: Incarcerated in Early America*, ed. Michele Lise Tarter and Richard Bell (Athens: University of Georgia Press, 2012), 124–48.

25. Scott Reynolds Nelson, *A Nation of Deadbeats: An Uncommon History of America's Financial Disasters* (New York: Knopf, 2012), chap. 5; Walter Johnson, *River of Dark Dreams: Slavery and Empire in the Cotton Kingdom* (Cambridge: Harvard University Press, 2013); Sven Beckert, *The Empire of Cotton: A Global History* (New York: Knopf, 2014); Brian Schoen, *The Fragile Fabric of Union: Cotton, Federal Politics, and the Global Origins of the Civil War* (Baltimore: Johns Hopkins University Press, 2009); C. A. Bayly, *The Birth of the Modern World, 1780–1914* (Oxford: Blackwell, 2004); Rowena

Olegario, *A Culture of Credit: Embedding Trust and Transparency in American Business* (Cambridge: Harvard University Press, 2006); Stanley Chapman, *Merchant Enterprise in Britain: From the Industrial Revolution to World War I* (Cambridge: Cambridge University Press, 1992), chaps. 2, 3, 5, and 6; Sheryllynne Haggerty, *The British-Atlantic Trading Community, 1760–1810: Men, Women, and the Distribution of Goods* (Leiden: Brill, 2006); Peter Maw, "Yorkshire and Lancashire Ascendant: England's Textile Exports to New York and Philadelphia, 1750–1805," *Economic History Review* 63.3 (August 2010): 734–68; R. C. Nash, "The Organization of Trade and Finance in the British Atlantic Economy, 1600–1830," in *The Atlantic Economy during the Seventeenth and Eighteenth Centuries: Organization, Operation, Practice, and Personnel*, ed. Peter A. Coclanis (Columbia: University of South Carolina Press, 2005), 95–151; Edwin J. Perkins, *Financing Anglo-American Trade: The House of Brown, 1800–1880* (Cambridge: Harvard University Press, 1975), chap. 1; Terence K. Hopkins and Immanuel Wallerstein, "Commodity Chains in the World-Economy prior to 1800," *Review* 10.1 (Summer 1986): 157–70; Ronald Bailey, "The Slave(ry) Trade and the Development of Capitalism in the United States: The Textile Industry in New England," *Social Science History* 14.3 (Autumn 1990): 373–414; Philip McMichael, "Slavery in Capitalism: The Rise and Demise of the U.S. Ante-Bellum Cotton Culture," *Theory and Society* 20.3 (June 1991): 321–49; Joseph C. Miller, *Way of Death: Merchant Capitalism and the Angolan Slave Trade, 1730–1830* (Madison: University of Wisconsin Press, 1988), chaps. 13, 16–18; Eric Williams, *Capitalism and Slavery* (1944; repr., Chapel Hill: University of North Carolina Press, 1994), chaps. 7–10.

26. Max Grivno, *Gleanings of Freedom: Free and Slave Labor along the Mason-Dixon Line, 1790–1860* (Urbana: University of Illinois Press, 2011), chap. 2.

27. Report of October 25, 1820, U.S. Customs Service, Port of Baltimore, Office of the Surveyor of Customs, Orders and Reports Concerning Slaves on Ships, folder February–December 1820, NARA-MA (quotations); Inward Slave Manifest, New Orleans, October 23, 1820 (*Unicorn*), NARA M1895, roll 1, images 590–91, 594–97; Inward Manifest, New Orleans, November 10, 1820 (*Unicorn*), NO–151, box 35, folder November 1820, NARA-SW; *Liverpool Mercury*, February 9, 1821, 263; February 23, 1821, 270; July 13, 1821, 15; August 3, 1821, 36; February 8, 1822, 255; Nelson, *A Nation of Deadbeats*, chap. 5; Perkins, *Financing Anglo-American Trade*, chaps. 1–2.

28. Brian Schoen, "Alternatives to Dependence: The Lower South's Antebellum Pursuit of Sectional Development through Global Interdependence," in *Global Perspectives on Industrial Transformation in the American South*, ed. Susanna Delfino and Michele Gillespie (Columbia: University of Missouri Press, 2005), 50–75; Robert J. Brugger, *Maryland: A Middle Temperament, 1630–1980* (Baltimore: Johns Hopkins University Press, 1988), chap. 5; Frank Richardson Kent, *The Story of Alexander Brown and Sons* (Baltimore: Alexander Brown and Sons, 1925), 109.

29. Report of November 16, 1820 (first quotation); Report of November 30, 1820 (second quotation); Report of March 15, 1820; Report of May 21, 1820; Report of September 11, 1820; Report of November 4, 1820, U.S. Customs Service, Port of Baltimore, Office of the Surveyor of Customs, Orders and Reports Concerning Slaves on Ships, folder

February–December 1820, NARA-MA; *Boston Daily Advertiser*, July 20, 1820, 2; *South Carolina City Gazette*, July 12, 1820, 3.

30. *Niles' Weekly Register*, July 21, 1821, 324 (quotations); Schoen, *Fragile Fabric of Union*; John T. Guertler, "Hezekiah Niles: Wilmington Printer and Editor," *Delaware History* 17.1 (Spring 1976): 37–53; Norval Neil Luxon, *Niles' Weekly Register: News Magazine of the Nineteenth Century* (Baton Rouge: Louisiana State University Press, 1947); Calderhead, "The Role of the Professional Slave Trader in a Slave Economy," 203–5; Philip Redding Smith, "Hezekiah Niles and American Economic Nationalism: A Political Biography" (PhD diss., University of Kansas, 1975).

31. Déborah Oropeza Keresey, "La Esclavitud Asiática en el Virreinato de la Nueva España, 1565–1673," *Historia Mexicana* 61.1 (2011): 5–57; Donald M. Sweig, "The Importation of African Slaves to the Potomac River, 1732–1772," *William and Mary Quarterly* 42.4 (1985): 507–24; Pieter C. Emmer, "The History of the Dutch Slave Trade: A Bibliographical Survey," *Journal of Economic History* 32 (1972): 728–29; Calvin Schermerhorn, "The Coastwise Slave Trade and a Mercantile Community of Interest," in *Slavery's Capitalism: A New History of American Economic Development*, ed. Sven Beckert and Seth Rockman (Philadelphia: University of Pennsylvania Press, forthcoming).

32. Johnson, *River of Dark Dreams*, 257.

33. Inward Manifest, New Orleans, June 9, 1819 (*Emilie*), NO–151, box 31, folder June 1819; Inward Manifest, New Orleans, December 14, 1819 (*Emilie*), NO–151, box 32, folder December 1819; Inward Manifest, New Orleans, March 28, 1820 (*Emilie*), NO–151, box 33, folder March 1820; Inward Manifest, New Orleans, July 2, 1820 (*Emilie*), NO–151, box 34, folder July 1820; Inward Manifest, New Orleans, October 9, 1820 (*Emilie*), NO–151, box 35, folder October 1820, NARA-SW; Inward Slave Manifest, New Orleans, January 4, 1819 (*Emilie*), NARA M1895, roll 1, image 184; Inward Slave Manifest, New Orleans, January 5, 1819 (*Emilie*), NARA M1895, roll 1, images 177–87; Inward Slave Manifest, New Orleans (*Emilie*), August 21, 1819, NARA M1895, roll 1, images 273–78, 300–301; Inward Slave Manifest, New Orleans (*Emilie*), November 27, 1819, NARA M1895, roll 1, images 344–45, 348–51; Works Progress Administration, Survey of Federal Archives in Louisiana, *Ship Registers and Enrollments of New Orleans, Louisiana*, vol. 1, 1804–1820 (University: Louisiana State University Library, 1941), 40; Ralph Clayton, *Cash for Blood: The Baltimore to New Orleans Domestic Slave Trade* (Bowie, Md.: Heritage Books, 2007), 625–39; Calvin Schermerhorn, "Capitalism's Captives: The Maritime United States Slave Trade, 1807–1850," *Journal of Social History* 47.4 (Summer 2014); Rothman, *Slave Country*, chap. 5; Robert H. Gudmestad, *Steamboats and the Rise of the Cotton Kingdom* (Baton Rouge: Louisiana State University Press, 2011), chaps. 1–2; John C. Clark, *New Orleans, 1718–1812: An Economic History* (Baton Rouge: Louisiana State University Press, 1970), chap. 14; Peter Maskell, "The Firm in Economic Geography," *Economic Geography* 77.4 (October 2001): 329–44; Erik Stam, "Why Butterflies Don't Leave: Locational Behavior of Entrepreneurial Firms," *Economic Geography* 83.1 (January 2007): 27–50; Ulrich B. Phillips, *Life and Labor in the Old South* (1929; repr., Columbia: University of South Carolina Press, 2007), 177.

34. Outward Slave Manifest, Annapolis, January 15, 1822 (*Charles*), Records of the Bureau of Customs, Annapolis, Md., Outward Coastwise Manifests, 1807–1832, box 3, folder 1822, NARA-MA; *Augusta Chronicle and Georgia Gazette*, May 2, 1822, 1; July 30, 1823, 1; May 29, 1824, 3; Outward Slave Manifest, Annapolis, May 3, 1819 (*Morris*), U.S. Collector of Customs, Baltimore, MS2383, folder 10, Maryland Historical Society, Baltimore; Inward Slave Manifest, Savannah, October 6, 1821 (*Gustavus*), NARA–Southeast Region (Atlanta); Coastwise Slave Manifests, 1801–1860, Record Group 36, Records of the U.S. Customs Service, www.ancestry.com (accessed August 30, 2013); Phillips, *Life and Labor in the Old South*, 177.

35. Clayton, *Cash for Blood*, 628–30; Martijn Konings, *The Development of American Finance* (New York: Cambridge University Press, 2011), chaps. 1–4; Peter L. Rousseau and Richard Sylla, "Emerging Financial Markets and Early U.S. Growth," *Explorations in Economic History* 42.1 (January 2005): 1–26.

36. Inward Slave Manifests, New Orleans, December 9–12, 1818 (*Temperance*), NARA M1895, roll 1, images 31–52; *Baltimore American and Commercial Daily Advertiser*, August 24, 1818, 1 (quotation); *Baltimore Price-Current*, June 15, 1816, 4; January 11, 1817, 4; April 11, 1818, 4; November 21, 1818, 1; December 5, 1818, 1; *Baltimore Patriot*, May 28, 1817, 1; April 10, 1818, 2; C. Keenan, *The Baltimore Directory, for 1822 and 1823* (Baltimore: Richard J. Matchett, 1822), 23, 154, 170; Schoen, *Fragile Fabric of Union*, 122; Charles W. Calomiris and Jonathan B. Pritchett, "Preserving Slave Families for Profit: Traders' Incentives and Pricing in the New Orleans Slave Market," *Journal of Economic History* 69.4 (December 2009): 986–1011; Dwight P. Lanmon, "The Baltimore Glass Trade, 1780–1820," *Winterthur Portfolio* 5 (1969): 15–48; Anderson Chenault Quisenberry, *Kentucky in the War of 1812* (Baltimore: Genealogical Publishing Co., 1969), 182; Robert E. Roeder, "Merchants of Ante-Bellum New Orleans," *Explorations in Entrepreneurial History* 10.3/4 (April 1958): 113–22; Scharf, *History of Baltimore City and County*, 372, 438–39.

37. Inward Slave Manifest, New Orleans, December 9, 1818 (*Temperance*), NARA M1895, roll 1, image 38 (quotation); Robert H. Gudmestad, "The Troubled Legacy of Isaac Franklin: The Enterprise of Slave Trading," *Tennessee Historical Quarterly* 62.3 (September 2003): 197.

38. *Baltimore Patriot*, December 3, 1818, 2; *Baltimore American and Commercial Daily Advertiser*, December 7, 1818, 3; Toni Ahrens, *Design Makes a Difference: Shipbuilding in Baltimore, 1765–1835* (Bowie, Md.: Heritage Books, 1998), 136; Writers' Program of the Works Projects Administration of the City of New York, *A Maritime History of New York* (Garden City, N.Y.: Doubleday, Doran, 1941), 125.

39. Benjamin Henry Latrobe, *The Journal of Latrobe, Being the Notes and Sketches of an Architect, Naturalist, and Traveler in the United States from 1796 to 1820*, ed. J. H. B. Latrobe (New York: D. Appleton, 1905), 152–53.

40. Ibid., 154–55 (quotations); J. B. Pritchett and H. Freudenberger, "A Peculiar Sample: The Selection of Slaves for the New Orleans Market," *Journal of Economic History* 52.1 (March 1992): 109–28; Andrew Tabak, *An Unimportant Ship: The Brig Pavilion, 1829–1863* (Charleston, S.C.: CreateSpace, 2011).

41. Robert Greenhalgh Albion, *Square-Riggers on Schedule: The New York Sailing Packets to England, France, and the Cotton Ports* (Princeton: Princeton University Press,

1938), 12 (first quotation); M. F. Maury, *Explanations and Sailing Directions to Accompany the Wind and Current Charts*, vol. 2 (Washington, D.C.: Cornelius Wendell, 1859), 1 (subsequent quotations); Ernest Obadele-Sparks, *Freebooters and Smugglers: The Foreign Slave Trade in the United States after 1808* (Fayetteville: University of Arkansas Press, 2007), 51.

42. Latrobe, *The Journal of Latrobe*, 157–58.

43. Ibid., 158.

44. Ibid., 159.

45. Richard Campanella, *Bienville's Dilemma: A Historical Geography of New Orleans* (Lafayette: Center for Louisiana Studies, 2008).

46. Latrobe, *The Journal of Latrobe*, 160–61 (quotation); Inward Slave Manifest, New Orleans, December 9, 1818 (*Temperance*), NARA M1895, roll 1, images 38–39.

47. Philippe Pedesclaux, vol. 19, Act 72, January 23, 1821; vol. 19, Act 6, January 3, 1821; vol. 22, Act 2090, November 29, 1821, NONA; *Orleans Gazette and Commercial Advertiser*, August 4, 1819, 1; *Louisiana Advertiser*, July 22, 1820, 2; Inward Slave Manifest, New Orleans, November 3, 1820 (*Intelligence*), NARA M1895, roll 1, images 621–22.

48. Inward Slave Manifest, New Orleans, December 9, 1818 (*Temperance*), NARA M1895, roll 1, images 35, 41–43; Philippe Pedesclaux, vol. 7, Act 135, February 17, 1819; vol. 24, Act 883, August 22, 1822; John Lynd, vol. 14, Act 4, February 18, 1819; Philippe Pedesclaux, vol. 15, Act 1229, June 28, 1820; vol. 18, Act 2033, December 22, 1820, NONA; 1830 U.S. Census, St. Martin Parish, Louisiana, 128, NARA, roll M19–44; Family History Film: 0009687, www.ancestry.com (accessed April 15, 2011).

49. Kenneth Morgan, "Remittance Procedures in the Eighteenth-Century British Slave Trade," *Business History Review* 79.4 (Winter 2005): 715–49.

50. Philippe Pedesclaux, vol. 13, Act 686, April 6, 1820; vol. 13, Act 710, April 10, 1820; vol. 15, Act 1296, July 12, 1820, NONA; Jessica M. Lepler, *The Many Panics of 1837: People, Politics, and the Creation of a Transatlantic Financial Crisis* (New York: Cambridge University Press, 2013), chap. 1; Kenneth Morgan, *Slavery, Atlantic Trade and the British Economy, 1660–1800* (Cambridge: Cambridge University Press, 2000); Robin Pearson and David Richardson, "Social Capital, Institutional Innovation and Atlantic Trade before 1800," *Business History* 50.6 (2008): 765–80; Robert Harms, *The Diligent: A Voyage through the Worlds of the Slave Trade* (New York: Basic Books, 2002), chap. 5.

51. Irene D. Neu, "J. B. Moussier and the Property Banks of Louisiana," *Business History Review* 35.4 (Winter 1961): 555; Hugues Lavergne, vol. 1, Act 4, July 27, 1819, NONA; *Baltimore Gazette and Daily Advertiser*, July 19, 1826, 2; Betsy Swanson, *Historic Jefferson Parish: From Shore to Shore* (Gretna, La.: Pelican, 2003), 152–53.

52. Inward Manifest, New Orleans, November 10, 1820 (*Margaret Wright*), NO–151, box 35, folder November 1820, NARA-SW; Inward Slave Manifest, New Orleans, October 14–20, 1820 (*Margaret Wright*), NARA M1895, roll 1, images 524–29, 584–88; *Norfolk (Va.) American Beacon*, November 7, 1820, 1; September 30, 1820, 3; October 10, 1820, 3; *Liverpool Mercury*, May 3, 1822, 351; November 1, 1822, 3.

53. Hugues Lavergne, vol. 4, Act 621, November 16, 1820; vol. 4, Act 623, November 22, 1820; vol. 4, Act 624, November 24, 1820; Philippe Pedesclaux, vol. 18, Act 1906,

November 15, 1820, NONA; Inward Slave Manifest, New Orleans, May 22, 1823 (*Brazillian*), NARA M1895, roll 3, images 166–68; John Maddox, *The Richmond Directory, Register and Almanac, for the Year 1819* (Richmond: John Maddox, 1819), 37; Works Progress Administration, Survey of Federal Archives in Louisiana, *Ship Registers and Enrollments of New Orleans, Louisiana*, vol. 2, *1821–1830* (University: Louisiana State University Library, 1942), 19; Lauren Benton, *A Search for Sovereignty: Law and Geography in European Empires, 1400–1900* (Cambridge: Cambridge University Press, 2009); Paul F. Lachance, "The Foreign French," in *Creole New Orleans: Race and Americanization*, ed. Arnold R. Hirsch and Joseph Logsdon (Baton Rouge: Louisiana State University Press, 1992), 120n.38.

54. *Richmond Enquirer*, October 29, 1824, 1 (first and second quotations); Inward Slave Manifest, New Orleans, December 9, 1824 (*Factor*), NARA M1895, roll 3, images 860–62 (third quotation); Inward Slave Manifest, New Orleans, October 21, 1822 (*Brazillian*), NARA M1895, roll 2, images 460–63; Hugues Lavergne, vol. 8, Act 1605, December 14, 1822, NONA; Alcée Fortier, *Louisiana, Comprising Sketches of Parishes, Towns, Events, Institutions, and Persons, Arranged in Cyclopedic Form*, vol. 3 (Madison, Wisc.: Century Historical Association, 1914), 298; Sylvia Neely, "The Politics of Liberty in the Old World and the New: Lafayette's Return to America in 1824," *Journal of the Early Republic* 6.2 (Summer 1986): 162; Margaret A. Peteraf, "The Cornerstones of Competitive Advantage: A Resource-Based View," *Strategic Management Journal* 14.3 (March 1993): 179–91; Robert M. Grant, "The Knowledge-Based View of the Firm," in *The Strategic Management of Intellectual Capital and Organizational Knowledge*, ed. Chun Wei Choo and Nick Bontis (New York: Oxford University Press, 2002), 133–48; David Waldstreicher, *In the Midst of Perpetual Fetes: The Making of American Nationalism, 1776–1820* (Chapel Hill: University of North Carolina Press, 1997); Gilbert C. Din, "The Offices and Functions of the New Orleans Cabildo," *Louisiana History: The Journal of the Louisiana Historical Association* 37.1 (Winter 1996): 5–30; Sally Kittredge Reeves, "Spanish Colonial Records of the New Orleans Notarial Archives," *LLA Bulletin* 55 (1992): 7–12; Joseph A. Scoville, *The Old Merchants of New York City*, vol. 1 (New York: Thomas R. Knox, 1885), 46–48.

55. Hugues Lavergne, vol. 12, Act 2284, March 6, 1824 (quotation); vol.7, Act 1195, April 5, 1822; vol. 7, Act 1283, June 23, 1822; vol. 7, Act 1348, June 8, 1822; vol. 11, Act 2193, December 31[?], 1823; Philippe Pedesclaux, vol. 24, Act 1140, December 27, 1822, NONA; Inward Slave Manifest, New Orleans, April 5, 1822 (*Hollon*), NARA M1895, roll 2, images 679–84.

56. Inward Slave Manifest, May 14, 1822 (*Hyperion*), NARA M1895, roll 2, images 290–91; *Baltimore American and Commercial Daily Advertiser*, May 31, June 21, June 26, July 2, and July 10, 1816; *Baltimore Patriot*, July 12, 13, 16, and 17, 1816; Robert Jackall, *Moral Mazes: The World of Corporate Managers* (New York: Oxford University Press, 2009); Salvatore Sciascia, Pietro Mazzola, Joseph H. Astrachan, and Torsten M. Pieper, "The Role of Family Ownership in International Entrepreneurship: Exploring Nonlinear Effects," *Small Business Economics* 38.1 (January 2012): 15–31.

57. Keenan, *The Baltimore Directory, for 1822 and 1823*, 82, 306 (first quotation); *Baltimore Patriot*, September 24, 1823, 3; December 12, 1823, 3 (second and third quotations);

Clayton, *Cash for Blood*, 61 (fourth and fifth quotations); *Baltimore Patriot*, July 27, 1821; *Matchett's Baltimore Director* (Baltimore, 1842), 408; *Niles' Weekly Register*, September 10, 1812, 46; Griffith, *Sketches of the Early History of Maryland*, 117–18; Miller, *Way of Death*, 295.

58. *Baltimore Patriot*, August 11, 1824, 3 (quotation); 1820 U.S. Census, Richmond County, Georgia, 217, NARA M33, roll 7, image 215, www.ancestry.com (accessed December 14, 2010); *Augusta Chronicle and Georgia Advertiser*, September 27, 1823, 3; July 11, 1827, 3; May 29, 1824, 3; *Maryland Federal Gazette*, November 18, 1818; *Baltimore Patriot*, November 30, 1818; *Republican Star and General Advertiser*, June 7, 1825, 3; September 27, 1825, 4; Carrow-Woolfolk, *Pioneers, Patriots and Planters*, 237–41; Rothman, *Slave Country*; Tadman, *Speculators and Slaves*, 275, 282; Dickson J. Preston, *Young Frederick Douglass: The Maryland Years* (Baltimore: Johns Hopkins University Press, 1980), 78–80.

59. Inward Slave Manifest, New Orleans, April 12, 1826 (*James Monroe*), NARA M1895, roll 4, images 220–21; *Easton (Md.) Republican Star and General Advertiser*, October 16, 1827, 1; January 29, 1828, 4; Solomon Northup, *Twelve Years a Slave: Narrative of Solomon Northup, a Citizen of New-York, Kidnapped in Washington City in 1841, and Rescued in 1853* (Auburn, N.Y.: Derby and Miller, 1853), chap. 3.

60. *Princess Anne (Md.) Village Herald*, January 7, 1831, quoted in Winfield Hazlitt Collins, *The Domestic Slave Trade of the Southern States* (New York: Broadway Publishing, 1904), 51; Carrow-Woolfolk, *Pioneers, Patriots and Planters*, 231; Bancroft, *Slave-Trading in the Old South*, 31–32; Gudmestad, *A Troublesome Commerce*, chap. 1.

61. *Augusta Chronicle and Georgia Gazette*, August 27, 1825, 4; Hugues Lavergne, vol.8, Act 1605, December 14, 1822; vol. 16, Act 3044, May 13, 1825, NONA; Inward Slave Manifest, New Orleans, March 25, 1825 (*Lady Monroe*), NARA M1895, roll 3, images 877–78; Alfred D. Chandler Jr., *The Visible Hand: The Managerial Revolution in American Business* (Cambridge: Harvard University Press, 1977), chap. 1.

62. Philippe Pedesclaux, vol. 23, Act 554, May 7, 1822; Hugues Lavergne, vol.12, Act 2264, March 15, 1824; vol. 18, Act 3449, March 11, 1826; vol. 18, Act 3450, March 18, 1826; vol. 18, Act 3621, June 17, 1826; vol. 18, Act 3636, June 29, 1826; vol. 18, Act 3372, January 18, 1826, NONA; Inward Slave Manifest, December 19, 1825 (*Virginia*), NARA M1895, roll 4, images 174–75; *Niles' Weekly Register*, August 20, 1825, 388; Shirley Elizabeth Thompson, *Exiles at Home: The Struggle to Become American in Creole New Orleans* (Cambridge: Harvard University Press, 2009).

63. *Louisiana Advertiser*, January 23, 1827, 2.

64. Schermerhorn, "Capitalism's Captives"; Clayton, *Cash for Blood*, 625–39; Pritchett and Freudenberger, "A Peculiar Sample."

65. J. Thomas Scharf, *The Chronicles of Baltimore, Being a Complete History of "Baltimore Town" and Baltimore City from the Earliest Period to the Present Time* (Baltimore: Turnbull Brothers, 1874), 483.

66. Inward Slave Manifest, New Orleans, May 15, 1828 (*Arctic*), NARA M1895, roll 5, images 523–24; Inward Slave Manifest, New Orleans, December 5, 1826 (*Hibernia*), NARA M1895, roll 4, images 657–59; *Baltimore Gazette and Daily Advertiser*, August 15, 1827, 3; Keenan, *The Baltimore Directory, for 1822 and 1823*, 220; Greg H. Williams,

The French Assault on American Shipping, 1793–1813: A History and Comprehensive Record of Merchant Marine Losses (Jefferson, N.C.: McFarland, 2009), 73; Clayton, *Cash for Blood*, 625–39; WPA, *Ship Registers and Enrollments of New Orleans*, 2:9.

67. Inward Slave Manifest, New Orleans, December 21, 24–27, 1827 (*Jefferson*), NARA M1895, roll 5, images 87–90, 145–50 (quotation 148); *Charleston (S.C.) City Gazette*, February 3, 1827, 2; December 31, 1827, 2; *Baltimore Torch Light*, December 27, 1827, 3; *Louisiana Advertiser*, March 9, 1827, 3; *Baltimore Gazette and Daily Advertiser*, June 6, 1827, 2; July 5, 1827, 2; November 27, 1827, 2; December 21, 1827, 2; *Baltimore Patriot*, March 28, 1828, 2.

68. *Genius of Universal Emancipation*, November 1832, quoted in Deyle, *Carry Me Back*, 179 (quotation); Merton L. Dillon, *Benjamin Lundy and the Struggle for Negro Freedom* (Urbana: University of Illinois Press, 1966), chaps. 3–7.

69. *Genius of Universal Emancipation*, July 4, 1825, 1; Inward Slave Manifest, New Orleans, March 25, 1825 (*Lady Monroe*), NARA M1895, roll 3, images 874–79; Hugh Gordon, vol. 1, Act 230, May 17, 1825, NONA; Adam Hochschild, *Bury the Chains: Prophets and Rebels in the Fight to Free an Empire's Slaves* (New York: Mariner Books, 2006).

70. *Genius of Universal Emancipation*, reprinted in the *Hartford Connecticut Courant*, August 9, 1825, 3 (quotation); *Niles' Weekly Register*, August 20, 1825, 388; *Connecticut Courant*, November 20, 1826, 2; December 8, 1829, 2; *New York Spectator*, August 12, 1825, 4; *Edwardsville (Ill.) Spectator*, August 13, 1825, 1.

71. *Baltimore Gazette and Daily Advertiser*, May 23, 1826, 2; Eric Robert Taylor, *If We Must Die: Shipboard Insurrections in the Era of the Atlantic Slave Trade* (Baton Rouge: Louisiana State University Press, 2006), 147.

72. *Baltimore Gazette and Daily Advertiser*, May 23, 1826, 2 (quotations); *Niles' Weekly Register*, May 20, 1826, 202; Taylor, *If We Must Die*, 147–50.

73. *Baltimore Gazette and Daily Advertiser*, May 23, 1826, 2 (quotation); *New York Commercial Advertiser*, May 19, 1826, 2; Taylor, *If We Must Die*, 148.

74. *Genius of Universal Emancipation*, reprinted in *Berks and Schuylkill (Pa.) Journal*, January 13, 1827, 1 (quotations); *New York Spectator*, August 12, 1825, 4; November 22, 1826, 3; W. David Sloan and Lisa Mullikin Parcell, *American Journalism: History, Principles, Practices* (Jefferson, N.C.: McFarland, 2002), 100.

75. *Niles' Weekly Register*, May 19, 1827, 205 (quotations).

76. Ibid. (quotations).

77. Mayer, *All on Fire*, 75; *Genius of Universal Emancipation*, September 12, 1825, 150–51 (quotation).

78. W. Caleb McDaniel, *The Problem of Democracy in the Age of Slavery: Garrisonian Abolitionists and Transatlantic Reform* (Baton Rouge: Louisiana State University Press, 2013); Susan Schulten, *Mapping the Nation: History and Cartography in Nineteenth-Century America* (Chicago: University of Chicago Press, 2012), chaps. 4–5; Mayer, *All on Fire*, chaps. 1–3; James Brewer Stewart, *Holy Warriors: The Abolitionists and American Slavery* (New York: Hill and Wang, 1997).

79. *Genius of Universal Emancipation*, November 13, 1829, quoted in Kevin C. Julius, *The Abolitionist Decade, 1829–1838: A Year-by-Year History of Early Events in the Antislavery Movement* (Jefferson, N.C.: McFarland, 2004), 47; Mayer, *All on Fire*, 76.

80. *Newburyport (Mass.) Herald*, November 17, 1829, 3; December 15, 1829, 3; *Baltimore Gazette and Daily Advertiser*, October 15, 1830, 2; Mayer, *All on Fire*, chap. 5.

81. *Genius of Universal Emancipation*, November 13, 1829, 75, quoted in Francis Jackson Garrison, *William Lloyd Garrison, 1805–1879: The Story of His Life, Told by His Children*, vol. 1, 1805–1835 (New York: Century, 1885), 165 (quotations); *Baltimore Gazette and Daily Advertiser*, May 30, 1829, 2; Mayer, *All on Fire*, 76.

82. Mayer, *All on Fire*, 84 (first quotation), 87 (second quotation); *Genius of Universal Emancipation*, October, 1830, 98; *Baltimore Gazette and Daily Advertiser*, October 15, 1830, 2.

83. Mayer, *All on Fire*, chap. 5; Paul Finkelman, ed., *Slavery, Race, and the American Legal System, 1700–1872*, ser. 4, vol. 1 (New York: Garland, 1988), 200.

84. McDaniel, *The Problem of Democracy in the Age of Slavery*, introduction; Fionnghuala Sweeney, *Frederick Douglass and the Atlantic World* (Liverpool: Liverpool University Press, 2007); Robert Fanuzzi, *Abolition's Public Sphere* (Minneapolis: University of Minnesota Press, 2003); Robert S. Levine, *Martin Delany, Frederick Douglass, and the Politics of Representative Identity* (Chapel Hill: University of North Carolina Press, 1997); William L. Andrews, *To Tell a Free Story: The First Century of Afro-American Autobiography* (Urbana: University of Illinois Press, 1988); William S. McFeely, *Frederick Douglass* (New York: W. W. Norton, 1991), chap. 10.

85. Douglass, *My Bondage and My Freedom*, 446–450; Gudmestad, *A Troublesome Commerce*, chap. 2; Calvin Schermerhorn, "Arguing Slavery's Narrative: Southern Regionalists, Ex-Slave Autobiographers, and the Contested Literary Representations of the Peculiar Institution, 1824–1849," *Journal of American Studies* 46.4 (2012): 1009–33; Scott Romine, *The Narrative Forms of the Southern Community* (Baton Rouge: Louisiana State University Press, 1999).

86. Joseph C. Miller, *The Problem of Slavery as History: A Global Approach* (New Haven: Yale University Press, 2012), chap. 4; David S. Reynolds, *Mightier Than the Sword: Uncle Tom's Cabin and the Battle for America* (New York: W. W. Norton, 2011); Sarah Meer, *Uncle Tom Mania: Slavery, Minstrelsy, & Transatlantic Culture in the 1850s* (Athens: University of Georgia Press, 2005); Eric Gardner, *Unexpected Places: Relocating Nineteenth-Century African American Literature* (Jackson: University Press of Mississippi, 2009); Michael T. Gilmore, *The War on Words: Slavery, Race, and Free Speech in American Literature* (Chicago: University of Chicago Press, 2010), 1–196; Augusta Rohrbach, *Truth Stranger Than Fiction: Race, Realism, and the U.S. Literary Marketplace* (New York: Palgrave, 2002); David Grimsted, *American Mobbing, 1828–1861: Toward Civil War* (New York: Oxford University Press, 1998).

87. Alejandro Portes, *Economic Sociology: A Systematic Inquiry* (Princeton: Princeton University Press, 2010), chaps. 3–6; Gregory Castle, *Reading the Modernist Bildungsroman* (Gainesville: University Press of Florida, 2006); Neil Fligstein, *The Architecture of Markets: An Economic Sociology of Twenty-First-Century Capitalist Societies* (Princeton: Princeton University Press, 2002), chaps. 1–4; Ronald S. Burt, *Structural Holes: The Social Structure of Competition* (Cambridge: Harvard University Press, 1992); Stanley F. Slater and John C. Narver, "Market Orientation and the Learning Organization," *Journal of Marketing* 59.3 (July 1995): 63–74.

88. *Baltimore Patriot*, September 9, 1831, 3; September 19, 1831, 3; September 26, 1831, 3; *Baltimore Gazette and Daily Advertiser*, October 15, 1831, 1; November 1, 1831, 1; Inward Slave Manifest, New Orleans, October 11, 1831 (*Brunswick*), NARA M1895, roll 6, images 1102–5; Inward Slave Manifest, New Orleans, November 11, 1831 (*Signet*), NARA M1895, roll 6, images 1111–13, 1159–60; Inward Slave Manifest, New Orleans, November 29, 1834 (*Isabella*), NARA M1895, roll 7, images 510–11; Hilary Breton Cenas, vol. 2, Act 23, January 12, 1835, NONA; Fortier, *Louisiana*, 3:85.

89. Carrow-Woolfolk, *Pioneers, Patriots and Planters*, 232–33; U.S. Bureau of Land Management, *Louisiana Land Records*, www.ancestry.com (accessed November 24, 2011); Jordan Dodd, *Maryland Marriages, 1655–1850*, www.ancestry.com (accessed November 14, 2011); William Samuel Slack and Charles Wesley Slack, *The Slack Family: More Particularly an Account of the Family of Eliphalet Slack and His Wife Abigail Cutter, Their Ascendants, Descendants and Relations* (Alexandria, La.: Standard Printing Co., 1930), 122–35.

90. Federal Writers' Project, *Louisiana: A Guide to the State* (Baton Rouge: Louisiana Library Commission, 1941), 572 (quotation); Anne Butler, *The Pelican Guide to Plantation Homes of Louisiana* (Gretna, La.: Pelican, 2009), 101.

91. *Daily National Intelligencer*, March 15, 1847, 3 (first quotation); Austin Woolfolk Will, Madison County, Tenn., Will Book 5, p. 65, http://homepages.rootsweb.ancestry.com/~woolfolk/documents/austinwoolfolkwill.htm (accessed November 14, 2011) (second quotation); Carrow-Woolfollk, *Pioneers, Patriots and Planters*, 235 (third quotation).

92. Alexis de Tocqueville, quoted in Louis P. Masur, *1831: Year of the Eclipse* (New York: Hill and Wang, 2002), 42; Rockman, *Scraping By*, chap. 7.

93. Gustave de Beaumont, *Marie; or, Slavery in the United States: A Novel of Jacksonian America*, trans. Barbara Chapman (Baltimore: Johns Hopkins University Press, 1998), 45–46 (all but last quotation); Alexis de Tocqueville, *Journey to America*, ed. J. P. Mayer, trans. George Lawrence (Westport, Conn.: Greenwood Press, 1981), 159–60 (last quotation).

CHAPTER 3. SWEET DREAMS AND SMUGGLING SCHEMES

1. *New York Courier*, November 7, 1815, 4; December 25, 1815, 2; January 22, 1816, 1; February 16, 1816, 4; June 21, 1816, 3; June 25, 1816, 1; *New York Evening Post*, November 4, 1815, 2; May 21, 1817, 3; Joseph A. Scoville, *The Old Merchants of New York City*, vol. 1 (New York: Carleton, 1863), 269–72; Bertram Wyatt-Brown, *Lewis Tappan and the Evangelical War against Slavery* (Cleveland: Case Western Reserve University Press, 1969), 42; Oliver E. Williamson, "Opportunism and Its Critics," *Managerial and Decision Economics* 14.2 (March–April 1993): 97–107; R. H. Coase, "The Problem of Social Cost," *Journal of Law and Economics* 3 (October 1960): 1–44.

2. Scott Reynolds Nelson, *A Nation of Deadbeats: An Uncommon History of America's Financial Disasters* (New York: Knopf, 2012), chap. 5; Walter Johnson, *River of Dark Dreams: Slavery and Empire in the Cotton Kingdom* (Cambridge: Harvard University Press, 2013); Edward E. Baptist, *The Half Has Never Been Told: Slavery and the Making of American Capitalism* (New York: Basic Books, 2014); Nelson Lichtenstein, *The*

Retail Revolution: How Wal-Mart Created a Brave New World of Business (New York: Henry Holt, 2009); Joseph C. Miller, Way of Death: Merchant Capitalism and the Angolan Slave Trade (Madison: University of Wisconsin Press, 1988), chaps. 13, 16–18; Ira Cohen, "The Auction System in the Port of New York, 1817–1837," Business History Review 45.4 (Winter 1971): 488–510.

3. Eric Homberger, The Historical Atlas of New York City: A Visual Celebration of 400 Years of New York City's History (New York: Henry Holt, 2005), 62; Michael Zakim, Ready-Made Democracy: A History of Men's Dress in the American Republic, 1760–1860 (Chicago: University of Chicago Press, 2003); Jedidiah Morse and Richard C. Morse, A New Universal Gazetteer; or, Geographical Dictionary (New Haven: Sherman Converse, 1821), 517; Daniel Rogers, The New-York City Hall Recorder for the Year 1818 (New York: Abraham Vosburgh, 1818), 87–91.

4. Bond of $4,918.74 by John C. Marsh, November 27, 1817, Avery Family Papers, 1796–1924, Iberia Parish, Louisiana (microfilm), series J., part 5, reel 10, RASP, microfilm; New York Courier, July 25, 1816, 1; New York Columbian, August 11, 1817, 3; New York National Advocate, September 22, 1817, 1; New-York Gazette, November 11, 1817, 2; New-York Daily Advertiser, March 31, 1818, 2; April 21, 1819, 1; Emil Wilbekin, "Hip Hop Hooray," Vibe 11.5 (May 2003): 28; Ann Patton Malone, Sweet Chariot: Slavery and Household Structure in Nineteenth-Century Louisiana (Chapel Hill: University of North Carolina Press, 2002), 92–103; Bruce H. Mann, Republic of Debtors: Bankruptcy in the Age of American Independence (Cambridge: Harvard University Press, 2002); Wyatt-Brown, Lewis Tappan, chap. 5; The Bank of America (New York: De Vinne Press, 1887), 107; Scoville, Old Merchants of New York City, 1:229–32; Lewis Tappan, The Life of Arthur Tappan (New York: Hurd and Houghton, 1870), chap. 4.

5. New York National Advocate, September 9, 1817, 2 (first three quotations); Niles' Weekly Register, June 28, 1817, 276 (final quotation).

6. Malone, Sweet Chariot, 92–103; Harnett T. Kane, The Bayous of Louisiana (New York: William Morrow, 1943), 122 (quotations); Samuel H. Lockett, Louisiana as It Is: A Geographical and Topographical Description of the State (Baton Rouge: Louisiana State University Press, 1969), 50, 97–99.

7. Henry Clay to unknown recipient, February 16, 1831, in The Private Correspondence of Henry Clay, ed. Calvin Colton (New York: A. S. Barnes, 1855), 294, 296 (quotations); New-York Herald, August 9, 1817, 4; New York Spectator, December 29, 1818, 4; Douglas A. Irwin, "Antebellum Tariff Politics: Regional Coalitions and Shifting Economic Interests," Journal of Law and Economics 51.4 (November 2008): 715–41; David O. Whitten, "Tariff and Profit in the Antebellum Louisiana Sugar Industry," Business History Review 44.2 (Summer 1970): 226–33; Mark D. Schmitz, "Economies of Scale and Farm Size in the Antebellum Sugar Sector," Journal of Economic History 37.4 (December 1977): 959–80.

8. Jesse McCall to Stone and Marsh, April 15, 1818, Avery Family Papers, series J., part 5, reel 10, RASP (quotation); Malone, Sweet Chariot, 92–93.

9. Joseph C. Miller, "Credit, Captives, Collateral and Currencies: Debt, Slavery and the Financing of the Atlantic World," in Debt and Slavery in the Mediterranean and Atlantic Worlds, ed. Gwyn C. Campbell and Alessandro Stanziani (London: Pickering

and Chatto, 2013), 105–22; Brian Schoen, *The Fragile Fabric of Union: Cotton, Federal Politics, and the Global Origins of the Civil War* (Baltimore: Johns Hopkins University Press, 2009), chap. 3.

10. James J. Gigantino Jr., "Trading in New Jersey Souls: New Jersey and the Interstate Slave Trade," *Pennsylvania History* 77.3 (June 2010): 281–302; Kenneth E. Marshall, *Manhood Enslaved: Bondmen in Eighteenth- and Early Nineteenth-Century New Jersey* (Rochester: University of Rochester Press, 2011); Edgar J. McManus, *Blacks in Bondage in the North* (Syracuse: Syracuse University Press, 1973), chap. 10; Isaac Holmes, *An Account of the United States of America Derived from Actual Observations during a Residence of Four Years in That Republic* (London: Caxton Press, 1823), 324.

11. Leslie M. Harris, *In the Shadow of Slavery: African Americans in New York City, 1626–1863* (Chicago: University of Chicago Press, 2003), chap. 4; Shane White, *Stories of Freedom in Black New York* (Cambridge: Harvard University Press, 2007), chap. 1; Scott A. Sandage, *Born Losers: A History of Failure in America* (Cambridge: Harvard University Press, 2005), chap. 1; Adam Rothman, *Slave Country: American Expansion and the Origins of the Deep South* (Cambridge: Harvard University Press, 2005), chap. 5; Amartya Sen, *Resources, Values, and Development*, exp. ed. (Cambridge: Harvard University Press, 1997), chaps. 2, 3, and 8.

12. Indenture of Ann Moore, August 28, 1818; Indenture of Susan Jackson, August 28, 1818; Indenture of Eliza Thompson, August 28, 1818; Indenture of Mary Harris, August 28, 1818; Indenture of Margaret Boss, September 9, 1818; Indenture of Julian Jackson, September 9, 1818, Avery Family Papers, series J., part 5, reel 10, RASP; 1870 U.S. Census, Ward 3, Iberia, La., roll M593_513, p. 200A, image 405; Family History Library Film 552012, www.ancestry.com (accessed December 7, 2013).

13. Indenture of Samuel Prince, September 14, 1818; Indenture of Edward Gilbert, September 22, 1818; Indenture of Samuel Peters, September 22, 1818; Indenture of Joseph Hendrickson, October 23, 1818 (quotation), Avery Family Papers, series J., part 5, reel 10, RASP; Robert A. Margo, *Wages and Labor Markets before the Civil War* (Chicago: University of Chicago Press, 2000), chaps. 3–5.

14. Frances D. Pingeon, "An Abominable Business: The New Jersey Slave Trade, 1818," *New Jersey History* 109.1/2 (February 1991): 19.

15. Gigantino, "Trading in New Jersey Souls," 285–86; Sue Eakin, *Solomon Northup's Twelve Years a Slave and Plantation Life in the South* (Lafayette: University of Louisiana Press, 2008), 412.

16. *Virginia Farmer's Repository*, August 12, 1818, 2 (quotations; emphasis in original); Pingeon, "An Abominable Business."

17. Gigantino, "Trading in New Jersey Souls," 286–87; *New York Evening Post*, March 7, 1818, 2; *Trenton Federalist*, August 3, 1818, 2.

18. *Trenton Federalist*, August 3, 1818, 2 (quotations); Gigantino, "Trading in New Jersey Souls," 287; Ernest Obadele-Starks, *Freebooters and Smugglers: The Foreign Slave Trade in the United States after 1808* (Fayetteville: University of Arkansas Press, 2007), 50–51.

19. *Trenton Federalist*, August 3, 1818, 3; Pingeon, "An Abominable Business," 27; Works Progress Administration, *Ship Registers and Enrollments of New Orleans, Louisiana*, vol. 1, *1804–1820* (University: Louisiana State University, 1941), 126.

20. *New York Columbian*, August 3, 1818, 2 (quotations); *Alexandria (Va.) Gazette*, October 27, 1819, 1; August 16, 1819, 1; November 3, 1819, 3; *New York Spectator*, August 7, 1818, 3; WPA, *Ship Registers and Enrollments of New Orleans*, 1:15; *National Messenger*, May 26, 1819, 3; Pingeon, "An Abominable Business," 29; Rothman, *Slave Country*, 193.

21. Gigantino, "Trading in New Jersey Souls," 286; Pingeon, "An Abominable Business," 27; Holmes, *An Account of the United States*, 324; Rothman, *Slave Country*, 191–93; Joshua D. Rothman, *Flush Times and Fever Dreams: A Story of Capitalism and Slavery in the Age of Jackson* (Athens: University of Georgia Press, 2012).

22. Memorandum of Consent (Cain), Court of Common Pleas, Middlesex County, N.J., October 6, 1818 (quotation); John G. Sanock to Lewis Compton, Bill of Sale of Cain, October 1, 1818; John Pettit to Lewis Compton, Bill of Sale of Hanna Johnson, July 29, 1818, Avery Family Papers, series J., part 5, reel 10, RASP; Clement Alexander Price, ed., *Freedom Not Far Distant: A Documentary History of Afro-Americans in New Jersey* (Newark: New Jersey Historical Society, 1980), 85–86; Malone, *Sweet Chariot*, 305n.108.

23. Memorandum of Consent (Peter), Court of Common Pleas, Middlesex County, N.J., October 21, 1818 (first quotation); Memorandum of Consent, Frank, Court of Common Pleas, Middlesex County, N.J., October 21, 1818 (second quotation); Bill of Sale, Jane, October 16, 1818; Memorandum of Consent, Jane, Court of Common Pleas, Middlesex County, N.J., October 21, 1818, Avery Family Papers, series J., part 5, reel 10, RASP; for accusations of bribery, see Malone, *Sweet Chariot*, 100, 303n.98.

24. *Delaware American Watchman*, June 24, 1818, 2 (quotation); Historical Census Browser, Geospatial and Statistical Center, University of Virginia, http://mapserver. lib.virginia.edu/ (accessed September 27, 2011).

25. William Stone to John C. Marsh, December 1818, Avery Family Papers, series J., part 5, reel 10, RASP (quotations); Laura F. Edwards, "Status without Rights: African Americans and the Tangled History of Law and Governance in the Nineteenth-Century U.S. South," *American Historical Review* 112.2 (April 2007): 365–93; Pingeon, "An Abominable Business," 27.

26. Shawn Cole, "Capitalism and Freedom: Manumissions and the Slave Market in Louisiana, 1725–1820," *Journal of Economic History* 65.4 (December 2005): 1008–27; Obadele-Starks, *Freebooters and Smugglers*, chap. 1; David L. Lightner, *Slavery and the Commerce Power: How the Struggle against the Interstate Slave Trade Led to the Civil War* (New Haven: Yale University Press, 2006).

27. Steven Deyle, "An 'Abominable' New Trade: The Closing of the African Slave Trade and the Changing Patterns of U.S. Political Power, 1808–60," *William and Mary Quarterly* 66.4 (October 2009): 833–52; Obadele-Starks, *Freebooters and Smugglers*, 50–52; John Craig Hammond, *Slavery, Freedom, and Expansion in the Early American West* (Charlottesville: University of Virginia Press, 2007), chap. 3; Ned Sublette, *The World That Made New Orleans: From Spanish Silver to Congo Square* (Chicago: Lawrence Hill Books, 2008), 258; Gilbert C. Din, "The Offices and Functions of the New Orleans Cabildo," *Louisiana History: The Journal of the Louisiana Historical Association* 37.1 (Winter 1996): 5–30; John M. Sacher, *A Perfect War of Politics: Parties,*

Politicians, and Democracy in Louisiana, 1824–1861 (Baton Rouge: Louisiana State University Press, 2003), chap. 1; John C. Clark, *New Orleans, 1718–1812: An Economic History* (Baton Rouge: Louisiana State University Press, 1970), 281.

28. Andrew Jackson to William C. C. Claiborne, September 20, 1814, quoted in Robert C. Vogel, "Jean Lafitte, the Baratarians, and the Battle of New Orleans: A Reappraisal," *Louisiana History: The Journal of the Louisiana Historical Association* 41.3 (Summer 2000): 264 (quotation); Gautham Rao, *At the Water's Edge: Customhouses, Politics, Governance and the Origins of the Early American State* (Chicago: University of Chicago Press, forthcoming); Matthew Salafia, *Slavery's Borderland: Freedom and Bondage along the Ohio River* (Philadelphia: University of Pennsylvania Press, 2013); Eberhard L. Faber, "Building the Land of Dreams: The American Transformation of New Orleans, 1795–1820" (PhD diss., Princeton University, 2012); Edward Bartlett Rugeme, *The Problem of Emancipation: The Caribbean Roots of the American Civil War* (Baton Rouge: Louisiana State University Press, 2008); Obadele-Starks, *Freebooters and Smugglers*, chap. 2; Alexander DeConde, *This Affair of Louisiana* (New York: Charles Scribner's Sons, 1976); Peter S. Onuf, *Jefferson's Empire: The Language of American Nationhood* (Charlottesville: University Press of Virginia, 2000); Frank L. Owsley Jr., *Struggle for the Gulf Borderlands: The Creek War and the Battle of New Orleans, 1812–1815* (Tuscaloosa: University of Alabama Press, 2000); Matthew E. Mason, "Slavery Overshadowed: Congress Debates Prohibiting the Atlantic Slave Trade to the United States, 1806–1807," *Journal of the Early Republic* 20.1 (Spring 2000): 59–81; William W. Freehling, *The Road to Disunion: Secessionists at Bay, 1776–1854* (New York: Oxford University Press, 1990), 136–39; Don E. Fehrenbacher, *The Slaveholding Republic: An Account of the Government's Relations to Slavery* (New York: Oxford University Press, 2001), 144–47; Peter J. Kastor, *The Nation's Crucible: The Louisiana Purchase and the Creation of America* (New Haven: Yale University Press, 2004); Lawrence N. Powell, *The Accidental City: Improvising New Orleans* (Cambridge: Harvard University Press, 2012); John Craig Hammond, "Slavery, Settlement, and Empire: The Expansion and Growth of Slavery in the Interior of the North American Continent, 1770–1820," *Journal of the Early Republic* 32.2 (Summer 2012): 175–206; Anne F. Hyde, *Empires, Nations, and Families: A History of the North American West* (Lincoln: University of Nebraska Press, 2011); Eliga H. Gould, *Among the Powers of the Earth: The American Revolution and the Making of a New World Empire* (Cambridge: Harvard University Press, 2012), chap. 4.

29. Proclamation of James Madison, February 6, 1815, quoted in Obadele-Starks, *Freebooters and Smugglers*, 33 (quotations); Peter Andreas, *Smuggler Nation: How Illicit Trade Made America* (New York: Oxford University Press, 2013), chap. 5; Matthew Warshauer, "The Battle of New Orleans Reconsidered: Andrew Jackson and Martial Law," *Louisiana History: The Journal of the Louisiana Historical Association* 39.3 (Summer 1998): 261–91; Jane Lucas De Grummond, *The Baratarians and the Battle of New Orleans* (Baton Rouge: Louisiana State University Press, 1961); Robert V. Remini, *Andrew Jackson: The Course of American Empire, 1767–1821*, vol. 1 (Baltimore: Johns Hopkins University Press, 1998), chap. 16.

30. Walter Johnson, "White Lies: Human Property and Domestic Slavery aboard the Slave Ship *Creole*," *Atlantic Studies* 5.2 (August 2008): 239 (first quotation); Georgia *Reflector*, December 15, 1818, 3 (subsequent quotations); Deyle, "An 'Abominable' New Trade"; Obadele-Starks, *Freebooters and Smugglers*, chaps. 2–3.

31. W. E. B. Du Bois, *The Suppression of the African Slave Trade to the United States of America, 1638–1870* (New York: Longmans, Green, 1896), 119 (quotation); Matthew Mason, "Keeping Up Appearances: The International Politics of Slave Trade Abolition in the Nineteenth Century Atlantic World," *William and Mary Quarterly* 66.4 (October 2009): 809–32; Joseph C. Miller, *Way of Death: Merchant Capitalism and the Angolan Slave Trade, 1730–1830* (Madison: University of Wisconsin Press, 1988), chaps. 10, 11, 14; Frances Stafford, "Illegal Importations: Enforcement of Slave Trade Laws along the Florida Coast, 1810–1828," *Florida Historical Quarterly* 46.2 (October 1967): 124–33; Johnson, "White Lies"; a notable exception is explored in Gene A. Smith, "U.S. Navy Gunboats and the Slave Trade in Louisiana Waters, 1808–1811," *Military History of the West* 23.2 (1993): 135–47; "Voyages: The Trans-Atlantic Slave Trade Database," #39023, #41571, www.slavevoyages.org/tast/database/search.faces (accessed January 20, 2012).

32. Jane Lucas De Grummond, *Renato Beluche: Smuggler, Privateer, and Patriot, 1780–1860* (Baton Rouge: Louisiana State University Press, 1983), chap. 12; Obadele-Starks, *Freebooters and Smugglers*, 48–50; De Grummond, *Renato Beluche*, 166.

33. De Grummond, *Renato Beluche*, 168–69 (quotation 168).

34. Ibid.

35. Philippe Pedesclaux, vol. 5, Act 644, July 31, 1818; vol. 5, Act 652, August 4, 1818 (first quotation); vol. 5, Act 652, August 4, 1818 (second quotation), NONA.

36. De Grummond, *Renato Beluche*, chap. 13; Hugh Thomas, *The Slave Trade: The Story of the Atlantic Slave Trade, 1440–1870* (New York: Simon and Schuster, 1997), 615; *Journal of the House of Representatives of the United States, Being the Second Session of the Nineteenth Congress* (Washington, D.C., 1826), 216; "Voyages: The Trans-Atlantic Slave Trade Database," #39023; Obadele-Starks, *Freebooters and Smugglers*, 48; Johnson, "White Lies"; De Grummond, *Renato Beluche*, 169–70.

37. Rothman, *Slave Country*, chap. 5.

38. William Halsted Jr., *Reports of Cases Argued and Determined in the Supreme Court of Judicature of the State of New-Jersey*, vol. 2 (Trenton: Joseph Justice, 1824), 260–61 (quotations); Inward Manifest, New Orleans, December 10, 1818 (*Schoharie*), NO–151, box 29, folder December 1818, NARA-SW; *American Beacon*, November 24, 1815, 3; September 26, 1816, 3; *New York Evening Post*, September 25, 1817, 2; Morse and Morse, *A New Universal Gazetteer*, 39; Forrest R. Holdcamper, comp., *List of American-Flag Merchant Vessels That Received Certificates of Enrollment or Registry at the Port of New York, 1789–1867*, vol. 2 (Washington, D.C.: Government Services Administration, 1968), 632.

39. Inward Manifest, New Orleans, December 10, 1818 (*Schoharie*), NO–151, box 29, folder December 1818, NARA-SW (quotation); Bill of Sale for Han [Hanna Johnson?], July 29, 1818; Bill of Sale for Jack, October 15, 1818, Avery Family Papers, series J., part 5, reel 10, RASP; 1870 U.S. Census, Ward 3, Iberia, La., roll M593_513, p. 200A, image

405; Family History Library Film 552012, www.ancestry.com (accessed December 7, 2013).

40. Inward Manifest, New Orleans, December 10, 1818 (*Schoharie*), NO–151, box 29, folder December 1818, NARA-SW.

41. Inward Slave Manifest, New Orleans, October 26, 1818 (*Schoharie*), NO–151, box 29, folder December 1818, NARA-SW; Mlada Bukovansky, "American Identity and Neutral Rights from Independence to the War of 1812," *International Organization* 51.2 (Spring 1997): 209–43.

42. Inward Manifest, New Orleans, December 10, 1818 (*Schoharie*), NO–151, box 29, folder December 1818, NARA-SW; Outward Slave Manifest of June 21, 1816, Outward Coastwise Slave Manifests, Savannah, Georgia, 1808–1820, image 51, www.ancestry.com; *New-York Daily Advertiser*, March 2, 1818, 2; *New York Mercantile Advertiser*, January 11, 1819, 2; *New York Columbian*, April 27, 1819, 2; Maurine Bergerie, *They Tasted Bayou Water: A Brief History of Iberia Parish* (Gretna, La.: Pelican, 2000), 64.

43. William Stone to John C. Marsh, December 1818, Avery Family Papers, series J., part 5, reel 10, RASP (quotations); Malone, *Sweet Chariot*, 103.

44. Jonas Marsh to John C. Marsh, February 9, 1820, Avery Family Papers, series J., part 5, reel 10, RASP; Philippe Pedesclaux, vol. 13, Act 621, March 10, 1820, NONA; C. Pollack, vol. 5, Act 229, July 25, 1820, NONA; *Louisiana Advertiser*, June 29, 1820, 2; *New York National Advocate*, September 7, 1820, 3; *Albany Gazette*, September 1, 1820, 2; *New York Commercial Advertiser*, June 23, 1829, 2; *New York Morning Herald*, February 3, 1830, 2; *Baltimore Gazette and Daily Advertiser*, December 24, 1835, 2; Inward Slave Manifest, New Orleans, June 25, 1820 (*Experiment*), M1895, roll 1, image 490; Outward Slave Manifest, Savannah, June 5, 1820 (*Experiment*), M1895, roll 1, image 414; WPA, *Ship Registers and Enrollments of New Orleans*, 1:43.

45. Anthony E. Kaye, "The Second Slavery: Modernity in the Nineteenth-Century South and the Atlantic World," *Journal of Southern History* 75.3 (August 2009): 627–50; Michael Tadman, "The Demographic Cost of Sugar: Debates on Slave Societies and Natural Increase in the Americas," *American Historical Review* 105.5 (December 2000): 1534–75; Jenny B. Wahl, "The Jurisprudence of American Slave Sales," *Journal of Economic History* 56.1 (March 1996): 143–69; Edward E. Baptist, "'Cuffy,' 'Fancy Maids,' and 'One-Eyed Men': Rape, Commodification, and the Domestic Slave Trade," *American Historical Review* 106.5 (December 2001): 1619–50.

46. Damian Alan Pargas, *The Quarters and the Fields: Slave Families in the Non-Cotton South* (Gainesville: University Press of Florida, 2010), chap. 2; H. Bakker, *Sugar Cane Cultivation and Management* (New York: Plenum Publishers, 1999), chaps. 7, 13–14; Samuel Henry Lockett and Lauren C. Post, *Louisiana as It Is: A Geographical and Topographical Description of the State* (Baton Rouge: Louisiana State University Press, 1969).

47. B. Cooke, "The Denial of Slavery in Management Studies," *Journal of Management Studies* 40.8 (December 2003): 1895–1918; Elizabeth Abbott, *Sugar: A Bittersweet History* (Toronto: Penguin Canada, 2008), 280–81; Richard Follett, *The Sugar Masters: Planters and Slaves in Louisiana's Cane World, 1820–1860* (Baton Rouge: Louisiana State University Press, 2005), chap. 1; John Alfred Heitmann, *The Modernization of the*

Louisiana Sugar Industry, 1830–1910 (Baton Rouge: Louisiana State University Press, 1987), chaps. 1–3.

48. Henry Goings, *Rambles of a Runaway from Southern Slavery*, ed. Calvin Schermerhorn, Michael Plunkett, and Edward Gaynor (Charlottesville: University of Virginia Press, 2012), 51 (quotations); Michael Tadman, *Speculators and Slaves: Masters, Traders, and Slaves in the Old South* (Madison: University of Wisconsin Press, 1996), chap. 3, app. 3.

49. Receipt of John Lee Jr., May 1, 1819, Avery Family Papers, series J., part 5, reel 10, RASP (quotation); 1820 U.S. Census, St Martin Parish, La., 148, NARA, roll M33_31, image 144, p. 148, www.ancestry.com (accessed September 21, 2011); Tadman, "The Demographic Cost of Sugar," 1537.

50. *Louisiana Advertiser*, June 29, 1820, 2; July 25, 1820, 2; *New-York Gazette*, September 27, 1820, 1; *New York Mercantile Advertiser*, May 9, 1820, 2; May 15, 1820, 2; October 11, 1820, 1; *New York Evening Post*, July 9, 1821, 2.

51. James K. Paulding, Washington Irving, and William Irving, *Salmagundi: or, the Whim-Whams and Opinions of Launcelot Langstaff, Esq., and Others*, vol. 1 (New York: David Longworth, 1814), xl (quotation); Philippe Pedesclaux, vol. 7, Acts 821–23, 824, October 11, 1819, NONA; *New York Mercantile Advertiser*, July 13, 1819, 2; August 9, 1819, 2; Jonas Marsh to John C. Marsh, February 9, 1820; Stewart C. Marsh to John C. Marsh, February 17, 1827, Avery Family Papers, series J., part 5, reel 10, RASP; Scoville, *The Old Merchants of New York City*, 1:172, 200, 273–75.

52. Robert Southey, "Poems concerning the Slave Trade, Sonnet III," in *The Poetical Works of Robert Southey* (Paris: A. and W. Galignani, 1829), 607 (quotations); Wendy A. Woloson, *Refined Tastes: Sugar, Confectionery, and Consumers in Nineteenth-Century America* (Baltimore: Johns Hopkins University Press, 2002), chap. 1; Sidney W. Mintz, *Sweetness and Power: The Place of Sugar in Modern History* (New York: Penguin, 1986), chap. 3; Adam Hochschild, *Bury the Chains: Prophets and Rebels in the Fight to Free an Empire's Slaves* (New York: Mariner Books, 2006), chaps. 13, 22.

53. *Freedom's Journal*, September 25, 1828, 7 (quotation); Graham Russell Gao Hodges, *David Ruggles: A Radical Black Abolitionist and the Underground Railroad in New York City* (Chapel Hill: University of North Carolina Press, 2010), 43, 80; Ruth Neurmberger, *The Free Produce Movement: A Quaker Protest against Slavery* (Durham: Duke University Press, 1942); Thomas C. Holt, "Marking: Race, Race-making, and the Writing of History," *American Historical Review* 100.1 (February 1995): 10; Henri Lefebvre, *Critique of Everyday Life: Foundations for a Sociology of the Everyday*, trans. John Moore (London: Verso, 2002); Robin Blackburn, *The Making of New World Slavery: From the Baroque to the Modern, 1492–1800* (London: Verso, 1997), introduction.

54. Jonas Marsh to John C. Marsh, December 25, 1818 (first two quotations); Jonas Marsh to John C. Marsh, February 9, 1820, (final quotation); Bill of Sale of William McClane by Jesse McCall, February 28, 1819; Indenture of Sally Cross, December 26, 1822; Indenture of Hannah Johnson, December 26, 1822, Avery Family Papers, series J., part 5, reel 10, RASP; 1850 U.S. Census, Slave Schedule, Fausse Point, St. Martin Parish, La., p. 5, image 3; 1850 U.S. Census, Fausse Pointe, St Martin, La., roll M432_240, p. 138B, image 281, www.ancestry.com (accessed October 11, 2011).

55. Bill of Sale, Perry and Joseph (quotation); Bill of Sale, Harriet, November 17, 1823, Bill of Sale, Edward Coursey, November 15, 1823, Avery Family Papers, series J., part 5, reel 10, RASP; Charles Keenan, *C. Keenan's Baltimore Directory for 1822 and 1823* (Baltimore: J. R. Matchett, 1822), 159; Inward Slave Manifest, New Orleans, November 18, 1823 (*Virginia*), NARA M1895, roll 3, images 268–73; *Baltimore Patriot*, November 18, 1823, 3; December 29, 1823, 2; January 18, 1824, 3; February 3, 1824, 3; John Thomas Scharf, *History of Baltimore City and County, From the Earliest Period to the Present Day* (Philadelphia: Louis H. Everts, 1881), 187, 214, 246, 407, 437–38, 577.

56. Bill of Sale, Chloe, June 10, 1826 (quotation); Bill of Sale, Silvia, April 20, 1826; Bill of Sale, Milley, April 23, 1826; Bill of Sale, Terry, April 18, 1826, Avery Family Papers, series J., part 5, reel 10, RASP; Inward Slave Manifest, New Orleans, February 6, 1826 (*Superior Hope*), NARA M1895, roll 4, images 192–95; John Adams Paxton, *New Orleans Directory and Register* (New Orleans: Benjamin Levy, 1822), http://files. usgwarchives.net/la/orleans/history/directory/1822nocd.txt (accessed June 13, 2014).

57. Bill of Sale, Augustus, Anenon, and Fanny, May 19, 1827, Avery Family Papers, series J., part 5, reel 10, RASP (quotation); Inward Slave Manifest, New Orleans, February 9, 1827 (*James Monroe*), NARA M1895, roll 4, images 330–31, 344–45, 603–5, 621–22; Calvin Schermerhorn, "Capitalism's Captives: The Maritime United States Slave Trade, 1807–1850," *Journal of Social History* 47.4 (Summer 2014).

58. Obadele-Starks, *Freebooters and Smugglers*, chap. 3; Steven Deyle, *Carry Me Back: The Domestic Slave Trade in American Life* (New York: Oxford University Press, 2005), app. A; George D. Green, *Finance and Economic Development in the Old South: Louisiana Banking, 1804–1861* (Stanford: Stanford University Press, 1972), chaps. 1–2; Howard Bodenhorn, *State Banking in Early America: A New Economic History* (New York: Oxford University Press, 2003), chaps. 10–11; Follett, *The Sugar Masters*, 33; Schmitz, "Economies of Scale and Farm Size"; David O. Whitten, "A Black Entrepreneur in Antebellum Louisiana," *Business History Review* 45.2 (Summer 1971): 201–19.

59. Malone, *Sweet Chariot*, 92–94; Mary Elizabeth Sanders, *St. Mary Parish, Louisiana, Heirship Series*, vol. 2, *Selected Annotated Abstracts of Marriage, Book 1, 1811–1829* (Gretna, La.: Pelican, 2002), 111–13.

60. 1870 U.S. Census, Ward 3, Iberia, La., roll M593_513, p. 200A, image 405; Family History Library Film 552012; Ward 4, Iberia Parish, La., roll M593_513, p. 244A, image 493; New Iberia, Iberia Parish, La., roll M593_513, p. 194B, image 394; Family History Library Film 552012, www.ancestry.com (accessed December 7, 2013); Inward Slave Manifest, New Orleans, April 11, 1834 (*Uncas*), NARA M1895, roll 7, image 403; Malone, *Sweet Chariot*, 103.

61. John Kennedy Toole, *A Confederacy of Dunces* (1980; repr., New York: Grove Press, 2002), xi.

CHAPTER 4. BANK BONDS AND BONDSPERSONS

1. *New York Commercial Advertiser*, July 5, 1828, 2 (quotation).

2. Stanley Clisby Arthur and George Campbell Huchet de Kernion, *Old Families of Louisiana* (1931; repr., Gretna, La.: Pelican, 1999), 59–61; Robert E. Wright, *The*

Wealth of Nations Rediscovered: Integration and Expansion of American Financial Markets, 1780–1850 (New York: Cambridge University Press, 2002), chap. 8; Richard Sylla, "Financial Systems and Economic Modernization," *Journal of Economic History* 62.2 (June 2002): 277–92; Peter L. Rousseau and Richard Sylla, "Emerging Financial Markets and Early U.S. Growth," *Explorations in Economic History* 42.1 (January 2005): 1–26; Martijn Konings, *The Development of American Finance* (New York: Cambridge University Press, 2011), chaps. 1–4.

3. Edward E. Baptist, "Toxic Debt, Liar Loans, Collateralized and Securitized Human Beings, and the Panic of 1837," in *Capitalism Takes Command: The Social Transformation of Nineteenth-Century America*, ed. Michael Zakim and Gary J. Kornblith (Chicago: University of Chicago Press, 2012), 69–92; John Matthews, *Complete American Armoury and Blue Book* (Baltimore: Genealogical Publishing Co., 1991), 105; R. Edward Freeman, *Strategic Management: A Stakeholder Approach* (1984; repr., New York: Cambridge University Press, 2010); George D. Green, *Finance and Economic Development in the Old South: Louisiana Banking, 1804–1861* (Stanford: Stanford University Press, 1972), chaps. 1–2.

4. *New York Commercial Advertiser*, July 30, 1828, 2; Robert G. Albion, The *Rise of New York Port, 1815–1860* (1939; repr., Hamden, Conn.: Archon Books, 1961), chap. 6; Emile P. Grenier, "The Early Financing of the Consolidated Association of the Planters of Louisiana" (MA thesis, Louisiana State University, 1938), chaps. 4–5.

5. Peter E. Austin, *Baring Brothers and the Birth of Modern Finance* (London: Pickering and Chatto, 2007), 21 (quotation); Howard Bodenhorn, *State Banking in Early America: A New Economic History* (New York: Oxford University Press, 2003), 253; Grenier, "The Early Financing of the Consolidated Association," 30–38; *New York Commercial Advertiser*, August 10, 1827, 2.

6. Baptist, "Toxic Debt, Liar Loans," 80; Bodenhorn, *State Banking in Early America*, 289; Scott Reynolds Nelson, *A Nation of Deadbeats: An Uncommon History of America's Financial Disasters* (New York: Knopf, 2012), chaps. 5–6; Steven Deyle, *Carry Me Back: The Domestic Slave Trade in American Life* (New York: Oxford University Press, 2005), app. A; Richard Follett, *The Sugar Masters: Planters and Slaves in Louisiana's Cane World, 1820–1860* (Baton Rouge: Louisiana State University Press, 2005), 20–22; Michael Tadman, "The Demographic Cost of Sugar: Debates on Slave Societies and Natural Increase in the Americas," *American Historical Review* 105.5 (December 2000): 1534–75; Green, *Finance and Economic Development in the Old South*, chaps. 1–2; Lewis Cecil Gray, *History of Agriculture in the Southern United States to 1860*, vol. 2 (Washington, D.C.: Carnegie Institution of Washington, 1933), 1026.

7. *New York Commercial Advertiser*, July 1, 1828, 3; July 14, 1828, 2; *New-York Daily Advertiser*, July 22, 1828, 1; Robert Greenhalgh Albion, *Square-Riggers on Schedule: The New York Sailing Packets to England, France, and the Cotton Ports* (Princeton: Princeton University Press, 1938), chaps. 2, 9; John Steele Gordon, A *Thread across the Ocean: The Heroic Story of the Transatlantic Cable* (New York: Walker, 2002), chaps. 6–11; Frank O. Braynard, *S.S. Savannah: The Elegant Steam Ship* (Athens: University of Georgia Press, 1963).

8. Adam Rothman, *Slave Country: American Expansion and the Origins of the Deep South* (Cambridge: Harvard University Press, 2005), chap. 5.

9. Ralph W. Hidy, *The House of Baring in American Trade and Finance: English Merchant Bankers at Work* (Cambridge: Harvard University Press, 1949), chaps. 3–4; Grenier, "The Early Financing of the Consolidated Association," chap. 4; Austin, *Baring Brothers and the Birth of Modern Finance*, 52–54.

10. George D. Green, "Public Policy toward Banking," in *Antebellum Louisiana, 1830–1860, Part A: Life and Labor*, ed. Carolyn E. DeLatte (Lafayette: Center for Louisiana Studies, 2004), 321; Follett, *The Sugar Masters*, chap.1; William J. Novak, *The People's Welfare: Law and Regulation in Nineteenth-Century America* (Chapel Hill: University of North Carolina Press, 1996), chap. 3; Stephen Bell and Andrew Hindmoor, *Rethinking Governance: The Centrality of the State in Modern Society* (New York: Cambridge University Press, 2009), chap. 6.

11. Victor Bulmer-Thomas, *The Economic History of the Caribbean since the Napoleonic Wars* (New York: Cambridge University Press, 2012), chap. 5; Cynthia Clark Northrup and Elaine C. Prange Turney, eds., *Encyclopedia of Tariffs and Trade in U.S. History*, vol. 3 (Westport, Conn.: Greenwood Press, 2003), 29; John M. Sacher, *A Perfect War of Politics: Parties, Politicians, and Democracy in Louisiana, 1824–1861* (Baton Rouge: Louisiana State University Press, 2003), 51. William J. Novak, "The Myth of the 'Weak' American State," *American Historical Review* 113.3 (June 2008), 752–72; Opelousas [pen name of Edmond Jean Forstall], "Louisiana Sugar," *DeBow's Review* 1.1 (1846): 56; *Savannah Georgian*, March 11, 1828, 2; June 7, 1828, 2; *Charleston Courier*, March 3, 1828, 2; *Boston Traveler*, March 11, 1828, 3.

12. Baptist, "Toxic Debt, Liar Loans"; Howard Bodenhorn, *A History of Banking in Antebellum America: Financial Markets and Economic Development in an Era of Nation-Building* (New York: Cambridge University Press, 2000), chap. 5; Edwin J. Perkins, *Financing Anglo-American Trade: The House of Brown, 1800–1880* (Cambridge: Harvard University Press, 1975), 154; Lawrence H. Officer, *Between the Dollar-Sterling Gold Points: Exchange, Rates, Parity, and Market Behavior* (New York: Cambridge University Press, 1996), 204.

13. Gilbert C. Din, "The Offices and Functions of the New Orleans Cabildo," *Louisiana History: The Journal of the Louisiana Historical Association* 37.1 (Winter 1996): 5–30; Sally Kittredge Reeves, "Spanish Colonial Records of the New Orleans Notarial Archives," *LLA Bulletin* 55 (1992): 7–12.

14. Hugues Lavergne to Thomas Baring, July 21, 1829, Hugues Lavergne Letterbooks, series H., reel 30, RASP (quotation); *Louisiana State Gazette*, February 11, 1826, 2; Larry Schweikart, *Banking in the American South from the Age of Jackson to Reconstruction* (Baton Rouge: Louisiana State University Press, 1987), 138; Reginald C. McGrane, *Foreign Bondholders and American State Debts* (New York: Macmillan, 1935), 172; Green, *Finance and Economic Development in the Old South*, 60; R. W. Hidy, "The Union Bank of Louisiana Loan, 1832: A Case Study in Marketing," *Journal of Political Economy* 47.2 (April 1939): 232–53; Bodenhorn, *State Banking in Early America*, 250.

15. Rothman, *Slave Country*, 159–60.

16. Joseph C. Miller, "Credit, Captives, Collateral and Currencies: Debt, Slavery and the Financing of the Atlantic World," in *Debt and Slavery in the Mediterranean and*

Atlantic Worlds, ed. Gwyn C. Campbell and Alessandro Stanziani (London: Pickering and Chatto, 2013), 105–22; Wright, *The Wealth of Nations Rediscovered*; Bodenhorn, *A History of Banking in Antebellum America*; Hidy, *The House of Baring in American Trade and Finance*, chap. 4; Baptist, "Toxic Debt, Liar Loans"; Green, "Public Policy toward Banking," 320–21.

17. Austin, *Baring Brothers and the Birth of Modern Finance*, chap. 1; Jay Sexton, *Debtor Diplomacy: Finance and American Foreign Relations in the Civil War Era, 1837–1873* (New York: Oxford University Press, 2005), chap. 1; Kenneth Pomeranz, *The Great Divergence: China, Europe, and the Making of the Modern World Economy* (Princeton: Princeton University Press, 2000), chap. 6.

18. *New Orleans Argus*, February 20, 1828, 2; September 5, 1828, 1; *Courrier de la Louisiane*, January 1, 1824, 3; *Liverpool Mercury*, August 8, 1828, 256; Jessica M. Lepler, *The Many Panics of 1837: People, Politics, and the Creation of a Transatlantic Financial Crisis* (New York: Cambridge University Press, 2013), chaps. 1, 2, 7; Austin, *Baring Brothers and the Birth of Modern Finance*, 53; Richard J. Salvucci, *Politics, Markets and Mexico's "London Debt," 1823–1887* (New York: Cambridge University Press, 2009), chaps. 2–3; Schweikart, *Banking in the American South*, 211–13; Irene D. Neu, "My Nineteenth-Century Network: Erastus Corning, Benjamin Ingham, Edmond Forstall," *Business and Economic History* 14 (1985): 1–14; Grenier, "The Early Financing of the Consolidated Association," chap. 4.

19. Hugues Lavergne and Alexander Gordon to Thomas Baring, August 19, 1828, Baring Papers, Ottawa, Canada, quoted in McGrane, *Foreign Bondholders and American State Debts*, 171–72 (quotations); Nelson, *A Nation of Deadbeats*, 115–16; Irene D. Neu, "Edmond Jean Forstall and Louisiana Banking," *Explorations in Economic History* 7 (Summer 1970): 383–98; Denise Gigante, *The Keats Brothers: The Life of John and George* (Cambridge: Harvard University Press, 2011), 238–41.

20. John Linnell, *Thomas Baring*, oil on canvas, 1841, PT019; George Richmond, *Thomas Baring*, chalk-tinted drawing, DR007, Baring Archive, London, www.baringarchive. org.uk/art_collection/browse/ (accessed May 7, 2012).

21. Hidy, *The House of Baring in American Trade and Finance*, 96; Grenier, "The Early Financing of the Consolidated Association," chap. 5.

22. Hugues Lavergne to Manuel Andry, September 3, 1828, translated by and quoted in Grenier, "The Early Financing of the Consolidated Association," 43.

23. Baptist, "Toxic Debt, Liar Loans"; Lepler, *The Many Panics of 1837*, chap. 1.

24. Baptist, "Toxic Debt, Liar Loans."

25. Amadée Ducatel, vol. 22, Act 8, February 18, 1840, NONA (first quotation); Hugues Lavergne to Alexander Gordon, March 6, 1829, Hugues Lavergne Letterbook, series H., reel 30, RASP (second and third quotations); Michael Tadman, *Speculators and Slaves: Masters, Traders, and Slaves in the Old South* (Madison: University of Wisconsin Press, 1996), chap. 2; Timothy Curtis Jacobson and George David Smith, *Cotton's Renaissance: A Study in Market Innovation* (New York: Cambridge University Press, 2001).

26. Joseph C. Miller, *Way of Death: Merchant Capitalism and the Angolan Slave Trade, 1730–1830* (Madison: University of Wisconsin Press, 1988), 224–25; Vincent Nolte,

Fifty Years in Both Hemispheres; or, Reminiscences of the Life of a Former Merchant (New York: Redfield, 1854), chap. 15; Bodenhorn, *State Banking in Early America,* 250–60; Officer, *Between the Dollar-Sterling Gold Points,* chap. 11.

27. Richard Holcombe Kilbourne Jr., *Debt, Investment, Slaves: Credit Relations in East Feliciana Parish, Louisiana, 1825–1885* (Tuscaloosa: University of Alabama Press, 1995), chap. 1; Joseph G. Tregel Jr., "Creoles and Americans," in *Creole New Orleans: Race and Americanization,* ed. Arnold R. Hirsch and Joseph Logsdon (Baton Rouge: Louisiana State University Press, 1992), 131–88; Green, "Public Policy toward Banking," 323; Naomi R. Lamoreaux, "Banks, Kinship, and Economic Development: The New England Case," *Journal of Economic History* 46.3 (September 1996): 647–67; Paul B. Trescott, *Financing American Enterprise: The Story of Commercial Banking* (New York: Harper and Row, 1963), 10–12; Directors' Minutes, October 31, 1829, Consolidated Association of the Planters of Louisiana Papers, Louisiana State University, quoted in Irene D. Neu, "J. B. Moussier and the Property Banks of Louisiana," *Business History Review* 35.4 (Winter 1961): 550–57.

28. Baptist, "Toxic Debt, Liar Loans," 80 (quotation); Henry Wiencek, *Master of the Mountain: Thomas Jefferson and His Slaves* (New York: Farrar, Straus and Giroux, 2012), 96–98; Bonnie M. Martin, "Slavery's Invisible Engine: Mortgaging Human Property," *Journal of Southern History* 76.4 (November 2010): 817–66.

29. Clerk of Court Records, Baton Rouge Parish, Mortgage Book J, 507. My thanks to Bonnie Martin for this document. Hugues Lavergne, vol. 4, Act 621, November 16, 1820; vol. 4, Act 623, November 22, 1820; vol. 4, Act 624, November 24, 1820; vol. 9, Act 1695, February 14, 1823, NONA.

30. Citizens' Bank Directors' Minutes, July 7, 1836, Canal Bank Papers, translated by and quoted in Neu, "J. B. Moussier and the Property Banks of Louisiana," 556 (quotation); *Zacharie and Co. versus Rogers and Harrison* (no number in original), Supreme Court of Louisiana, Eastern District, 19 La. 223, 1841 La. Lexis 397, LexisNexis Academic, accessed March 7, 2013; Neu, "J. B. Moussier and the Property Banks of Louisiana," 555.

31. Amadée Ducatel, vol. 13, Act 103, October 28, 1839; Act 104, October 28, 1839; Act 105, October 28, 1839; Act 106, October 31, 1839; Act 107, October 31, 1839, NONA; Salvucci, *Politics, Markets and Mexico's "London Debt,"* chaps. 2–3; Hidy, *The House of Baring in American Trade and Finance,* 96; Grenier, "The Early Financing of the Consolidated Association," chap. 5.

32. Consolidated Association of the Planters of Louisiana, 1836 bond, $1,000 (collection of the author); Neu, "Edmond Jean Forstall and Louisiana Banking," 387–89; Stephen Mihm, *A Nation of Counterfeiters: Capitalists, Con Men, and the Making of the United States* (Cambridge: Harvard University Press, 2007), prologue.

33. Edmond J. Forstall to Baring Brothers and Company, February 27, 1829, reel 51, Baring Papers, Manuscripts Division, Library of Congress, quoted in Lepler, *The Many Panics of 1837,* 11 (quotation); Bodenhorn, *State Banking in Early America,* 253–54; Green, "Public Policy toward Banking," 320–21.

34. *New York Evening Post,* November 8, 1830, 2; Schweikart, *Banking in the American South,* 211; Lepler, *The Many Panics of 1837,* chap. 1.

35. Nelson, *A Nation of Deadbeats,* 96 (quotation).

36. Hidy, "The Union Bank of Louisiana Loan, 1832."
37. Baptist, "Toxic Debt, Liar Loans," 82; Neu, "J. B. Moussier and the Property Banks of Louisiana"; Neu, "Edmond Jean Forstall and Louisiana Banking"; Hidy, "The Union Bank of Louisiana Loan, 1832"; *Niles' Weekly Register*, October 6, 1832, 87.
38. Edmond Forstall to Thomas Wren Ward, November 19, 1832, Baring Papers, Ottawa, Canada, quoted in McGrane, *Foreign Bondholders and American State Debts*, 171 (quotations); Historical Census Browser, University of Virginia, Geospatial and Statistical Data Center, http://mapserver.lib.virginia.edu/index.html (accessed June 13, 2014); Gelien Matthews, *Caribbean Slave Revolts and the British Abolitionist Movement* (Baton Rouge: Louisiana State University Press, 2013); Gad Heuman, "A Tale of Two Jamaican Rebellions," *Jamaican Historical Review* 19 (1996): 1–8.
39. Adolphe Mazureau, vol. 5, Act 118, November 23, 1832; vol. 5, Act 134, November 28, 1832, NONA; Nelson, *A Nation of Deadbeats*, 115–16; Bodenhorn, *State Banking in Early America*, chap. 11; Malcolm Rohrbough, *The Land Office Business: The Settlement and Administration of American Public Lands, 1789–1837* (New York: Oxford University Press, 1968), chaps. 10–13.
40. Inward Slave Manifest, New Orleans, October 28, 1831 (*Industry*), NARA M1895, roll 6, image 1139.
41. Vol. 2, R. C. Ballard and Co. Invoice Book, series 5, folder 417; vol. 38, Ledger, Ballard and Co., 1831–1834, subseries 5, folder 463, Rice C. Ballard Papers, Southern Historical Collection, UNC.
42. Bodenhorn, *State Banking in Early America*, 289; Nelson, *A Nation of Deadbeats*, chaps. 5–6; Deyle, *Carry Me Back*, app. A; Follett, *The Sugar Masters*, 20–22; Tadman, "The Demographic Cost of Sugar"; Green, *Finance and Economic Development in the Old South*.
43. Adolphe Mazureau, vol. 5, Act 139, November 28, 1832, NONA; Purchase Book, vol. 4, 1832–1834, series 5, folder 420; "Sales of R. C. Ballard and Co," vol. 4, series 5, folder 421, Ballard Papers, UNC; Eugene Choo and Jean Eid, "Interregional Price Difference in the New Orleans Auctions Market for Slaves," *Journal of Business and Economic Statistics* 26.4 (October 2008): 486–509; Scott P. Marler, *The Merchants' Capital: New Orleans and the Political Economy of the Nineteenth-Century South* (New York: Cambridge University Press, 2013), 32–35; Mark D. Schmitz, "Economies of Scale and Farm Size in the Antebellum Sugar Sector," *Journal of Economic History* 37.4 (December 1977): 959–80; David O. Whitten, "Tariff and Profit in the Antebellum Louisiana Sugar Industry," *Business History Review* 44.2 (Summer 1970): 226–33.
44. Adolphe Mazureau, vol. 9, Act 711, June 29, 1833; vol. 9, Act 852, October 5, 1833, NONA; Henry L. Ellsworth, *A Digest of Patents Issued by the United States from 1790 to January 1, 1839* (Washington, D.C., 1840), 160; Saunders, "Report of the Joint Committee on the Affairs of the Union Bank of Louisiana," 11; Kilbourne, *Debt, Investment, Slaves*.
45. Adolphe Mazureau, vol. 5, Act 134, November 28, 1832; vol. 5, Act 136, November 28, 1832; vol. 5, Act 139, November 28, 1832 (quotation), NONA; Herman de Bachellé Seebold, *Old Louisiana Plantation Homes and Family Trees*, vol. 2 (Gretna, La.: Pelican, 2004), 11–15.

46. Opelousas, "Louisiana Sugar," 56 (quotation); Follett, *The Sugar Masters*, chaps. 1–2; Christopher E. G. Benfey, *Degas in New Orleans: Encounters in the Creole World of Kate Chopin and George Washington Cable* (New York: Knopf, 1997), 26–30; David O. Whitten, "A Black Entrepreneur in Antebellum Louisiana," *Business History Review* 45.2 (Summer 1971): 201–19.

47. *New Orleans Advertiser*, March 27, 1834, quoted in *Niles' Weekly Register*, May 10, 1834, 174 (quotation); Follett, *The Sugar Masters*, 26–28.

48. Richard E. Sylla, Jack Wilson, and Robert E. Wright, "Trans-Atlantic Capital Market Integration, 1790–1845," *Review of Finance* 10.4 (2006): 613–44; Paul B. Trescott, *Financing American Enterprise: The Story of Commercial Banking* (New York: Harper and Row, 1963).

49. Stephen A. Caldwell, *A Banking History of Louisiana* (Baton Rouge: Louisiana State University Press, 1935), 48–49; Schweikart, *Banking in the American South*, 211–12; Hannah J. Francis, "Investing in Citizenship: Free Men of Color of Color and the Case against Citizens Bank ~ Antebellum Louisiana" (MA thesis, University of New Orleans, 2011), 23–26.

50. Theodore Seghers, vol. 9, Act 434, August 19, 1834; vol. 11, Act 158, March 23, 1835 (quotation); vol. 15, Act 555, June 27, 1836, NONA; Scott P. Marler, *The Merchants' Capital: New Orleans and the Political Economy of the Nineteenth Century* (New York: Cambridge University Press, 2013), 33n.27; Joshua D. Rothman, *Flush Times and Fever Dreams: A Story of Capitalism and Slavery in the Age of Jackson* (Athens: University of Georgia Press, 2012); Ana Carolina Castillo Grimm, *De León: A Tejano Family History* (Austin: University of Texas Press, 2003), 178.

51. Bodenhorn, *State Banking in Early America*, 30, 254–55; Schweikart, *Banking in the American South*, 211–13.

52. Bodenhorn, *State Banking in Early America*, 251–52; Schweikart, *Banking in the American South*, 51, 197–98, table 10; Michael G. Schene, "Robert and John Grattan Gamble: Middle Florida Entrepreneurs," *Florida Historical Quarterly* 54.1 (July 1975): 61–73; Edward E. Baptist, *Creating an Old South: Middle Florida's Plantation Frontier before the Civil War* (Chapel Hill: University of North Carolina Press, 2002), chap. 4.

53. Bodenhorn, *State Banking in Early America*, chap. 10; Green, *Finance and Economic Development in the Old South*, 1–32; Marler, *The Merchants' Capital*, 32–35; Baptist, "Toxic Debt, Liar Loans"; Schmitz, "Economies of Scale and Farm Size."

54. Bodenhorn, *State Banking in Early America*, 252–55; Baptist, "Toxic Debt, Liar Loans."

55. McGrane, *Foreign Bondholders and American State Debts*, 22; Hidy, *The House of Baring in American Trade and Finance*, 283–85, 316–17.

56. Schweikart, *Banking in the American South*, chap. 5; Lepler, *The Many Panics of 1837*, chap. 4; Bodenhorn, *A History of Banking in Antebellum America*, chap. 2.

57. Bodenhorn, *State Banking in Early America*, 257–60; John Alfred Heitmann, *The Modernization of the Louisiana Sugar Industry, 1830–1910* (Baton Rouge: Louisiana State University Press, 1987), chaps. 1–2; George D. Green, "The Citizens Bank of Louisiana: Property Banking in Troubled Times, 1833–1842," paper presented at the fifteenth annual meeting of the Business History Conference, Indiana University, 1968; Gray, *History of Agriculture in the Southern United States*, 2:1033.

58. Walter Johnson, *River of Dark Dreams: Slavery and Empire in the Cotton Kingdom* (Cambridge: Harvard University Press, 2013), chap. 10; Roulhac Toledano, Mary Louise Christovich, Robin Derbes, and Betsy Swanson, *New Orleans Architecture*, vol. 6, *Faubourg Tremé and the Bayou Road* (Gretna, La.: Pelican, 2003), 44; Bodenhorn, *State Banking in Early America*, 257–60.

59. Inward Slave Manifest, New Orleans, October 28, 1831 (*Industry*), NARA M1895, roll 6, images 1139–42; "Slaves Owned by the Citizens Bank and New Orleans Canal and Banking Company, 1831–1865," http://www2.bankone.com/upload/docs/presents/2005_01_19_ownership_list.pdf (accessed October 23, 2013); Stephen L. Esquith, *The Political Responsibilities of Everyday Bystanders* (State College: Pennsylvania State University Press, 2010), chap. 3.

60. Lacy K. Ford, *Deliver Us from Evil: The Slavery Question in the Old South* (New York: Oxford University Press, 2009), 457; Bodenhorn, *State Banking in Early America*, 257–60 (quotation 260); Lepler, *The Many Panics of 1837*, chap. 5.

61. Bodenhorn, *State Banking in Early America*, 258–59.

62. *New Orleans Times-Picayune*, February 16, 1843, 2 (first and second quotations); *Alexandria (Va.) Gazette*, February 28, 1843, 3 (third quotation); *New Orleans Times-Picayune*, February 16, 1843, 2 (fourth quotation); *Morning Chronicle* (London), March 17, 1843, 2 (fifth quotation); *Connecticut Courant*, March 4, 1843, 1; Arthur and Kernion, *Old Families of Louisiana*, 61–62.

CHAPTER 5. "THE SLAVE-FACTORY OF FRANKLIN & ARMFIELD"

1. Isaac Franklin to Rice C. Ballard, March 30, 1834, series 1, folder 13 (first quotation); Isaac Franklin to Col. Rice C. Ballard, May 22, 1834, series 1, folder 14 (second quotation); Isaac Franklin to Rice C. Ballard, April 9, 1834, series 1, folder 14, (third quotation); Rice C. Ballard Papers, Southern Historical Collection, UNC; Jan E. Stets and Michael J. Carter, "A Theory of the Self for the Sociology of Morality," *American Sociological Review* 77.1 (February 2012): 120–40; Robert H. Gudmestad, *A Troublesome Commerce: The Transformation of the Interstate Slave Trade* (Baton Rouge: Louisiana State University Press, 2003), 18–32; Robert H. Gudmestad, "The Troubled Legacy of Isaac Franklin: The Enterprise of Slave Trading," *Tennessee Historical Quarterly* 62.3 (September 2003): 192–217; Steven Deyle, *Carry Me Back: The Domestic Slave Trade in American Life* (New York: Oxford University Press, 2005), 100–138; Steven Deyle, "Rethinking the Slave Trade: Slave Traders and the Market Revolution in the South," in *The Old South's Modern Worlds*, ed. L. Diane Barnes, Brian Schoen, and Frank Towers (New York: Oxford University Press, 2011), 104–19; Edward E. Baptist, "'Cuffy,' 'Fancy Maids,' and 'One-Eyed Men': Rape, Commodification, and the Domestic Slave Trade in the United States," *American Historical Review* 106.5 (December 2001): 1619–50; Eyüp Özveren, "The Shipbuilding Commodity Chain, 1590–1790," in *Commodity Chains and Global Capitalism*, ed. Gary Gereffi and Miguel Korzeniewicz (Westport, Conn.: Praeger, 1994), 20–34; Douglass C. North, *Institutions, Institutional Change, and Economic Performance* (Cambridge: Cambridge University Press, 1990), chap. 1; Terrence K. Hopkins and Immanuel Wallerstein, "Commodity Chains in the

World-Economy prior to 1800," *Review* 10.1 (Summer 1986): 157–70; Immanuel Wallerstein, "American Slavery and the Capitalist World-Economy," in Wallerstein, *The Capitalist World-Economy* (1979; repr., Cambridge: Cambridge University Press, 1997), 202–21.

2. Wendell Stephenson, *Isaac Franklin: Slave Trader and Planter of the Old South* (Baton Rouge: Louisiana State University Press, 1938), 14 (quotation); 22–23.

3. Isaac Franklin to Rice C. Ballard, November 1, 1833, series 1, folder 12 (first quotation); Isaac Franklin to Rice C. Ballard, May 30, 1831, series 1, folder 1, Ballard Papers, UNC (subsequent quotations); Stephenson, *Isaac Franklin*, 15–16, 69–70; Richard P. Rumelt, "Toward a Strategic Theory of the Firm," in *Competitive Strategic Management*, ed. Robert Boyden Lamb (Englewood Cliffs, N.J.: Prentice-Hall, 1984), 556–70.

4. Ulrich B. Phillips, *American Negro Slavery* (1918; repr., Baton Rouge: Louisiana State University Press, 1966), 194–96; Frederic Bancroft, *Slave-Trading in the Old South* (Baltimore: J. H. Furst, 1931), 50–64, 275–76; Stephenson, *Isaac Franklin*; Michael Tadman, *Speculators and Slaves: Masters, Traders, and Slaves in the Old South* (Madison: University of Wisconsin Press, 1996), 77–86; Phillip Davis Troutman, "Slave Trade and Sentiment in Antebellum Virginia" (PhD diss., University of Virginia, 2000), chaps. 1–2; Tomoko Yagyu, "Slave Traders and Planters in the Expanding South: Entrepreneurial Strategies, Business Networks, and Western Migration in the Atlantic World, 1787–1859" (PhD diss., University of North Carolina, Chapel Hill, 2006), chaps. 2–3; Jim Barnett and H. Clark Burkett, "The Forks of the Road Slave Market at Natchez," *Journal of Mississippi History* 63.3 (September 2001): 168–87.

5. Stephenson, *Isaac Franklin*, 56; Yagyu, "Slave Traders and Planters in the Expanding South," 139–41; Midori Takagi, *"Rearing Wolves to Our Own Destruction": Slavery in Richmond, Virginia, 1782–1865* (Charlottesville: University Press of Virginia, 1999), 17; *Virginia Herald*, May 13, 1829, 1; June 10, 1829, 3.

6. *Daily National Intelligencer*, July 2, 1833, quoted in Bancroft, *Slave-Trading in the Old South*, 59; *Baltimore Republican*, July 3, 1833, quoted in Bancroft, *Slave-Trading in the Old South*, 39; Deyle, *Carry Me Back*, 102–4, 316n.18; Caitlin Rosenthal, "From Memory to Mastery: Accounting for Control in America, 1750–1880" (PhD diss., Harvard University, 2012).

7. Teppo Felin and William S. Hesterly, "The Knowledge-Based View, Nested Heterogeneity, and New Value Creation: Philosophical Considerations on the Locus of Knowledge," *Academy of Management Review* 32.1 (January 2007): 195–218; Naomi R. Lamoreaux, Daniel M. G. Raff, and Peter Temin, "Beyond Markets and Hierarchies: Toward a New Synthesis of American Business History," *American Historical Review* 108.2 (April 2003): 404–33; Thomas Welskopp, "Class Structures and the Firm: The Interplay of Workplace and Industrial Relations in Large Capitalist Enterprises," in *Authority and Control in Modern Industry: Theoretical and Empirical Perspectives*, ed. Paul L. Robertson (New York: Routledge, 1999), 73–119; David J. Teece, Gary Pisano, and Amy Shuen, "Dynamic Capabilities and Strategic Management," *Strategic Management Journal* 18.7 (August 1997): 509–33; Raphael Amit and Paul J. H. Schoemaker, "Strategic Assets and Organizational Rent," *Strategic Management*

Journal 14.1 (January 1993): 33–46; Pierre Bourdieu, *The Logic of Practice*, trans. Richard Nice (Stanford: Stanford University Press, 1990), chaps. 3–5; Philip Scranton, *Proprietary Capitalism: The Textile Manufacture at Philadelphia, 1800–1885* (Cambridge: Cambridge University Press, 1983); Alfred D. Chandler Jr., "The United States: Seedbed of Managerial Capitalism," in *Managerial Hierarchies: Comparative Perspectives on the Rise of the Modern Industrial Enterprise*, ed. Alfred D. Chandler Jr. and Herman Daems (Cambridge: Harvard University Press, 1980), 9–40.

8. Isaac Franklin to Rice C. Ballard, November 1, 1833, series 1, folder 12 (first, third, and fourth quotations); John Armfield to Rice C. Ballard, March 26, 1832, series 1, folder 5 (second quotation), Ballard Papers, UNC; Joseph C. Miller, *The Problem of Slavery as History: A Global Approach* (New Haven: Yale University Press, 2012), chap. 1; Pankaj Ghemawat, "Competition and Business Strategy in Historical Perspective," *Business History Review* 76.1 (Spring 2002): 37–74; Kathleen R. Conner and C. K. Prahalad, "A Resource-Based Theory of the Firm: Knowledge versus Opportunism," *Organizational Science* 7.5 (September–October 1996): 477–501; Margaret A. Peteraf, "The Cornerstones of Competitive Advantage: A Resource-Based View," *Strategic Management Journal* 14.3 (March 1993): 179–91; Jay B. Barney, "Firm Resources and Sustained Competitive Advantage," *Journal of Management* 17.1 (1991): 99–120; Joseph Schumpeter, *Capitalism, Socialism, and Democracy* (1942; repr., Oxford: Routledge, 2006).

9. Vol. 2, R. C. Ballard and Co. Invoice Book, series 5, folder 417, Ballard Papers, UNC; *Alexandria Phenix Gazette*, May 10, 1833, 1 (quotation).

10. Vol. 38, Ballard and Co. Ledger, 1831–1834, subseries 5, folder 463, Rice C. Ballard Papers, Southern Historical Collection, UNC; Thomas Longworth, *Longworth's American Almanac, New York Register, and City Directory* (New York: Thomas Longworth, 1827), 202, 322, 329; *New-York Daily Advertiser*, May 23, 1826, 3; July 14, 1826, 3; *New York National Advocate*, November 13, 1822, 1; *New York Evening Post*, January 10, 1827, 2; March 11, 1830, 1; *New York Commercial Advertiser*, September 27, 1831, 3; Ian Hunter, "Commodity Chains and Networks in Emerging Markets: New Zealand, 1880–1910," *Business History Review* 79.2 (Summer 2005): 275–304; Kenneth Morgan, "Remittance Procedures in the Eighteenth-Century British Slave Trade," *Business History Review* 79.4 (Winter 2005): 715–49; Richard C. McKay, *South Street: A Maritime History of New York* (New York: G. P. Putnam's Sons, 1934), 194–95; Walter Barrett, *Old Merchants of New York City* (New York: Carleton, 1863), 327.

11. Isaac Franklin to Rice C. Ballard, October 26, 1831, series 1, folder 2, Ballard Papers, UNC (quotation); Ballard and Co. Ledger, 1831–1834; Howard Bodenhorn, *State Banking in Early America: A New Economic History* (New York: Oxford University Press, 2003), chap. 3; Robert E. Wright, *The Wealth of Nations Rediscovered: Integration and Expansion of American Financial Markets, 1780–1850* (New York: Cambridge University Press, 2002), chaps. 5–8; Sven Beckert, *The Monied Metropolis: New York City and the Consolidation of the American Bourgeoisie* (New York: Cambridge University Press, 2001); Marie-Thérèse Boyer-Xambeu, Ghislain Deleplace, and Lucien Gillard, *Private Money and Public Currencies: The 16th-Century Challenge*, trans. Azizeh Azodi (Armonk, N.Y.: M. E. Sharpe, 1994).

12. Ballard and Co. Ledger, 1831–1834 (quotation); David L. Lightner, *Slavery and the Commerce Power: How the Struggle against the Interstate Slave Trade Led to the Civil War* (New Haven: Yale University Press, 2006), 8; Deyle, *Carry Me Back*, 98–100; Jonathan Levy, *Freaks of Fortune: The Emerging World of Capitalism and Risk in America* (Cambridge: Harvard University Press, 2012), chap. 2; Miller, *The Problem of Slavery as History*, chap 4; Robert E. Wright and Christopher Kingston, "Corporate Insurers in Antebellum America," *Business History Review* 86.3 (Autumn 2012): 447–76; Herman Freudenberger and Jonathan B. Pritchett, "The Domestic United States Slave Trade: New Evidence," *Journal of Interdisciplinary History* 21.3 (1991): 447–77.

13. *Ithaca (N.Y.) Journal*, September 21, 1831, 3; Matthew Jaremski, "Bank-Specific Default Risk in the Pricing of Bank Note Discounts," *Journal of Economic History* 71.4 (December 2011): 950–75.

14. Inward Slave Manifest, New Orleans, October 28, 1831 (*Industry*), NARA M1895, roll 6, images 1138–43.

15. Inward Slave Manifest, New Orleans, November 15, 1831 (*Ajax*), NARA M1895, roll 6, image 1137; Inward Slave Manifest, New Orleans, October 22, 1831 (*Betsey*), NARA M1895, roll 6, images 986, 991, 994; R. C. Ballard and Co. Invoice Book; *Charleston (S.C.) City Gazette*, December 1, 1831, 2; Susan Eva O'Donovan, "Universities of Social and Political Change: Slaves in Jail in Antebellum America," in *Buried Lives: Incarcerated in Early America*, ed. Michele Lise Tarter and Richard Bell (Athens: University of Georgia Press, 2012), 124–48; Freudenberger and Pritchett, "The Domestic United States Slave Trade."

16. Joseph Holt Ingraham, *The South-West by a Yankee*, vol. 2 (New York: Harper and Brothers, 1835), 196 (first quotation), 192 (second quotation); Ariela J. Gross, *Double Character: Slavery and Mastery in the Antebellum Southern Courtroom* (Athens: University of Georgia Press, 2006), chap. 1; Baptist, "'Cuffy,' 'Fancy Maids,' and 'One-Eyed Men'"; Barnett and Burkett, "The Forks of the Road Slave Market at Natchez"; George D. Green, *Finance and Economic Development in the Old South: Louisiana Banking, 1804–1861* (Stanford: Stanford University Press, 1972), chap. 2.

17. Isaac Franklin to Rice C. Ballard, December 14, 1831, series 1, folder 3, Ballard Papers, UNC (quotation); Joshua D. Rothman, *Flush Times and Fever Dreams: A Story of Capitalism and Slavery in the Age of Jackson* (Athens: University of Georgia Press, 2012); Eugene Genovese and Elizabeth Fox Genovese, *Fatal Self-Deception: Slaveholding Paternalism in the Old South* (New York: Cambridge University Press, 2011).

18. Isaac Franklin to Rice C. Ballard, January 11, 1834, series 1, folder 13 (first quotation); Isaac Franklin to Rice C. Ballard, January 9, 1832, series 1, folder 4 (second quotation), Ballard Papers, UNC; Green, *Finance and Economic Development in the Old South*, chap. 1; Joseph C. Miller, "Credit, Captives, Collateral and Currencies: Debt, Slavery and the Financing of the Atlantic World," in *Debt and Slavery in the Mediterranean and Atlantic Worlds*, ed. Gwyn C. Campbell and Alessandro Stanziani (London: Pickering and Chatto, 2013), 105–22.

19. Isaac Franklin to Rice C. Ballard, March 10, 1834, series 1, folder 13, Ballard Papers, UNC (quotation); Matthew Sweeney, *The Lottery Wars: Long Odds, Fast Money, and the Battle over an American Institution* (New York: Bloomsbury, 2009), 34–38;

Mark Casson, "The Nature of the Firm Reconsidered: Information Synthesis and Entrepreneurial Organization," *MIR: Management International Review* 36 (1996): 55–94; Howard Bodenhorn, *A History of Banking in Antebellum America: Financial Markets and Economic Development in an Era of Nation-Building* (New York: Cambridge University Press, 2000), 180; R. W. Hidy, "Credit Rating before Dun and Bradstreet," *Bulletin of the Business Historical Society* 13.6 (December 1939): 81–88.

20. Isaac Franklin to Rice C. Ballard, January 9, 1832, series 1, folder 4, Ballard Papers, UNC (quotations); T. K. Das and Noushi Rahman, "Determinants of Partner Opportunism in Strategic Alliances: A Conceptual Framework," *Journal of Business Psychology* 25.1 (March 2010): 55–74; Henry Wiencek, *The Hairstons: An American Family in Black and White* (New York: St. Martin's Press, 1999), chap. 4; Deyle, *Carry Me Back*, chap. 4.

21. James Franklin to Rice C. Ballard, January 18, 1832, series 1, folder 4, Ballard Papers, UNC.

22. Isaac Franklin to Rice C. Ballard, January 9, 1832, series 1, folder 4, Ballard Papers, UNC (quotations); *Succession of Isaac Franklin*, 7 La. Ann. 395 (1852), 330; Barnett and Burkett, "The Forks of the Road Slave Market at Natchez"; Green, *Finance and Economic Development in the Old South*, xi, 74–75.

23. James Franklin to Rice C. Ballard, March 27, 1832, series 1, folder 5, Ballard Papers, UNC (quotations); Bodenhorn, *State Banking in Early America*, chap. 10.

24. Isaac Franklin to Rice C. Ballard, December 14, 1831, series 1, folder 3; James and Isaac Franklin to Rice C. Ballard, April 24, 1832, series 1, folder 6; Isaac Franklin to Rice C. Ballard, May 19, 1832, series 1, folder 6; James and Isaac Franklin to Rice C. Ballard, June 9, 1832, series 1, folder 7; Ballard and Co. Ledger, 1831–1834; Richard L. Booker to Rice C. Ballard, April 18, 1833, series 1, folder 11; Isaac Franklin to Rice C. Ballard, November 5, 1833, series 1, folder 12; James R. Franklin to Rice C. Ballard, November 14, 1833, series 1, folder 12, Ballard Papers, UNC; *New York Spectator*, March 5, 1830, 2; Richard Holcombe Kilbourne Jr., *Slave Agriculture and Financial Markets: The Bank of the United States in Mississippi, 1831–1852* (London: Pickering and Chatto, 2006); Richard Sylla, "Shaping the US Financial System, 1690–1913: The Dominant Role of Public Finance," in *The State, the Financial System and Economic Modernization*, ed. Richard Sylla and Richard Tilly (New York: Cambridge University Press, 1999), 249–70; Joshua D. Rothman, "The Hazards of the Flush Times: Gambling, Mob Violence, and the Anxieties of America's Market Revolution," *Journal of American History* 95.3 (December 2008): 651–77; John Joseph Wallis, "Answering Mary Shirley's Question; or, What Can the World Bank Learn from American History?" in *Political Institutions and Financial Development*, ed. Stephen Haber, Douglass C. North, and Barry R. Weingast (Stanford: Stanford University Press, 2008), 103–9; Jeffery W. Markham, *A Financial History of the United States*, vol. 2, *From J. P. Morgan to the Institutional Investor (1900–1970)* (Armonk, N.Y.: M. E. Sharpe, 2002), 64–65.

25. Rice C. Ballard to Isaac Franklin, September 7, 1832, series 1, folder 7, Ballard Papers, UNC.

26. Isaac Franklin to Rice C. Ballard, October 5, 1832, series 1, folder 7; John Armfield to Rice C. Ballard, December 29, 1832, series 1, folder 9; Ballard and Co. Ledger, 1831–1834.

27. Richard L. Booker to Rice C. Ballard, April 18, 1833, series 1, folder 11 (first quotation); Isaac Franklin to Rice C. Ballard, March 30, 1834, series 1, folder 13 (second quotation); Isaac and James Franklin to Rice C. Ballard, December 20, 1832, series 1, folder 9; Ballard and Co. Ledger, 1831–1834; Naomi R. Lamoreaux, "Banks, Kinship, and Economic Development: The New England Case," *Journal of Economic History* 46.3 (September 1996): 647–67; Paul Duguid, "Networks and Knowledge: The Beginning and End of the Port Commodity Chain, 1703–1860," *Business History Review* 79.3 (Autumn 2005): 493–526; Ralph W. Hidy, *The House of Baring in American Trade and Finance: English Merchant Bankers at Work, 1763–1861* (Cambridge: Harvard University Press, 1949), 109–10; Ralph W. Hidy, "The Union Bank of Louisiana Loan, 1832: A Case Study in Marketing," *Journal of Political Economy* 47.2 (1939): 232–53.

28. E. A. Andrews, *Slavery and the Domestic Slave-Trade in the United States* (Boston: Light and Stearns, 1836), 136 (first quotation); G. W. Featherstonhaugh, *Excursion through the Slave States, from Washington on the Potomac to the Frontier of Mexico: With Sketches of Popular Manners and Geological Notices*, vol. 1 (London: John Murray, 1844), 152–53 (second quotation); Stephenson, *Isaac Franklin*, 22–24; Isabel Howell, *John Armfield of Beersheba Springs* (Beersheba Springs, Tenn.: Beersheba Springs Historical Society, 1983), 18; Deyle, *Carry Me Back*, 100–101.

29. Richard Whitley, *Business Systems and Organizational Capabilities: The Institutional Structuring of Competitive Practices* (Oxford: Oxford University Press, 2007).

30. Inward Slave Manifest, New Orleans, February 12–15, 1827 (*Jefferson*), NARA M1895, roll 4, images 352–64; Inward Slave Manifest, New Orleans, October 18–20, 1828 (*Jefferson*), NARA M1895, roll 5, images 748–60; Inward Slave Manifest, New Orleans, January 18, 1828 (*United States*), NARA M1895, roll 5, image 80; Inward Slave Manifest, New Orleans, October 22, 1828 (*United States*), NARA M1895, roll 5, images 617–25; *New Orleans Argus*, May 19, 1828, 2; May 28, 1828, 2; *Louisiana Advertiser*, May 2, 1827, 3; *Liverpool Mercury*, June 29, 1827, 207; July 20, 1827, 231; *New York Commercial Advertiser*, August 30, 1827, 3; October 8, 1827, 2; January 31, 1828, 2; *Alexandria Phenix Gazette*, October 3, 1828, 3; October 8, 1828, 3; *New Orleans Argus*, April 8, 1828, 2; August 7, 1828, 1; *Louisiana Advertiser*, March 27, 1827, 3; Walter Johnson, *River of Dark Dreams: Slavery and Empire in the Cotton Kingdom* (Cambridge: Harvard University Press, 2013), chap. 1; Robert Gudmestad, *Steamboats and the Rise of the Cotton Kingdom* (Baton Rouge: Louisiana State University Press, 2011), 155; Deyle, *Carry Me Back*, 315n.14; Forrest R. Holdcamper, comp., *List of American-Flag Merchant Vessels That Received Certificates of Enrollment or Registry at the Port of New York, 1789–1867*, vol. 2 (Washington, D.C.: Government Services Administration, 1968), 700; Robert Greenhalgh Albion, *Square-Riggers on Schedule: The New York Sailing Packets to England, France, and the Cotton Ports* (Princeton: Princeton University Press, 1938), chaps. 1–2; Stephenson, *Isaac Franklin*, 64, 92.

31. *Alexandria Phenix Gazette*, March 30, 1830, 2 (first quotation); March 2, 1831, 3; March 4, 1831, 3; March 10, 1831, 1 (second quotation); *Daily National Intelligencer*, April 5,

1830, 4; Inward Slave Manifest, New Orleans, March 10, 1831 (*James Monroe*), NARA M1895, roll 6, images 885–90; Calvin Schermerhorn, "Capitalism's Captives: The Maritime United States Slave Trade, 1807–1850," *Journal of Social History* 47.4 (Summer 2014); James A. McMillin, *The Final Victims: Foreign Slave Trade to North America, 1783–1810* (Columbia: University of South Carolina Press, 2004), app. B.

32. Isaac Franklin to Rice C. Ballard, February 28, 1831, series 1, folder 1, Ballard Papers, UNC (quotations); Inward Slave Manifest, New Orleans, February 27, 1829 (*Comet*), NARA M1895, roll 6, images 168–75.

33. John Armfield to Rice C. Ballard, January 26, 1832, series 1, folder 4, Ballard Papers, UNC (quotations; emphasis in original); *Acts Passed at the First Session of the Ninth Legislature of the State of Louisiana* (New Orleans: John Gibson, 1829), 38–50; Stephen Mihm, *A Nation of Counterfeiters: Capitalists, Con Men, and the Making of the United States* (Cambridge: Harvard University Press, 2007), chap. 2; Judith Kelleher Schafer, *Slavery, the Civil Law, and the Supreme Court of Louisiana* (Baton Rouge: Louisiana State University Press, 1997), 165–68; Gudmestad, *A Troublesome Commerce*, 109–10.

34. Works Progress Administration, Survey of Federal Archives in Louisiana, *Ship Registers and Enrollments of New Orleans, Louisiana*, vol. 2, *1821–1830* (University: Louisiana State University Library, 1942), 3; Inward Slave Manifest, New Orleans, February 8, 1832 (*Ajax*), NARA M1895, roll 7, images 31–40, 283–85, 301; John Armfield to Rice C. Ballard, January 26, 1832, series 1, folder 4, Ballard Papers, UNC (first and second quotations); Ballard and Co. Ledger, 1831–1834 (third quotation).

35. Jon Meacham, *American Lion: Andrew Jackson and the White House* (New York: Random House, 2008), 418n.211.

36. Andrew Tabak, *An Unimportant Ship: The Brig Pavilion, 1829–1863* (Charleston, S.C.: CreateSpace Publishing, 2011), 20–60.

37. Ballard and Co. Ledger, 1831–1834; Inward Slave Manifest, New Orleans, January 7, 1822 (*Intelligence*), NARA M1895, roll 2, images 128–29; Inward Slave Manifest, New Orleans, December 8–9, 1829 (*Ajax*), NARA M1895, roll 5, images 890–903; Tabak, *An Unimportant Ship*, 20, 32–33; WPA, *Ship Registers and Enrollments of New Orleans*, 2:3.

38. Tabak, *An Unimportant Ship*, 34–35; Holdcamper, *List of American-Flag Merchant Vessels*, 2:687; Works Progress Administration, Survey of Federal Archives in Louisiana, *Ship Registers and Enrollments of New Orleans, Louisiana*, vol. 3, *1831–1840* (University: Louisiana State University Library, 1942), 211; Inward Slave Manifest, New Orleans, February 26, 1835 (*Tribune*), NARA M1895, roll 7, images 679–83; *Alexandria Phenix Gazette*, November 12, 1831, 3.

39. Bancroft, *Slave-Trading in the Old South*, 275.

40. Ballard and Co. Ledger, 1831–1834 (quotation); Bill of Sale, Customs Collector's Office, Alexandria, October 23, 1833, series 1, folder 11, Ballard Papers, UNC; R. C. Ballard and Co. Invoice Book; William M. Lytle and Forrest R. Holdcamper, *Merchant Steam Vessels of the United States, 1807–1868* (Mystic, Conn.: Steamship Historical Society of America, 1952), 72; *New-Orleans Commercial Bulletin*, June 3, 1833, 1; October 18, 1833, 3.

41. John Armfield to Rice C. Ballard, March 26, 1832, series 1, folder 5 (quotations); vol. 2, 1831–1833, series 5, folder 417, Ballard Papers, UNC; Inward Slave Manifest, New Orleans, March 19, 1832 (*Tribune*), NARA M1895, roll 7, images 77, 78, 81–84, 87; *Alexandria Phenix Gazette*, November 5, 1832, 5; David J. Libby, *Slavery and Frontier Mississippi, 1720–1835* (Jackson: University Press of Mississippi, 2008), 66; Phillips, *American Negro Slavery*, 194–95.

42. James R. Franklin to Rice C. Ballard, March 27, 1832, series 1, folder 5, Ballard Papers, UNC (quotation; emphasis in original); Laura F. Edwards, "Status without Rights: African Americans and the Tangled History of Law and Governance in the Nineteenth-Century U.S. South," *American Historical Review* 112 (2007): 365–93; Anthony E. Kaye, *Joining Places: Slave Neighborhoods in the Old South* (Chapel Hill: University of North Carolina Press, 2007); Stephanie M. H. Camp, *Closer to Freedom: Enslaved Women & Everyday Resistance in the Plantation South* (Chapel Hill: University of North Carolina Press, 2004); Dylan C. Penningroth, *The Claims of Kinfolk: African American Property and Community in the Nineteenth-Century South* (Chapel Hill: University of North Carolina Press, 2003); Joshua D. Rothman, *Notorious in the Neighborhood: Sex and Families across the Color Line in Virginia, 1787–1861* (Chapel Hill: University of North Carolina Press, 2003).

43. James R. Franklin to Rice C. Ballard, March 27, 1832, series 1, folder 5, Ballard Papers, UNC (quotations; emphasis in original); Inward Slave Manifest, New Orleans, November 17, 1831 (*Tribune*), NARA M1895, roll 6, image 1213; Baptist, "'Cuffy,' 'Fancy Maids,' and 'One-Eyed Men,'" 1633; Walter Johnson, *Soul by Soul: Life inside the Antebellum Slave Market* (Cambridge: Harvard University Press, 1999), chaps. 4–5.

44. James Franklin to Rice C. Ballard, March 4, 1832, series 1, folder 5, Ballard Papers, UNC.

45. James and Isaac Franklin to Rice C. Ballard, April 24, 1832, series 1, folder 6; Isaac and James Franklin to Rice C. Ballard, April 20, 1832, series 1, folder 6, Ballard Papers, UNC (quotations); Libby, *Slavery and Frontier Mississippi*, 33.

46. James Franklin to Rice C. Ballard, May 13, 1832, series 1, folder 6 (first four quotations; emphasis in original); Isaac Franklin to Rice C. Ballard, November 1, 1833, series 1, folder 12 (fifth quotation), Ballard Papers, UNC; *Alexandria Phenix Gazette*, March 31, 1832, 3; Joseph Martin, *A Comprehensive Description of Virginia and the District of Columbia* (Richmond: J. W. Randolph, 1830[?]), 113–14.

47. Isaac Franklin to Rice C. Ballard, December 8, 1832, series 1, folder 8, Ballard Papers, UNC (quotations); Gudmestad, *A Troublesome Commerce*, 93.

48. *Alexandria Phenix Gazette*, January 23, 1833, 3; February 16, 1833, 3; February 26, 1833, 3; March 9, 1833, 3; March 16, 1833, 3; April 29, 1833, 3; October 19, 1833, 1 (quotation); Memorandum of October 23, 1833, series 1, folder 11, Ballard Papers, UNC; WPA, *Ship Registers and Enrollments of New Orleans*, 3:213.

49. *Genius of Universal Emancipation*, December 1830, 131 (first and second quotations); Lightner, *Slavery and the Commerce Power*, 102 (third quotation); Ralph Clayton, *Cash for Blood: The Baltimore to New Orleans Domestic Slave Trade* (Bowie, Md.: Heritage Books, 2007), 625–39; J. B. Pritchett and H. Freudenberger, "A Peculiar Sample: The Selection of Slaves for the New Orleans Market," *Journal of Economic*

History 52.1 (March 1992): 109–27; Freudenberger and Pritchett, "The Domestic United States Slave Trade"; Donald M. Sweig, "Northern Virginia Slavery: A Statistical and Demographic Investigation" (PhD diss., College of William and Mary, 1982), chap. 3; Allan Pred, "Manufacturing in the American Mercantile City: 1800–1840," *Annals of the Association of American Geographers* 56.2 (1966): 310; William Jay, *Slavery in America; or, An Inquiry into the Character and Tendency of the American Colonization and American Anti-Slavery Societies* (New York: R. G. Williams, 1837), 157–62.

50. Jay, *Slavery in America*, 158 (first quotation); James G. Blakey to Rice C. Ballard, June 15, 1834, series 1, folder 15 (second quotation), Ballard Papers, UNC; Ballard and Co. Ledger, 1831–1834; Baptist, "'Cuffy,' 'Fancy Maids,' and 'One-Eyed Men,'" 1628; Kathleen M. Eisenhardt, "Agency Theory: An Assessment and Review," *Academy of Management Review* 14.1 (January 1989): 57–74.

51. *Richmond Enquirer*, April 5, 1831, 1; Ballard and Co. Ledger, 1831–1834.

52. Ira Berlin, *Generations of Captivity: A History of African-American Slaves* (Cambridge: Harvard University Press, 2003), chap. 4; Marie Jenkins Schwartz, *Birthing a Slave: Motherhood and Medicine in the Antebellum South* (Cambridge: Harvard University Press, 2006); Nell Irvin Painter, *Soul Murder and Slavery* (Waco, Tex.: Baylor University Press, 1995).

53. Ballard and Co. Ledger, 1831–1834; *Alexandria Phenix Gazette*, March 7, 1833, 2; Troutman, "Slave Trade and Sentiment," chap. 1; Tadman, *Speculators and Slaves*, chap. 5; Jaime Amanda Martinez, "The Slave Market in Civil War Virginia," in *Crucible of the Civil War: Virginia from Secession to Commemoration*, ed. Edward L. Ayers, Gary W. Gallagher, and Andrew J. Torget (Charlottesville: University of Virginia Press, 2006), 106–35.

54. *Richmond Enquirer*, March 19, 1833, 1.

55. Ballard and Co. Ledger, 1831–1834; Negro Board Book, series 5, vol. 3, folder 418, Ballard Papers, UNC; Donald M. Sweig, "Reassessing the Human Dimension of the Interstate Slave Trade," *Prologue* 12.1 (Spring 1980): 5–21.

56. *Richmond Enquirer*, March 22, 1833, 1; Lytle and Holdcamper, *Merchant Steam Vessels of the United States*, 177.

57. *Alexandria Phenix Gazette*, March 16, 1833, 3; March 22, 1833, 3; "Sales of R. C. Ballard and Co," vol. 4, series 5, folder 421, Ballard Papers, UNC; Inward Slave Manifest, New Orleans, December 9, 1829 (*Comet*), NARA M1895, roll 6, images 454–59; Edward B. Rugemer, "Robert Monroe Harrison, British Abolition, Southern Anglophobia and Texas Annexation," *Slavery and Abolition* 28.2 (August 2007): 169–91.

58. Howard I. Chapelle, *The Search for Speed under Sail* (New York: W. W. Norton, 1967), 298–304; *Albany Evening Journal*, February 20, 1836, 2 (quotations).

59. Ingraham, *The South-West*, 2:234–35.

60. *Alexandria Phenix Gazette*, April 29, 1833, 3; *Albany Evening Journal*, February 20, 1836, 2; William Jay, *Miscellaneous Writings on Slavery* (Boston: J. P. Jewett and Company, 1853), 157–58; Gudmestad, *Steamboats and the Rise of the Cotton Kingdom*, chap. 3.

61. *Natchez Courier and Adams, Jefferson and Franklin Advertiser*, April 12, 1833, 1–4.

62. Ingraham, *The South-West*, 2:193 (quotations); Tadman, *Speculators and Slaves*, chap. 4.

63. Ingraham, *The South-West*, 2:193.

64. Ibid., 197 (quotations); Michael B. Miller, *The Bon Marché: Bourgeois Culture and the Department Store, 1869–1920* (Princeton: Princeton University Press, 1981).

65. Ingraham, *The South-West*, 2:245.

66. Purchase Book, vol. 4, 1832–1834, series 5, folder 420, (first three quotations); Isaac Franklin to Rice C. Ballard, November 1, 1833, series 1, folder 12 (subsequent quotations), Ballard Papers, UNC.

67. "Sales of R. C. Ballard and Co."

68. Gudmestad, *A Troublesome Commerce*, 93–94; *New York Evening Post*, May 20, 1833, 2 (quotation).

69. *Natchez Courier and Adams, Jefferson and Franklin Advertiser*, April 26, 1833, 2 (quotations); *New York Evening Post*, May 20, 1833, 2; *Niles' Weekly Register*, May 25, 1833, 196; Gudmestad, *A Troublesome Commerce*, 93.

70. *Natchez Courier and Adams, Jefferson and Franklin Advertiser*, April 26, 1833, 2.

71. Ibid., 3; May 3, 1833, 2 (quotations); Gudmestad, *A Troublesome Commerce*, 93–94.

72. Isaac Franklin to Rice C. Ballard, February 28, 1831, series 1, folder 1, Ballard Papers, UNC (quotation); Alfred D. Chandler Jr., *The Visible Hand: The Managerial Revolution in American Business* (Cambridge: Harvard University Press, 1977).

73. Partnership Agreement, May 1833, Rice C. Ballard and Co., enclosure, vol. 4, series 5, folder 421 (first two quotations); Memorandum of August 26, 1833, series 1, folder 11; Isaac Franklin to Rice Ballard, August 26, 1833, series 1, folder 11 (third quotation), Ballard Papers, UNC.

74. *Succession of Isaac Franklin*, 274–300, 348–69; William Cronon, *Nature's Metropolis: Chicago and the Great West* (New York: W. W. Norton, 1991), chap. 5; Michael G. Jacobides, "How Capability Differences, Transaction Costs, and Learning Curves Interact to Shape Vertical Scope," *Organization Science* 19.2 (March–April 2008): 306–26; Harold C. Livesay and Patrick G. Porter, "Vertical Integration in American Manufacturing, 1899–1948," *Journal of Economic History* 29.3 (September 1969): 494–500.

75. Scott Reynolds Nelson, *A Nation of Deadbeats: An Uncommon History of America's Financial Disasters* (New York: Knopf, 2012), chaps. 5–6; Bray Hammond, *Banks and Politics in America from the Revolution to the Civil War* (1957; repr., Princeton: Princeton University Press, 1991), 419; Michael F. Holt, *The Rise and Fall of the American Whig Party* (New York: Oxford University Press, 1999), 23–24.

76. *Succession of Isaac Franklin*, 298 (first quotation); 369 (second quotation); Martijn Konings, *The Development of American Finance* (New York: Cambridge University Press, 2011), chap. 3; Daniel Walker Howe, *What Hath God Wrought: The Transformation of America, 1815–1848* (New York: Oxford University Press, 2007), chap. 10.

77. Isaac Franklin to Rice C. Ballard, November 5, 1833, series 1, folder 12, Ballard Papers, UNC.

78. R. C. Ballard and Co., Accounts, vol. 6, series 5, folder 424; Isaac Franklin to Rice C. Ballard, November 5, 1833, series 1, folder 12 (quotations), Ballard Papers, UNC.

79. Isaac Franklin to Rice C. Ballard, November 5, 1833, series 1, folder 12 (quotation); R. C. Ballard and Co., Accounts, vol. 6, series 5, folder 424, Ballard Papers, UNC; *New-Orleans Commercial Bulletin*, November 6, 1833, 2; November 7, 1833, 2.

80. Isaac Franklin to Rice C. Ballard, November 6, 1833, series 1, folder 12, Ballard Papers, UNC (quotations); Inward Slave Manifest, New Orleans, October 16, 1833 (*Tribune*), NARA M1895, roll 7, images 332–35; *Alexandria Phenix Gazette*, November 21, 1833, 3.

81. Isaac Franklin to Rice C. Ballard, November 7, 1833, series 1, folder 12 (first quotation); James R. Franklin to Rice C. Ballard, November 14, 1833, series 1, folder 12 (subsequent quotations; emphases in original), Ballard Papers, UNC.

82. Stephenson, *Isaac Franklin*, 70; Maurie D. McInnis, *Slaves Waiting for Sale: Abolitionist Art and the American Slave Trade* (Chicago: University of Chicago Press, 2011), chap. 6; William Calderhead, "The Role of the Professional Slave Trader in a Slave Economy: Austin Woolfolk, a Case Study," *Civil War History* 23 (September 1977): 195–211.

83. James R. Franklin to Rice C. Ballard, December 9, 1833, series 1, folder 12 (first quotation); James R. Franklin to Rice C. Ballard, December 13, 1833, series 1, folder 12 (subsequent quotations; emphasis in original), Ballard Papers, UNC.

84. James R. Franklin to Rice C. Ballard, December 19, 1833, series 1, folder 12, Ballard Papers, UNC.

85. Isaac Franklin to Rice C. Ballard, December 25, 1833, series 1, folder 12, Ballard Papers, UNC.

86. Isaac Franklin to Rice C. Ballard, December 25, 1833, series 1, folder 12, Ballard Papers, UNC (quotations); *Alexandria Phenix Gazette*, November 29, 1833, 3; January 17, 1834, 3; Charles R. Schultz, "New Orleans in December 1860," *Louisiana History: The Journal of the Louisiana Historical Association* 9.1 (Winter 1968): 60

87. Isaac Franklin to Rice C. Ballard, January 11, 1834, series 1, folder 13, Ballard Papers, UNC.

88. Ballard and Co. Ledger, 1831–1834 (first quotation); Isaac Franklin to Rice C. Ballard, January 11, 1834, series 1, folder 13, Ballard Papers, UNC (second quotation); Joshua D. Rothman, *Notorious in the Neighborhood: Sex and Families across the Color Line in Virginia, 1787–1861* (Chapel Hill: University of North Carolina Press, 2003), 130–32.

89. Isaac Franklin to Rice C. Ballard, January 11, 1834, series 1, folder 13, Ballard Papers, UNC (quotations); H. B. Croom, "Some Account of the Agricultural Soil and Products of Middle Florida, in a Letter to the Editor," *Farmers' Register* 2.1 (June 1834): 1–3.

90. Isaac Franklin to Rice C. Ballard, January 11, 1834, series 1, folder 13, Ballard Papers, UNC (quotations); *Alexandria Phenix Gazette*, January 27, 1834, 3.

91. Isaac Franklin to Rice C. Ballard, January 11, 1834, series 1, folder 13, Ballard Papers, UNC (quotations); Troutman, "Slave Trade and Sentiment," 46n.54.

92. James R. Franklin to Rice C. Ballard, February 2, 1834, series 1, folder 13, Ballard Papers, UNC (quotations); Laurence J. Kotlikoff, "The Structure of Slave Prices in New Orleans, 1804–1862," *Economic Inquiry* 17.4 (October 1979): 496–98.

93. James R. Franklin to Rice C. Ballard, February 2, 1834, series 1, folder 13, Ballard Papers, UNC.

94. James R. Franklin to Rice C. Ballard, March 7, 1834, series 1, folder 13 (first and second quotations); Isaac Franklin to Rice C. Ballard, November 1, 1833, series 1, folder 12 (third quotation); James R. Franklin to Rice C. Ballard, March 27, 1832, series 1, folder 5 (fourth quotation; emphasis in original), Ballard Papers, UNC.

95. Katherine Osburn, *Choctaw Resurgence in Mississippi: Race, Class, and Nation Building, 1830–1977* (Norman: University of Oklahoma Press, 2014), chap. 1; Jessica M. Lepler, *The Many Panics of 1837: People, Politics, and the Creation of a Transatlantic Financial Crisis* (New York: Cambridge University Press, 2013); Johnson, *River of Dark Dreams*, chap. 1; Howard Bodenhorn, "Entry, Rivalry and Free Banking in Antebellum America," *Review of Economics and Statistics* 72.4 (November 1990): 682–86; Kotlikoff, "The Structure of Slave Prices in New Orleans"; Hammond, *Banks and Politics in America from the Revolution to the Civil War*, 453.

96. Isaac Franklin to Rice C. Ballard, March 10, 1834, series 1, folder 13 (first, second, fifth, and sixth quotations); Isaac Franklin to Rice C. Ballard, April 9, 1834, series 1, folder 14 (third and fourth quotations), Ballard Papers, UNC.

97. Isaac Franklin to Rice C. Ballard, March 10, 1834, series 1, folder 13, Ballard Papers, UNC.

98. Isaac Franklin to Rice C. Ballard, April 9, 1834, series 1, folder 14, Ballard Papers, UNC.

99. Ibid.

100. Ibid. (quotations); *Richmond Whig*, November 15, 1844, 2.

101. Isaac Franklin to Rice C. Ballard, March 30, 1834, series 1, folder 13, Ballard Papers, UNC.

102. James R. Franklin to Rice C. Ballard, April 16, 1834, series 1, folder 14, Ballard Papers, UNC (quotations); Judith Herman, *Trauma and Recovery: The Aftermath of Violence from Domestic Abuse to Political Terror* (New York: Basic Books, 1992).

103. Isaac Franklin to Rice C. Ballard, May 13, 1834, series 1, folder 14 (first two quotations); Isaac Franklin to Rice C. Ballard, May 22, 1834, series 1, folder 15 (third quotation), Ballard Papers, UNC; Gudmestad, *A Troublesome Commerce*, 206; Stephenson, *Isaac Franklin*, 16

104. John Armfield to Rice C. Ballard, September 19, 1834, series 1, folder 15, Ballard Papers, UNC (quotation); *New York Spectator*, June 25, 1832, 1; August 9, 1832, 3; September 6, 1832, 4; *South Carolina Southern Patriot*, May 25, 1825, 3; *Baltimore Gazette and Daily Advertiser*, September 17, 1832, 2; *Portland (Maine) Eastern Argus*, July 3, 1833, 3; Charleston (S.C.) Courier, July 8, 1833, 3; June 4, 1834, 3; June 23, 1834, 2; *New York Commercial Advertiser*, July 22, 1833, 1; June 17, 1834, 2; *Alexandria Phenix Gazette*, August 21, 1833, 3; July 2, 1834, 3; July 14, 1834, 3.

105. Chapelle, *The Search for Speed under Sail*, 302–3.

106. *New-Orleans Commercial Bulletin*, October 29, 1835, 3; Michael Stammers, *Figureheads & Ship Carving* (Annapolis: Naval Institute Press, 2005), chap. 6; Deyle, *Carry Me Back*, 98–120; Toni Ahrens, *Design Makes a Difference: Shipbuilding in Baltimore, 1765–1835* (Bowie, Md.: Heritage Books, 1998), 66, 151; Works Progress Administration, Survey of Federal Archives in Louisiana, *Ship Registers and Enrollments of New Orleans, Louisiana*, vol. 4, *1831–1840* (University: Louisiana State University Library, 1942), 106.

107. *Daily National Intelligencer*, January 1, 1836, 2; *Washington (D.C.) Globe*, January 2, 1836, 1; David J. Teece, "Explicating Dynamic Capabilities: The Nature and Microfoundations of (Sustainable) Enterprise Performance," *Strategic Management Journal* 28.13 (December 2007): 1319–50; Ciarán O'Kelly and Sally Wheeler, "Internalities and the Foundations of Corporate Governance," *Social & Legal Studies* 21.4 (December 2012): 469–89; Joel M. Podolny and James N. Baron, "Resources and Relationships: Social Networks and Mobility in the Workplace," *American Sociological Review* 62.5 (October 1997): 673–93; Miller, *The Problem of Slavery as History*, chap. 4.

108. Inward Slave Manifest, New Orleans, September 28, 1838 (*Isaac Franklin*), NARA M1895, roll 8, images 277–79; Inward Slave Manifest, New Orleans, February 21, 1839 (*Isaac Franklin*), NARA M1895, roll 8, images 463–65; Inward Slave Manifest, New Orleans, October 17, 1840 (*Isaac Franklin*), NARA M1895, roll 8, images 773–76; *Richmond Enquirer*, January 2, 1836, 1; *Alexandria Phenix Gazette*, April 4, 1837, 2; *Daily National Intelligencer*, July 23, 1838, 4; *Baltimore Sun*, November 18, 1838, 4; Isabel Howell, *John Armfield of Beersheba Springs* (Beersheba, Tenn.: Beersheba Springs Historical Society, 1983), 21; Bancroft, *Slave-Trading in the Old South*, 28n.26, 91, 120n.2.

109. W. E. F. Ward, *The Royal Navy and the Slavers: The Suppression of the Atlantic Slave Trade* (New York: Pantheon Books, 1969), 156–57 (first three quotations); *New York Spectator*, May 15, 1844, 1 (fourth quotation); Outward Slave Manifest, Alexandria, October 9, 1840 (*Uncas*), New-York Historical Society SC B–05 F–16 015, http://cdm128401.cdmhost.com/cdm/landingpage/collection/p15052coll5 (accessed December 7, 2013); Inward Slave Manifest, New Orleans, November 19, 1839 (Uncas), NARA M1895, reel 8, images 517–20; WPA, *Ship Registers and Enrollments of New Orleans*, 3:106, 211, 213, 4:282, 285; "Voyages: The Trans-Atlantic Slave Trade Database," #3484, #4940, www.slavevoyages.org/tast/database/search.faces (accessed December 9, 2013); Clayton R. Barrow Jr., *America Spreads Her Sails: U.S. Seapower in the 19th Century* (Annapolis: Naval Institute Press, 1973), 96–97; Leonardo Marques, "Slave Trading in a New World: The Strategies of North American Slave Traders in the Age of Abolition," *Journal of the Early Republic* 32.2 (Summer 2012): 233–60.

110. *Richmond Enquirer*, May 29, 1847, 4; *Richmond Whig*, July 18, 1854, 4; Kelly Houston Jones, "'A Rough, Saucy Set of Hands to Manage': Slave Resistance in Arkansas," *Arkansas Historical Quarterly* 71.1 (Spring 2012): 1–21; Michael Germana, *Standards of Value: Money, Race, and Literature in America* (Iowa City: University of Iowa Press, 2009), chap. 1; William Kauffman Scarborough, *Masters of the Big House: Elite Slaveholders of the Mid-Nineteenth-Century South* (Baton Rouge: Louisiana State University Press, 2003), chap. 5.

111. Gudmestad, *A Troublesome Commerce*, 204 (first and second quotations); John Armfield to Rice C. Ballard, April 29, 1859, subseries 1.3, folder 313, Ballard Papers, UNC (third and fourth quotations); Steven Deyle, *Carry Me Back*, 86–132; Howell, *John Armfield of Beersheba Springs*, 24–38.

112. *Succession of Isaac Franklin*, 298–99 (first three quotations), 279 (fourth and fifth quotations), 284 (sixth quotation).

113. Howell, *John Armfield of Beersheba Springs*, 21; Gudmestad, "The Troubled Legacy of Isaac Franklin," 193; Gudmestad, *A Troublesome Commerce*, 201–7; Stephenson, *Isaac Franklin*, 18–19; *Succession of Isaac Franklin*, 277 (quotation).

114. *Mississippi Free Trader and Natchez Gazette*, December 30, 1846, 1 (first quotation); October 21, 1846, 4 (second quotation); Isaac Franklin to Rice C. Ballard, May 22, 1834, series 1, folder 14, Ballard Papers, UNC (third quotation).

CHAPTER 6. CHAINS OF VIOLENCE

1. Inward Slave Manifest, New Orleans, April 27, 1841 (*Orleans*), NARA M1895, roll 8, image 910 (quotation); Solomon Northup, *Twelve Years a Slave: Narrative of Solomon Northup, a Citizen of New-York, Kidnapped in Washington City in 1841, and Rescued in 1853* (Auburn, N.Y.: Derby and Miller, 1853), 17–27, 99; David Fiske, Clifford W. Brown, and Rachel Seligman, *Solomon Northup: The Complete Story of the Author of Twelve Years a Slave* (Santa Barbara: Praeger, 2013), chap. 2; David Fiske, *Solomon Northup: His Life before and after Slavery* (Ballston Spa, N.Y.: the author, 2012), 9–21; Edith Hay Wyckoff, *The Autobiography of an American Family* (Fort Edward, N.Y.: Washington County Historical Society, 2000), chap. 12.

2. Northup, *Twelve Years a Slave*, 31 (quotation); Fiske, *Solomon Northup*, 15–19, 47.

3. Fiske, *Solomon Northup*, 16–19; William W. Freehling, *Road to Disunion*, vol. 1, *Secessionists at Bay*, 1776–1854 (New York: Oxford University Press, 1990), chap. 20.

4. Fiske, *Solomon Northup*, 47.

5. Joseph C. Miller, "Credit, Captives, Collateral and Currencies: Debt, Slavery and the Financing of the Atlantic World," in *Debt and Slavery in the Mediterranean and Atlantic Worlds*, ed. Gwyn C. Campbell and Alessandro Stanziani (London: Pickering and Chatto, 2013), 105–22; Jessica M. Lepler, *The Many Panics of 1837: People, Politics, and the Creation of a Transatlantic Financial Crisis* (New York: Cambridge University Press, 2013); Walter Johnson, *River of Dark Dreams: Slavery and Empire in the Cotton Kingdom* (Cambridge: Harvard University Press, 2013); Anthony E. Kaye, "The Second Slavery: Modernity in the Nineteenth-Century South and the Atlantic World," *Journal of Southern History* 75.3 (August 2009): 627–50; Carroll Pursell, *The Machine in America: A Social History of Technology*, 2nd ed. (Baltimore: Johns Hopkins University Press, 2007), chaps. 2–4; Aaron Marrs, *Railroads in the Old South: Pursuing Progress in a Slave Society* (Baltimore: Johns Hopkins University Press, 2009), chap. 3; Nick Dyer-Witheford, *Cyber-Marx: Cycles and Circuits of Struggle in High-Technology Capitalism* (Urbana: University of Illinois Press, 1999), chap. 5.

6. William G. Thomas, *The Iron Way: Railroads, the Civil War, and the Making of Modern America* (New Haven: Yale University Press, 2011), chap. 1; John Majewski, "Toward a Social History of the Corporation: Shareholding in Pennsylvania, 1800–1840," in *The Economy of Early America: Historical Perspective and New Directions*, ed. Cathy D. Matson (State College: Pennsylvania State University Press, 2007), 294–316; Gregg D. Kimball, *American City, Southern Place: A Cultural History of Antebellum Richmond* (Athens: University of Georgia Press, 2000); Craig Miner, *A Most Magnificent Machine: America Adopts the Railroad, 1825–1862* (Lawrence:

University Press of Kansas, 2010); Frank Towers, *The Urban South and the Coming of the Civil War* (Charlottesville: University of Virginia Press, 2004), chap. 2; Alasdair Roberts, *America's First Great Depression: Economic Crisis and Political Disorder after the Panic of 1837* (Ithaca: Cornell University Press, 2012); Dale W. Tomich, *Through the Prism of Slavery: Labor, Capital, and World Economy* (Lanham, Md.: Rowman and Littlefield, 2004), chap. 3.

7. Northup, *Twelve Years a Slave*, 75.

8. *Theophilus Freeman v. W. H. Finnall et al.* (no number in original), Supreme Court of Mississippi, 1 Miss. 623, 1842 Miss. Lexis 12, 1 S.&M. 623, Lexis-Nexis Academic (accessed October 6, 2012) (quotation); Frederic Bancroft, *Slave-Trading in the Old South* (Baltimore: J. H. Furst, 1931), 26; John C. Rives, ed., *Appendix to the Congressional Globe for the Second Session, Thirty-Third Congress* (Washington, D.C., 1855), 436; Ranjay Gulati, "Network Location and Learning: The Influence of Network Resources and Firm Capabilities on Alliance Formation," *Scientific Management Journal* 20.5 (May 1999): 397–420; Birger Wernerfelt, "A Resource-Based View of the Firm," *Strategic Management Journal* 5 (April–June, 1984): 171–80; Erbon W. Wise, *The Bridwell Family in America* (Sulphur, La.: Wise Publications, 1978), 25.

9. E. A. Andrews, *Slavery and the Domestic Slave-Trade in the United States* (Boston: Light and Stearns, 1836), 164–65 (first four quotations); L. Minor Blackford, *Mine Eyes Have Seen the Glory: The Story of a Virginia Lady, Mary Berkeley Minor Blackford, 1802–1896* (Cambridge: Harvard University Press, 1954), 42 (fifth quotation); Robert H. Gudmestad, *A Troublesome Commerce: The Transformation of the Interstate Slave Trade* (Baton Rouge: Louisiana State University Press, 2003), 140.

10. Will Mackintosh, "'Ticketed Through': The Commodification of Travel in the Nineteenth Century," *Journal of the Early Republic* 32 (Spring 2012): 61–89; Frank J. Byrne, *Becoming Bourgeois: Merchant Culture in the South, 1820–1865* (Lexington: University Press of Kentucky, 2006), chaps. 1–3; Joel M. Podolny, "Market Uncertainty and the Social Character of Economic Exchange," *Administrative Science Quarterly* 39.3 (September 1994): 458–83; Eric Sheppard, "The Spaces and Times of Globalization: Place, Scale, Networks, and Positionality," *Economic Geography* 78.3 (July 2002): 307–30; Ronald S. Burt, *Structural Holes: The Social Structure of Competition* (Cambridge: Harvard University Press, 1992); Bruno Latour, *Science in Action: How to Follow Scientists and Engineers through Society* (Cambridge: Harvard University Press, 1987), chap. 4; Mark S. Granovetter, "The Strength of Weak Ties: A Network Theory Revisited," *Sociological Theory* 1 (1983): 201–33; Michel Callon and John Law, "On Interests and Their Transformation: Enrolment and Counter-Enrolment," *Social Studies of Science* 12.4 (1982): 615–25.

11. *Natchez Daily Courier*, January 7, 1839, 1; *Mississippi Free Trader and Natchez Daily Gazette*, August 14, 1838, 1; *Theophilus Freeman, for the use of George W. Barnes v. E[mile] Profilet* (no number in original), Supreme Court of Louisiana, Eastern District, New Orleans, 1845 La. Lexis 190, 11 Rob. 33; *Theophilus Freeman v. William H. Malcom et al.* (no number in original), Supreme Court of Mississippi, 19 Miss. 53, 1848 Lexis 155, 11 S. & M. 5, Lexis-Nexis Academic (accessed October 7, 2012); Johnson, *River of Dark Dreams*, chap. 1; Lewis C. Gray, *History of Agriculture in the Southern United*

States to 1860, vol. 2 (New York: Peter Smith, 1941), 1026–27; Alan L. Olmstead and Paul W. Rhode, "Biological Innovation and Productivity Growth in the Antebellum Cotton Economy," *Journal of Economic History* 68.4 (December 2008): 1123–71; Laurence J. Kotlikoff, "The Structure of Slave Prices in New Orleans, 1804–1862," *Economic Inquiry* 17.4 (October 1979): 496–518.

12. *Liberator*, December 2, 1842, 190 (quotations); Stephen Mihm, *A Nation of Counterfeiters: Capitalists, Con Men, and the Making of the United States* (Cambridge: Harvard University Press, 2007), 13–14.

13. *Liberator*, July 21, 1837, 120 (first quotation); December 2, 1842, 190 (second and third quotations); Jason Rhodes, *Somerset County, Maryland: A Brief History* (Charleston, S.C.: History Press, 2007), 52–53; Inward Slave Manifest, New Orleans, November 21, 1835 (*Ajax*), NARA M1895, roll 7, images 893–96.

14. *Daily National Intelligencer*, November 10, 1835, 4 (quotation); Northup, *Twelve Years a Slave*, 43; Winfield Hazlitt Collins, *The Domestic Slave Trade of the Southern States* (New York: Broadway, 1904), 51.

15. *Liberator*, December 2, 1842, 190; Inward Slave Manifest, New Orleans, October 21, 1839 (*Orleans*), NARA M1895, roll 8, images 511–13; Sharon Ann Holt, "Symbol, Memory, and Service: Resistance and Family Formation in Nineteenth-Century African America," in *Working toward Freedom: Slave Society and Domestic Economy in the American South*, ed. Larry E. Hudson (Rochester: University of Rochester Press, 1994), 192–210.

16. Northup, *Twelve Years a Slave*, 41 (quotation); Bancroft, *Slave-Trading in the Old South*, 56–57; Walter Johnson, *Soul by Soul: Life inside the Antebellum Slave Market* (Cambridge: Harvard University Press, 1999), 161.

17. Northup, *Twelve Years a Slave*, 38 (first quotation); Inward Slave Manifest, New Orleans, April 27, 1841 (*Orleans*), NARA M1895, roll 8, image 910 (second quotation).

18. Northup, *Twelve Years a Slave*, 50–54; Lawrence L. Langer, *Versions of Survival: The Holocaust and the Human Spirit* (Albany: State University of New York Press, 1982), 100; Ben Schiller, "US Slavery's Diaspora: Black Atlantic History at the Crossroads of 'Race,' Enslavement, and Colonisation," *Slavery and Abolition* 32.2 (July 2011): 199–212; Annette Gordon-Reed, *The Hemingses of Monticello: An American Family* (New York: W. W. Norton, 2008), chap. 4; William W. Freehling, *The Road to Disunion*, vol. 2, *Secessionists Triumphant, 1854–1861* (New York: Oxford University Press, 2007), 222–27.

19. Northup, *Twelve Years a Slave*, 56.

20. "Rates of Fare for the Transportation of Passengers on the Richmond, Fredericksburg and Potomac Railroad," January 27, 1837, cited in John B. Mordecai, *A Brief History of the Richmond, Fredericksburg and Potomac Railroad* (Richmond: Old Dominion Press, 1941), 12 (quotation); Sarah H. Gordon, *Passage to Union: How the Railroads Transformed American Life, 1829–1929* (Chicago: Ivan R. Dee, 1996), chap. 7; Mackintosh, "'Ticketed Through.'"

21. *Twenty-Second Annual Report of the Board of Public Works to the General Assembly of Virginia* (Richmond: Thomas Ritchie, 1838), 90–92; *Baltimore Patriot*, December 4, 1829, 2; Mordecai, *A Brief History of the Richmond, Fredericksburg and Potomac*

Railroad, 10, 17, 20, 28, 37; Marrs, *Railroads in the Old South*, chap. 3; Edward E. Baptist, "Toxic Debt, Liar Loans, Collateralized and Securitized Human Beings, and the Panic of 1837," in *Capitalism Takes Command: The Social Transformation of Nineteenth-Century America*, ed. Michael Zakim and Gary J. Kornblith (Chicago: University of Chicago Press, 2012), 82; James D. Dilts, *The Great Road: The Building of the Baltimore and Ohio, the Nation's First Railroad, 1828–1853* (Stanford: Stanford University Press, 1993), 303; Richard Boyse Osborne, *Professional Biography of Moncure Robinson, Civil Engineer* (Philadelphia: J. B. Lippincott, 1889); Darwin H. Stapleton, "Moncure Robinson: Railroad Engineer, 1828–1840," in *Benjamin Henry Latrobe & Moncure Robinson: The Engineer as Agent of Technology Transfer*, ed. Barbara E. Benson (Wilmington, Del.: Eleutherian Mills–Hagley Foundation, 1975), 33–60.

22. Mordecai, *A Brief History of the Richmond, Fredericksburg and Potomac Railroad*, 17 (quotation); Calvin Schermerhorn, *Money over Mastery, Family over Freedom: Slavery in the Antebellum Upper South* (Baltimore: Johns Hopkins University Press, 2011), chap. 5; Marrs, *Railroads in the Old South*, 5.

23. Thomas, *The Iron Way*, chap. 1; William G. Thomas, "'Swerve Me?': The South, Railroads, and the Rush to Modernity," in *The Old South's Modern Worlds: Slavery, Region, and Nation in the Age of Progress*, ed. L. Diane Barnes, Brian Schoen, and Frank Towers (New York: Oxford University Press, 2011), 166–88; Maximilian Rabl and Johann Stocklausner, *Österreichische Personenwaggons: Entwicklung, Konstruktion und Betreib seit 1832* (Vienna: Josef Otto Slezak, 1982); Anthony J. Bianculli, *Trains and Technology: The American Railroad in the Nineteenth Century*, vol. 3, *Track and Structures* (Cranbury, N.J.: Associated University Presses, 2003), 87–88.

24. Northup, *Twelve Years a Slave*, 58 (quotation); *Richmond Whig*, March 5, 1841, 1; Mordecai, *A Brief History of the Richmond, Fredericksburg and Potomac Railroad*, 10, 17, 26.

25. Northup, *Twelve Years a Slave*, 66 (first quotation), 58 (subsequent quotations); T. Tyler Potterfield, *Nonesuch Place: A History of the Richmond Landscape* (Charleston, S.C.: History Press, 2009), 45–49.

26. Northup, *Twelve Years a Slave*, 60.

27. Ibid., 61.

28. Ibid., 61–63 (quotations); Inward Slave Manifest, New Orleans, May 1, 1841 (*Orleans*), NARA M1895, roll 8, image 919.

29. Northup, *Twelve Years a Slave*, 62 (quotation); Inward Slave Manifest, New Orleans, April 27, 1841 (*Orleans*), NARA M1895, roll 8, image 910.

30. Northup, *Twelve Years a Slave*, 62–63 (quotations); Inward Slave Manifest, New Orleans, April 27, 1841 (*Orleans*), NARA M1895, roll 8, image 910.

31. Jonathan Levy, *Freaks of Fortune: The Emerging World of Capitalism and Risk in America* (Cambridge: Harvard University Press, 2012), chap. 2; Phillip D. Troutman, "Grapevine in the Slave Market: African American Geopolitical Literacy and the 1841 Creole Revolt," in *The Chattel Principle: Internal Slave Trade in the Americas*, ed. Walter Johnson (New Haven: Yale University Press, 2004), 209–10.

32. Northup, *Twelve Years a Slave*, 63 (quotations); Works Progress Administration, Survey of Federal Archives in Louisiana, *Ship Registers and Enrollments of New*

Orleans, Louisiana, vol. 3, *1831–1840* (University: Louisiana State University Library, 1942), 218–19; Works Progress Administration, Survey of Federal Archives in Louisiana, *Ship Registers and Enrollments of New Orleans, Louisiana*, vol. 4, *1841–1850* (University: Louisiana State University Library, 1942), 217; Samuel Hazard, ed., *Hazard's United States Commercial and Statistical Register*, vol. 2 (Philadelphia: William F. Geddes, 1840), 15.

33. *Liberator*, December 2, 1842, 190; Inward Slave Manifest, New Orleans, January 19–22, 1841 (*Orleans*), NARA M1895, roll 8, images 1104–8; Inward Slave Manifest, New Orleans, October 21, 1839 (*Orleans*), NARA M1895, roll 8, images 511–15; *New-York Spectator*, December 2, 1839, 1; Inward Slave Manifest, New Orleans, January 19–22, 1841 (*Creole*), NARA M1895, roll 8, images 954–56; Troutman, "Grapevine in the Slave Market," 203–33; Virginius Dabney, *Richmond: The Story of a City* (Garden City, N.Y.: Doubleday, 1976), 136.

34. Inward Slave Manifest, New Orleans, April 27, 1841 (*Orleans*), NARA M1895, roll 8, image 910 (quotations); Johnson, *Soul by Soul*, 12.

35. *Richmond Whig*, August 11, 1843, 3 (quotation); *Baltimore Sun*, November 19, 1838, 2; October 3, 1840, 2; *Baltimore Patriot*, December 14, 1831, 1; *New Orleans Daily Picayune*, March 24, 1840, 3; Inward Slave Manifest, New Orleans, October 25, 1843 (*Bachelor*), NARA M1895, roll 9, images 643–44; Inward Slave Manifest, New Orleans, November 29, 1843 (*Josephine*), NARA M1895, roll 9, image 595; Inward Slave Manifest, October 15, 1840 (*Orleans*), NARA M1895, roll 8, images 531–35; Inward Slave Manifest, New Orleans, October 21, 1843 (*Orleans*), NARA M1895, roll 9, images 624–25; Inward Slave Manifest, New Orleans, November 26, 1838 (*Orleans*), NARA M1895, roll 8, images 311–17; Richard McMillan, "A Journey of Lost Souls: New Orleans to Natchez Slave Trade of 1840," *Gulf Coast Historical Review* 13.2 (1998): 53; H. K. Ellyson, *Richmond Directory and Business Advertiser for 1856* (Richmond: H. K. Ellyson, 1856), 224; Saul S. Friedman, *Jews and the American Slave Trade* (Piscataway, N.J.: Transaction, 1997), 218.

36. Northup, *Twelve Years a Slave*, 71 (quotation); James Walvin, *The Zong: A Massacre, the Law and the End of Slavery* (New Haven: Yale University Press, 2011); Marcus Rediker, *The Slave Ship: A Human History* (New York: Viking, 2007).

37. Northup, *Twelve Years a Slave*, 66–67 (quotations); Saidiya V. Hartman, *Scenes of Subjection: Terror, Slavery, and Self-Making in Nineteenth-Century America* (New York: Oxford University Press, 1997), chaps. 2–3; Carol Wilson, *Freedom at Risk: The Kidnapping of Free Blacks in America, 1800–1865* (Lexington: University of Kentucky Press, 1994); Inward Slave Manifest, New Orleans, May 1, 1841 (*Orleans*), NARA M1895, roll 8, image 919.

38. Northup, *Twelve Years a Slave*, 65–67 (quotations); Inward Slave Manifest, New Orleans, May 1, 1841 (*Orleans*), NARA M1895, roll 8, image 919; William I. Bowditch, *Slavery and the Constitution* (Boston: Robert F. Wallcut, 1849), 88; Hartman, *Scenes of Subjection*, 87.

39. *Thomas McCargo v. the New Orleans Insurance Company*, 1845 La. Lexis 122, 10 Rob. 202, Lexis-Nexis Academic (accessed April 29, 2011); Levy, *Freaks of Fortune*, chap. 2; Walter Johnson, "White Lies: Human Property and Domestic Slavery aboard the Slave

Ship *Creole*," *Atlantic Studies* 5.2 (August 2008): 241–42; Troutman, "Grapevine in the Slave Market"; Eric Robert Taylor, *If We Must Die: Shipboard Insurrections in the Era of the Atlantic Slave Trade* (Baton Rouge: Louisiana State University Press, 2006), 147–51.

40. Speech of Henry Stanton, in *Proceedings of the New-England Anti-Slavery Convention: Held in Boston, on the 27th, 28th, and 29th of May, 1834* (Boston: Garrison and Knapp, 1834), 33.

41. Northup, *Twelve Years a Slave*, 67; Stephanie Smallwood, "African Guardians, European Slave Ships, and the Changing Dynamics of Power in the Early Modern Atlantic," *William and Mary Quarterly* 64.4 (October 2007): 679–716.

42. Northup, *Twelve Years a Slave*, 66–67.

43. Ibid., 68.

44. Benjamin Drew, *A North-Side View of Slavery; or, The Narratives of Fugitives in Canada. Related by Themselves, with an Account of the History and Condition of the Coloured Population of Upper Canada* (Boston: J. P. Jewett, 1856), 83–84 (quotations); Northup, *Twelve Years a Slave*, 68–71; Emma Christopher, *Slave Ship Sailors and Their Captive Cargoes* (Cambridge: Cambridge University Press, 2006), chap. 1.

45. Northup, *Twelve Years a Slave*, 71–72.

46. Ibid., 74 (quotation); Christopher, *Slave Ship Sailors and Their Captive Cargoes*, 33; Daniel Vickers and Vince Walsh, *Young Men and the Sea: Yankee Seafarers in the Age of Sail* (New Haven: Yale University Press, 2005), chap. 6; *Army and Navy Chronicle*, July 30, 1835, 248; Hyman G. Weintraub, *Andrew Furuseth: Emancipator of the Seamen* (Berkeley: University of California Press, 1959), chap. 1

47. Inward Slave Manifest, New Orleans, May 1, 1841 (*Orleans*), NARA M1895, roll 8, image 919 (first two quotations); Northup, *Twelve Years a Slave*, 75 (third quotation); Outward Slave Manifest, New Orleans, June 7, 1841 (*Orleans*), NARA M1895, roll 23, images 196–97; Fiske, Brown, and Seligman, *Solomon Northup*, 90–92.

48. Northup, *Twelve Years a Slave*, 75–76.

49. *New Orleans Times-Picayune*, May 11, 1841, 2.

50. James Davidson, "A Journey through the South in 1836: Diary of James D. Davison," ed. Herbert A. Kellar, *Journal of Southern History* 1.3 (August 1935): 358.

51. Ibid., 357–58 (first quotation); Northup, *Twelve Years a Slave*, 76 (second quotation); Maurie D. McInnes, *Slaves Waiting for Sale: Abolitionist Art and the American Slave Trade* (Chicago: University of Chicago Press, 2011), 160–62; Judith Kelleher Schafer, *Slavery, the Civil Law, and the Supreme Court of Louisiana* (Baton Rouge: Louisiana State University Press, 1994), 137; Robert Sobel, *The Money Manias: The Eras of Great Speculation in America, 1770–1970* (Frederick, Md.: Beard Books, 2000), 94–96; Steven Deyle, *Carry Me Back: The Domestic Slave Trade in American Life* (New York: Oxford University Press, 2005), 323n.118; Gudmestad, *A Troublesome Commerce*, 31; Bancroft, *Slave-Trading in the Old South*, 277n.26, 314.

52. Northup, *Twelve Years a Slave*, 78–79 (quotations); Luke 1:3; Acts 1:1.

53. Northup, *Twelve Years a Slave*, 79.

54. Ibid., 79–80 (quotations); McInnes, *Slaves Waiting for Sale*, 164; Leonard V. Huber, *New Orleans: A Pictorial History from the Earliest Times to the Present Day* (1971; repr., Gretna, La.: Pelican, 1991), 79, 83–84.

55. Adolphe Mazureau, vol. 75, Act 75, 1841, NONA.

56. Northup, *Twelve Years a Slave*, 81 (quotations); Kotlikoff, "The Structure of Slave Prices in New Orleans," 498; 1870 U.S. Census, Baton Rouge, Ward 9, East Baton Rouge, La., roll M593_512, p. 158B [manuscript page 74], image 320; Family History Library Film 552011, www.ancestry.com (accessed October 29, 2012).

57. Inward Slave Manifest, New Orleans, April 27, 1841 (*Orleans*), NARA M1895, roll 8, image 910; *New Orleans Times-Picayune*, June 4, 1841, 2; Jonathan B. Pritchett and Myeong-Su Yun, "The In-Hospital Mortality Rates of Slaves and Freemen: Evidence from Touro Infirmary, New Orleans, Louisiana, 1855–1860," *Explorations in Economic History* 46 (April 2009): 241–52; Richard C. Wade, *Slavery in the Cities: The South, 1820–1860* (New York: Oxford University Press, 1964), 135; Jennifer Lee Carrell, *The Speckled Monster: A Historical Tale of Battling Smallpox* (New York: Penguin, 2004), chap. 3.

58. Northup, *Twelve Years a Slave*, 85.

59. Davidson, "A Journey through the South in 1836," 358.

60. Northup, *Twelve Years a Slave*, 86–87 (first and third quotations); Executive Committee of the American Anti-Slavery Society, *Slavery and the Internal Slave Trade in the United States of North America* (London: Thomas Ward, 1841), 67 (second quotation).

61. *New-York Gazette*, October 12, 1812, 2 (quotation); Johnson, *Soul by Soul*, 114; Ivan Goncharov, *Oblomov*, trans. Natalie Duddington (1859; repr., New York: Everyman's Library, 1992).

62. *Mississippi Free Trader*, October 16, 1850, 2 (quotation); Northup, *Twelve Years a Slave*, 87–88; Schermerhorn, *Money over Mastery, Family over Freedom*, chap. 3; Ben Schiller, "Selling Themselves: Slavery, Survival, and the Path of Least Resistance," *49th Parallel* 23 (Summer 2009), www.49thparallel.bham.ac.uk/back/issue23/schiller.pdf (accessed November 22, 2013).

63. Joshua D. Rothman, *Flush Times and Fever Dreams: A Story of Capitalism and Slavery in the Age of Jackson* (Athens: University of Georgia Press, 2012); Adam Rothman, *Slave Country: American Expansion and the Origins of the Deep South* (Cambridge: Harvard University Press, 2005); Edward Luttwak, *Turbo-Capitalism: Winners and Losers in the Global Economy* (New York: HarperCollins, 1999), chap. 7; William M. Lytle and Forrest R. Holdcamper, *Merchant Steam Vessels of the United States, 1790–1868*, ed. C. Bradford Mitchell with Kenneth R. Hall (Staten Island: Steamship Historical Society of America, 1975), 187.

64. Robert Gudmestad, *Steamboats and the Rise of the Cotton Kingdom* (Baton Rouge: Louisiana State University Press, 2011); Johnson, *River of Dark Dreams*, chap. 3.

65. *New Orleans Times-Picayune*, March 20, 1841, 3; May 7, 1841, 2; June 20, 1841, 2; December 8, 1841, 2; Gudmestad, *Steamboats and the Rise of the Cotton Kingdom*, chap. 7.

66. Northup, *Twelve Years a Slave* (quotation), 293; Johnson, *River of Dark Dreams*, chaps. 3, 7, 9–10.

67. *New Orleans Times-Picayune*, August 7, 1838, 2 (quotations); Marrs, *Railroads in the Old South*, 4–5; Elizabeth Kilbourne Dart, "Working on the Railroad: The West

Feliciana, 1828–1842," in *Antebellum Louisiana, 1830–1860, Part A: Life and Labor*, ed. Carolyn DeLatte (Lafayette: Center for Louisiana Studies, 2004), 443–64.

68. *New Orleans Jeffersonian Republican*, December 13, 1845, 4 (quotations); *James Drummond v. The Commissioners of the Clinton and Port Hudson Railway Company* (1844) (no number in original), Supreme Court of Louisiana, Eastern District, New Orleans, 1844 La. Lexis 391, 7 Rob. 234, Lexis-Nexis Academic (accessed November 23, 2012); Charles Bowen, *The American Almanac and Repository of Useful Knowledge for the Year 1837* (Boston: Charles Bowen, 1836), 323; Franz von Gerstner, *Early American Railroads: Franz Anton Ritter von Gerstner's Die innern Communicationen (1842–1843)*, ed. Frederick C. Gamst, trans. David Diephouse and John C. Decker (Stanford: Stanford University Press, 1997), 762; Marrs, *Railroads in the Old South*, 4–5; Lawrence E. Estaville Jr., "A Small Contribution: Louisiana's Short Rural Railroads in the Civil War," *Louisiana History: The Journal of the Louisiana Historical Association* 18.1 (Winter 1977): 87–103.

69. *New-Orleans Commercial Bulletin*, April 6, 1836, 2; Miller, "Credit, Captives, Collateral, and Currencies"; Merl E. Reed, "Government Investment and Economic Growth: Louisiana's Ante Bellum Railroads," *Journal of Southern History* 28.2 (May 1962): 183–201.

70. *Fayetteville (N.C.) Observer*, January 19, 1837, quoted in Miner, *A Most Magnificent Machine*, 67 (quotations; emphasis in original); *New-Orleans Commercial Bulletin*, October 29, 1835, 2; *Acts Passed at the First Session of the Twelfth Legislature of the State of Louisiana* (New Orleans: Jerome Bayon, 1835), 39–52; Ann Patton Malone, *Sweet Chariot: Slave Family and Household Structure in Nineteenth-Century Louisiana* (Chapel Hill: University of North Carolina Press, 1992), 305.

71. A. A. Parker, *Trip to the West and Texas* (Concord, N.H.: White and Fisher, 1835), 123 (first quotation); Northup, *Twelve Years a Slave*, 155 (second and third quotations); Richard P. Tucker, *Insatiable Appetite: The United States and the Ecological Degradation of the Tropical World* (Lanham, Md.: Rowman and Littlefield, 2007), chap. 5; Louis C. Hunter, *Steamboats on the Western Rivers: An Economic and Technological History* (Cambridge: Harvard University Press, 1949), chap. 7.

72. Northup, *Twelve Years a Slave*, 159 (quotations); Robbie Ethridge, *From Chicaza to Chickasaw: The European Invasion and the Transformation of the Mississippian World, 1540–1715* (Chapel Hill: University of North Carolina Press, 2010); J. Daniel Rogers and George Sabo III, "Caddo," in *Handbook of North American Indians*, vol. 14, *Southeast*, ed. Raymond Fogelson and William C. Sturtevant (Washington, D.C.: Smithsonian Institution, 2004), 616–31; Frank H. Gille, ed., *Encyclopedia of Texas Indians*, vol. 1 (St. Clair Shores, Mich.: Somerset, 1999), 91–92.

73. Northup, *Twelve Years a Slave*, 92; Walter M. Lowrey, "The Red," in *The Rivers and Bayous of Louisiana*, ed. Edwin Adams Davis (Baton Rouge: Louisiana Research Association, 1968), 53.

74. Gudmestad, *Steamboats and the Rise of the Cotton Kingdom*, 131–32; LeeAnna Kieth, *The Colfax Massacre: The Untold Story of Black Power, White Terror, and the Death of Reconstruction* (New York: Oxford University Press, 2008), 4; Lytle and Holdcamper, *Merchant Steam Vessels of the United States*, 157; Benjamin Brad Dison, "The

Steamboat's Contribution to the Development of Shreveport's Railroads, 1840–1890," *North Louisiana History* 42.3/4 (Summer/Fall 2011): 113–28.

75. Northup, *Twelve Years a Slave*, 98–99; Trish Loughran, *The Republic in Print: Print Culture in the Age of U.S. Nation Building, 1770–1870* (New York: Columbia University Press, 2007), 399–404.

76. Northup, *Twelve Years a Slave*, 97 (quotations); Johnson, *River of Dark Dreams*, chap. 6.

77. Thomas Carlyle, "Signs of the Times," *Edinburgh Review* 98 (June 1829): 442 (quotation); I. T. King, "Political Economy and the 'Laws of Beauty': Aesthetics, Economics, and Materialism in Marx," in *Karl Marx's Social and Political Thought*, ed. Bob Jessop and Russell Wheatley (London: Routledge, 1999), 334–46.

78. Karl Marx, *Karl Marx on America and the Civil War*, ed. Saul K. Padover (New York: McGraw-Hill, 1972), 36 (quotations); Walter Johnson, "The Pedestal and the Veil: Rethinking the Capitalism/Slavery Question," *Journal of the Early Republic* 24 (Summer 2004): 301–10.

79. Thomas Carlyle, *The Works of Thomas Carlyle*, vol. 30, *Critical and Miscellaneous Essays, V*, ed. Henry Duff Traill (New York: Cambridge University Press, 2010), 6 (quotation); W. Caleb McDaniel, *The Problem of Democracy in the Age of Slavery: Garrisonian Abolitionists and Transatlantic Reform* (Baton Rouge: Louisiana State University Press, 2013), chap. 3; Scott Reynolds Nelson, *A Nation of Deadbeats: An Uncommon History of America's Financial Disasters* (New York: Knopf, 2012), chap. 7; Ralph Jessop, "Shooting the Enlightenment: A Brave New Era for Carlyle?" in *Thomas Carlyle Resartus: Reappraising Carlyle's Contribution to the Philosophy of History, Political Theory, and Cultural Criticism*, ed. Paul E. Kerry and Marylu Hill (Madison, N.J.: Fairleigh Dickinson University Press, 2010), 62–84; Loughran, *The Republic in Print*, chap. 7.

80. Susan Schulten, *Mapping the Nation: History and Cartography in Nineteenth-Century America* (Chicago: University of Chicago Press, 2012), chaps. 4–5; George M. Fredrickson, *Racism: A Short History* (Princeton: Princeton University Press, 2002), chap. 2; Edward E. Baptist, "'Cuffy,' 'Fancy Maids,' and 'One-Eyed Men': Rape, Commodification, and the Domestic Slave Trade in the United States," *American Historical Review* 106.5 (December 2001): 1619–50; Walter Johnson, "The Slave Trader, the White Slave, and the Politics of Racial Determination in the 1850s," *Journal of American History* 87.1 (June 2000): 13–38; A. A. M. van der Linden, *A Revolt against Liberalism: American Radical Historians, 1959–1976* (Amsterdam: Rodopi B.V., 1996), chaps. 13–14; William W. Freehling, *The Reintegration of American History: Slavery and the Civil War* (New York: Oxford University Press, 1994), chap. 5.

81. Kenneth Pomeranz, *The Great Divergence: China, Europe, and the Making of the Modern World Economy* (Princeton: Princeton University Press, 2001), chap. 6; Georg Borgstrom, *The Hungry Planet: The Modern World at the Edge of Famine* (New York: Macmillan, 1965), chap. 5; Lepler, *The Many Panics of 1837*; Deyle, *Carry Me Back*, chap. 2; Amy Kaplan, *The Anarchy of Empire in the Making of U.S. Culture* (Cambridge: Harvard University Press, 2002), chap 1.

82. Northup, *Twelve Years a Slave*, 310 (quotations); Fiske, Brown, and Seligman, *Solomon Northup*, 191n.61; *John Petway v. John Goodin and another* (no number in original),

Supreme Court of Louisiana, Eastern District, New Orleans, 1846, La. Lexis 227, 12 Rob. 445, Lexis-Nexis Academic (accessed October 12, 2012).

83. *The Bank of Kentucky v. Conner et al.*, Supreme Court of Louisiana, New Orleans, 4 La. Ann. 365, 1849 La. Lexis 223 (1849); *Theophilus Freeman, for the use of George W. Barnes, v. E. Profilet*; *Courrier de la Louisiane*, January 9, 1845; *New Orleans Times-Picayune*, July 3, 1845, 2.

84. *Mississippi Free Trader*, June 16, 1852, 3 (quotations); *New Orleans Times-Picayune*, August 2, 1851, 2; *State v. Sarah Connor, f.w.c.* Supreme Court of Louisiana, New Orleans, 7 La. Ann. 379, 1852 La. Lexis 186; *Theophilus Freeman v. His Creditors*, Supreme Court of Louisiana, New Orleans, 15 La. Ann. 397, 1860 La. Lexis 724 (1860), Lexis-Nexis Academic (accessed November 28, 2012).

85. Northup, *Twelve Years a Slave*, 312; Templeman and Goodwin Account Book, M–3508, UNC; Fiske, Brown, and Seligman, *Solomon Northup*, 108–10; 125–41; McInnes, *Slaves Waiting for Sale*, chap. 4.

86. Northup, *Twelve Years a Slave*, 319–20 (quotations); Fiske, *Solomon Northup*, 25–34.

CHAPTER 7. MACHINES OF EMPIRE

1. Sven Beckert, *The Monied Metropolis: New York City and the Consolidation of the American Bourgeoisie* (New York: Cambridge University Press, 2001), 20–24; James P. Baughman, *Charles Morgan and the Development of Southern Transportation* (Nashville: Vanderbilt University Press, 1968); Richard Y. Francaviglia, *From Sail to Steam: Four Centuries of Texas Maritime History, 1500–1900* (Austin: University of Texas Press, 1998), chaps. 5–6.

2. Michael Tadman, *Speculators and Slaves: Masters, Traders, and Slaves in the Old South* (Madison: University of Wisconsin Press, 1996), 12; C. Allan Jones, *Texas Roots: Agriculture and Rural Life before the Civil War* (College Station: Texas A&M University Press, 2005), chap. 9.

3. Works Progress Administration, Survey of Federal Archives in Louisiana, *Ship Registers and Enrollments of New Orleans, Louisiana*, vol. 5, *1851–1860* (University: Louisiana State University Library, 1942), 178; Airbus S.A.S., "Dimensions and Key Data" for Airbus A330–300, www.airbus.com/aircraftfamilies/passengeraircraft/a330family/a330–300/specifications/ (accessed November 27, 2013); *List of American-Flag Merchant Vessels That Received Certificates of Enrollment, Port of New York, 1789–1867*, vol. 2 (Washington, D.C.: Government Services Administration, 1968), 478; Outward Slave Manifest, New Orleans, January 6–7, 1853 (*Mexico*), NARA M1895, roll 26, images 999–1006, 1009–37; *New Orleans Daily Picayune*, February 5, 1853, 2; Ira Berlin, *The Making of African America: The Four Great Migrations* (New York: Viking, 2010), chaps. 1–3; Louis C. Hunter, *Steamboats on the Western Rivers: An Economic and Technological History* (Cambridge: Harvard University Press, 1949), 606–9; Abigail Curlee, "A Study of Texas Slave Plantations, 1822 to 1865" (PhD diss., University of Texas, 1932), 47–48.

4. T. Edward Bowdich, "Mission from the Cape Coast Castle to Ashantee, with a Statistical Account of that Kingdom, and Geographical Notices of Other Parts of the

Interior of Africa," *Quarterly Review* 22.44 (January 1820): 298 (first quotation); *New Orleans Daily Picayune*, March 15, 1854, 1 (second and third quotations); Steven Deyle, *Carry Me Back: The Domestic Slave Trade in American Life* (New York: Oxford University Press, 2005), chap. 1.

5. 1860 U.S. Census, Fort Bend, Tex., roll M653_1294, p. 376, image 246, www.ancestry. com (accessed February 10, 2011); Outward Slave Manifest, New Orleans, January 27, 28, 31, February 1, 1854 (*Mexico*), NARA M1895, roll 28, images 177–211.

6. 1860 U.S. Census, Fayette County, Tex., roll M653_1294, p. 324, image 136; p. 356, image 201; 1860 U.S. Census, Slave Schedule, Fayette County, Tex., image 36, 47, www.ancestry.com (accessed February 10, 2011).

7. Curlee, "A Study of Texas Slave Plantations," 50 (quotation); Walter Johnson, *Soul by Soul: Life Inside the Antebellum Slave Market* (Cambridge: Harvard University Press, 1999), 45–46.

8. *New Orleans Daily Picayune*, February 10, 1854, 1; February 15, 1854, 5; William M. Lytle and Forrest R. Holdcamper, *Merchant Steam Vessels of the United States, 1790–1868*, ed. C. Bradford Mitchell with Kenneth R. Hall (Staten Island: Steamship Historical Society of America, 1975), 33, 131, 170, 210; Outward Slave Manifest, New Orleans, February 2–4, 1854 (*Louisiana*), NARA M1895, roll 28, images 214–30, 232–33; Outward Slave Manifest, New Orleans, February 7–9, 1854 (*Perseverance*), NARA M1895, roll 28, images 234–51; Outward Slave Manifest, New Orleans, February 13, 1854 (*Charles Morgan*), NARA M1895, roll 28, images 252–54; Outward Slave Manifest, New Orleans, February 13–14, 1854 (*Mexico*), NARA M1895, roll 28, images 255–66.

9. John F. O'Sullivan, "The Great Nation of Futurity," *United States Magazine and Democratic Review* 6.23 (November 1839): 426 (quotation; emphasis in original); Steven E. Woodworth, *Manifest Destinies: America's Westward Expansion and the Road to Civil War* (New York: Knopf, 2011); Alfred F. Young, *The Democratic Republicans of New York: The Origins, 1763–1797* (Chapel Hill: University of North Carolina Press, 1967).

10. Julian Go, *Patterns of Empire: The British and American Empires, 1688 to the Present* (New York: Cambridge University Press, 2011); Thomas R. Hietala, *Manifest Design: American Exceptionalism and Empire* (1985; repr., Ithaca: Cornell University Press, 2003), chap. 6; Peter S. Onuf, *Jefferson's Empire: The Language of American Nationhood* (Charlottesville: University Press of Virginia, 2000); Baughman, *Charles Morgan and the Development of Southern Transportation*, 113–16, 245–46; Joseph C. Miller, *Way of Death: Merchant Capitalism and the Angolan Slave Trade, 1730–1830* (Madison: University of Wisconsin Press, 1988), chaps. 13–19; P. C. Emmer, *The Dutch Slave Trade, 1500–1850*, trans. Chris Emery (Oxford: Berghahn Books, 2006), chaps. 2, 6; Kenneth Morgan, *Slavery, Atlantic Trade, and the British Economy, 1660–1800* (Cambridge: Cambridge University Press, 2000); Alan J. Singer, *New York Slavery: Time to Teach the Truth* (Albany: State University of New York Press, 2008), chap. 9; Douglas C. North, *Institutions, Institutional Change, and Economic Performance* (Cambridge: Cambridge University Press, 1990), introduction; Beckert, *The Monied Metropolis*, chap. 7; Harold D. Woodman, *King Cotton and His Retainers: Financing and Marketing the Cotton Crop of the South, 1800–1925* (Lexington: University of

Kentucky Press, 1968), chaps. 12–14; Stephen Fox, *Transatlantic: Samuel Cunard, Isambard Brunel, and the Great Atlantic Steamships* (New York: HarperCollins, 2003), chap. 1; Robert G. Albion, *The Rise of New York Port, 1815–1860* (1939; repr., Hamden, Conn.: Archon Books, 1961), 254.

11. David J. Teece, *Dynamic Capabilities and Strategic Management: Organizing for Innovation and Growth* (New York: Oxford University Press, 2009); Baughman, *Charles Morgan and the Development of Southern Transportation*, chaps. 1–6.

12. *Charleston Southern Patriot*, February 20, 1838, 2 (quotation); Works Progress Administration, Survey of Federal Archives in Louisiana, *Ship Registers and Enrollments of New Orleans, Louisiana*, vol. 3, *1831–1840* (University: Louisiana State University Library, 1942), 154; John K. Mahon, *History of the Second Seminole War, 1835–1842* (Gainesville: University of Florida Press, 1967).

13. Roger G. Kennedy, *Cotton and Conquest: How the Plantation System Acquired Texas* (Norman: University of Oklahoma Press, 2013); Francaviglia, *From Sail to Steam*, chap. 5; David G. Surdam, "The Antebellum Texas Cattle Trade across the Gulf of Mexico," *Southwestern Historical Quarterly* 100.4 (April 1997): 477–92; Edward L. Miller, *New Orleans and the Texas Revolution* (College Station: Texas A&M University Press, 2004).

14. *DeBow's Review*, February 1847, 98 (quotations); Michael F. Holt, *The Fate of Their Country: Politicians, Slavery Extension, and the Coming of the Civil War* (New York: Hill and Wang, 2004), chap. 1; Tom Chaffin, *Fatal Glory: Narciso López and the First Clandestine U.S. War against Cuba* (Charlottesville: University Press of Virginia, 1996); William W. Freehling, *The Reintegration of American History: Slavery and the Civil War* (New York: Oxford University Press, 1994), chap. 8.

15. Outward Slave Manifest, New Orleans, January 16, 1847 (*Palmetto*), NARA M1895, roll 24, images 576–77; *Victoria (Tex.) Advocate*, October 10, 1850, 2–3; Francaviglia, *From Sail to Steam*, chap. 5; Baughman, *Charles Morgan and the Development of Southern Transportation*, 46–47, 69, 74, 88; WPA, *Ship Registers and Enrollments of New Orleans*, 3:44.

16. Gary Clayton Anderson, *The Conquest of Texas: Ethnic Cleansing in the Promised Land, 1820–1875* (Norman: University of Oklahoma Press, 2005), chaps. 11–12; Baughman, *Charles Morgan and the Development of Southern Transportation*, chap. 1.

17. WPA, *Ship Registers and Enrollments of New Orleans*, 3:59, 64, 75, 96, 115, 119, 146, 154; Inward Slave Manifest, New Orleans, February 9, 1838 (*Adelaide*), NARA M1895, roll 8, image 198; Inward Slave Manifest, New Orleans, October 8, 1834 (*Washington*), NARA M1895, roll 7, image 434; Francaviglia, *From Sail to Steam*, 128.

18. Fox, *Transatlantic*, chap. 7; Christopher F. Jones, *Routes of Power: Energy and Modern America* (Cambridge: Harvard University Press, 2014); Donna J. Souza, *The Persistence of Sail in the Age of Steam: Underwater Archaeological Evidence from the Dry Tortugas* (New York: Plenum Press, 1998); Patricia Bellis Bixel, *Sailing Ship Elissa* (College Station: Texas A&M University Press, 1998); C. Knick Harley, "Ocean Freight Rates and Productivity, 1740–1913: The Primacy of Mechanical Invention Reaffirmed," *Journal of Economic History* 48.4 (December 1988): 851–76; Alfred D. Chandler Jr., "Anthracite Coal and the Beginnings of the Industrial Revolution in the United

States," *Business History Review* 46.2 (Summer 1972): 141–81; Robert Gudmestad, *Steamboats and the Rise of the Cotton Kingdom* (Baton Rouge: Louisiana State University Press, 2011), chap. 6.

19. *Telegraph and Texas Register*, December 27, 1843, www.texasslaveryproject.org (accessed December 17, 2013) (quotation); Outward Slave Manifest, New Orleans, December 15–16, 1843 (*Neptune*), NARA M1895, roll 23, images 871–80; Outward Slave Manifest, New Orleans, December 14, 1843 (*Rover*), NARA M1895, roll 23, image 867; Works Progress Administration, Survey of Federal Archives in Louisiana, *Ship Registers and Enrollments of New Orleans, Louisiana*, vol. 4, *1841–1850* (University: Louisiana State University Library, 1942), 205, 249; Herbert T. Hoover, "Ashbel Smith on Currency and Finance in the Republic of Texas," *Southwestern Historical Quarterly* 71 (January 1968): 419–24; Francaviglia, *From Sail to Steam*, 130; WPA, *Ship Registers and Enrollments of New Orleans*, 3:154; Baughman, *Charles Morgan and the Development of Southern Transportation*, 112–13.

20. Baughman, *Charles Morgan and the Development of Southern Transportation*, 57–69.

21. Ibid., chap. 6, app. 3.

22. *Civilian and Galveston Gazette*, January 11, 1839, 4 (first quotation); *Weekly Houston Telegraph*, April 17, 1839, 3 (second quotation); Chaffin, *Fatal Glory*, 25 (third quotation); Robert W. Johannsen, *Stephen A. Douglas* (1973; repr., Urbana: University of Illinois Press, 1997), 304–32; Francaviglia, *From Sail to Steam*, 131; Baughman, *Charles Morgan and the Development of Southern Transportation*, chap. 2; Richard Whitley, *Divergent Capitalisms: The Social Structuring and Change of Business Systems* (Oxford: Oxford University Press, 1999), chaps. 1–2; T. J. Stiles, *The First Tycoon: The Epic Life of Cornelius Vanderbilt* (New York: Knopf, 2009), 175; Patrick Regnér and Udo Zander, "Knowledge and Strategy Creation in Multinational Companies: Social-Identity Frames and Temporary Tension in Knowledge Combination," *MIR: Management International Review* 51.6 (2011): 821–50; Jack B. Irion and David A. Ball, "The *New York* and the *Josephine*: Two Steamships of the Charles Morgan Line," *International Journal of Nautical Archaeology* 30.1 (2001): 48–56; Lytle and Holdcamper, *Merchant Steam Vessels of the United States*, 78.

23. Baughman, *Charles Morgan and the Development of Southern Transportation*, chap. 3; Chaffin, *Fatal Glory*, chap. 1.

24. Outward Slave Manifest, New Orleans, December 30, 1846 (*Palmetto*), NARA M1895, roll 24, image 546; Outward Slave Manifest, New Orleans, August 3, 1850 (Palmetto), NARA M1895, roll 26, image 67; Lytle and Holdcamper, *Merchant Steam Vessels of the United States*, 156, 167; Baughman, *Charles Morgan and the Development of Southern Transportation*, 46–50.

25. H. Wilson, *Trow's New York City Directory* (New York: John F. Trow, 1859), 574; Peter Mathias, "Risk, Credit and Kinship in Early Modern Enterprise," in *The Early Modern Atlantic Economy*, ed. John J. McCusker and Kenneth Morgan (Cambridge: Cambridge University Press, 2000), 5–35; Jay P. Barney and Delwyn N. Clark, *Resource-Based Theory: Creating and Sustaining Competitive Advantage* (New York: Oxford University Press, 2007); Oliver Gottschlag and Maurizio Zollo, "Interest Alignment

and Competitive Advantage," *Academy of Management Review* 32.2 (April 2007): 418–37; Mary Poovey, *Genres of the Credit Economy: Mediating Value in Eighteenth- and Nineteenth-Century Britain* (Chicago: University of Chicago Press, 2008); Baughman, *Charles Morgan and the Development of Southern Transportation*, 54–56.

26. Baughman, *Charles Morgan and the Development of Southern Transportation*, 54–58; David J. Teece, "Explicating Dynamic Capabilities: The Nature and Microfoundations of (Sustainable) Enterprise Performance," *Scientific Management Journal* 28.13 (December 2007): 1319–50.

27. *New Orleans Daily Picayune*, December 24, 1849, 3; *DeBow's Review*, October 1858, 460–61; Baughman, *Charles Morgan and the Development of Southern Transportation*, 50–53.

28. Lytle and Holdcamper, *Merchant Steam Vessels of the United States*, 78, 86, 176, 234; Baughman, *Charles Morgan and the Development of Southern Transportation*, 46–47, 86–88; Outward Slave Manifest, New Orleans, November 16, 1850 (*Galveston*), NARA M1895, roll 26, images 245–46; Outward Slave Manifest, New Orleans, October 15, 1850 (*Portland*), NARA M1895, roll 26, image 153; Outward Slave Manifest, New Orleans, April 29, 1852 (*Yacht*), NARA M1895, roll 13, image 770; Outward Slave Manifest, New Orleans, December 25, 1850 (*Globe*), M1895, roll 26, image 394; Inward Slave Manifest, New Orleans, October 26, 1860 (*Arizona*), NARA M1895, roll 16, images 743–44; Inward Slave Manifest, New Orleans, May 29, 1852 (*Louisiana*), NARA M1895, roll 13, image 715; Outward Slave Manifest, New Orleans, August 3, 1850 (*Palmetto*), NARA M1895, roll 26, image 67; Outward Slave Manifest, New Orleans, April 26, 1858 (*Calhoun*), NARA M1895, roll 30, image 301; Outward Slave Manifest, New Orleans, December 15, 1858 (*Magnolia*), NARA M1895, roll 30, image 671; Outward Slave Manifest, New Orleans, November 20, 1855 (*Charles Morgan*), NARA M1895, roll 28, image 1353; Outward Slave Manifest, New Orleans, April 9, 1856 (*Nautilus*), NARA M1895, roll 29, image 226; Outward Slave Manifest, New Orleans, December 16, 1851 (*Meteor*), NARA M1895, roll 26, image 808; Outward Slave Manifest, New Orleans, February 23, 1853 (*Perseverance*), NARA M1895, roll 26, images 1302–3; *Boston Evening Transcript*, May 13, 1850, 2; *New Orleans Daily Picayune*, September 2, 1852, 2; December 1, 1852, 2; *New York Herald*, November 7, 1858, 8; WPA, *Ship Registers and Enrollments of New Orleans*, 4:116, 220, 234–35; WPA, *Ship Registers and Enrollments of New Orleans* 5:20, 37, 44–45, 48–49, 98, 160, 174, 178, 187, 188, 199–200, 207, 247, 252, 280.

29. George P. Rawick, ed., *The American Slave: A Composite Autobiography*, vol. 5, *Texas Narratives, Parts 3–4* (Westport, Conn.: Greenwood Press, 1972), 252–53 (quotations); James M. Smallwood and Barry A. Crouch, "Texas Freedwomen during Reconstruction, 1865–1874," in *Black Women in Texas History*, ed. Bruce A. Glasrud and Merline Pitre (College Station: Texas A&M University Press), 57.

30. Craig E. Colton, *An Unnatural Metropolis: Wresting New Orleans from Nature* (Baton Rouge: Louisiana State University Press, 2005), chaps. 2–3.

31. *Victoria (Tex.) Advocate*, October 10, 1850, 2 (quotations; emphasis in original); Brian Phillips Murphy, *Building the Empire State: Political Economy in the Early Republic* (Philadelphia: University of Pennsylvania Press, forthcoming); Ernest Obadele-Starks,

Freebooters and Smugglers: The Foreign Slave Trade in the United States after 1808 (Fayetteville: University of Arkansas Press, 2007), 154–55.

32. Matilda C. F. Houstoun, *Hesperos; or, Travels in the West*, vol. 2 (London: John W. Parker, 1850), 97.

33. Ibid., 97.

34. Teresa Griffin Vielé, *"Following the Drum": A Glimpse of Frontier Life* (1858; repr., Austin: Steck-Vaughn, 1968), 76–78 (emphasis in original).

35. Vielé, *"Following the Drum,"* 82–83 (quotations); Inward Slave Manifest, New Orleans, March 5, 1851 (*Globe*), NARA M1895, roll 13, image 131; Inward Slave Manifest, New Orleans, April 18, 1851 (*Globe*), NARA M1895, roll 13, image 201; Inward Slave Manifest, New Orleans, April 1, 1851 (*Globe*), NARA M1895, roll 13, image 184; Inward Slave Manifest, New Orleans, May 1, 1851 (Globe), NARA M1895, roll 13, image 226.

36. Houstoun, *Hesperos*, 2:98–99.

37. Rawick, *The American Slave*, 252–53.

38. Houstoun, *Hesperos*, 2:99–100 (quotations); *DeBow's Review*, February 1855, 239; Robert S. Shelton, "Slavery in a Texas Seaport: The Peculiar Institution in Galveston," *Slavery & Abolition* 28.2 (August 2007): 155–68.

39. Philip Paxton, *A Stray Yankee in Texas* (New York: Redfield, 1853), chap. 22; Marian Jean Barber, "How the Irish, Germans, and Czechs Became Anglo: Race and Identity in the Texas-Mexico Borderlands" (PhD diss., University of Texas, Austin, 2010); Shelton, "Slavery in a Texas Seaport,"158; Suzanne L. Summers, "Public Policy and Economic Growth in Antebellum Texas: The Role of Houston-Galveston Merchants," *Essays in Economic and Business History* 16 (1998): 127–46.

40. Paxton, *A Stray Yankee in Texas*, 232–33 (quotation); Gary Cartwright, *Galveston: A History of the Island* (New York: Macmillan, 1991), chap. 9.

41. Randolph B. Campbell, *An Empire for Slavery: The Peculiar Institution in Texas, 1821–1865* (Baton Rouge: Louisiana State University Press, 1989), chap. 6; 1860 U.S. Census, McLennan County, Tex., roll M653_1300, p. 386, image 196; 1860 U.S. Census, Slave Schedule, McLennan County, Tex., p. 1, image 1, www.ancestry.com (accessed April 21, 2011).

42. Mrs. [Matilda C.] Houstoun, *Texas and the Gulf of Mexico; or, Yachting in the New World* (Philadelphia: G. B. Zieber, 1845), 114, 117.

43. Ibid., 179 (emphasis in original).

44. Ibid., 179–81 (emphasis in original).

45. Ibid., 183.

46. Pekka Hämäläinen, *The Comanche Empire* (New Haven: Yale University Press, 2008), 253 (quotation); Andrew J. Torget, *Cotton Empire: Slavery, the Texas Borderlands, and the Origins of the U. S.–Mexican War* (Chapel Hill: University of North Carolina Press, forthcoming); Brian DeLay, *War of a Thousand Deserts: Indian Raids and the U.S.–Mexican War* (New Haven: Yale University Press, 2008); James F. Brooks, *Captives and Cousins: Slavery, Kinship, and Community in the Southwest Borderlands* (Chapel Hill: University of North Carolina Press, 2001), 327.

47. Mark Goldberg, "Making Bodies, Linking Chains: Comanche Captivity, Black Chattel Slavery, and Empire in Antebellum Central Texas," paper presented at the

Uniting the Histories of Slavery in North America Symposium, School for Advanced Research, Santa Fe, N.M., October 12–13, 2012; *New York Commercial Advertiser*, November 4, 1848, 2 (quotation); William R. Nester, *From Mountain Man to Millionaire: The "Bold and Dashing Life" of Robert Campbell*, rev. ed. (Columbia: University of Missouri Press, 2011), 189–91; George R. Nielsen, "Torrey's Frontier Post No. 2: A Business History," *Business History Review* 37.3 (Autumn 1963): 200–216; Thomas T. Smith, *The U.S. Army and the Texas Frontier Economy, 1845–1900* (College Station: Texas A&M University Press, 1999), app. 2.

48. *Houston Telegraph*, August 14, 1850, 3 (quotations); September 11, 1850, 4; Outward Slave Manifest, New Orleans, September 14, 1850 (*Galveston*), NARA M1895, roll 26, images 116–17; Outward Slave Manifest, New Orleans, November 16, 1850 (*Galveston*), NARA M1895, roll 26, images 245–46; Outward Slave Manifest, New Orleans, September 6, 1851 (*Louisiana*), NARA M1895, roll 26, image 578; Outward Slave Manifest, New Orleans, January 22, 1853 (*Mexico*), NARA M1895, roll 26, image 1131; Outward Slave Manifest, New Orleans, February 18, 1853 (*Texas*), NARA M1895, roll 26, images 1281–82; WPA, *Ship Registers and Enrollments of New Orleans*, 5:178; 1860 U.S. Census, Houston, Ward 3, Harris County, Tex., roll M653_1296, p. 413, image 271, www.ancestry.com (accessed January 29, 2013); Curlee, "A Study of Texas Slave Plantations," 49; 1850 U.S. Census, Houston, Harris County, Tex., roll M432_911, p. 7A, image 19; 1850 U.S. Census Slave Schedule, Houston, Harris County, Tex., p. 2, www.ancestry.com (accessed January 29, 2013); Joe R. Feagin, *Free Enterprise City: Houston in Political-Economic Perspective* (New Brunswick, N.J.: Rutgers University Press, 1988), 240–41, 264.

49. *Galveston Civilian*, July 23, 1842, 4 (first quotation); *Galveston Weekly Journal*, June 4, 1852, 2 (second quotation); Outward Slave Manifest, New Orleans, May 1, 1852 (*Mexico*), NARA M1895, roll 13, image 766; Outward Slave Manifest, New Orleans, December 30, 1846 (*Palmetto*), NARA M1895, roll 24, image 546; Fred L. McGhee, "The Black Crop: Slavery and Slave Trading in Nineteenth Century Texas" (PhD diss., University of Texas, Austin, 2000), 221; Joe E. Ericson, *Banks and Bankers in Early Texas, 1835–1875* (New Orleans: Polyanthos, 1976), 133; Howard Barnstone, Henri Cartier-Bresson, and Ezra Stoller, *The Galveston That Was* (New York: Macmillan, 1965).

50. O. F. Allen, *The City of Houston from Wilderness to Wonder* (Temple, Tex.: the author, 1936), 45 (quotation); David G. McComb, *Galveston: A History* (Austin: University of Texas Press, 1986), 57, 86; Gary Cartwright, *Galveston: A History of the Island* (New York: Macmillan, 1991), 79; Earl Wesley Fornell, *The Galveston Era: The Texas Crescent on the Eve of Secession* (Austin: University of Texas Press, 1961), 115–16.

51. *Trinity (Tex.) Advocate*, August 11, 1858, 1 (first quotation); *Galveston Weekly Journal*, September 17, 1852, 4 (second quotation); Fornell, *The Galveston Era*, 230–31; Curlee, "A Study of Texas Slave Plantations," 49–52.

52. Margaret Swett Henson, *Samuel May Williams: Early Texas Entrepreneur* (College Station: Texas A&M University Press, 1976), 3 (quotation); Howard Bodenhorn, *A History of Banking in Antebellum America: Financial Markets and Economic Development in an Era of Nation-Building* (New York: Cambridge University Press, 2000), chap. 2.

53. Curlee, "A Study of Texas Slave Plantations," 43; Ericson, *Banks and Bankers in Early Texas*, 2–6; Rebecca Szucs, *The Long Lingering Shadow: Slavery, Race, and Law in*

the American Hemisphere (Athens: University of Georgia Press, 2013); Brian Norris, "Culture, Religion, Modernization and the Development of Modern Popular Credit Institutions in Texas and Bolivia, ca. 1800–2000" (PhD diss., Johns Hopkins University, 2010), 158–59, 168–70; Henson, *Samuel May Williams*, introduction; Lawrence L. Grant and Joseph M. Crum, *The Development of State-Chartered Banking in Texas: From Predecessor Systems until 1970* (Austin: University of Texas Press, 1978); Edwin J. Perkins, *Financing Anglo-American Trade: The House of Brown, 1800–1880* (Cambridge: Harvard University Press, 1975), 164.

54. Suzanne L. Summers, "Banking in Houston, 1840–1914," *Houston Review* 12.1 (1990): 37–41; Curlee, "A Study of Texas Slave Plantations," 53–54.

55. Frederick Law Olmsted, *A Journey through Texas; or, A Saddle-Trip on the South-Western Frontier* (New York: Dix, Edwards, 1857), 240.

56. William W. Freehling, *The Road to Disunion*, vol. 2, *Secessionists Triumphant, 1854–1861* (New York: Oxford University Press, 2007), chap. 11; Chaffin, *Fatal Glory*, 174; Jay Sexton, *The Monroe Doctrine: Empire and Nation in Nineteenth-Century America* (New York: Hill and Wang, 2011), chap. 2; Sam W. Haynes, *Unfinished Revolution: The Early American Republic in a British World* (Charlottesville: University of Virginia Press, 2010), chap. 12; Dale W. Tomich, *Through the Prism of Slavery: Labor, Capital, and World Economy* (Lanham, Md.: Rowman and Littlefield, 2004), chap. 3.

57. David I. Folkman Jr., *The Nicaragua Route* (Salt Lake City: University of Utah Press, 1972), 163; Winthrop Marvin, *The American Merchant Marine—Its History and Romance from 1620–1902* (New York: Charles Scribner's Sons, 1902), 284, 353, 380.

58. Gonzales, *Harvest of Empire*, 48–49; Brady Harrison, *Agent of Empire: William Walker and the Imperial Self in American Literature* (Athens: University of Georgia Press, 2004), chap. 2; Baughman, *Charles Morgan and the Development of Southern Transportation*, 61–64; T. J. Stiles, *The First Tycoon: The Epic Life of Cornelius Vanderbilt* (New York: Knopf, 2009), 175.

59. Stiles, *The First Tycoon*, 221 (quotation); Baughman, *Charles Morgan and the Development of Southern Transportation*, 70–72; Richard P. Rumelt, "Theory, Strategy, and Entrepreneurship," in *The Competitive Challenge: Strategies for Industrial Innovation and Renewal*, ed. David Teece (Cambrige, Mass.: Ballinger Publishing, 1987), 137–58; Freehling, *The Road to Disunion*, 2: chap. 11; Chaffin, *Fatal Glory*, 174.

60. William O. Scroggs, *Filibusters and Financiers: The Story of William Walker and His Associates* (New York: Macmillan, 1916), 128 (first quotation); *New York Times*, January 5, 1877, 2 (second quotation); Walter Johnson, *River of Dark Dreams: Slavery and Empire in the Cotton Kingdom* (Cambridge: Harvard University Press, 2013), chap. 13; Sexton, *The Monroe Doctrine*; Stephen Dando-Collins, *Tycoon's War: How Cornelius Vanderbilt Invaded a Country to Overthrow America's Most Famous Military Adventurer* (Cambridge, Mass.: Da Capo Press, 2008), 30–31; Joseph A. Stout Jr., *Schemers and Dreamers: Filibustering in Mexico, 1828–1921* (Fort Worth: Texas Christian University Press, 2002); Baughman, *Charles Morgan and the Development of Southern Transportation*, 73–78; Folkman, *The Nicaragua Route*, 49–51, 163.

61. *New Orleans Daily Creole*, December 15, 1856, 2 (quotation); *San Francisco Bulletin*, January 2, 1856, 2; Lytle and Holdcamper, *Merchant Steam Vessels of the United*

States, 33, 131, 144, 170; Baughman, *Charles Morgan and the Development of Southern Transportation*, 84–85, 95.

62. Thomas North, *Five Years in Texas; or, What You Did Not Hear during the War from January 1861 to January 1866* (Cincinnati: Elm Street Printing, 1871), 52–53 (quotations); Baughman, *Charles Morgan and the Development of Southern Transportation*, 96–103; Lawrence H. Larsen, "New Orleans and the River Trade: Reinterpreting the Role of the Business Community," *Wisconsin Magazine of History* 61.2 (Winter 1977–78): 112–24.

63. *New Orleans Daily Creole*, December 24, 1856, 2 (quotation); Baughman, *Charles Morgan and the Development of Southern Transportation*, 96–105.

64. *San Francisco Bulletin*, November 22, 1856, 1; Outward Slave Manifest, March 16, 1857 (*Daniel Webster*), NARA M1895, roll 29, images 939–41; Lytle and Holdcamper, *Merchant Steam Vessels of the United States*, 51; Baughman, *Charles Morgan and the Development of Southern Transportation*, 96–105.

65. Alvin Edwin Brizzard, *Looking Back at Morgan City, Louisiana: Two Hundred Years in Retrospect*, vol. 1, *To 1900* (Los Angeles: Stuart F. Cooper Co., 2004); Baughman, *Charles Morgan and the Development of Southern Transportation*, 82–85; Scroggs, *Filibusters and Financiers*, chaps. 12–13.

66. Steve Hoyt, "Is Shipwreck at Indianola the *Perseverance?*" *Current Archaeology in Texas* 7.2 (November 2005): 1–6; Francaviglia, *From Sail to Steam*, 177; Lytle and Holdcamper, *Merchant Steam Vessels of the United States*, 131; Baughman, *Charles Morgan and the Development of Southern Transportation*, 88, 95, 105.

67. *Alexandria (Va.) Gazette*, March 28, 1859, 2 (first and second quotations); *Weekly Houston Telegraph*, February 2, 1859, 3 (third quotation); Herman Freudenberger and Jonathan B. Pritchett, "The Domestic United States Slave Trade: New Evidence," *Journal of Interdisciplinary History* 21.3 (1991): 447–77.

68. *New Orleans Bee*, reprinted in *Massachusetts Spy*, April 8, 1857, 1 (quotation); Laird W. Bergad, "American Slave Markets during the 1850's: Slave Price Rises in the United States, Cuba, and Brazil in Comparative Perspective," in *Slavery in the Development of the Americas*, ed. David Eltis, Frank D. Lewis, and Kenneth Sokoloff (Cambridge: Cambridge University Press, 2004), 219–35.

69. Jacques D. Bagur, *Antebellum Jefferson, Texas: Everyday Life in an East Texas Town* (Denton: University of North Texas Press, 2012), 129; Jacques D. Bagur, *A History of Navigation on Cypress Bayou and the Lakes* (Denton: University of North Texas Press, 2001), introduction; Ulrich B. Phillips, *Life and Labor in the Old South* (1929; repr., Columbia: University of South Carolina Press, 2007), 177.

70. *Marshall (Tex.) Star State Patriot*, May 29, 1852, 9 (quotation); Maurie D. McInnes, *Slaves Waiting for Sale: Abolitionist Art and the American Slave Trade* (Chicago: University of Chicago Press, 2011), chap. 4; Philip J. Schwarz, "Hector Davis (1816–1863)," Virginia Memory, Library of Virginia, www.virginiamemory.com/online_classroom/union_or_secession/people/hector_davis (accessed December 17, 2013).

71. *Texas Republican*, March 17, 1860, 2 (first quotation); January 28, 1860, 2 (second and third quotations), www.uttyler.edu/vbetts/marshall_texas_republican_1860.htm (accessed January 25, 2013); *Alexandria (Va.) Gazette*, March 28, 1859, 2 (final quotation).

72. *Columbus (Ga.) Daily Enquirer*, January 19, 1860, 2 (quotations); Michael J. Gagnon, *Transition to an Industrial South: Athens, Georgia, 1830–1870* (Baton Rouge: Louisiana State University Press, 2012); Mark Fiege, *The Republic of Nature: An Environmental History of the United States of America* (Seattle: University of Washington Press, 2012), 230–32; Charles B. Dew, *Ironmaker to the Confederacy: Joseph R. Anderson and the Tredegar Iron Works* (New Haven: Yale University Press, 1966), chaps. 1–2; Ulrich Bonnell Phillips, *American Negro Slavery: A Survey of the Supply, Employment and Control of Negro Labor as Determined by the Plantation Regime* (1918; repr., Baton Rouge: Louisiana State University Press, 2002), 375.

73. Johnson, *River of Dark Dreams*, chaps. 11–12; Robert D. Sampson, *John L. O'Sullivan and His Times* (Kent: Kent State University Press, 2003); Nicole Etcheson, *Bleeding Kansas: Contested Liberty in the Civil War Era* (Lawrence: University Press of Kansas, 2004); Christopher Childers, *The Failure of Popular Sovereignty: Slavery, Manifest Destiny, and the Radicalization of Southern Politics* (Lawrence: University Press of Kansas, 2012); Joel H. Silbey, *Storm over Texas: The Annexation Controversy and the Road to Civil War* (New York: Oxford University Press, 2007); Amy S. Greenberg, *A Wicked War: Polk, Clay, Lincoln, and the 1846 U.S. Invasion of Mexico* (New York: Knopf, 2012); Gretchen Murphy, *Hemispheric Imaginings: The Monroe Doctrine and Narratives of U.S. Empire* (Durham: Duke University Press, 2005), chap. 2; Robert E. May, *The Southern Dream of a Caribbean Empire, 1854–1861* (Baton Rouge: Louisiana State University Press, 1973); Albert K. Weinberg, *Manifest Destiny: A Study of Nationalist Expansionism in American History* (Baltimore: Johns Hopkins University Press, 1935).

74. William Walker, *The War in Nicaragua* (Mobile: S. H. Goetzel and Co., 1860), 409 (quotation); May, *The Southern Dream of a Caribbean Empire*, 75; Chaffin, *Fatal Glory*, chap. 1; Baughman, *Charles Morgan and the Development of Southern Transportation*, 81–83.

75. Lytle and Holdcamper, *Merchant Steam Vessels of the United States*, 33, 127; Baughman, *Charles Morgan and the Development of Southern Transportation*, 119–21.

CONCLUSION

1. Georg Borgstrom, *The Hungry Planet: The Modern World at the Edge of Famine* (New York: Macmillan, 1965), chap. 5; Kenneth Pomeranz, *The Great Divergence: China, Europe, and the Making of the Modern World Economy* (Princeton: Princeton University Press, 2000); Edward E. Baptist, "Toxic Debt, Liar Loans, Collateralized and Securitized Human Beings, and the Panic of 1837," in *Capitalism Takes Command: The Social Transformation of Nineteenth-Century America*, ed. Michael Zakim and Gary J. Kornblith (Chicago: University of Chicago Press, 2012), 69–92.

2. Edmund S. Morgan, *American Slavery, American Freedom* (New York: W. W. Norton, 1975), 10 (quotation); William W. Freehling, *The Road to Disunion*, vol. 2, *Secessionists Triumphant, 1854–1861* (New York: Oxford University Press, 2007).

3. Cornel West, *Democracy Matters: Winning the Fight against Imperialism* (New York: Penguin, 2004), 22 (quotation).

4. Heather Andrea Williams, *Help Me to Find My People: The African American Search for Family Lost in Slavery* (Chapel Hill: University of North Carolina Press, 2012); Walter Johnson, Eric Foner, and Richard Follett, *Slavery's Ghost: The Problem of Freedom in the Age of Emancipation* (Baltimore: Johns Hopkins University Press, 2011); Susan Eva O'Donovan, "Traded Babies: Enslaved Children in America's Domestic Migrations, 1820–1860," in *Children in Slavery through the Ages*, ed. Gwyn Campbell, Suzanne Miers, and Joseph C. Miller (Athens: Ohio University Press, 2009), 88–102; Susan Eva O'Donovan, *Becoming Free in the Cotton South* (Cambridge: Harvard University Press, 2007); Bruce Sacerdote, "Slavery and the Intergenerational Transmission of Human Capital," *Review of Economics and Statistics* 87.2 (May 2005): 217–34; Ira Berlin, *Generations of Captivity: A History of African-American Slaves* (Cambridge: Harvard University Press, 2003), chaps. 3–4.

5. Saidiya V. Hartman, *Scenes of Subjection: Terror, Slavery, and Self-Making in Nineteenth-Century America* (New York: Oxford University Press, 1997); R. H. Coase, "The Problem of Social Cost," *Journal of Law and Economics* 3 (October 1960): 1–44; Henry Watson, *Narrative of Henry Watson, a Fugitive Slave* (Boston: Bela Marsh, 1848).

6. Frederick Douglass, *My Bondage and My Freedom* (New York: Miller, Orton, and Mulligan, 1855), 448.

7. Federal Writers' Project, *Slave Narratives: A Folk History of Slavery in the United States from Interviews with Former Slaves*, vol. 16, *Texas Narratives, Part 3* (Washington, D.C., 1941), http://www.gutenberg.org/files/35380/35380-h/35380-h.html (accessed January 6, 2014).

8. William W. Freehling, *Becoming Lincoln* (forthcoming); Walter Johnson, *River of Dark Dreams: Slavery and Empire in the Cotton Kingdom* (Cambridge: Harvard University Press, 2013).

9. Edmund Ruffin, *The Diary of Edmund Ruffin*, vol. 1, *Toward Independence, October, 1856–April, 1861*, ed. William Kauffman Scarborough (Baton Rouge: Louisiana State University Press, 1972), 535 (first and second quotations); James L. Nicholson and Robert E. Corlew, *Grundy County* (Memphis: Memphis State University Press, 1982), 46 (third quotation).

10. Philip S. Foner, *Business and Slavery: The New York Merchants and the Irrepressible Conflict* (Chapel Hill: University of North Carolina Press, 1941).

11. Howard Jones, *Blue and Gray Diplomacy: A History of Union and Confederate Foreign Relations* (Chapel Hill: University of North Carolina Press, 2010), chap. 9; John D. Bennett, *The London Confederates: The Officials, Clergy, Businessmen, and Journalists Who Backed the American South during the Civil War* (Jefferson, N.C.: McFarland, 2008), chap. 2; Sven Beckert, *The Empire of Cotton: A Global History* (New York: Knopf, 2014); Roger L. Ransom and Richard Sutch, *One Kind of Freedom: The Economic Consequences of Emancipation*, 2nd ed. (Cambridge: Cambridge University Press, 2001), 190.

INDEX

Page numbers in *italics* indicate illustrations.

Northup, Solomon: auctioning of, 190; autobiography *Twelve Years a Slave*, 200, 202, 251; as consequence of capitalist development, 200; failed on-board uprising, 186–87; at Ford's plantation, 197–99; kidnapping of, 169–70, 175, 248; life before kidnapping, 169; name change, 175–76, 182–83; in New Orleans, 188–90, 243; in private jail, 179–82; rescue of, 201–3; return home, 203; sea voyage, 182–88; smallpox contracted by, 191; trip up-river, 192–96, 205, 236; violence against, 7–8, 175, 181; violin playing of, 169, 190
Nullification Crisis, 145, 148

Olmsted, Frederick Law, 228
Omohundro, Silas, 144, 192
Orleans (merchant ship), 182–88, 191
Orr, Nathaniel, 202
O'Sullivan, John L., 208–9, 238
Overley, Thomas W., 56, 174

Pacific Mail Steamship Company, 215
packet lines, 98–99, 137, 183, 209–10, 214
Packwood, George, 22
Palmetto (steamship), 211, 216
Parks, Benjamin J., 113, 128, 144
Parnell, Caroline, 181, 190
Paulding, James Kirke, 37–38
Peïllon, Stephen, 50
Pennington, James W. C., 31
Pennoyer, James, 212, 213, 214, 216
Perrault, J. B., 135
Persac, Marie Adrien, *Port and City of New Orleans*, 218
Perseverance (steamship), 208, 232, 234
Peters, Samuel, 75
Petersburg, Virginia, 10–11, 14, 18, 32, 250
Petersburg Railroad, 32
Peyton Mason and Company, 11–18, 22, 24, 27–28, 31–32, 126
Phenix Bank of New York, 133
Philadelphia and Reading Railroad, 177

Planters' Bank of Mississippi, 133, 148, 173
Polk, James K., 205, 215–16
Port Lavaca, Texas, 206, 217
postal service, U.S.: post roads and, 14–15; steamships contracted by, 217, 230, 232, 233
Potomac (steamboat), 146
Pottsville and Danville Railroad, 177
Prime, Ward, King, and Company, 112, 134
Prince, Samuel, 75
Princess Anne Village Herald, 39
private jails: in Baltimore, 40–41, 44, 48, 55–56, 60; in New Orleans, 188–92; in Virginia, 29, 126, 127, 128, 129–30, 136, 145–46, 172–73, 175, 179–82
protective nationalism, 19–20
Purvis, James, 127, 140, 153, 165, 183

Quakers (Society of Friends), 42, 43, 59–64, 91, 135
Quitman, John A., 24

R. and I. Smith, 174
Radburn, Ebenezer, 175
railroads, nineteenth-century development of, 32, 176–79, 194–95, 203, 232–33, 235–36, 243
Raleigh, North Carolina, 10, 13
Randolph, J. Beverly, 52
Randolph, John, 13–14
Ray, Clemens, 176, 181
Raynal, William Theophilus, 190
Real Estate Bank of Arkansas, 119
Reed, James, 212, 213, 214, 216
Republican Star and General Advertiser, 39
Richmond, Fredericksburg and Potomac Railroad, 176–79
Richmond, Henry, 118
Richmond, Virginia, slaving activities in, 28–29, 52–56, 126–29, 145–47, 175, 179–82, 235–36
Richmond and Petersburg Railroad, 177
Rillieux, Edmond, 116–17

Rillieux, Norbert, 116–17
Rillieux, Vincent, 117
Rives, Francis Everod, 6, 11–18, 24–25, 28, 29, 31–32, 240–41, 246, 250
Rives, Nathaniel, 54
roads, nineteenth-century development of, 6, 10, 13–15; local residents and, 13–14; military, 15–16; post roads and turnpikes, 14–15, 32, 240; routes, 14
Robert (bondsman), 180, 183, 185
Robertson, Minerva, 150
Robertson, Thomas B., 50
Robinson, Abner, 122
Robinson, Mariah, 218–24, 238, 248–49
Robinson, Moncure, 177–78
Robinson, Peter, 248–49
Rodolph (steamboat), 192–93
Rogers and Harrison, 53
Roman, André Bienvenue, 157
Roosevelt, Franklin Delano, 90
Roosevelt, Isaac, 90
Ruffin, Edmund, 250
Ruggles, David, 91
Russell, Joseph, 169–70

San Antonio, Texas, 212, 224, 227
San Francisco, California, 8
Sanders, Robert, 56, 174
Schoharie (merchant ship), 85–90
Scranton, Fred, 225
Second Bank of the United States: branches of, 26–27, 129; foreign exchange business, 103, 105, 112, 242; growth of, 26–27; Jackson's curtailing of, 7, 111, 120, 134, 145, 153, 159, 160; as largest U.S. merchant bank, 43, 51; regulatory function of, 107; slaveholders' interests promoted by, 100–101
Second Seminole War, 209–10
Sel, François, 54
Seminole nation, 209–10
Shaben and Brother, 226
Shawnee nation, 19
Shelton, Lethe, 181, 188, 190

shipwrecks, 48, 181–82, 211, 221, 234
Shreve, Henry Miller, 197
Shreveport, Louisiana, 198, 236
Silas, Harriet, 86
Simms, William Gilmore, 66
Singleton, Cuffee, 185–86
Singleton, David, 181, 190
Singleton, Mary, 181
Slack, Eliphalet, 118
Slatter, Hope Hull, 165
slave markets and auctions, 172; commodity value and, 24–25, 30, 141, 148–50; in Houston, 207, 226; monetary instruments used, 24–25; in Natchez, 22–25, 29–30, 124, 130–31, 137–38, 140–42, 148–52, 155–63; in New Orleans, 188–90; in Richmond, 179–82; "training" for, 189–90
slave revolts and uprisings, 60–62, 112, 246
slave smugglers: as defenders of New Orleans, 69, 81–82; in New Jersey, 6–7, 69, 73–80, 85–88, 91–92, 94
slave traders: advertising and marketing strategies, 6, 35–40, 43–44, 58, 174–75; Baltimore-based, 6, 33–68, 92, 126, 127; as banknote disseminators, 27–28; as bogeymen, 246; borders and, 4; captives' casualties and health problems, 49, 54, 141–42, 146, 150–51, 155–56, 180, 191; domestication of trade, 85, 241; innovations of, 6, 240–46; interstate credit network, 126, 128; Latin American, 164; Natchez-based, 22–25, 29–30, 92, 127, 132–33, 139–40, 202; New Orleans-based, 51–53, 92, 115, 126–27, 157–62, 172–75, 201–3; operating costs of, 40–41, 49, 126, 146, 147, 151–52, 156, 181; private jails of, 29, 40–41, 44, 48, 55–56, 60, 127, 128, 129–30, 136, 172–73, 175, 179–82; railroads promoted by, 195; Virginia-based, 11–32, 113, 115, 169–83, 203, 235–36
slaves. *See* bondspersons